IMMIGRATION
RECONSIDERED

IMMIGRATION RECONSIDERED

History, Sociology, and Politics

Edited by

Virginia Yans-McLaughlin

New York   Oxford

OXFORD UNIVERSITY PRESS

1990

Oxford University Press

Oxford   New York   Toronto
Delhi   Bombay   Calcutta   Madras   Karachi
Petaling Jaya   Singapore   Hong Kong   Tokyo
Nairobi   Dar es Salaam   Cape Town
Melbourne   Auckland

and associated companies in
Berlin   Ibadan

Copyright © 1990 by The Statue of Liberty Ellis Island Foundation

Published by Oxford University Press, Inc.,
200 Madison Avenue, New York, New York 10016

Oxford is a registered trademark of Oxford University Press

Library of Congress Cataloging-in-Publication Data
Immigration reconsidered : history, sociology, and politics
edited by Virginia Yans-McLaughlin.
p.   cm.
"This book of essays grew out of a conference . . . sponsored by
the Statue of Liberty Ellis Island Foundation, the Alfred P. Sloan Foundation,
and the New York Council for the Humanities . . . which was
held at the New York Public Library on October 24–25, 1986"—P.
ISBN 0-19-505510-1
ISBN 0-19-505511-X (pbk)
1. United States—Emigration and immigration—History—Congresses.
2. United States—Emigration and immigration—Government policy—Congresses.
I. Yans-McLaughlin, Virginia, 1943– II.
Statue of Liberty-Ellis Island Foundation, Inc.
III. Alfred P. Sloan Foundation.
IV. New York Council for the Humanities.
JV6450.I57   1990   89-22923   304.8'73—dc20

Parts of Chapter 6 were published previously in
Annual Review of Sociology 13 (1987), and are reprinted
by permission of the publishers.

9   8   7   6   5   4   3   2

Printed in the United States of America
on acid-free paper

In Memory of

Herbert G. Gutman
and
Warren I. Susman,

*Who would certainly have had
something to say*

CONTENTS

THE STUDY OF IMMIGRATION

NEW APPROACHES TO THE STUDY OF IMMIGRATION

THE POLITICS OF IMMIGRATION

Acknowledgments

This book of essays grew out of a conference generously sponsored by the Statue of Liberty Ellis Island Foundation, the Alfred P. Sloan Foundation, and the New York Council for the Humanities. The purpose of the conference, which was held at the New York Public Library on October 24–25, 1986, was to create a forum for scholarly commentary during the year of the Statue's centenary and to prepare for the upcoming centennial of Ellis Island in 1992. I particularly wish to thank William B. May, president of the Statue of Liberty Ellis Island Foundation, for his understanding that the reflections of scholars add a sober but necessary dimension to such moments of national celebration. Joan M. Jensen and Louise Ano Nuevo Kerr of the Statue of Liberty Ellis Island History Committee added their imaginative minds to help me develop the basic concept of the conference and to identify the talented scholars who could fulfill it. Other members of the History Committee also deserve thanks, including the chair, Rudolph J. Vecoli, Kathleen N. Conzen, Jay P. Dolan, Roger Daniels, Victor Greene, F. Ross Holland, Alan Kraut, Bara Levin, Dwight Pitcaithley, and Moses Rischen. Sally Jones and Gary Kelley of the Statue of Liberty Ellis Island Foundation added indispensable fund-raising and management assistance. Michael S. Teitelbaum of the Sloan Foundation believed in the significance of the conference idea and participated in its deliberations. Jay Kaplan of the New York Council for the Humanities is to be thanked for understanding the importance of bringing this scholarly agenda to the general public and for his reliability in providing the last bit of support needed to make a project such as this happen. The Institute for Research in History organized the conference. Acting on its behalf, Barbara Abrash and Marjorie Lightman expertly and stylishly oversaw the conference, which confirmed the idea that a book was indeed to be born. William Zeisel, our editor, did his magic by helping each author in this book to turn a conference paper into an essay. I would like to thank all conference participants, and especially Sune Åkerman, Lucie Cheng, and Lydio Tomasi, whose comments could not be included in this book but who contributed to the intellectual richness of the collective effort that it represents. At Oxford University Press, Nancy Lane lent her professional guidance as we walked through all stages of production, and Paul Schlotthauer and David Roll of Oxford also deserve appreciation. Finally, warmest thanks go to Lutz Rath, himself an immigrant, for his usual agreeable sense of proportion when I took time from one to write about thousands of immigrants.

New York, January 1990   V. Y.-McL.

IMMIGRATION RECONSIDERED

INTRODUCTION

Virginia Yans-McLaughlin

Since about the middle of the sixteenth century, one hundred million people have emigrated from their homelands to new places. Across the Atlantic and Pacific oceans they went, to what are now the world's multinational societies—to the United States of America and Canada, to Latin America, Australia, and New Zealand. Some Europeans and Asians chose to remain on their own continents, buffeted about from countryside to city, drawn unwittingly into the turbulent change created first by mercantile capitalism, later by the nineteenth century's industrial expansion. Still others—entrepreneurs, rascals, or scoundrels—saw this great shuffling of human traffic, here and there, about the world, as an opportunity to turn a profit. Slave traders, labor agents, and steamship company representatives, they captured, contracted, and transported enslaved Africans or laborers to plantations, towns, and mines on the periphery of the developing world—forsaken places, rough-and-tumble outposts, and frontier cities, where local hands could not meet the demand for labor.

By chance or by choice, almost half of these world travelers settled in the United States; the free men among them, at least, were hinging their hopes on democracy, rich natural resources, and American enterprise. It was not, it seemed, an unreasonable dream. Believers in the really tall tales about America, English or Irish, Arab or Jew, Chinese or Japanese, were joined as fools when they learned that the streets held no precious metals, that the "golden mountain" did not yield its riches equally to newcomers with darker skins, slanted eyes, strange tongues, and peculiar names. Still, newly chastened or calculating from the start, many immigrants found enough to keep them here, enough for the ambitious to tool a better life for themselves in the promised land.

New York City's Ellis Island Immigration Station, one of several federal processing centers established at the turn of the twentieth century, was, depending upon where one stood in the world, a model of bureaucratic efficiency, a target for reform, or the first chance for a job. Its uniformed officials, translators, and clerks processed sixteen million immigrants, most of them Europeans of exceedingly modest means who traveled steerage passage because they could afford no better.

I would like to thank my colleague Samuel Baily for his helpful comments on this introduction.

In 1992, the centennial year of Ellis Island, Americans will celebrate these doughty wayfarers, the country they made, and the country they hoped to find. In the United States, the figure of the common man bound for glory—whether an immigrant clutching the remains of his former life in a bursting cardboard suitcase, or a seedy frontiersman in coonskin cap—cuts a potent and sentimental populist symbol. A fanfare for these ordinary immigrant men and women is a fitting finale to the 1980s, a decade that obstinately resurrected traditional beliefs in hard work, individualism, and enterprise, and in the economic autonomy and infinite capacity for growth of the United States, even as the nation confronted disturbing evidence of shrinking environmental resources and the realities of global interdependence.

The American people and the American mission are an intimately married couple in the structure of our national consciousness. Scholars of immigration and ethnicity have participated in the design of this national self-portrait. Peering back from the vantage point of the 1990s to the work of historians, we see, for example, some ironic twists and turns in their perceptions of national identity and ethnic amalgamation. In multivolume syntheses of the American past, early twentieth-century gentlemen historians, such as William Ellery Channing and John Bach McMaster, generally accepted the superiority of the Anglo-Saxon culture, even as they assumed that immigrants would conform to it.[1] By the 1970s, however, the "decade of the ethnics," many scholars and intellectuals, themselves descendants of immigrants, put aside this inexorable teleology of assimilation. Instead, they defended "ethnic pluralism," the right—and the actuality—of separate ethnic-group identity in this nation of immigrants.[2]

The subject of immigration continues to arouse public and scholarly controversy, much of it rooted in these different descriptions of, or prescriptions for, national identity. Not immune from the passions and prejudices of laypersons, scholars bring disciplinary training and theory to these debates, for in a contemporary Western democracy, the practice of scholarship also implies a commitment to objectivity confirmed through research and the open exposure of findings to an audience of experts. The exposure of methodologies, theories, and sources of information can at once serve to demystify any authority inappropriately extended to scholarly texts and to lead the lay public and policymakers toward sophisticated interpretations of immigration. This book brings together a group of scholars whose essays reveal or directly explain how the disciplines and methodologies of history, sociology, and political science interpret a broad scope of immigration issues, including restriction policy, individual and ethnic group experience and the place of American immigration itself in the history of the world. The book will familiarize readers with essential facts about immigration and its history as well as the scholar's habits of interpreting and reinterpreting them.

I invited many of the authors represented in this collection to write essays because they are well-known immigration specialists. I also wanted this collection to reflect broader trends in the historical and social science scholarship of the 1970s and 1980s, and hoped to encourage a timely union of the immigration specialist's acuity with the generalist's breathtaking power to assemble short, particular stories and locate them within broad contexts of history and meaning. Because I believed that the breadth and scope of their knowledge could not help but energize the field of immigration studies, I invited distinguished scholars working outside the field, as it is conventionally understood — scholars such as historian of slavery Philip Curtin and the sociologist Charles Tilly — to add their reflections to the joint endeavor. Curtin's deft treatment of slavery in the tropical world and Tilly's synthesis of these essays and other recent scholarship illustrate the dominant tone for the entire book. These authors move between local and global perspectives, constantly contextualize the topic of immigration, and unabashedly place the North American immigration experience on the periphery of human history.

It is possible to identify scholars who assume American exceptionalism, that is, the uniqueness of United States history, individual achievement, and the great "melting pot" as the givens of the immigrant experience. Their viewpoint stands in easy harmony with the new political consensus of the 1980s.[3] In organizing this book, however, I attempted to provide a framework for contemporary specialists, whose innovative work does not partner easily with accepted national mythologies, to initiate their synthesis. The new scholarship represented in this book heavily emphasizes global patterns and comparative methods, and broadens a European-centered study to include people from other continents: African slaves and their descendants, recent Mexican and Latin American migrants, and Asians. This work is, of course, an appropriate accommodation to the realities of recent immigration streams to North America. Readers will see, however, that these authors convincingly suggest the universality of their model, and extend both the comparative method and a global perspective back in time to the ancient world and to almost all regions of the globe.

The innovations required to move immigration studies forward involve interdisciplinary work, a condition that all of the scholars in this book happily meet. Most move with amazing agility from one discipline to another. A few have been formally trained in more than one discipline. Ewa Morawska, for example, holds advanced degrees in history and sociology, and Sucheng Chan began her career in political science but now publishes in the field of history. Aristide Zolberg and Lawrence Fuchs, both of whom offer essays on immigration policy, are equally adept managing the tools of history and political science. Fuchs, as executive director of the House of Representatives Select Commission on Immigration and Refugee Policy from 1979 to 1981, has also been exposed to the public-policy world. Five of the scholars — Samuel Baily, Sucheng Chan, Suzanne Model, Ewa Morawska, and Charles Tilly — regularly employ sociological and historical methods in their writings. The sociologists in this group are more likely than their predecessors of two or three decades ago to turn their attention to the historical contexts of immigration, and historians such as Samuel Baily, Philip Curtin, and Kerby Miller share the sociologist's enthusiasm for broad comparisons. Finally, several of the essays represented here pattern themselves after natural science, most notably in their use of aggregate statistical data and in their search for broad explanatory models. But this collection also presents the views of a contemporary vocal minority of scholars, mostly ethnographers, historians, and a few sociologists, who continue to believe that human consciousness and human subjectivity are legitimate objects for study. And, it also reflects very recent criticism that, by exposing unacknowledged power relations between social science "experts" and their subjects or informants, also questions the supposed objective production of social science and historical texts. My essay on the use of oral narratives in immigration studies elaborates on both of these themes, and Kerby Miller's work on nineteenth-century Irish immigrants, though concerned with real historical events and real human struggles for power, nevertheless assumes the significance of values, ideology, and human consciousness in historical explanation. If this collection of essays represents scholarship of the 1980s for its extraordinary disciplinary integration and for its synthesis of new perspectives on immigration, it also stands as testimony to the pluralism of American social scientific and historical thought.

The most striking revisionism offered by these essays as a group is the chilling distance they establish from the accepted myths of individual and national autonomy as unquestioned attributes of the American experience. Instead of individuals making their way toward Americanization on their own, these scholars portray collective strategies of family, ethnic group, or class. Instead of open labor markets, free competition, and equal opportunity for all, they reveal discrimination and unequal positioning of different ethnic groups. Instead of a unified class of working men and women joined in common purpose, they expose alliances between capital and labor to restrict immigration. Along with assimilation to American culture, they portray a variety of actively chosen options, including repatriation and return to the homeland. For America as the special haven of the downtrodden, they substitute America as one point on the periphery of an expanding system of world capitalism. Most important, these scholars understand immigration, whether it refers to free individuals, slaves, contract laborers, *braceros*, or guest workers, as a form of labor recruitment in an international labor market. The reader will be struck by an overwhelming affirmation of the individual's contingency upon national and international conditions that, if they did not control human fate, set the stage for its enactment. Even historians like Kerby Miller and me, who are interested in the analysis of class consciousness and cultural mentalities, ground these in the material circumstances of immigrant life. Neither William Ellery Channing's dreams of a "melting pot" nor the "ethnic pluralism" of the 1970s can accommodate the complex processes described in this new paradigm.

The revisions of accepted wisdom proposed in this volume turn around three points: the international ecology of migration; a questioning of the classical assimilation model, which proposes a linear progression of immigrant culture toward a dominant American national character; and, through references to other national experiences in Asia and Latin America, a denial of American exceptionalism. Pursued separately by the authors, these lines of analysis are related aspects of the new paradigm. The contextualization of American immigration within a continuing global process, clearly accomplished by the 1980s by these and other scholars, itself eroded the classical assimilation theory. For example, once the United States is viewed as only one point on the periphery of an expanding world economy, the alternatives to Americanization become apparent. One frequently exercised option was the decision to repatriate: 25 percent to 60 percent of immigrants returned to their homelands.[4] Or, as Samuel Baily's work shows, thousands chose to emigrate elsewhere, such as the Italians who chose Argentina as their new home.

Scholars recognized global migration patterns and the inadequacy of the assimilation paradigm for at least thirty years, but a synthesis has only recently emerged. In may be useful, therefore, to review some of the ideas that contributed to this shift toward an alternative synthesis. In his short, prophetic, and brilliantly argued essay published in 1960, "Migration from Europe Overseas in the Nineteenth and Twentieth Centuries," the historian Frank Thistlethwaite drew upon the work of his contemporaries in history, sociology, economics, and demography to initiate a new agenda.[5] Perhaps Thistlethwaite's most significant conclusion was his insistence that conventional disciplinary categories required rethinking. He was particularly concerned with revising scholarly stereotypes of immigrants as an undifferentiated group of peasants or as an "inchoate ethnic mass." He sketched a much more complex and stratified labor market, organized by occupation and village ties; these bonds underlaid networks of immigrants in circular systems crossing back and forth across broad regions, oceans, and continents. Although Thistlethwaite understood the conventional scholarly practice of exploring immigration within national contexts as the logical outcome of European political and administrative history, he believed that it inhibited understanding. He insisted that European historians, concerned only with what went on within national boundaries, could not possibly understand the dynamics of migration; nor could Americanists who were almost exclusively preoccupied with immigrant adjustment and focused on only one geographic point in a world system. The Americanists' parochialism led to the assumption that the United States was the ultimate and final destination of all immigration, a point easily refuted with statistical data.

As an antidote to this ineptly bounded field, Thistlethwaite cited works such as historian Marcus Lee Hansen's *The Atlantic Migration, 1607–1860* (1940) and economist Brinley Thomas's *Migration and Economic Growth: A Study of Great Britain and the Atlantic Economy* (1952), which initiated a shift toward a global perspective.[6] He acknowledged, of course, the legitimacy of studying migration within certain European regional and local economies, such as the Mediterranean basin, and of continuing intracontinental movements between rural and urban places throughout the world. He was primarily interested in refocusing study on the entire North Atlantic region. "The Atlantic economy," he wrote, "was concerned with exploiting the grasslands of North America by means of European capital and labor in the interests of cheaper cotton and wheat for Europe and overseas markets for European manufacturers. The migration of the twin factors of capital investment and labor was the key to it and emigrants essential to its operation." Thistlethwaite concluded that because there was such free movement for the factors of production, "we can hardly distinguish the two principal countries concerned, Britain and the United States, as separate, closed economies."[7] He proposed a merging of studies of nineteenth- and early twentieth-century immigration with Atlantic studies, a feat that could not have been achieved without the basic scholarly monographs written during the past thirty years.

In line with his emphasis upon the artificiality of national boundaries, Thistlethwaite urged the exploration of causal relationships between American restriction or "Open Door" policies and the "international mobility of labor." Finally, in attempting to remedy the "elusiveness" of "anonymous" individuals such as immigrants, he urged historians to apply the statistical and demographic data used by social scientists as a solution to the search for data. Thistlethwaite's agenda coupled a global perspective on immigration with consideration of local and regional economies; his emphasis upon statistical data and a natural science model of analysis directed attention away from subjective experiences toward structural conditions. Readers of these essays will recognize that many are direct descendents of these parts of Thistlethwaite's agenda.

In the thirty years since Thistlethwaite and his contemporaries published their work, scholars have grappled with many of the issues they raised. The study of the evolution of world capitalism from the sixteenth century[8] has profoundly altered immigration studies: it has reframed the immigration story within the broad context of the emerging industrial regions that established a world market for immigrant labor and transformed the feudal relations of nearby rural areas. In the 1970s scholars such as Josef Barton pioneered in explaining how local economies in southern and eastern Europe, on the edge of the developed European world but not isolated from capitalist markets or the commercialization of arable land, fed into cross-continental networks of migrating workers.[9] In *The Transplanted* John Bodnar has recently synthesized a number of monographs focused on European migration and related their findings to the broad sweep of developing industrial capitalism.[10]

Essays in this book by Charles Tilly and Sucheng Chan elaborate and refine these earlier efforts. Tilly points out that by the early nineteenth century, evolving capitalist economic and property relations—notably the spread of wage labor, the separation of households from the means of production, and the rising productivity of commercial agriculture—had combined with diminishing land resources and an expanding demand for labor in urban-industrial areas to make long-distance migration a logical choice for many Europeans. Recent scholars of European emigration generally agree that local conditions, including land-tenure patterns, agricultural requirements, and resource management, profoundly influenced rates of emigration and return as well as the kinds of people who emigrated.[11] The poorest could not afford to emigrate. Those from regions, such as certain parts of southern Italy, where land ownership was still possible hoped to use American wages to purchase land upon their return. The sons of west Norwegian cattle farmers, shut out from ownership by rules of impartible inheritance designed to maintain sizable grazing lands, along with fairly-well-off farmers seeking larger farms, also left Europe. Emigration was a means to avoid loss of social status or to improve it. Kerby

Miller's essay emphasizes class differences among Irish immigrants to explain both the dynamics of immigration and the resulting Irish-American culture. Thistlethwaite's suggestion that emigrants were not an inchoate ethnic or "peasant mass" certainly holds up under these recent close analyses of European migration.

The essays in this book carry Thistlethwaite's agenda even further by expanding the chronology and the geography of immigration to include Asia, Africa, Latin America, and the tropical world. Curtin's essay, "Migration in the Tropical World," locates European and African migration to North America in the long continuum of migrations throughout thousands of years of human history. He connects the geographic locus of migration and the occurrence of slave migration, indenture contracts, and free migration to changing demands for forced and free labor at various stages of regional economic development. Although the United States was certainly a focal point for European migration, and the descendants of Africans are a significant part of its present population, the United States stood on the periphery of the slave trade, and absorbed less than 10 percent of its product. The great population movements throughout the tropical world and Asia that followed the abolition of the slave trade completely evaded North America. Not until after World War II did movements of tropical peoples from what is now known as the Third World direct themselves to highly developed regions like North America and Europe.

Sucheng Chan, in her comparison of European and Asian immigration to the United States from 1820 to 1920, expands our understanding of immigration to include the Eastern Hemisphere. She establishes immigration as a two-way process by focusing on both the United States and the "sending nations," and thus directs attention to the Asian continent as a migration source. Chan imaginatively synthesizes a newly developing literature on China, Japan, India, and Korea that, like recent scholarship on European migrations, identifies advancing world capitalism and local political conditions as forces driving global migrations. According to Chan, two streams of Cantonese gold rush emigrants, who traveled overseas as free emigrants or contract laborers to the Pacific Coast and Australia before the middle of the nineteenth century, were most likely using emigration to accumulate savings to be used upon return to enhance family ownership of land in the fertile Pearl River Delta region. Skilled craftsmen from urban Canton also left in this period. The impoverished individuals who left after the 1850s, however, as "coolie" labor for Cuba and Peru were, Chan says, more likely victims of hopeless situations, such as natural disasters, debt bondage, land dispossession, war, or imperialistic policies. In the case of British India and China, local political conditions that stimulated migration were themselves related to Western capitalist expansion. Instead of the usual emphasis upon distinctive national or continental experiences, Chan emphasizes similar originating causes for Asian, European, and Latin American emigration.

Alejandro Portes locates the most recent Hispanic minorities in the United States—Mexicans, Puerto Ricans, and various Caribbean peoples from Cuba and Santo Domingo—at still another point in the development of world capitalism. To understand the formation of these ethnic groups, he examines their immigration to North America and the expansion of the United States into colonial and postcolonial communities on its immediate periphery. Mexico, Puerto Rico, and Cuba offer different examples of the latter theme: the exploitation of local resources including labor, as in Mexico and Puerto Rico, or direct United States political intervention, as occurred more recently in Cuba, Puerto Rico, and Santo Domingo. The result, as Portes points out, appears to be a paradox: certain immigrant groups were actually Americanized before they came to the United States. In short, Portes shows the need to examine economic and political relations between sending and receiving nations along with local economic conditions when seeking explanations of contemporary immigration.

All the authors in this book regard emigration and immigration as means of providing a reserve labor supply. Although they are often concerned with the relocation of European, Third World, and Hispanic populations to the United States, a similar case could be made for internal migration of rural southern blacks into northern cities beginning when World War I blocked overseas migration to the United States. And, as Aristide Zolberg points out, Algerians in France, Turkish "guest workers" in Germany, Moroccans in Belgium, and the nineteenth-century Irish in Britain also constituted a reserve labor supply. Technology and the organization of agriculture and industry determined whether the migrating labor supply would be free, indentured, or enslaved. The advent of steamships that could carry large numbers of people across the Atlantic and return with a cargo of goods provided a cheap supply of unskilled European labor for the American economy, which also benefited from not having to make long-term investments in developing an indigenous labor force. Slave labor was inconsistent with the demands of industrial economies. Instead, in these highly developed economies, free market allocation of housing, health, education, and community resources, the ecology of cities, and intermittent labor demands made exploitation of workers through the wage system a more rational choice.

Aristide Zolberg and Lawrence Fuchs make clear, in their essays on immigration policy and coalition politics, that labor-market surpluses and shortages have always driven debates about restriction. After the abolition of slavery, Zolberg observes, agricultural and industrial employers used a variety of "back-door" techniques to bypass restrictions on immigration and bring temporary Asian, European, and Mexican workers to the United States. Contract labor and the Mexican *bracero* program allowed agricultural employers simply to import workers, like goods, and export them when they were no longer needed. Zolberg points out that the Constitution as written, considered imported laborers a category of imported things, not people. When restrictionist policy made labor scarce, for example, when the Chinese Exclusion Act of 1882 and the 1924 Restriction Act reduced Asian and European labor supplies, employers found substitutes such as Mexican laborers.

Labor and the unemployed, frequently opposed the "back-door" policies on the grounds that imported labor would diminish their own opportunities.

This was the case, as Fuchs ironically demonstrates, with black leaders who supported restrictive legislation. For some Americans, the battle over restriction implied a control of national identity and of the nature of their political life. Both Zolberg and Fuchs point to "odd-couple" coalitions that resulted from this alliance of race purists, black political leaders, and organized laborers. Fuchs shows that men like Frederick Douglass and Booker T. Washington were restrictionists, a position only recently abandoned by North American black leaders when they formed a coalition with Mexican-Americans regarding the 1986 immigration reform legislation. Fuchs implies that Afro-American political leaders see their reversal and attempts at coalition building as a means to win support among recent black immigrant groups, as a civil rights program, and as a potential basis for future continuing coalitions with Hispanic groups. Zolberg attributes the success of the coalition-building maneuvers preceding the 1986 Immigration Reform and Control Act to the fact that everyone got something: employer sanctions pleased restrictionists and those who wished to protect labor from foreign competition; Hispanics and civil rights groups got their amnesty; and employers retained the possibility of keeping an open door to seasonal farm workers at least for a few years.

Ewa Morawska's essay offers a lucid, detailed analysis of work by historians and sociologists over the past fifteen years that has revised the older, two-part paradigm of American immigration. One half of that paradigm emerged in the 1920s from Chicago school sociologists such as Robert Park. The Chicago school proposed what I referred to earlier as the classical assimilation model, which essentially assumed a linear progression from Old World traits toward Americanization.[12] A related part of the old paradigm, "human-capital theory," posited that individual actions or assets such as educational level, language skills, or family cohesion, contributed to economic achievement, assimilation, or inability to adapt. For a generation, the two-part paradigm not only dominated scholarly discourse on immigration but reinforced the popular American ideology of the "melting pot" and the individual's responsibility for successes and failures.

The two models also fit coherently into the nationally focused framework that Thistlethwaite wanted revised. This paradigm was incorporated, in whole or in part, into the work of influential historians of the 1950s who concerned themselves with the question of American identity, and whose works were read outside the historical profession. Charles Tilly observes that when Oscar Handlin published his general history of the United States, he called it *The Americans: A New History of the People of the United States* (1963),[13] a title grounded in his underlying premise that United States history is a continuing story of many people becoming one people, a process that would continue if all received an equal opportunity. Tilly correctly points out that a liberal political agenda shaped Handlin's vision of ethnicity and national character. Yet, the object of study for Handlin and for many of his generation was not the immigrant or the phenomenon of immigration, as it was for Hansen and Thistlethwaite, but the American polity itself.

As for the allied "human-capital theory," in accepting the terms of the

American ideology of achievement, it assumed that the individual goal of self-improvement and the strategies to achieve it were the proper objects for studies of immigration. Curiously, then, nationally bounded studies of immigration and immigrant groups often revealed more about national ideologies and national politics than they did about immigration. As Thistlethwaite and his colleagues hoped, the recent international focus and emphasis upon such structural factors as regional economies and occupational groupings have eroded that tendency.

Morawska and Tilly point out, for example, that the recent shift to structural analysis has successfully drawn attention away from the individual toward collective transformations. Even as individual motivation, action, and resources decline in significance in this scheme, groups assume a more active role. This is not a simple case of the modern sociologist's preferences for the study of group over individual behavior. Nor is it simply a case of transferring to the group that which was once attributed to the individual. Rather, attention seems to focus upon the web of connections among groups, and upon the functions and transformations of this web. As internationalism has moved the immigration paradigm away from the nation-state toward a global field, this new scholarship has moved away from both individual and group agency toward the social relations of exchange. So, instead of individuals assimilating or achieving, we have group strategies and networks. What we might call a network-exchange theory seems to be emerging as a potential alternative to assimilation and human-capital theory. In network-exchange theory, an ethnic group's human capital is not simply transported from one place to another by individuals who fold their riches into the American system. Although it is true that the groups are sometimes portrayed as holders of assets, these are transformed to new purposes; indeed, immigrant groups seem capable of creating new advantages for themselves. The network structure that originally functioned as the grid connecting Old World kin might, for example, transform itself in ethnic subeconomies to provide jobs, housing, or even business opportunities. Kerby Miller's essay, in which he discusses Irish-American nationalism in the United States as a form of group cohesion, provides an instance of a newly created ideology lending cohesion to the group. Within the ethnic subeconomy we can observe immigrant groups not only accumulating but creating wealth despite, or perhaps even as a result of, exclusion from mainstream economic resources. Sucheng Chan, for instance, argues that legal and occupational discrimination against the Chinese forced them to remain in ethnic enclaves. As in the case of early twentieth-century Jews and, as Portes points out, of later Cuban immigrants, the Chinese accumulated real economic and human capital within their own groups. The very fact that the American economy was closed, not open, to them may have allowed second and later generations of these groups to compete vigorously in the American success game and position themselves to enter white-collar and professional jobs.

Suzanne Model's essay comparing European immigrants and native-born blacks points out that the situation seems to have worked in the reverse for black urban migrants. In contrast to Europeans, blacks were unable to achieve labor-union membership, and by the early twentieth century were losing access to such occupations as bootblacking and barbering, which they traditionally occupied. Blacks were forced into service jobs that allowed little mutual assistance in job recruitment. Unable to aid one another in finding work, they had to resort to individual job searches; fathers, for example, could seldom place their sons in jobs. Blacks were less successful than immigrants in their work searches, even though, ironically, they followed the favored individualistic American strategy. Model also looks to differences in employment opportunities, not the frequently cited cultural legacy of slavery, to explain why black families appear less cohesive than families of white immigrants in the job market and at home. Morawska's survey of the recent literature and Chan's survey of Asian immigrants supports the notion that labor market conditions, including the points at which groups are able to enter into the labor market, not individual incentive or family resources, explain individual and group success or failure and probably determine how quickly, if at all, a group can enhance its own resources.

Although the scholars in this book agree on a new paradigm for immigration studies, areas of disagreement and omission remain. Most of the authors stress structural conditions as the initial point of analysis, but several scholars here and elsewhere have evolved alternative notions such as "playing within structures" and "ethnic resilience." Proponents of the last two ideas, who are likely to find the structural emphases limited or deterministic, are interested in the persistence or adaptability of ethnic group cultural life and social organizations. The idea of "playing within structures," as Morawska points out, exposes the complexity of the assimilation process and analyzes the way in which immigrants and their families coped with "structural limitations by maneuvering within them." This, Morawska believes, is still a "structural solution." Kerby Miller, arguing that neither the assimilation model nor the ethnic resilience model is adequate, offers the concept of "cultural hegemony." His project is not to examine how powerful groups or circumstances can dominate but why subordinate groups, such as Irish peasants and workers, accepted dominant values. Miller examines how the transcontinental developing capitalist system produced *bourgeois* ideals that working-class Irish immigrants ultimately came to embrace. The Irish middle class, though a small segment of the immigrant stream, played a leading role in forging Irish-American identity, just as middle-class Irishmen in Ireland played a leading role in forging Irish nationalism. Miller reveals that Irish nationalism among peasants and workers, here and abroad, was grounded in traditional middle-class values of home, family, religion, and consumption. His point is simply that explanations that attempt neat alignments of social structure, culture, and ideology cannot adequately accommodate historical reality. He searches for a dialectical explanation that does accommodate the contradictions and muddles of human pursuits.

A number of historians and social scientists are proposing methodologies that allow for both structural and symbolic interpretation. For reasons discussed in greater detail in my own contribution to this volume, this dual analysis has been abandoned by most American sociologists, including those represented in this book. As Morawska suggests, this seems to follow from the sociologist's preoccupation with model building and comfort with statistical data, a situation that, given the landscape of American sociological inquiry, is unlikely to change. But as Morawska also points out, the social scientist's emphasis on the objective, "as opposed to the subjective factors influencing the immigrant's actions and their outcomes appears at times overdrawn," and a "difference in research methods also influences the outcome."

Historians more willingly entertain the dual analysis of subjectivity and objective conditions, possibly because they are not, as Morawska points out, always equally bent on comprehensive model building, and because their craft routinely requires acceptance of a more inclusive universe of documentation from statistics to immigrant letters.[14] Contemporary historical methodology, which incorporates both structural and comparative analysis, embraces a greater variety of sources, including the use of personal documents and, more recently, analysis of the construction of narratives and documents themselves. The analysis of cultural texts has led many scholars to examine the scholarly texts they themselves create, and to reevaluate their own discourse. Logically, in the human sciences and history, ethnographers and oral historians whose field-work practices require careful attention to intersubjective analysis, seem most willing to involve themselves in this self-scrutiny.

The sociologist's work, it seems to me, cannot be considered immune from such epistemological questions and the political issues they imply. As James Clifford and others have pointed out in relation to ethnographic practices, the social scientist's texts themselves are a "strategy of authority," for they involve "an unquestioned claim to appear as the purveyor of truth." And, these texts are, as critics of colonial ethnography and immigration history have shown, created in "specific historical relations of dominance."[15] It is no coincidence that the American-centered theories of assimilation and immigration appeared in the 1920s and 1950s, when the United States enjoyed enormous prosperity and the unquestioned status of a gigantic world power. Today, increasing attention is being paid to global sources of migration at precisely the moment when the United States is confronting serious challenges to economic and political hegemony even from friendly Asian and European powers. The use of aggregate data, the emphasis upon theory building, and the exclusion of subjective information, although in keeping with the proven efficacy of natural science conventions, seem unnecessarily rigid restrictions, inconsistent with efforts to correct ethnocentric biases in immigration studies, with sophisticated methodological advances in the assessment of narrative sources and subjective documents, and with the inescapable pluralism of today's global culture. I hope that this collection, in posing a new synthesis, but not a methodological consensus, will stimulate solutions to these limitations.

The study of gender has had a major impact in the social sciences and the humanities since the 1960s, but only Suzanne Model's discussion of the black family and my discussion of immigrant autobiographical narratives refer to gender in any depth. My efforts to identify a suitable essay for this volume relating gender and migration proved frustratingly disappointing. Perhaps it is premature to expect the necessary partnership required for such a project. Although, as Samuel Baily's contribution to this volume suggests, immigration studies have moved to the point where we can anticipate not only synthesis but comparative analysis, studies of immigrant women are still very much in the case study stage.[16] Feminist scholars, moreover, remain divided on what should be studied about immigrant women and how it should be studied. Many consider the study of women within patriarchal structures — including of course, the family — to be regressive.[17] They prefer to study women as wage earners, writers, labor organizers, and political leaders. Other feminists stress that immigrant women's lives were lived almost exclusively as family lives; they argue that the family should be the centerpiece of analysis. The new paradigm already discussed, which emphasizes such collective strategies as the family economy, the family wage, and the immigration process itself as a family affair, sustains this judgment. Scholars who look at women within the family, like those who study the adaptation of kin groups, are also studying how people "play within structures." Thus, although it is true that some Irish women immigrated to the United States alone, many of them also hoped to enhance their marriage opportunities. German women who married with special prenuptial agreements to use their dowries to escape from Europe were also working within given family practices. Women who took in boarders were earning for the family, but they performed their work at home.[18] All of these women were playing within patriarchal structures, even as many of them shaped those structures to their own ends. Finally, it seems that to sever the immigrant woman's reproductive role from her other roles simply fails to respect the reality of her life.

Still, there is plenty of room for revision of the current structural paradigm, which unnecessarily and incorrectly ignores gender. The reader of almost any scholarly work on labor migration will leave it assuming that all immigrants were, and are, men. Until 1930, when female immigrants actually began to outnumber males, free female migration to the United States was indeed a secondary migration: women followed men as wives or as future wives, and there were fewer of them in the migrant streams. With a few exceptions, most notably the shift to female predominance after 1930 in the United States, this has been a consistent worldwide pattern.[19] Yet, we know that women participated in these flows, and that, as Thistlethwaite pointed out for migrants in general, they were not an undifferentiated mass. Very little is known about women's roles in the decision to migrate either by themselves or as part of family groups. Slave women, of course, did not come as family members, nor did those nineteenth-century Chinese women, who came as indentured prostitutes to serve male Chinese laborers. Many Irish women seemed to have come, like Irish men, to better their lives and possibly to escape arranged marriages. Contemporary Hispanic women use immigration as a means to find work. Other variations no doubt existed; they await scholarly examination.[20] A joining together of immigration studies and gender studies could also explore how the demographics of immigrant sex ratios related to the demographics and politics of the wider society. The relationship between immigration restriction and women's reproductive role is a likely place to begin. The use of male contract labor, a temporary labor force likely to leave wives and families at home, also functioned to control the "browning" of America and what nineteenth-century Americans called "race suicide." As yet, however, no studies consider this obvious point, nor the effects of restrictive legislation on either immigrant assimilation or the host society.

Writers in this volume who emphasize collective strategies and the significance of structural determinants still disagree concerning primary causal explanations. It is no coincidence that three of the scholars who specialize in the study of formerly colonized groups — Portes, Chan, and Miller — incorporate the consequences of imperialism in their analyses of world migration. Portes and Miller, for example, include collective activities in their understanding of immigrant adjustment, but instead of locating the origin of migrations and the formation of ethnic communities in such collective decisions, they see geopolitical interests and their consequences in colonial or postcolonial Ireland, Mexico, Cuba, and Puerto Rico as causes of primary significance. Chan observes that the status of Asian immigrants in this country was profoundly and negatively influenced if their homeland had not achieved nationhood, a situation that she compares with the nineteenth-century Irish. Men and women without a country — Asian Indians before independence, the Irish, and Koreans — continued to suffer from their ambiguous legal status and legal discrimination, both of which reduced their potential for assimilation.

As an antidote to these and other disputes over priority of causation, Samuel Baily's essay offers a systematic cross-cultural and cross-national comparison of host or receiving countries. His essay summarizes the logic of comparative studies, and his own work on Italian immigration to Buenos Aires and New York City from 1870 to 1914, and proposes what may be a coming agenda for immigration studies, a comparative typology of immigrant adjustment. Although this book considers both European and Asian premigration history, and Afro-American and Euro-American experiences within a comparative context, more work of this kind is needed. As Baily points out, we need more synthetic treatments that would historicize the experiences of all immigrating peoples — something Chan has done in her essay comparing various Asian and European groups. My distinguished colleagues, who graciously agreed to join together in creating this book, have provided a point of departure for that task.

NOTES

1. Edward N. Saveth, *American Historians and European Immigrants, 1875-1925* (New York: Russel & Russel, 1965), p. 200.
2. For a discussion of the scholarly literature, see Rudolph J. Vecoli, "The Resurgence of American Immigration History," *American Studies International* 12 (Winter 1979): 46-71; see also Michael Novak, *The Rise of the Unmeltable Ethnics: Politics and Culture in the Seventies* (New York: MacMillan, 1971).

3. The economist Thomas Sowell provides a sophisticated discussion in *Race and Economics* (New York: David McKay, 1975). In his presidential address to the American Historical Association, Carl Degler discussed the issue as well; see his "In Pursuit of an American History," *American Historical Review* 92 (February, 1987): 10. See also John Higham, "Current Trends in the Study of Ethnicity," *Journal of American Ethnic History* 2 (Fall 1982): 5–15.

4. John Bodnar, *The Transplanted: A History of Immigrants in Urban America* (Bloomington: Indiana University Press, 1985), p. 53.

5. Frank Thistlethwaite, "Migration from Europe Overseas in the Nineteenth and Twentieth Centuries," reprinted in *Population Movements in Modern European History*, ed. Herbert Moller (New York: Macmillan, 1964), pp. 73–92.

6. Marcus Lee Hansen, *The Atlantic Migration, 1607–1860* (Cambridge: Harvard University Press, 1940). Although this is Hansen's major synthetic work, Thistlethwaite actually cited other examples of his work. Brinley Thomas, *Migration and Economic Growth: A Study of Great Britain and the Atlantic Economy* (Cambridge: Cambridge University Press, 1952).

7. Thistlethwaite, "Migration from Europe Overseas," p. 85.

8. See, for example, Immanuel Wallerstein, *The Modern World-System: Capitalist Agriculture and the Origins of the European World-Economy in the Sixteenth Century* (New York: Academic Press, 1974), and its sequel, *The Modern World-System II: Mercantilism and the Consolidation of the European World-Economy, 1600–1750* (New York: Academic Press, 1980). This controversial work is discussed, in Steve J. Stern, "Feudalism, Capitalism, and the World-System in the Perspective of Latin America and the Caribbean," *American Historical Review* 93 (October 1988): 829–72; see also further comments by Wallerstein and Stern, pp. 873–85.

9. Josef Barton, *Peasants and Strangers: Italians, Rumanians, and Slovaks in an American City, 1890–1950* (Cambridge: Harvard University Press, 1975); other examples of this kind of work include Kristan Hvidt, *Flight to America: The Social Background of 300,000 Danish Emigrants* (New York: Academic Press, 1975), and later works in this tradition, such as Dino Cinel, *From Italy to San Francisco* (Stanford: Stanford University Press, 1982).

10. Bodnar, *The Transplanted*, chap. 1.

11. In addition to such works as Barton, *Peasants and Strangers*, and Cinel, *From Italy to San Francisco*, see Jon Gjerde, *The Migration from Balestrand, Norway, to the Upper Middle West* (Cambridge: Cambridge University Press, 1985).

12. See Stow Persons, *Ethnic Studies at Chicago, 1905–45* (Urbana: University of Illinois Press, 1987).

13. Oscar Handlin, *The Americans: A New History of the People of the United States* (Boston: Little, Brown, 1963).

14. Samuel Baily, one of the historians contributing to this collection who is, like sociologists, interested in model building, has recently edited a book of letters documenting the immigration experience of an Italian family. See Samuel Baily and Franco Ramella, eds., *One Family Two Worlds: An Italian Family's Correspondence across the Atlantic, 1901–22* (New Brunswick: Rutgers University Press, 1988). As this book of essays was being prepared for publication, Charles Tilly was preparing a research project comparing Italian immigrants in the United States and France that would include both statistical analysis and oral history interviews. Perhaps the recent work of these scholars indicates a shift to a more integrated portrait of immigration history.

15. James Clifford, *The Predicament of Culture: Twentieth Century Ethnography, Literature and Art* (Cambridge: Harvard University Press, 1988), pp. 25, 23.

16. Attempts at synthesis include Charlotte Baum, Paula Hyman, and Sonya Michel, *The Jewish Woman in America* (New York: New American Library, 1975); Louise Lamphere, *From Working Daughters to Working Mothers: Immigrant Women in a New England Industrial Community* (Ithaca: Cornell University Press, 1987).

17. For a recent discussion of women's history and family history, see Louise A. Tilly, "Women's History and Family History: Fruitful Collaboration or Missed Connection?" *Journal of Family History* 12, nos. 1–3 (1987): 303–15. Immigration experts almost always see women within the family context, but scholars who are primarily concerned with gender issues tend to focus upon the women themselves. Examples of the latter are Joanne Meyerowitz, "Women and Migration: Autonomous Female Migrants to Chicago, 1880–1930," *Journal of Urban History* 13 (February 1987): 197–206, and her *Women Adrift: Independent Wage-Earners in Chicago, 1880–1930* (Chicago: University of Chicago Press, 1988). There are many examples of the other perspective. For general bibliographies on immigrant women, see Joseph Cardasco, *The Immigrant Woman in North America: An Annotated Bibliography* (Metuchen, N.J.: Scarecrow Press, 1985), and Mary Garcia Castro, Margaret Gill, and Margaret Jean Gearing, *Women in Migration: A Selective Annotated Bibliography*, Occasional Paper 2 (Gainesville: Center for Latin American Studies, University of Florida, 1983). Specific examples of the immigration scholar's emphasis upon the family context include my own book, *Family and Community: Italian Immigrants in Buffalo, 1880–1930* (Ithaca: Cornell University Press, 1977), and a work by another contributor to this volume, Ewa Morawska, *For Bread with Butter: Life-Worlds of East Central Europeans in Johnstown, Pennsylvania, 1890–1940* (New York: Cambridge University Press, 1985). Morawska's essay contains further thoughts on the issue of the family.

18. There is a substantial literature on women wage earners, much of which reflects the split between those who see women as individuals apart from the family and those who see women functioning primarily as contributors to the family economy. See Alice Kessler Harris, *Out to Work: A History of Wage-Earning Women in the United States* (New York: Oxford University Press, 1982); Carol Groneman and Mary Beth Norton, eds., *To Toil the Livelong Day: America's Women at Work, 1780–1980* (Ithaca: Cornell University Press, 1987); Viki L. Ruiz, *Cannery Women, Cannery Lives: Mexican Women, Unionization and the California Food Processing Industry, 1930–1950* (Albuquerque: University of New Mexico Press, 1987), for recent examples of this literature.

19. See Marion F. Houstoun, Roger G. Kramer, and Joan Mackin Barrett, "Female Predominance in Immigration to the United States since 1930: A First Look," *International Migration Review* 18 (Winter 1984): 908–63.

20. The literature on slave women as migrants is thin. For a general discussion of slave women, see Deborah G. White, *'Arn'n't I A Woman?' Female Slaves in the Plantation South* (New York: Norton, 1985); see also Richard S. Dunn, "A Tale of Two Plantations: Slave Life at Mesopotamia in Jamaica and Mount Airy in Virginia, 1799–1828," *William & Mary Quarterly* 34 (1977): 32–65. On Asian women, see Lucie Cheng Hirata, "Free, Indentured, Enslaved: Chinese Prostitution in Nineteenth Century America, *Signs: Journal of Women in Culture and Society* 5 (Autumn 1979): 3–29; Yuji Ichicka, "Ameyuki-san: Japanese Prostitutes in Nineteenth Century America," *Amerasia Journal* 4 (1977): 1–21. On Irish immigrant women, see Hasia Diner, *Erin's Daughters in America: Irish Immigrant Women in the Nineteenth Century* (Baltimore: Johns Hopkins University Press, 1983). On Hispanic women, see Marta Tienda, ed., *Hispanic Origin Workers in the United States Labor Market: Comparative Analysis of Employment and Earnings* (Washington, D.C.: U.S. Department of Labor, Employment and Training Administration, 1981); Georges Borjas and Marta Tienda, eds., *Hispanics in the United States Economy* (Orlando and New York: Academic Press, 1985).

MIGRATION PATTERNS IN WORLD HISTORY: THE TROPICAL WORLD, ASIA, AND THE UNITED STATES

1

Migration in the Tropical World

Philip D. Curtin

Ellis Island stands as a symbol of the peopling of the United States from Europe. It *was* the prominent gateway through which millions of immigrants from Europe passed on their way to become Americans. And the United States *was* the main destination for the great movement of Europeans overseas in the nineteenth century and early twentieth century. Ellis Island received these at their maximum flow. The median date of arrival for immigrants to the United States from Europe was about 1900. By that date, half had come, and half were still to come. On the other hand, many Americans arrived by other routes as a part of other patterns of intercontinental migration, and with other timing. Most of our African ancestors came with the slave trade, and with quite different timing. The median date of arrival for the ancestors of present-day Afro-Americans lay further back in the past—in about the 1770s. Indeed, it was not until the 1840s that more Europeans than Africans crossed the Atlantic to the New World.[1]

The movements of Euro- and Afro-Americans to the United States were different in other respects as well. North America was the goal and principal destination of the great transatlantic migration; it was only a minor destination for the slave trade from Africa, and it was even further removed from the great migrations through the tropical world after the slave trade ended. Understanding something of these other population movements helps to keep migration to the United States in world perspective.

Population movement is so obvious in world history that many historians have paid little attention to it until recently.[2] All humankind is now thought to have come from a single center, presumably somewhere in eastern Africa. Hunting and fishing peoples populated most of the earth before about 10,000 B.C., as small bands in search of new hunting, gathering, or fishing grounds. This form of migration—into lands with no human occupants, as opposed to sparsely occupied lands like pre-Colombian North America—continued much later than we sometimes realize. Overland migrations had reached most of the world's land masses even before the development of agriculture, but off-shore islands had to wait for the development of appropriate maritime technology. The Polynesian peoples began to spread across the Pacific only in the last millennium B.C., and most of their movement actually took place after the birth of Christ.[3]

Another maritime-based population movement had similar timing: Indonesian navigators moved west across the Indian Ocean to the east coast of Africa and on to Madagascar, that gigantic but previously uninhabited island the size of California and Oregon combined. Later immigrants came from the nearby coasts of Africa, but the initial (and comparatively small) intercontinental movement of Indonesians set patterns of culture and language. The Malagasy today speak a Malayo-Polynesian language, more than three thousand miles from any other language in that group.

Other population movements rested on technical capacities of other kinds — often agricultural or military. The expansion of the Chinese language and culture from the Yellow River valley into the Yangtze basin and further south was made possible by the superiority of Chinese farming techniques. Between about 300 B.C. and A.D. 1300, in much the same way, Germanic-speaking people moved outward in all directions from the plains of northwestern Germany to occupy much of north-central Europe. They moved eastward along the Baltic, into northern France and Italy, into parts of the British Isles, and southeastward into the upper Danube basin. The moldboard plow, the essential technique in this case, made it possible to turn over the heavy soil of the north-European valleys, where excellent agricultural land had previously been forested and unplanted. Some of these migrants later adopted Romance languages, but the extent of Germanic languages in northern Europe today reflects this early population movement.

At about the same time, the Bantu-speaking peoples spread across the whole of central and southern Africa. Linguistic evidence suggests they must have come from east-central Nigeria, where closely related languages are still spoken. Today Bantu languages are as similar to one another as the Germanic languages of Europe are to one another, though they extend over a much wider area. Historians once thought the expansion was made possible by a combination of iron-age technology and new plants from southeast Asia, such as taro or cocoyams, bananas, and coconut palms. It is even possible that these plants came across the Indian Ocean with the same mariners who settled Madagascar. The evidence, however, is quite inconclusive. Mariners of many different origins were able to cross the Indian Ocean by the second century B.C., and techniques for smelting iron seem to have entered sub-Saharan Africa by several different routes.[4] In any event, the Bantu-speakers populated central and southern Africa in much the same way that Polynesians spread across the central Pacific, though southern Africa had previous inhabitants and the Pacific did not.

Still another form of early migration is associated with pastoral nomadism and the age-old struggle between nomadic and sedentary peoples for control over the lands that were marginal to either. In the Afro-Eurasian land mass, the historical scene for this struggle was the great arid and semiarid belt that stretches from the Atlantic coast of Mauritania eastward across Africa, the Red Sea, Arabia, Central Asia, and Mongolia to the Sea of Okhotsk north of Manchuria. Nomads and sedentary peoples each had their own peculiar advantages. Sedentary societies had wealth. Nomads had mobility and the military advantage that came with it; they could mobilize to attack with speed and force at a weak point. If successful, they could seize booty and withdraw, or seize the marginal land with its superior pasture, or even establish control over the sedentary society, as Ghengiz Khan did in founding the Yüan dynasty in thirteenth-century China, or Muhammad's successors did in riding north out of Arabia to establish the first Muslim caliphate.

The sedentary-nomadic conflict involved migration, at least on a small scale, when the nomads won and moved in to control the sedentary society, but they tended to move for other reasons as well. The poverty of their home territory made them nomads in the first place. Population growth forced them to seek more or better land, and their habit of seasonal movement made it easy to move on and not return. Nomads who failed to keep their grazing rights tended to move toward more favorable regions, which set up what William McNeill has called a "geographic gradient," meaning that people tended to move outward over the centuries and in all direction from such unfavorable environments as Mongolia and Arabia. Speakers of the Semitic branch of the Afro-Asiatic language family came out of the desert into Mesopotamia before 2000 B.C.[5] Some no doubt moved even earlier, and such movements continued up to the comparatively recent past. Ancestors of the principal Arabic-speaking peoples of the Maghrib in Africa drifted westward along the northern rim of that continent beginning as late as the eleventh century.

In all of these migrations, people moved in an apparent response to perceived self-interest. They were self-directed as migrants, or at least directed by the leadership of the migrating community. Other, "induced" migrations, however, took place on the orders of people who were not themselves migrants. In most early societies this implied a slave trade. The historical record shows an enormous variety of social subordinations: helots, women, serfs, debt peons, and the list could go on. Slavery is one of these forms, marked off from the others by the fact that the superior has property rights in people. Any of the other forms may serve to extract material goods from the inferiors or to secure other advantages, but slavery alone makes it possible to transfer these rights to a third party. It could therefore serve conveniently as an institution for forcibly moving people from one place to another. Slavery and the slave trade were therefore the principal institutions for induced migration in early societies.

In many societies in which the enslavement of war prisoners was the normal practice, a slave held in captivity close to his or her original home might easily escape. Such a slave's value on the market would therefore be comparatively low. The slave trade provided a way to increase that value by moving the slave so far from home that escape would be difficult and the expectation of finding the way home would be slight.[6] Large-scale forced migration, however, seems to grow out of population shortages, which often occurred in occupations other than normal subsistence food production. Periclean Athens, for example, had a population estimated at 25 to 35 percent slave, but comparatively few worked the land. Many were employed in craft work in the city, and an estimated 15 to 30 percent of the slave force worked the silver mines at Laurion.[7]

Roman slavery was different. It was the best-developed system of which we have detailed knowledge. Roman military expansion drew free farmers into the cities — creating a labor shortage in the countryside — and military expansion made possible the enslavement of the conquered as a new labor force for the countryside. This circular changeover from free to slave labor in the countryside was most common on the Italian peninsula, in southern France, and in Spain, where latifundia — large estates employing hundreds and sometimes thousands of slaves — became the dominant form of agricultural organization. Estimates place the slave population of Italy in the early empire at nearly a third of the total population.[8] It is uncertain how many of the newly enslaved were military captives on the frontiers or how many came from farther away, but beyond the region of border wars the largest external source was the Slavic peoples of the present-day southeastern Soviet Union, north and east of the Black Sea.[9]

The fall of the Roman Empire in the West in the fifth century saw the institutions of slavery and the slave trade pass to Rome's three principal successors: the kingdoms of the Christian West, the Byzantine Empire, and the Muslim societies to the south and southeast. Each of these modified the Roman slave system in its own way. Slavery in the West and in Byzantium declined drastically, partly through manumissions, partly because the flow of slaves from the frontiers dried up as conquest ceased, and partly because the economic demand for the products of the latifundia declined.

In the Muslim world as well slaves were far less important than they had been at the height of Roman power. From the eighth century onward, as a distinct Muslim society took shape in North Africa and the Middle East, some forms of Roman slavery continued, but the large-scale use of slaves in agriculture and industry disappeared, with a few regional and temporary exceptions in Tunisia and southern Mesopotamia. Instead, the set of institutions sometimes called Muslim service slavery became more important. Slaves came to be thought of essentially as strangers to Muslim culture and Muslim society. They were therefore used in occupations that were better left to strangers. Domestic service of a peculiarly intimate sort was one of these, including the service of concubines, castrated harem guards, or women slaves kept for prostitution.

Another kind of service appropriate to strangers was service to the sultan, even military service or high office. A local person was likely to have kinship ties or other interests within society that might run contrary to those of the ruler. A slave owned by the ruler, on the other hand, was free of such ties, and could more easily identify his own interests with those of his master. Slaves of this higher group of servants served in the slave armies that became nearly ubiquitous in the Muslim world: the Janissaries, Mamluks, and the black 'abid of the sultans of Morocco. Because these slaves were valued as strangers, their descendants rarely remained slaves. They had to be replaced by a flow of new slaves from beyond the frontiers — from the Caucasus mountains, from black

Africa, and especially from the great plains to the north of the Black Sea, the most important external sources of Roman slaves as well.[10]

The slave trade out of southern Russia also flowed to the West, largely by way of Byzantium. Slaves were still used in the Christian Mediterranean, especially in domestic service, long after slavery had given way to a variety of serfdoms north of the Alps. When the Crusaders reached the Levant, they took control of the local agricultural production through forms of social subordination that gave them a part of the product, but they usually left the management of production to the peasants themselves.

Things were different with sugar. The Crusaders took over the Muslim techniques for growing and refining sugar but kept the management of sugar production in their own hands, partly because sugar required important new capital investment in grinding and refining equipment, and partly because the semi-refined sugar was destined for the distant European market.[11]

Sugar was also a labor-intensive crop, often planted on comparatively large tracts of land not already in use. This required labor that was not locally available. At first, the Frankish sugar producers exacted more-or-less forced labor from the peasants under their control, but this labor was too scarce to meet the long-term need. The existing slave trade provided exactly the kind of forced migration they wanted.

In the setting of the twelfth, thirteenth, and early fourteenth centuries, slaves were drawn mainly from the Muslim world and from the region north of the Black Sea. Many were Tatars, Circassians, and other non-Slavs, but the medieval Latin word for Slav, *sclavus,* became the word for slave as well, replacing the *servetus* of classical Latin. The new word worked its way into European languages and lasted into the period when most slaves in Western-controlled societies were Africans, not Russians.

In any event, the Mediterranean sugar industry established a link between the slave trade and new agricultural enterprises under European control but beyond Europe. This association between sugar and forced migration was to last almost a thousand years and to reach nearly every corner of the tropical world.

The first move was a migration of the European-controlled sugar industry outward from the Mediterranean. For maximum production, sugar cane requires hot weather the year round and a plentiful supply of water, from either rainfall or irrigation. The Mediterranean basin met these conditions poorly. Tropical islands in the trade-wind belt did much better, and the maritime revolution of the late fifteenth century and the sixteenth century made such lands available to European entrepreneurs.

The earliest Western sugar industry in the Mediterranean had been concentrated on eastern islands like Crete and Cyprus. As the expulsion of the Crusaders drove the Franks from the Levant, they began acquiring control of the formerly Muslim sugar estates in Sicily, southern Spain, and Portugal. Then, in the fifteenth century, Spanish and Portuguese maritime expansion carried them out to the Atlantic islands — especially the Madeiras and Canaries north of the equator and the distant island of São Thomé in the Gulf of Guinea, tucked under the western bulge of Africa—islands that were superior sugar-growing areas in most respects and were also closer to sub-Saharan Africa as a source of labor. The Turkish capture of Constantinople in 1453 had made access to the Black Sea slave ports difficult for Christian ships, just at a time when Europeans established maritime access to the coasts of Africa.

When European mariners landed on the West African coast, as they did increasingly from the 1440s onward they found a network of trade routes already carrying a variety of African goods: kola nuts, shea butter, salt, textiles, iron and iron tools, and also some slaves. African societies enslaved war captives, as many early societies did. The same considerations applied here as elsewhere in the world: once enslaved, a captive near home was less valuable than one far from home, simply because he or she might escape. A form of forced migration was thus already in existence, and North African traders from across the Sahara had already tapped into that supply to fill the demands of Muslim service slavery.

The European role in the African slave trade in its early decades was somewhat ambiguous. The Europeans came down the African coast for gold, not slaves. They also bought a few slaves for export to Europe or the Atlantic islands—about 1,300 a year to Europe and 500 to the various Atlantic islands just before 1500. But they also sold slaves in some circumstances. After 1480 the Portuguese had a fortified post on the coast of present-day Ghana, to protect gold awaiting export. The Akan of the hinterland wanted slaves to work the placer deposits, and the Portuguese obliged by acting as sea-borne middlemen. They bought war captives from the expansive kingdoms of Benin (in present-day Nigeria) and Kongo (in present-day Zaïre). They sold some of these slaves on the Gold Coast, some to Europe, but the great majority to the expanding sugar plantations on nearby São Thomé.

Forced migration *on* the Atlantic had clearly begun by about 1450, but extensive forced migration *across* the Atlantic came a century later. The first slave ship direct from Africa to the West Indies sailed only in 1532. Direct trade to Brazil came only after 1550, when the westward march of the European-directed sugar industry reached the mainland. During the following half century, Brazil emerged as the most important single source of European sugar. After the 1630s, the sugar migration moved on to the Caribbean, with Barbados, St. Kitts, and other of the Lesser Antilles as the first centers. In the second half of the seventeenth century, it moved once more to the larger islands, especially Jamaica and the western or French-controlled end of Hispaniola or Santo Domingo. As sugar moved, the slave trade from Africa increased until, after the 1690s, slaves became the most important single export from western tropical Africa, a position the trade was to hold until about 1850.

The Atlantic slave trade is the best known of all forced migrations in world history. It is nevertheless hard for us to comprehend an economic and social order based on values so different from the present ones. Because many have heard of the slave trade only in the context of the American past, they tend to think of it as a special link between Africa and the United States. In fact, it was a much broader movement within the tropical world with antecedents in other forms of migration and in earlier forced migrations. And it had successors after Africa ceased to be the principal source of plantation labor. In fact, only about 6 percent of all the slaves arriving in the Atlantic slave trade between the fifteenth century and the nineteenth century came to what was to be the United States. About half went to the Caribbean islands and mainland, and about a third went to Brazil. The part that came here was to be important in United States history and for its contribution to American society today, but it was only an offshoot of the larger migration.[12]

Even the size of this population movement is hard for us to grasp. At around nine and a half million people arriving in the Americas, it was tiny compared with the population movements in twentieth-century monsoon Asia; and it was tiny compared with the great outpouring of Europeans in the nineteen and twentieth centuries, but it was still the largest known migration over such a distance in world history up to that time.

The European emigration of the late nineteenth century seems to be associated with the industrialization of Europe and North America, but the forced migration from Africa occurred too soon for any such connection. It seems instead to fit into a transitional phase between the preindustrial and the industrial eras.

One important element is sugarcane as a crop. It not only was labor-intensive but also differed from ordinary food crops like rice or wheat or potatoes in being nutritionally more specialized than the normal starchy staples that form the base of most human diets. It could not, therefore, be the main source of food, which meant that it had to be produced in small quantities or exported for consumption elsewhere. These facts link sugar to societies capable of engaging in long-distance trade. In early times it was so expensive that it was more nearly a drug than a food. It could be sold to distant markets because of its high value-to-bulk ratio, in circumstances when ordinary food products with low value-to-bulk could not justify the cost of transportation. This meant that a sugar-producing work force had to exist close to a complementary source of food. Put another way, adding sugar production to an agricultural economy required increased population density, just as a city or a mine put new demands on the surrounding peasantry. New sugar production thus called for increased population, which in early centuries was found the same way mining populations were found: through the slave trade.

As technological changes in production and ocean shipping brought down the price, sugar consumption increased enormously. In economic terms, from the sixteenth century to the late nineteenth, the price elasticity of sugar consumption was close to unity and sometimes higher. That is, a given drop in price brought an equivalent increase in per capita consumption. By the early twentieth century, however, the price of sugar had fallen so low and available incomes in the Western world had risen so much that most people bought all the sugar they wanted regardless of price. Today, price changes of double or half will hardly change consumption patterns. But in earlier periods, the rise of European prosperity brought with it an inordinate demand for sugar, which ran far beyond the increase in European or world population.[13]

A second factor behind the Atlantic slave trade was the pattern of disease and demography in the tropical Atlantic. The most intensely intercommunicating regions of the Afro-Eurasian land mass had achieved, by 1500 or so, a broad disease environment that included most of the endemic diseases known to any society from Western Europe through the Middle East, South Asia, and on to China. Tropical Africa had most of these diseases, but it also had yellow fever and falciparum malaria, the most frequently fatal species of malaria, and it had the most dangerous mosquitos to serve as vectors of malaria from one person to another.

The New World, on the other hand, had been separated from the intercommunicating zone for such a long time that it lacked most of Europe's endemic diseases, probably lacked falciparum malaria, and may have lacked yellow fever as well. This meant that after Columbus, as newcomers brought in unfamiliar diseases from both Europe and Africa, a series of epidemics devastated the Native Americans. Broadly speaking, the peoples of the tropical lowlands were wiped out by the end of the sixteenth century. Peoples of the Andean and Middle American highlands lost up to 80 or 90 percent of their population during the first 100 to 150 years of contact. The more isolated peoples of the Argentine pampas and of the North American plains sustained similar losses, but later, sometimes as late as the nineteenth century.[14]

Europeans faced their own problems with disease. They had some degree of immunity against the main Asian diseases, but less against those in the tropical Americas and still less against those found in tropical Africa. Mortality rates were erratic, because epidemics came and went, but a European death rate of 250 per 1,000 in eighteenth-century Africa was ordinary. Death rates of Europeans at 100 per 1,000 in the West Indies were normal and could run much higher during yellow fever epidemics. Africans, on the other hand, had some immunity to the main tropical diseases and some immunity to the endemic diseases of Europe. The death rates of Africans newly arrived in the West Indies were also variable, but about 40 per 1,000 appears to have been common.

These differential death rates had a number of important demographic and economic consequences. Most important for the history of migration, the death of the Native Americans left the tropical Americas with enormous potential for agriculture and very few people to work the land. The Europeans had a remedy. They already had experience with plantation slavery and the slave trade; they had the maritime technology required to move people from the Old World to the New; and that same maritime expertise could assure the distant distribution of a specialized food product like sugar. The underlying situation was one of underpopulation (in light of available technology and resources), and underpopulation could be corrected by moving people. Similar conditions were to bring about the great postindustrial European migrations of the nineteenth century. The preindustrial version of those conditions foreshadowed the kinds of migration that were to come with the industrial age. They took place before the true beginnings of industrialization, partly because even preindustrial Europe had the maritime skills needed to move people and products in large quantities over long distances, and partly because the European-managed sugar estate represented a ruthless but technologically efficient way to produce food—a precursor of the organization of labor and machinery that came with the early factory system.

One demographic aspect of this early transatlantic migration was peculiar. It used up people—not just their labor but the people themselves. For Europeans, mortality rates in the tropics were high. One study of servants of the Royal African Company serving in Africa showed that for every ten men sent out for a three-year tour of duty, only one lived to return to England.[15] For such a population to be self-sustaining, births would have to replace deaths. In this instance, low birth rates negated the possibility. Most European planters left their women at home. The fertility rates of the overseas-European population was thus unusually low.[16] Few human societies in history have managed a gross fertility rate of more than 50 per 1,000. Yet the death rates for Europeans in the American tropics substantially exceeded this maximum potential, rendering natural replacement impossible. Europeans simply were not reproducing themselves. For slaves, the normal net natural decrease in the American tropics was notorious, usually in the range of 2 to 5 percent per year everywhere in the belt of territory between northeast Brazil to coastal Mexico.[17] This meant that simply to maintain the tropical American sugar industries at a given level—leaving aside growth—required a continuous stream of migrants from Africa, alongside smaller but still significant streams of migrants from Europe for a one-way trip to the African coast or the West Indies.

This demographic pattern was not unusual for the preindustrial age. Epidemiological theory suggests that people acquire a set of immunities in childhood, but these are at their most effective only in the childhood disease environments. Cities, for example, had usually been consumers of people from the countryside who met new conditions of crowding, filth, and unfamiliar diseases.[18] The population mobility built into the tropical plantation system simply reproduced these unfavorable conditions on a vastly greater scale.

Toward the end of the eighteenth century, a whole set of changes began in Western and world society, connected directly or indirectly to the growing industrialization of the West. The changes influenced tropical migration in a number of ways. One was the rise of humanitarian protest against the slave trade and against slavery itself. Scholars disagree about the nature and strength of any possible connection between capitalist industrialization, abolitionism, and the end of the slave trade. Some intellectual roots of the antislavery movement are traceable to evangelical Protestantism; others, to the "rights-of-man" philosophy of the early eighteenth century. Neither phenomenon is clearly associated with industrialism.

Some people of influence came to believe that the slave system of the Caribbean was not worth the salvage, and some of their ideas did reflect concerns arising from industrialization.[19] From a combination of motives, Britain, the United States, the Netherlands, and Denmark made their part of the slave trade illegal by the first decade of the nineteenth century. Britain, with some help later from France and the United States, began to suppress the trade at sea with naval patrols, not merely the English trade but in time the trade of other nations as well. The slave trade nevertheless continued to grow until the 1840s, its all-time peak decade, followed by sharp decline in the 1850s and effective extinction by the 1870s.

After about 1780, Western populations began to grow faster than any others in recent experience. Western standards of living also began to rise with the products of industrialization, thus increasing the demand for sugar, coffee, and other plantation products. Rising demand might have called forth rising prices, but prices fell instead with improvements in the technology of production, manufacture, and transportation. Demand from the industrial world therefore increased many times over.

Sugar planting began to expand beyond its familiar territory in the tropical Americas. From the 1790s to the 1890s significant new sugar industries appeared in Cuba, British Guiana, and Trinidad in the West Indies and in new parts of Brazil. Sugar also spread to Hawaii, Fiji, coastal Peru, Queensland in Australia, and Natal in South Africa. On the Indian Ocean islands of Mauritius and Réunion, where sugar planting had begun in the eighteenth century with slave labor from Africa, it increased enormously from the mid-nineteenth century onward with contract labor from India.[20]

Demand for other tropical crops increased at the same time, again driven by industrial Europe's new need for raw material and tropical exotics in quantities larger than every before: for tea from Assam, coffee from Brazil and Sri Lanka, cloves from Zanzibar, and later on rubber from Malaya. All of these changes redoubled the demand for labor in the plantation areas, just as sugar had done.

Advancing European technology now made it cheaper and easier to supply the demand from a distance. Even before the era of iron ships and steam power, improved sailing ships made the passage with slaves from Africa to the Americas faster and more secure. The health of the slaves could be better protected than had been possible in earlier centuries, partly through better food and space allocation and control at least of scurvy. The mortality rates for slaves on the middle passage declined from around 20 percent in the seventeenth century to under 5 percent in the early nineteenth, and mortality rates for passengers on other sea routes dropped in a similar fashion.[21] After the 1850s iron sailing ships and larger ships designed to carry people in bulk — troops, contract workers, and the like — come into common use. From the 1870s onward, steamships provided still shorter passages and lower mortality rates. By the 1880s immigrant ships carrying workers on the long voyage from India to British Guiana sustained a mortality rate of only 1 to 2 percent among the passengers. Throughout the century, however, individual voyages, through luck or ill management, sometimes sustained much higher losses.[22]

Even before the slave trade ended, planters began exploring sources of labor outside Africa. This was partly a response to the antislavery movement, but slave prices in Africa had been rising steeply and systematically since the late seventeenth century, which may account for the small flow of slaves from India to the Mascarene Islands in the eighteenth century.[23] As early as 1810, a

Brazilian planter imported a number of Chinese "coolies" under contract.[24] In the first half of the nineteenth century, various West Indian governments experimented with the induced contract immigration of Germans, Portuguese from the Azores, and black North Americans, among others.

By the 1830s, however, the immigrants of choice were from India, with China more prominent later in the century. Some free migrants were always present, but legal indenture for a period of years replaced enslavement as the typical device for securing workers and keeping them in bondage. Though the system was specifically designed to quiet possible objections from the antislavery camp, the reality was remarkably close to the formal slavery it replaced. The sugar industry had already migrated into the Atlantic, carried by technical personnel from the last centers of production, and it continued to migrate in the nineteenth century, again carried by technicians hired at first from the West Indies and then from secondary centers of dispersion like Mauritius or Queensland. Ingrained habits of command, and ingrained ideas about race and a "correct" social order traveled with the technicians. Even though the new enterprises were geographically dispersed, they could not begin with a clean slate. The old way had been the slave trade and the slave plantation, and the people who ran the new institutions tended to run them as nearly in the old way as they could.

Migration from India was mainly under some form of government regulation. The difference in law was that a worker signed an indenture as a voluntary act — at least in theory. Once signed, the worker was bound to serve three, five, or ten years in a distant sugar colony under overseers accustomed to the slave regime. The recruiting agency, often the government of the importing colony, could sell the contract to a third party without the worker's consent, and the contract was enforceable by penal sanctions. If the worker disobeyed orders, the state could step in and send him or her to prison at hard labor. A hundred different devices prevented the worker from receiving even the meager pay and privileges the contract promised. Contracts often included the promise of transportation back to India at the end of the specified term, but most workers never made it home. The same epidemiology of migration operated with contract workers as with the slave trade. The relatively small numbers of women guaranteed that these migrants were rarely a self-sustaining population during the period of the contract, though the remnant population of time-expired workers became capable of natural growth. It formed, indeed, the basis of significant communities of Indian culture scattered through the tropical world.[25]

Whether or not enlistment was "voluntary," it was coerced either directly or indirectly, though circumstances differed with time and place. In the early decades, many north Indian recruits were "hill coolies" — non-Hindu tribal people forced down to the plains in search of work, and there recruited for still more distant labor. In Madras Presidency, many of the recruits were untouchables, already reduced by caste oppression to a position of virtual, and sometimes legal, slavery, from which recruitment for overseas work may well have been a step out, if not up. In the best of circumstances, however, the "voluntary" recruit rarely had any idea what future conditions of labor would actually be.[26]

In the disorder of nineteenth-century China, recruitment was more violent, with a high incidence of outright kidnapping and coolies held in baracoons against their will — even the word *baracoon* was a carryover from the West African slave pens. The export of laborers was contrary to Chinese law most of the time, but the provisions were hard to enforce and the "coolie trade" could pass through Macao with comparative ease. The illegality of the trade, for that matter, worked against the interests of the coolies who *were* captured because the Chinese government could not enforce even the modest regulations imposed by the government of India. The labor recruiters often followed contractual forms, but the reality could very enormously. Many of the immigrants from China to Australia and California paid their own way and chose freely among employers who offered work. Those who went to Cuba and Peru were slaves in all but name.[27]

In the British sphere, the West Indian colonies as a whole imported 536,000 migrants between 1834 and 1918 (430,000 of them from India), but the vast majority of these went to the new sugar-growing areas on Trinidad and in British Guiana.[28] In addition, about 150,000 Chinese contract workers went to Cuba between 1849 and 1875.[29] The new stream of contract workers was, in short, somewhat larger than the 600,000 African slaves imported into Cuba and Puerto Rico (the only significant West Indian destinations for African slaves after about 1830) during the roughly equivalent and slightly overlapping period, 1811–1870.[30]

To shift the comparison, the *whole* transatlantic slave trade from Africa over the period 1801 to 1867 has been estimated at an export of about 3,300,000 people.[31] By contrast, the export of Indian contract workers to territories *outside Asia* from 1834 to 1916 came to about one-third of that number.[32] But that intercontinental migration was only a small part of the Indian contribution to the new migration flows within the tropical world, especially from India to other parts of Asia. Estimates of total emigration from India over the period 1834 to 1937 vary from about 31 million to as high as 45 million.[33] Emigration from Madras to Burma, Malaya, and Ceylon together came to 325,000 in 1900 alone.[34] Numbers almost as large left from Calcutta or moved overland to the tea plantations of Assam. Over the span from 1786 to 1957, an estimated 4,250,000 Indian immigrants entered Malaya — roughly half the size of the whole Atlantic slave trade. Over the same period, about 15 million Chinese arrived in Malaya,[35] or a good deal more than the whole of the Atlantic slave trade.

The distance in either case was only about a quarter of the Atlantic crossing from Africa; the important difference was the new technology of transportation, which not only made such large-scale migrations possible but also enabled many of the migrants to return home. Estimates of Indian returnees vary greatly from one territory to another; overall they may have been about one-quarter of the total.[36] Comparatively few returned from the sugar colonies, like the West Indies or Fiji, but more than two-thirds returned from Malaya during the years 1786 to 1957.[37] In some cases the proportion returning was greater still; virtually all of the surviving contract workers on the Uganda Railway of the 1890s returned to India.

The Chinese contribution to these migrations is harder to establish accurately. The movement into Southeast Asia was obviously much larger than any strand of the nineteenth-century Indian emigration, simply on the evidence of the present-day overseas-Chinese populations there, even though it has not yet been carefully studied. Other strands of the Chinese migration are known in much greater detail, like the temporary labor of some 100,000 Chinese in South Africa mines between 1902 and 1910. At its peak the Chinese migration accounted for 40 percent of all South African mine workers. In the end, however, the British government insisted on total repatriation. Although South Africa today has a small minority population of Chinese origin, it came in other ways, and the great mine-labor migration had little influence on South African culture.[38] But all of the old sugar colonies, indeed, from Jamaica and Cuba through to Hawaii, Fiji, and Mauritius, received a scattering of Chinese, the ancestors of the present Chinese communities.[39]

Then, between the onset of the Great Depression and the end of World War II, migration within the tropical world passed through a transition. The dominant flows before 1930 were from labor-surplus to labor-deficient regions within the tropical world—not entirely voluntary, but economically motivated, at least for the organizer. After 1945 political factors became more important in such mass moves as the exchange of refugees between India and Pakistan after independence, the expulsion of Indians from Uganda, the recent flow of refugees from Ethiopia into the Sudan or from Kampuchea into Thailand. But economically motivated migrations continued and grew in size. The economic motives were now those of the migrants themselves, not the organizers. The element of coercion, indeed, dropped steeply after World War I.

The migrations after 1945 took a new direction as well—no longer within the tropical world but out of the tropical countries, now called the Third World, to centers of economic development in the United States, Canada, Europe, and the Persian Gulf. The United States still received more immigrants than any other single country, but they came overwhelmingly from Mexico, followed by other places in Latin America. In Europe the countries that had once sent migrants across the North Atlantic now became targets of immigration from the South: Surinamese and Indonesians to the Netherlands, Pakistanis and Jamaicans to Great Britain, Turks to West Germany, Italians to Switzerland, Algerians and West Africans to France.

Just as the number of migrants had increased with each new phase—a giant step to the era of the slave trade, and another to the broadened flows of partly coerced migrants of the later nineteenth century—it increased once more after World War II. The change was a function partly of industrialization and partly of the population superexplosion of the tropical world in recent decades. Whereas a growth rate of 1.7 percent per year was considered explosive in nineteenth-century Europe, several modern tropical countries have growth rates approaching 4 percent. And the movement shows no sign of stopping or changing direction, in spite of prohibitions by particular countries like Japan, or unsuccessful efforts to stem the tide by others like the United States.[40]

Although the United States was clearly a central goal for the overseas movement of Europeans since the nineteenth century, it was peripheral to the massive movements of people through the tropical world. The slave trade introduced a significant part of the American population, but the United States was only on the edge of the Atlantic slave trade as a whole. With the phase of contract labor, only Hawaii (and then mainly before U.S. annexation) was even on the fringes of the movement. (Nineteenth-century Chinese migration to California does not fall into the semislave category.) From the 1950s onward, however, the United States was again the principal goal—both for the latest phases of the longstanding stream of migration from Europe and, more important still, for the newer and greater stream of migration toward the most developed parts of the industrial world.

NOTES

1. David Eltis, "Free and Coerced Transatlantic Migrations: Some Comparisons," *American Historical Review* 88 (1982): 251–80.

2. For surveys of early migration, see Kinglsey Davis, "The Migrations of Human Population," *Scientific American* 23 (1974): 93–105; William H. McNeill, "Human Migration in World Perspective," *Population and Development Review* 10 (1984): 1–18.

3. For early migrations in general, see Irving Rouse, *Migrations in Prehistory: Inferring Population Movement from Cultural Remains* (New Haven: Yale University Press, 1986).

4. Christopher Ehret, "Linguistic Inferences about Early Bantu History," in *The Archaeological and Linguistic Reconstruction of African History*, ed. C. Ehret and M. Posnansky (Berkeley: University of California Press, 1982), pp. 57–65; Christopher Ehret and Merrick Posnansky, "An Overview of Eastern and Southern Africa," in *The Archaeological and Linguistic Reconstruction of African History*, ed. C. Ehret and M. Posnansky (Berkeley: University of California Press), pp. 99–103; Jan Vansina, "Western Bantu Expansion," *Journal of African History* 25 (1984): 129–45.

5. McNeill, "Human Migration in World Perspective," pp. 4–5.

6. Orlando Patterson, *Slavery and Social Death: A Comparative Study* (Cambridge: Harvard University Press, 1982), p. 149; Philip D. Curtin, *Economic Change in Pre-Colonial Africa* (Madison: University of Wisconsin Press, 1975), pp. 154–56.

7. Davis, "The Migrations of Human Population," p. 95.

8. William D. Phillips, Jr., *Slavery from Roman Times to the Early Transatlantic Trade* (Minneapolis: University of Minnesota Press, 1985), pp. 18–19.

9. Patterson, *Slavery and Social Death,* pp. 150–52.

10. Phillips, *Slavery from Roman Times*, pp. 66–78. For Muslim military slavery, see Patricia Crone, *Slaves on Horses: The Evolution of the Islamic Polity* (New York: Cambridge University Press, 1980); Daniel Pipes, *Slave Soldiers and Islam: The Genesis of a Military System* (New Haven: Yale University Press, 1981).

11. J. H. Galloway, "The Mediterranean Sugar Industry," *Geographical Review* 67 (1977): 177–92, at pp. 188–90.

12. For the size and distribution of the Atlantic slave trade, see P. D. Curtin, *The Atlantic Slave Trade: A Census* (Madison: University of Wisconsin Press, 1969), to be read along with revised quantitative estimates based on later research in Paul S. Lovejoy, *Transformations in Slavery: A History of Slavery in Africa* (Cambridge: Cambridge University Press, 1983).

13. For a general study of sugar in society, see Sidney W. Mintz, *Sweetness and Power: The Place of Sugar in Modern History* (New York: Viking, 1985).

14. P. D. Curtin, "Epidemiology and the Slave Trade," *Political Science Quarterly* 83 (1968): 190–216.

15. K. G. Davies, "The Living and the Dead: White Mortality in West Africa, 1684–1732," in *Race and Slavery in the Western Hemisphere: Quantitative Studies*, ed. S. Engerman and E. Genovese (Princeton: Princeton University Press, 1974).

16. West Indian and presumably Brazilian populations of European origin apparently were self-sustaining in places like the Spanish part of Hispaniola, Puerto Rico, and Cuba because the native-born acquired appropriate immunities. The European populations of sugar colonies, however, were more transient and retained a net natural decrease.

17. See Curtin, *The Atlantic Slave Trade*, index, under "Population, slave, growth rates of."

18. William H. McNeill, "Human Migration: A Historical Overview," in *Human Migration: Patterns and Policies,* ed. W. M. McNeill and Ruth S. Adams (Bloomington: Indiana University Press, 1978), pp. 3–19.

19. The controversy, however, goes back at least as far as C.L.R. James, *The Black Jacobins: Toussaint L'Ouverture and the San Domingo Revolution* (New York: Vintage, 1938), and Eric Williams, *Capitalism and Slavery* (Chapel Hill: University of North Carolina Press, 1944). Seymour Drescher, *Econocide: British Slavery in the Era of Abolition* (Pittsburgh: University of Pittsburgh Press, 1977), presents another point of view. A survey of still more recent views is Barbara Solow and Stanley Engerman, eds., *British Capitalism and Caribbean Slavery: The Legacy of Eric Williams* (New York: Cambridge University Press, 1988).

20. Sugar production after the 1820s declined in most West Indian colonies, and increased only slightly in Barbados, but sugar production on Mauritius rose by more than 500 percent between the 1820s and 1850s. M. D. North-Coombes, "From Slavery to Indenture: Forced Labour in the Political Economy of Mauritius," in *Indentured Labour in the British Empire 1834–1920*, ed. Kay Saunders (London and Canberra: Croom Helm, 1984), p. 80.

21. Hebert S. Klein, *The Middle Passage: Comparative Studies in the Atlantic Slave Trade* (Princeton: Princeton University Press, 1978), esp. pp. 83–94.

22. Hugh Tinker, *A New System of Slavery: The Export of Indian Labour Overseas, 1830–1920* (London: Oxford University Press, 1974), pp. 145–76, especially p. 165.

23. Tinker, *A New System of Slavery*, pp. 44–46.

24. K. Whinnom, "The International Movement of Labour in the 19th Century," *Ekonami dan Keuangan Indonesia* 2 (February 1954): 78–88, at pp. 79–80.

25. Tinker, *A New System of Slavery,* is a valuable study of emigration from India to the sugar colonies, and especially to Mauritius. It can be supplemented by other studies of Indian migration within Asia itself, such as Kernial Singh Sandhu, *Indians in Malaya: Some Aspects of Their Immigration and Settlement (1786–1957)* (Cambridge: Cambridge University Press, 1969), and K. L. Gillion, *Fiji's Indian Migrants: A History to the End of Indenture in 1920* (Melbourne: Oxford University Press, 1962), or the cooperative works on nineteenth-century tropical migration in general: Kay Saunders,

ed., *Indentured Labour in the British Empire, 1834-1920* (London and Canberra: Croom Helm, 1984); and Shula Marks and Peter Richardson, eds. *Studies in International Labour Migration: Historical Perspectives* (London: MacMillan, 1984).

26. Tinker, *A New System of Slavery*, pp. 47–55, 16–45; Saunders, *Indentured Labour in the British Empire*, pp. 128–30, 168–69.

27. See Robert L. Irick, *Ch'ing Policy toward the Coolie Trade* (San Francisco: Chinese Materials Center, 1982), especially p. 29; Stewart Watt, *Chinese Bondage in Peru: A History of the Chinese Coolie in Peru, 1849-1874* (Durham, N.C.: Duke University Press, 1951), especially pp. 25–54; Persia Crawford Campbell, *Chinese Coolie Emigration to the Countries within the British Empire* (London B.S. King and Sons 1923), pp. 27–36; M.R.S. Coolidge, *Chinese Immigration*, new ed. (New York: Arno Press, 1909).

28. G. W. Roberts and J. Byrne, "Summary Statistics on Indenture and Associated Migration Affecting the West Indies," Research Paper 4 (Port of Spain: Trinidad and Tobago Central Statistical Office, 1967), pp. 59–68.

29. Irick, *Ch'ing Policy toward the Coolie Trade*, p. 8.

30. Curtin, *The Atlantic Slave Trade*, p. 234.

31. Lovejoy, *Transformations in Slavery*, p. 141.

32. Total Indians emigrating to destinations outside Asia were as follows:

Mauritius	453,063
Guyana	238,909
Natal	152,184
Trinidad	143,939
Jamaica	36,412
Surinam	34,304
East Africa	32,000

Ravindra K. Lal, "Labouring Men and Nothing More: Some Problems of Indian Indenture in Fiji," in *Indentured Labour in the British Empire, 1834-1920*, ed. Kay Saunders (London and Canberra: Croom Helm, 1941), p. 152.

33. Sandhu, *Indians in Malaya,* p. 152.

34. Tinker, *A New System of Slavery*, p. 57.

35. Sandhu, *Indians in Malaya*, p. 152.

36. Tinker, *A New System of Slavery*, p. 232.

37. Estimates indicate 3,012,000 returned out of a total migration of 4,250,000 – a net migration of 29 percent. Sandhu, *Indians in Malaya*, pp. 310–17.

38. Peter Richardson, "Chinese Indentured Labour in the Transvaal Gold Mining Industry, 1904–1910," in *Indentured Labour in the British Empire, 1834-1920*, ed. Kay Saunders (London and Canberra: Croom Helm, 1984), pp. 260–90, and "Coolies, Peasants, and Proletarians: The Origin of Chinese Indentured Labour in South Africa, 1904-07," in *Studies in International Labour Migration: Historical Perspectives*, ed. Shula Marks and Peter Richardson (London: MacMillan, 1984), pp. 167–85.

39. These communities and others like them have not yet been equally well studied, but see Clarence E. Glick, *Sojourners and Settlers: Chinese Migrants in Hawaii* (Honolulu: University Press of Hawaii, 1980); Ronald Takaki, *Pau Hana: Plantation Life and Labor in Hawaii* (Honolulu: University Press of Hawaii, 1983).

40. This phase is outlined in Davis, "The Migrations of Human Populations," pp. 102–5; still more recently by Alan Dowty, *Closed Borders: The Contemporary Assault on Freedom of Movement* (New Haven: Yale University Press, 1987). Various aspects are discussed by the contributors to W. H. McNeill and Ruth S. Adams, eds., *Human Migration: Patterns and Policies* (Bloomington: Indiana University Press, 1978).

2

European and Asian Immigration into the United States in Comparative Perspective, 1820s to 1920s

Sucheng Chan

Four separate streams of people migrated to the Americas to join Native Americans: the Spanish and Portuguese, who colonized Mesoamerica and South America and intermarried with the indigenous people to create mixed-blood Latinos; other Europeans, who crossed the Atlantic as colonists, indentured servants, and immigrants; Africans, brought to the New World by slave traders; and Asians, who crossed the Pacific to labor in mines, fields, and construction projects. As the immigrants came in ever larger waves, the indigenous population declined in numbers as a result of conquest, subjugation, and death from diseases introduced from the Old World, so that eventually non-natives outnumbered natives in most of the Western Hemisphere.

The movements of these peoples have seldom been studied in a comparative manner. The Euro-American tradition of viewing peoples of color as inferior beings has distorted our understanding of world history, and the study of many topics—including immigration into the United States—has suffered from constricted angles of vision.[1] Recent studies have begun to redress the balance by placing increased emphasis on the influx of people from Asia, Central America, and the Caribbean.[2] Nevertheless, attempts to analyze the coming of white and nonwhite immigrants—especially in the pre-1968 period—as an equally important phenomenon must still overcome two challenges: the need for a conceptual framework inclusive enough to permit treating the experiences of white and nonwhite immigrant groups meaningfully together, and the unearthing of reliable sources that will provide answers to similar questions about the history of African, European, Latin American, Asian, and Pacific migrations. Certain new developments in the historiography of immigration now make it possible to sketch a common framework of analysis, although the lack

37

of sound empirical information about many immigrant groups is an obstacle that will take years to overcome.

I shall confine my remarks to European and Asian immigration into the United States during the hundred years between the 1820s and the 1920s, a period when immigration was a visible and important factor in American national life. (Contemporary immigration, though an influential force in American society today, is taking place under conditions different from those that prevailed in the century following 1820.[3]) I shall pay more attention to the conditions in the sending regions and countries and to the international political context in which the migrations occurred, and less to the receiving countries, to provide a counterpoint to the existing literature, which, until recently, has focused almost exclusively on the social, economic, and cultural incorporation of immigrants. Only by looking at the emigration end of the story will we fully understand the motivation of emigrants, and until we know what impelled millions of people to undertake often risky transoceanic voyages, it will be difficult for us to place the emigrants/immigrants themselves at the center of our research. My purpose here is to suggest points of departure for comparing European and Asian immigration, and not to review the literature or classify theories of migration, for others have already done so.[4] I shall demonstrate how conclusions reached in studies of one group may be used to generate hypotheses to guide the investigation of other groups, even though they may hail from different continents.

Any meaningful comparison of European and Asian immigration must acknowledge an unfortunate tendency by scholars and others to dichotomize Asians and Europeans who have come to the United States as "sojourners" and "immigrants," respectively. With the single word *sojourner*, some oft-quoted scholars have banished Asians completely from the realm of immigration history.[5] By arguing that all Asians were temporary migrants who came to the United States only to earn money, nativists and scholars alike have justified efforts to exclude them from immigrating altogether and from participating in American social and political life. To be sure, many of the early Asian immigrants did return to their homelands, but as recent scholarship on European emigration has shown, so did many of those who crossed the Atlantic. The phenomenon of return migration among Italians — more than 60 percent of whom returned to Italy — is well known,[6] but even among the English, the return rate was as high as 30 percent in certain periods.[7] In comparison, between 1848 and 1882, when Chinese could enter freely, approximately 322,000 arrived and 151,000 departed, giving us a crude return rate of 47 percent.[8] Between 1909 and 1924, when the "Gentlemen's Agreement" governed Japanese immigration, some 119,000 immigrants (and 70,000 nonimmigrants) entered, while 39,000 emigrants (and 129,000 nonemigrants) left. If we consider only the immigrant and emigrant figures, the crude return rate was 33 percent.[9] Clearly, Asian and European immigrants cannot be differentiated according to their return migration rates. Moreover, the return rates reflect a *composite* set of factors and should not be read only as an indication of immigrant intentions. In some instances, regardless of what the immigrants themselves might have desired, circumstances dictated their final action. Thus, for example, in the 1899–1924 period, Jews had the lowest return migration rate of all immigrant groups (5.2 percent) because they were fleeing pogroms in Europe and had nothing to return to. Armenians, who were also escaping persecution, likewise had a low return rate (14.7 percent), as did the Irish (12.4 percent), who were forced out by circumstances to be discussed below.[10]

To counteract the tendency to dichotomize European and Asian immigrants, I shall discuss several clusters of characteristics that may be used to compare them. Instead of placing people from the two continents into mutually exclusive binary categories, I shall situate groups along particular "axes" or dimensions, and I shall begin my analysis by making three propositions.

1. The economic geography of a region — its topography and patterns of natural resource endowment, ownership, and exploitation — and certain prevailing social arrangements, such as kinship and inheritance patterns, strongly affect the rate of emigration and also the kind of people who leave and their subsequent behavior, including whether or not they ever return. Such economic and social "ecological" characteristics are the primary determinants of emigration at the local or regional level.

2. At the national level, political factors come into play. Immigrants from colonized lands are likely to put greater effort into freeing their homelands from subjugation than into building the communities they establish in the new country. Consequently, their rate of upward socioeconomic mobility may be retarded, unless at some point they are able to use their political skills to advance themselves in the host society. In other words, nationalist concerns for the homeland may be an important factor in perpetuating their "entry-level" occupational status as well as in preserving their ethnic identity.

3. Immigrants from colonized countries are more likely to be mistreated than those from sovereign nations because they do not have a homeland government to defend their interests. Discrimination comes not only in the form of economic exploitation but also as legally sanctioned subordination. In the case of Asian immigrants, the legal system has functioned even more effectively than the labor market as a sorting mechanism to determine their standing in American society.

The foregoing propositions are not exhaustive, but they provide starting points for placing Asian and European immigration on an equal analytical footing. Given the many gaps in our knowledge, my discussion can be only suggestive. I shall highlight the effect of ecological and economic conditions by comparing several studies of Italian and Norwegian emigration with what is currently known about Chinese and Japanese entry into the United States. To illustrate the effect of colonialism, I shall discuss the coming of Koreans and Asian Indians alongside the Irish influx. In neither set of comparisons are the numbers equivalent. Over 4,000,000 Italians and some 700,000 Norwegians entered the United States between 1860 and 1920; only 300,000-plus Chinese arrived between 1850 and 1882 and some 400,000 Japanese came between 1885 and 1924. (The Chinese and Japanese figures include people who went to Hawaii.) The numerical disparity between the Irish and Koreans and Asian

Indians is even greater: more than 4,000,000 Irish disembarked in American ports between 1840 and 1920, but only 7,000 Koreans came between 1902 and 1905 and a similar number of Asian Indians arrived between 1908 and 1917. These numerical differences notwithstanding, it is instructive to compare the groups because the circumstances that spurred them to leave their homelands were very similar and greatly influenced their subsequent behavior in the United States. I shall conclude with a discussion of how, despite many initial similarities, the status of European and Asian immigrants in the United States ultimately differed, and why.

Ecology and Economy

It is important to look at regional ecologies and economies because most transnational migrations have been geographically selective. Before the advent of modern transportation, in each sending country a relatively small number of localities sent large numbers of people abroad, and initially, at least, these migrants tended to settle in contiguous clusters (if not actual colonies) in the host societies. Specific ecological and economic conditions, combined with certain social practices, made some areas, and not others, into emigrant regions. For example, in a comparative study of Italians, Rumanians, and Slovaks in Cleveland, Josef Barton examines the regions from which they came and concludes that migration served not to sever the peasants' connections with their villages but to enhance their positions there.[11] Barton differentiates between regions characterized by household agriculture, where land was fairly broadly distributed and a variety of crops were grown by numerous small holders, and areas with commercial agriculture practiced on large estates, where "unequal cultivators" existed in a "hierarchical social structure." In the three homelands investigated — regions that eventually became Italy, Rumania, and Czechoslovakia — people in areas dominated by household agricultural organization dealt with their economic problems through emigration; those in areas dominated by commercial agriculture confronted their oppressed working conditions through political militancy. In southern Italy, especially, migration rates were highest in regions where property was most widely distributed. Although these regions had the lowest per capita income, that was not what impelled people to leave. Rather, Barton suggests, the availability of land for purchase and the widespread existence of sharecropping, which offered cultivators a stake in the products from the soil, gave people the incentive to work overseas so they could send money home for land acquisition.

In a study of Italians in San Francisco, Dino Cinel shows that the emigration rate was highest in areas where Italian land could be purchased with U.S. money. Where no small parcels were available for sale, few people emigrated across the Atlantic, and those who left seldom returned. In areas with purchasable land, the out-migration was large, and the number of returning migrants in the years before World War I often exceeded two-thirds the number of emigrants. People went abroad to earn the cash needed to buy the available plots because there were few ways to accumulate savings at home. According to one report that Cinel cites, "Most returnees said their decision to return to Italy had been based on economic plans made before they had departed for the first time. . . . The returnees were for the most part neither rejected by American society nor spurred by nostalgia. Rather they were individuals actively pursuing goals they had set before departing."[12]

The availability of land, though important, was not the only critical factor associated with different rates of emigration. The land-use pattern and its relationship to the system of inheritance also mattered. According to Jon Gjerde, in Norway, which before 1890 had the highest per capita rate of emigration of any European country except Ireland, there was "a strong correlation between the type of agriculture practiced in a locality and the propensity of its residents to move to the New World."[13] The broad, flat grain lands in eastern Norway and Trøndelag differed from the mountain and fjord regions of the West, where people relied on the sea and the high pastures for sustenance. In the grain-growing East, a region of large farms, where landowners and landless laborers were two clearly demarcated classes, the landowners had few reasons to emigrate, and the landless laborers seldom found the means to do so. Western Norway, on the other hand, contained two kinds of subregions: strips of arable land along the coast and mountain pastures in the interior. Partible inheritance was practiced along the coast, and over the centuries, farms were subdivided into ever-smaller plots, until most of them could no longer sustain families; people survived by fishing, seafaring, shipbuilding, trading, and lumbering. Out-migrants from coastal settlements usually went to other parts of Norway. In the mountain pastures, animal husbandry and dairying provided a living. Because cattle raising required large tracts, impartible inheritance was the rule, which meant that few young people could hope to inherit or buy land. Norwegian custom did not allow young people to marry until they could support a family, so an increasing number of individuals in each succeeding generation encountered greater difficulty in earning a living and felt doomed to celibacy, or had to resort to procreation out of wedlock. One way for families to avoid generational decline in social status was for some of their members to leave Norway altogether.

The first emigrants from the cattle-raising areas, however, were not individuals without prospects of landed inheritance; rather, fairly-well-to-do farmers with money for passage, in search of larger farms at lower prices, led the exodus to the United States. Their departure made it possible for the less-well-endowed to follow. Upon arrival in the American Midwest, where the majority of them settled, the pioneer immigrants discovered there was a shortage of labor. They dealt with this problem either by engaging in a different form of agriculture — cereal cultivation, which required less labor than animal husbandry — or by seeking help from home. They often sent back prepaid tickets to encourage young relatives and village mates with strong backs but insufficient funds to cross the Atlantic. Furthermore, the depopulation of localities where emigration fever hit made labor scarcer and wages consequently higher, so that now, even landless workers could accumulate money for steamship fares.

Emigration for these Norwegians was less a flight from poverty than a rational means to avoid socioeconomic decline. Moreover, settling abroad enabled them to improve and maintain their social institutions. The relative ease with which land could be purchased in the United States made it possible for young Norwegian emigrants to marry and form families and, in the process, to retain certain beliefs and practices — especially those based on people's abiding relationship to the land. For both the Italians and the Norwegians, emigration was a conservative act.

Like Europeans, Asians also emigrated from a limited number of areas. An overwhelming proportion of the nineteenth-century Chinese emigrants to the Pacific Coast of the United States and Canada came from the area around Guangzhou (Canton), the capital of Guangdong (Kwangtung) province. These emigrants can be further divided into people from San-i (Sam Yup in the Cantonese dialect, meaning the "Three Districts"), located to the west of the provincial capital; Si-i (Sze Yup in Cantonese, meaning the "Four Districts"), to the southwest of San-i; and the lone district of Xiangshan (Heungsan in Cantonese), south of San-i. For almost a thousand years before mass emigration from Guangdong, Chinese from that province and its neighbor, Fujian (Fukien), had sailed to the island of Taiwan and to various parts of Southeast Asia to trade and to settle. No definitive study has yet been done of nineteenth-century Cantonese emigration, but it seems safe to say that it differed from earlier Chinese emigration because of certain distinctive features of the economic and political history of the Guangzhou area.[14]

The city of Guangzhou had a long history of being China's main — indeed, sometimes sole — port open to foreign commerce. Before the Song (Sung) dynasty, it hosted thousands of foreign merchants, but from the ninth century to the last quarter of the eighteenth, the Chinese government favored Quanzhou (Ch'uanchou) in Fujian province as the locus of international commerce. Quanzhou was farther north on the China coast and therefore closer to Hanzhou (Hanchou), the center of silk production in central China, and, in addition, government officials believed they could control the collection of customs and port duties more tightly in Quanzhou, where the merchants (presumably) did not have as great a penchant to act independently as the Cantonese merchants did. However, in 1760 Guangzhou regained its status as the only port open to foreign trade, and traders from different parts of the world were allowed to do business there with designated Chinese merchants in specified localities in the city. Given such a history, Cantonese had more experience than Chinese from other parts of the Middle Kingdom in interacting with Westerners. They probably had less fear of traveling to faraway places like California, Hawaii, and Australia — the major destinations of Cantonese emigrants — in contrast to Fujianese, who also had centuries of experience in foreign trade and other maritime activities but preferred to migrate to Southeast Asia, where they had already established numerous settlements and extensive commercial networks.

Contact between Chinese and Westerners increased during the seventeenth century as a result of the worldwide commercial and colonial expansion of

Europe. The Chinese government's restrictive trade policies and practices led the British to begin "opening" China to commerce and Christian proselytization. The desire of foreign traders, particularly the Europeans, to obtain a vast array of Chinese goods, initially put the balance of trade in China's favor. The British tried to reduce the balance by importing opium into China, which they encouraged Chinese to use. The trade balance reversed and large amounts of silver bullion began to flow out of China, to the alarm of the government. When a Chinese official confiscated and destroyed thousands of chests of opium that English merchants were holding in storage in Guangzhou, the British fought a war with China in 1839–1842, followed by another in 1856–1860. Defeat forced China to accept the continued influx of opium, pay huge indemnities, limit the amount of duties it could charge foreign imports — all of which adversely affected its monetary system and trade balance — and cede territories to European control.

The effects of these concessions fell most heavily on the environs of Guangzhou. As taxes rose to help pay for the indemnities and the continued opium imports, many farmers suffered. Small landowners who could not pay the increased taxes lost their property and became tenants. Tenants who were unable to pay the higher rents became landless laborers. Laborers found it harder to earn a living because of rising unemployment as dockhands, boatsmen, and those who transported goods inland on foot lost their jobs once Guangzhou lost its monopoly over foreign trade. Peasant households also suffered because the products of their cottage industries could not compete with cheap, factory-produced, imported goods. At the same time, the presence of European soldiers and the carving out of an enclave in Chinese territory that was no longer subject to Chinese law enabled labor recruiters and agents of shipping companies to operate freely. (Soon after the Manchus conquered China and established the Qing [Ch'ing] dynasty [1644–1911], they promulgated a series of edicts prohibiting emigration, partly as a precaution against efforts by those loyal to the preceding Ming dynasty to form armies abroad to overthrow the Manchus.) Chinese who wished to defy the law now could also ignore their own officials, because the foreign enclaves served as sanctuaries to which they could escape. As a gesture of accommodation, the governor of Liangguang (the "two Guang" — Guangdong and Guangxi — provinces) took it upon himself to sign an agreement with the foreign officials to allow Chinese to be recruited as laborers for employment abroad.[15] Cession of the island of Xianggang (Hong Kong) to Great Britain after the first Opium War gave European and American sea captains access to another harbor, in addition to Aomen (Macao), which the Portuguese had acquired in the sixteenth century, where they could dock their ships while awaiting passengers. Chinese who wanted to emigrate as well as kidnappers of coolies[16] found it relatively easy to make their way to the waiting ships.

Another factor in emigration was a series of upheavals: the Taiping Rebellion (1850–1864), a millenarian movement led by a self-proclaimed younger brother of Jesus Christ during which an estimated ten million people perished; the Bendi-Kejia (Punti-Hakka) feuds, which raged in the 1860s between two dialect groups and devastated a large part of the Pearl River Delta; and the Red Turban uprisings led by secret societies that also cost an untold number of lives. Although the historiography presents these as important "push" factors, it is difficult to correlate them with migration out of particular districts.

The ecology of specific localities in Guangdong Province was probably related to the pattern of emigration in a way that has not yet been investigated. Guangzhou sits astride the Pearl River Delta, one of the richest agricultural areas in China, where the amount of arable land was increased by diking and draining the swamps to create polders. In the less fertile hilly areas, peasants planted sweet potatoes, which became one of their main staples as paddy acreage decreased with the expansion in the acreage devoted to nonstaple commercial crops.[17] These agricultural activities were carried out under a variety of landholding and labor-organization patterns, but it is not clear how they affected emigration or were themselves influenced by the larger political and economic developments discussed above.

Of the two streams of Cantonese who ventured overseas, those who traveled as free or semifree emigrants to the gold rushes in California, the Pacific Northwest, and Australia were probably upwardly mobile people who saw emigration as a way to obtain the funds that would enable them to benefit from the expansion of commercial agriculture, while those who left under the coercive conditions of the "coolie trade" to Cuba and Peru, as well as the ones who went to California *after* the placer mines there had given out, were more likely victims of imperialism, war, land dispossession, debt bondage, and natural disasters. San-i people from the delta were probably the bulk of the former, and Si-i folk who left out of dire necessity, or Kejia people who were taken prisoners in the Bendi-Kejia feuds and were sold to coolie traders, probably made up a large portion of the latter. Overall, the majority of the emigrants came from Si-i, where the land was hilly and barren.

Sources published in English in California confirm that the first Chinese arrivals there were merchants and skilled artisans. The merchants who had already established themselves in San Francisco, before the mass immigration of Chinese began with the influx of over 20,000 persons in 1852, made a favorable impression with their urbanity and ability to interact easily with white Americans. It is fairly certain that most of them were San-i people, because San-i merchants dominated U.S. Chinatowns until the 1890s, when some Si-i merchants began to challenge them.[18] We also know that Chinese carpenters and joiners showed up very early: they erected the Parrott building (using precut granite imported from China) on the corner of California and Montgomery streets in 1852.[19] It is quite possible that these skilled craftsmen were also San-i people who had gained their experience in the building trades in Guangzhou city. The immigrants who came after 1852, however, probably came from diverse districts, all lured by the glitter of gold. Eventually, poor Si-i people overwhelmed their more-well-to-do San-i peers as mining declined and Chinese came mainly to work as common laborers.

Regardless of what motivated their departure, many emigrants managed to save enough from their earnings to send sizable remittances home. Such funds enabled their families to survive and even to buy land, and also contributed substantially to the physical "uplift" of the emigrant communities: ancestral temples and halls were repaired, and schools and houses (and even China's first railroad) were built with overseas money.[20] Their contributions to the development of their communities of origin were quite similar to those made by Italian emigrants, who built numerous American-style "modern" houses that transformed the looks of many Italian villages.[21]

Japan was not forcibly "opened" as China had been, but the leaders who came to power after the Meiji Restoration of 1868 began to industrialize and modernize their country to prevent Japan from suffering at the hands of European imperialists. The changes they imposed on their society and economy affected peasants profoundly. A new taxation system placed the major burden on small landowners, tenant farmers, and landless laborers, who now had to pay taxes based on the value of the land instead of on the size of the harvest. In addition, inflation in the late 1870s, followed by deflation in the early 1880s, made life erratic for many. Between 1883 and 1900, some 367,000 farmers were dispossessed of their land for failure to pay taxes. The tenancy rate reached over 40 percent by 1892.

Such conditions caused the Japanese government to reevaluate its ban on emigration. For more than two centuries before the Meiji Restoration, Japan's rulers had followed a policy of seclusion, partly because a group of Japanese who revolted in 1637–1638 on the Shimabara peninsula had proclaimed themselves Christian rebels. Christianity, which had been introduced by Francis Xavier into Japan in 1549, thus became part of the subversive foreign influences that had to be wiped out. All foreign traders except the Chinese, Koreans, and Dutch were expelled. Chinese were allowed to trade only through the Ryukyu Islands (Okinawa), Koreans at Tsushima Island, and the Dutch at Deshima Island. Japanese subjects were forbidden to go abroad. However, in 1868 Europeans successfully smuggled several hundred Japanese out of the country to Guam, Hawaii, and California. But these Japanese were ill-treated, so the new Meiji government prohibited any further unauthorized departures. By the mid-1880s, having consolidated its power, the central government became more responsive to the requests of foreign labor recruiters who desired Japanese workers because it thought emigration might provide a safety valve during a period of economic hardship. The first shipment of contract laborers left for Hawaii in 1885.[22]

But economic considerations alone do not explain why the vast majority of the emigrants came from only a few prefectures in southwestern Japan: Yamaguchi, Hiroshima, Okayama, and Wakayama on Honshu Island, and Fukuoka, Nagasaki, Saga, Kumamoto, and Kagoshima on Kyushu Island. The usual explanation for this geographical distribution is the one offered by Hilary Conroy.[23] According to Conroy, Foreign Minister Inoue Kaoru and the president of Mitsui Bussan, an important import-export firm, Masuda Takashi, both of whom came from Yamaguchi prefecture, had told Robert W. Irwin, an American businessman in Japan who was consul general, commissioner of immigration, and special agent of the Board of Immigration of the then-independent Kingdom of Hawaii, as well as foreign adviser to Mitsui Bussan, that Yamaguchi and neighboring Hiroshima would be the best places from which to recruit Japanese laborers for Hawaii's developing sugar plantations. Irwin negotiated the terms under which Japanese would travel to Hawaii and work as contract laborers, and his agents did most of their recruiting in the southwestern prefectures listed above. By the time the so-called Irwin convention system ended, a chain migration process had been set in motion. From 1894 to 1908, private emigration companies controlled Japanese emigration to Hawaii and the Pacific Coast. According to Alan Moriyama, agents of these companies went from one village to the next, which also helps to account for the clustering of emigrant villages.[24]

Conroy's very reasonable explanation does not tell quite the whole story. One intriguing unexamined question is whether the political settlement following the Meiji Restoration had any impact on the pattern of emigration (apart from the personal predictions of Inoue Kaoru). During the Tokugawa period, *han* (feudal domains or fiefs) were grouped into three categories, *fudai*, *tozama*, and *shimpan*, based on the relationship of the *daimyo* (lord) to the Tokugawa *shogun*. *Fudai daimyo* came from clans that had become vassals of the Tokugawa before the first *shogun* unified Japan in 1600; during the shogunate period, they ruled their own *han* and simultaneously staffed the *shogun's* administration. *Tozama daimyo* belonged to houses that had not been vassals of the Tokugawa before 1600. (Their status was based on the vassalage relationship, not on whether they had fought on the side of the Tokugawa in the critical battle at Sekigahara. The ancestors of some *tozama daimyo* had fought against the Tokugawa, others had remained neutral, and yet others had been allies.) *Shimpan daimyo* came from branch houses of the Tokugawa, whose members were also eligible to serve as *shogun*. But like the *tozama daimyo*, they governed only their own *han*.[25] Superimposed on the *han* territorial divisions were provinces, whose boundaries did not always coincide with those of the *han*.

Following the Meiji Restoration, the *daimyo* were required in 1869 to turn over their registers of land and people to the new central government. Two years later the feudal domains were abolished and replaced by administrative units known as *ken* (prefectures), whose boundaries followed roughly those of the former *han*. With the single exception of Wakayama, all the other major emigrant *ken* had been *tozama han*, and *samurai* from Choshu and Satsuma (which became Yamaguchi and Kagoshima *ken*, respectively) had led the Meiji Restoration. Surely that fact has some as-yet-unexplored bearing on the pattern of emigration. Could it be that Inoue had recommended Yamaguchi and its neighboring *ken* to Irwin not only because he was trying to please the Hawaiian government, which sought sturdy peasants — after all, peasants could be found everywhere in agrarian Japan — but also because he wanted only inhabitants from *ken* he trusted to be recruited? Was the new taxation system applied uniformly throughout Japan, or did it affect the former *fudai*, *tozama*, and *shimpan han* differently? Did the central government's new leaders, virtually all of whom were natives of former *tozama han*, favor their own *ken* in any way? How did the landownership and land-use patterns change in each kind of *han* after they became *ken*? Finding answers to some of these questions would move the study of Japanese emigration to a new level of sophistication.

Regarding the emigrants themselves, we have already begun to discover answers to important questions. One is whether Asian and European emigrants were motivated by similar considerations about the desire to buy land and to avoid socioeconomic decline. That such motivations might indeed have been present among the Japanese is suggested by a number of recent studies. Although Japanese and Western scholars alike have generally followed the fight-from-poverty-and-disaster line of reasoning in discussing emigration from Japan, the findings of Kodama Masaaki, who studied emigrant districts in Hiroshima, and Ishikawa Tomonori, who focused more narrowly on four villages, are similar to those of Cinel and Barton for Europe. The existence of primogeniture in Japan suggests that, logically, sons destined to inherit their parents' fields and houses would be less likely to emigrate than their siblings, who had to find nonlanded means of livelihood. However, according to Ishikawa and Kodama, most of the contract laborers from the districts they studied in Hiroshima who went to Hawaii were "successor" sons from families that farmed small plots as owner-operators or as tenants.[26] This finding is corroborated by the results of a retrospective survey carried out by the Japanese American Research Project, which found that eldest sons outnumbered younger sons among the *Issei* (immigrant-generation Japanese) respondents.[27]

Why did so many "successor" sons emigrate? The answer probably lies in the fact that commercial as well as subsistence agriculture was practiced in southwestern Japan. Cotton was one of the commercial crops grown there, but during the 1880s domestically grown cotton had to compete with cotton imported from the United States in supplying Japan's developing textile industry. Cotton growers suffered as the price of Japanese cotton fell. "Successor" as well as "nonsuccessor" sons had to worry about making a living, though their reasons for emigration very likely differed. Those who were responsible for the preservation of their lineages looked to earnings abroad to help maintain their families' socioeconomic standing. Although no studies have been done of how the pattern of remittances among Japanese emigrants correlated with their birth order, it is likely that "successor" sons sent money home regularly to help pay taxes and mortgages, to redeem lost holdings, or to buy new plots. "Nonsuccessor" sons who emigrated, on the other hand, may have been less faithful in sending remittances home. A great many also probably planned never to return because there was no place for them in the land of their birth. Future studies will have to explore whether my hypothesis that "successor" sons resembled Italian emigrants and "nonsuccessor" sons acted more like Norwegian emigrants is correct.

Colonial Domination

Just as findings on the economic and ecological aspects of European emigration raise questions about Asian emigration that merit further study, so applying the insights gained from an analysis of the political dimensions of Asian

international migrations will sharpen our understanding of European movements across the seas. International politics were particularly salient in Asian
emigration and immigration because the colonial domination of Asia during
the peak period of emigration from that continent had important ramifications
on how Asians behaved and were treated in the United States and other "white
men's countries," such as Canada and Australia.[28] By contrasting the way
Japanese immigrants were handled with the reception given other Asian
groups—as I shall do in the last section of this essay—we can see that the
relatively stronger position of Japan in the family of nations forced the United
States federal government to be more sensitive in its dealings with Japan than
with China, Korea, India, or the Philippines. The relative standing of emigrant
nations mattered because subjects from strong and independent nations could
appeal to their homeland governments for help if they encountered discrimination abroad, but those from colonized or externally dominated lands had no
similar recourse.

Compared to other aspects of European migration, relatively little attention
has been paid to the question of whether colonialism had any effect on the
behavior and treatment of immigrants from subjugated European countries,
probably because we normally think of European countries as colonizing, and
not colonized, nations. Yet, the Baltic states of Estonia, Latvia, and Lithuania
had been absorbed into the Russian Empire and Poland had been partitioned
three times by the end of the eighteenth century; the six Balkan nations of
Bulgaria, Croatia, Macedonia, Montenegro, Serbia, and Slovenia had been
conquered by the Turkish Ottoman, the Russian, and the Austro-Hungarian
empires, and Greece had fallen under Turkish rule before mass emigration
began; and the Irish had suffered under English control for some eight centuries before the potato famine. Irish emigration provides a particularly useful
prism for examining the linkage between colonial domination and emigrant
behavior and treatment among European immigrants because the Irish influx
into the United States has been so extensively documented and studied.

How colonial rule in certain parts of Asia affected the lives of emigrants
from those lands can be seen most clearly in the case of Koreans and Asian
Indians (formerly called East Indians). In contrast to Chinese, Japanese, and
European emigration, local economic and ecological arrangements had relatively little to do with the departure of Koreans from their homeland. Rather,
emigration resulted primarily from the efforts of Americans to recruit Korean
workers.[29] At the beginning of the twentieth century, sugar plantation owners
in Hawaii turned to Korea as a possible source of labor because, by then,
Japanese workers, who constituted two-thirds of the total plantation work
force in the islands, had become militant and were engaging in work stoppages
and spontaneous strikes. In 1902 the Hawaiian Sugar Planters' Association met
with Horace N. Allen, an American medical missionary who had proselytized
in Korea since 1884, when he stopped in Hawaii en route back to Korea from a
visit to the United States. Allen had become quite involved in Korean affairs,
having gained the confidence of Emperor Kojong, whom he served as personal
physician. Desiring a more formal role in Korean politics, he managed, with

the help of George Nash, a friend of President William McKinley's, to get himself appointed as the United States minister to Korea. Nash was the stepfather of David Deshler, an American businessman in Korea, with whom Allen subsequently entered into a partnership to recruit Koreans for Hawaii's plantations.

Several steps had to be taken before emigration could begin. First, Allen persuaded the Korean monarch to set up a bureau of emigration. The emperor agreed to do so because famine had stalked several northern provinces in 1902; he thought emigration might provide some relief. Meanwhile, Deshler opened a bank in which the Hawaiian Sugar Planters' Association was the sole depositor. The Deshler Bank lent money to aspiring emigrants for their passage as well as to meet the requirement set by the U.S. government that immigrants had to possess $50 upon arrival, as proof that they were not contract laborers. Few Koreans responded to the recruitment efforts, however, until the Reverend George Heber Jones persuaded members of his congregation that life for them as Christians would be more pleasant in Hawaii, a Christian land. About half of the first shipment that left, in December 1902, were members of Jones's church. Another missionary, Homer Hulbert, who published the *Korea Review*, also urged Koreans to emigrate in the pages of his magazine. As a result of the active role that missionaries played, an estimated 40 percent of the more than seven thousand Koreans who eventually landed in Hawaii were converts to Protestant Christianity.

The emigrants originated from scattered locations and diverse socioeconomic backgrounds. Although there is no definitive information on exactly where they came from or what occupations they had followed prior to departure, most were probably laborers, former soldiers, peasants, and artisans from the areas around Inchon and Suwon. They traveled on ships owned by Deshler to Kobe, Japan, where they were medically examined before they set sail for Hawaii. More than six hundred of the emigrants were women and more than five hundred were children, figures that indicate that quite a large proportion probably intended to settle overseas. Eventually, about one thousand returned to Korea and another thousand or so reemigrated to the United States mainland to join the small number of Koreans — mostly merchants and students — who had gone there directly.

Emigration ended suddenly in 1905, in the midst of the Russo-Japanese War (1904–1905). When victory seemed imminent for Japan, which had desired control of the Korean peninsula for several decades, its representatives in Korea closed the emigration office that the emperor had set up and banned further departures in an effort to protect Japanese laborers in Hawaii, whose strikes were often broken by the sugar plantation owners' use of scabs of other nationalities, including Koreans. Winning the war enabled Japan to declare Korea its new sphere of influence. The Japanese resident-general in Korea, Ito Hirobumi, became the de facto ruler of Korea.[30] The new Japanese administration revised existing laws to allow Japanese to purchase land freely in Korea and reformed the currency to facilitate economic transactions between the two countries. Thousands of Japanese agricultural colonists settled in Korea; Japanese entrepreneurs obtained fishing, mining, timbering, and railroad construction concessions there; and Korean-grown rice, silk, and cotton were exported in increasing amounts to Japan. In the face of several popular uprisings, the Japanese administrators disbanded the Korean army and monopolized all instruments of physical coercion and channels of communication.

In 1910 Japan annexed Korea outright. Terauchi Masatake, the Japanese minister of war, became the governor-general of Korea, and to secure the goodwill of the Korean people, he announced that he would waive the unpaid taxes and unrepaid grain loans that Korean farmers had accumulated since 1908. This was mere window dressing, however, for those who did not provide the information requested in a land survey lost their holdings, as did farmers who did not pay their taxes after 1910. The Japanese also systematically tightened their control by increasing police surveillance, closing down several newspapers, suppressing all groups suspected of resisting Japanese rule, importing thousands of teachers from Japan to replace the Korean language with Japanese as the medium of instruction in schools, and passing laws to control Buddhist as well as Christian churches, lest they become centers of resistance. Meanwhile, droves of Japanese merchants and financiers flooded the country, opening businesses and banks and squeezing Koreans out of these enterprises altogether.

To escape the clutches of the Japanese secret police, Korean nationalists either went underground or fled abroad. The vast majority of those who escaped went to the maritime provinces of Russia, Manchuria, and China, but several hundred also found their way to Europe and the United States. Korean émigré communities around the world provided these anti-Japanese activists with shelter and financial support. Korean immigrants in Hawaii and the continental United States, though small in number and poor, supplied a large proportion of the funds.

The three best-known U.S.-based Korean expatriate leaders were Ahn Chang-ho (1878–1938), Park Yong-man (1881–1928), and Syngman Rhee (1875–1965).[31] Ahn, who believed in salvation through cultural renewal, had arrived in San Francisco in 1899, before Korean laborers started going to Hawaii and California. Four years later, he established the first social organization among Koreans in California, the Chin' mok-hoe (Friendship Society). He visited the homes of Koreans in the city and urged them to cleanse and beautify their dwellings because he thought cleanliness was a manifestation of moral rectitude; he also set up an employment agency to supply Korean laborers to Americans. Returning to Korea in 1907, he set up schools and organized secret societies, but he fled the country in 1910 when the Japanese fully took it over. Back in California, while earning a living as a general construction worker and a cleaner of hotel rooms—an unheard of occupation for an educated, upper-class Korean—Ahn formed the Hung Sa Dan (Young Korean Academy) in 1913 in San Francisco. He believed that the first step toward regaining Korean independence involved the "regeneration" of the Korean people through the development of their character.

On March 1, 1919, thousands gathered in Seoul and other Korean cities to proclaim the independence of their country. As demonstrators marched through the streets shouting "Man Sei!" ("Long live [Korea]!"), the Japanese military police fired into the crowd. Fighting broke out between the protestors and the authorities. The movement spread rapidly to the countryside, where eventually an estimated one million persons of all ages and classes joined the effort to oust their Japanese overlords. The movement was ruthlessly suppressed, and Koreans who managed to escape to the Chinese mainland formed a provisional government in Shanghai to provide centralized planning for the overthrow of Japanese rule. Korean leaders exiled in various parts of the world made their way to Shanghai to work in the new organization. Ahn Chang-ho was among them. He served first as the secretary of the interior and later as the secretary of labor in the provisional government. Arrested in 1935 by Japanese police (who maintained surveillance of Korean nationalists even on foreign soil), he was thrown in jail and died three years later shortly after being released. But the organization he founded in California, the Hung Sa Dan, continued to attract Korean immigrants in the United States into its ranks for a decade after his death.

Park Yong-man, in contrast to Ahn, believed in using military means to promote the cause of independence. In 1904 he came to the United States, where he studied political and military science at the University of Nebraska. Upon graduation in 1909, he remained in Nebraska to set up a Korean Youth Military Academy to train twenty-seven Korean cadets. Eventually, four other military academies for Korean youth were opened in Claremont and Lompoc, California; Kansas City; and Superior, Wyoming. An airplane-pilot-training program was also established in Willows, California, the expense of which was underwritten by Kim Jong-lim, the Korean "Rice King." After the Korean National Association set up military training centers in Hawaii, Park went there in 1912 and consolidated the different groups of cadets into the Korean National Brigade, which exceeded three hundred members and was headquartered at the Ahumanu Plantation in Kailua, Oahu. Park himself served as the brigade's military commander. Going to Shanghai in 1919, Park was selected as minister of foreign affairs, but resigned the post when Syngman Rhee, with whom he had longstanding political disagreements, arrived to serve as president of the provisional government. He then devoted his energies to setting up military training programs for Koreans in Manchuria until he was assassinated in 1928.

Syngman Rhee came to the United States in 1905, received an M.A. degree from Harvard and a Ph.D. degree in politics from Princeton, then went to Seoul to serve as secretary of the YMCA for a year before returning to the United States in 1911. Invited by Park Yong-man to Hawaii in 1913, Rhee taught at the Korean Community School and became its principal. Park and Rhee soon parted over political strategy because Rhee opposed the use of military force in the nationalist struggle and instead advocated winning over American public opinion. The conflict between Park and Rhee divided the

Korean immigrant communities in both Hawaii and the mainland for decades. To push for his own program, Rhee formed the Donji-hoe (Comrade Society) in 1921, established a separate church, called the Korean Christian Church, and published his own magazine, the *Pacific Weekly*. He went to Shanghai in 1919 to become the first president of the Korean provisional government but soon returned to the United States, where during the 1920s and 1930s he lobbied in Washington, D.C., and elsewhere, using funds donated by Korean immigrants who supported his faction. Rhee became the first president of independent Korea after World War II but was ousted by student radicals in 1960. He died in retirement in Hawaii in 1965.

The efforts of Ahn, Park, and Rhee were all supported by Korean immigrants, who turned over every bit of savings they could muster. In that way, Hawaii, California, and other localities in the United States, along with Manchuria and Shanghai, became bases from which Korean expatriates launched their struggle for national independence. The major community organization formed by Korean immigrants, the Korean National Association, had as its main purpose the overthrow of the Japanese colonial regime in Korea. It was formed in 1909 in San Francisco by the merger of the Mutual Assistance Society in California and the United Korean Society in Hawaii, amid efforts to defend two Koreans accused of assassinating Durham Stevens, an American whom the Japanese government had foisted on the Korean government as a foreign affairs adviser. In this capacity Stevens was sent to Washington, D.C., to explain the Japanese position to the United States government. While passing through San Francisco in March 1908, Stevens made a statement, published in local newspapers, to the effect that Japanese rule was for the benefit of the Korean people. Outraged, the Koreans in San Francisco gathered at a mass meeting and chose four delegates to meet with Stevens at the Fairmont Hotel. Stevens refused to honor the delegation's request that he retract his statement. On March 23, as Stevens emerged from a limousine in the company of the Japanese consul general, he was attacked by two Koreans, one of whom shot him dead. The Korean who had fired the fatal shots declared at trial that "to die for having shot a traitor is a glory because I did it for my people."[32] He was sentenced to twenty-five years in prison. During the several months when the trial was in progress, Koreans throughout the United States rallied behind the accused and raised funds for their defense. Having experienced the efficacy of collective political action, they formed the Korean National Association to defend and promote their own interests. Rich and poor alike who participated in these struggles found their lives deeply colored by the experience. Mutual dependence acted as a social leveler and at the same time made the suffering everyone endured as an immigrant more tolerable.

The plowing of so many resources into efforts to liberate Korea also retarded the development of Korean immigrant communities in the United States, for unlike the Chinese and Japanese, who opened stores to cater to the needs of their compatriots and for whom ethnic enclaves became a channel of upward socioeconomic mobility, few Korean immigrants went into business. The donating of so much of their savings to the nationalist effort meant that little capital could be accumulated. Moreover, few merchants had emigrated during the short period when Koreans could leave their country, and the Japanese had forbidden Koreans to participate in the import-export trade, one of the keystones of immigrant entrepreneurship. Political channels of upward mobility in the United States were also closed to them because they were denied the right of naturalization and could not vote. With virtually every avenue of access to the larger society blocked, their fierce involvement in the Korean independence struggle was at once a cause and a result of the circumstances under which they lived.

The desire to liberate their country likewise obsessed many Asian Indian immigrants. The long and complicated history of how the British colonized India began in 1600, when the crown granted a monopoly of trading rights to the East India Company, a chartered group of merchants who sent their first ships to Indian ports in 1608, set up their first permanent trading post at Surat in 1613, began trading in Bengal in 1634, and established a fort at Madras in 1639.[33] They encountered in India an empire ruled by the Islamic Mughal dynasty, which during the seventeenth century was beginning to disintegrate because of internal problems.

The scramble to carve up the old empire gave the English merchants an opening to solidify their place in Indian life and commerce. In retaliation for the sacking of the company's settlement in Calcutta in 1756, the company's private army fought and defeated the nawab of Bengal in the battle of Plassey the following year. After decisively overcoming the French, with whom they had vied for supremacy in India for several decades, the British forced the Mughal emperor to turn over the *diwani*, or revenue administration, of Bengal to them in 1765. This gave them entrée to the governing of Indian territory, for the *diwani* also carried the right to administer civil justice. Under successive governors-general, the British expanded their empire through military conquest, annexation, and the formation of alliances with local rulers. They fought their final war against the Marathas in 1817–1819; failed to subdue the Afghans in 1839–1842; annexed Sind (the lower Indus Valley) in 1843; and conquered the Punjab in 1849. By the middle of the nineteenth century, they had become masters of the entire subcontinent, often through local princes who publicly acknowledged English sovereignty.

The British Parliament paid relatively little attention to the East India Company during the first century and a half of its existence. However, as the company began to conquer Indian territory, an increasing number of lucrative appointments became available in India. Then, as the costs of military campaigns and the siphoning of profits into private pockets mounted, the company began to lose money and had to apply to Parliament for relief. In return for bailing it out, Parliament passed the India Act of 1784, which allowed the government to supervise the company's political operations more strictly, although its commercial affairs remained autonomous. The 1813 Charter Act finally proclaimed the "undoubted sovereignty of the Crown of the United

Kingdom over British India," though the company was not liquidated until 1858.

The company's officers and later the crown's colonial administrators both asserted that they desired to leave Indian social, cultural, and even economic institutions intact, but the British presence profoundly affected many spheres of Indian life. Among the most significant changes was the introduction in the 1793 Settlement Act of a concept of land ownership that replaced the traditional system of ownership and usufruct with outright ownership to those who paid the company's revenue. Other changes affected the tax-collecting structure, the pattern of foreign trade and industrial production, judicial administration (even when existing Moslem and Hindu legal precepts were preserved), and cultural forms, particularly with the introduction of Christianity and the use of the English language as the medium of instruction in higher education. Through these various means, the British managed to govern a vast territory with an army of only two hundred thousand (two-thirds of them Indian) and an Indian civil service staffed by only about one thousand Englishmen, supervising thousands of Indian bureaucrats, with the aid of a modern communications network of roads, railways, and telegraph lines.

As elsewhere in the world, the colonization of India led to emigration, but with a special twist.[34] None of the several million Indian indentured servants who were shipped to labor on sugar, rubber, coconut, coffee, tea, and other plantations in the far-flung British Empire in the first half of the nineteenth century landed in North America. Instead, the thousands of Indians who came to the New World originated from the Punjab, the last area of India that the British conquered. The Punjabis, adherents of the Sikh faith, had greatly impressed the British officers with their fierce military prowess. (The British had to fight three wars before they could impose colonial rule on the Punjabis' homeland in northwestern India.) After the area was finally pacified, the colonial administrators recruited the hefty Punjabis into their army and police force and sent them throughout the empire to preserve law and order. After completing their service, many of them used their savings to travel farther afield in search of economic opportunities. Among those who came to North America, some had worked in various places in Asia, such as Rangoon, Singapore, Hong Kong, Shanghai, Tianjin (Tientsin), and Manila.

The pioneers could not have persuaded clansmen and fellow villagers to follow them to the New World had conditions in the Punjab not been ripe for such a chain migration. The region's once productive agriculture had suffered from a series of famines. After the British conquered the area and built a network of canals and opened new land to agriculture, the food situation improved, but the introduction of a new system of private landownership, which concentrated landholding into fewer hands and caused an increase in tenancy, forced many smallholders off the land. As the ties to the soil were loosened, many landless Punjabis listened more receptively to the enticing tales told by labor recruiters and shipping agents.

British Columbia became a common destination for Punjabis, who were recruited to work there, but local opposition against them soon became significant. Within a few years of their arrival, their immigration was curtailed by Canada with the reluctant approval of the British colonial office. Because India and Canada were both within the British Empire, Indians, as British subjects, had the right to travel freely to other parts of the empire, so excluding them from Canada was a delicate matter. Canada's goal was achieved in 1908 with a law that barred immigrants who did not come by "continuous journey" from their country of origin: there was then no direct steamship service between India and the western coast of North America.

Indian immigration into the United States, which began in 1904 as a trickle from British Columbia, increased after 1908 when Punjabis started coming directly. U.S. officials, goaded by the Asiatic Exclusion League, quickly stopped that influx, first by executive means and then by legislation. A clause in the 1917 Immigration Act delineated a "barred zone" on the world map, with a line that circled most of Asia, from which immigrants could not come. Because Chinese and Japanese had already been kept out by other arrangements, the main group affected was Indians.

In the decade when entry was possible, approximately 7,000 landed at ports in Washington, Oregon, and California. Most were peasants, former soldiers, or small craftsmen who became farm workers, but there were also some students (some of whom entered via the East Coast) among them. Though under normal circumstances these two classes of Indians would have had little to do with each other, the like manner in which white Canadians and Americans treated them eventually awakened them to their common fate. Just as Korean expatriates relied on immigrant workers to sustain the independence movement, so Indian intellectuals who articulated nationalist sentiments found a ready audience among their plebeian compatriots.

Several incidents crystallized the Indians' realization that as the despised subjects of a colonized country, they had no protection of any sort against racial discrimination. In September 1907, lumber-mill hands in Bellingham, Washington, attacked and expelled dozens of "Hindus" (a misnomer; most of the Indians were Sikhs) from their town. A few days later, mob violence injured Chinese, Japanese, and Indians in Vancouver, British Columbia, and caused substantial property damages.[35] But the event that galvanized Indians up and down the Pacific Coast occurred in 1914, when a Japanese ship, the *Komagata Maru*, which had been chartered by a Sikh to take Indians to Vancouver directly in an effort to circumvent the continuous-journey provision, was refused permission to dock. All the passengers were kept aboard for two months while negotiations took place and food and water ran low. Vancouver Sikhs raised funds to pay the balance of the money due for chartering the vessel and sent telegrams to the British monarch, the viceroy of India, and Indian leaders in England and India in an effort to persuade the port authorities to allow the passengers to land, all to no avail. The ship was finally forced to leave—its departure a symbol of the powerlessness of Indians in North America.[36]

The Indians refused to accept the status assigned them, however. They began a twin struggle to achieve Indian independence and better treatment in North America. The two most active spokespersons during the first phase of

nationalist activities among Indians in North America were Tarak Nath Das
(1884–1958) and Har Dayal (1884–1939).[37] There were many parallels between
them and their Korean counterparts: their willingness, both out of necessity
and for ideological reasons, to mingle with working-class countrymen; their
far-flung travels; their use of publications to spread their message; and their
somewhat quixotic belief that military means might accomplish the ends they
sought.

Das withdrew from college in 1905 to agitate against British rule. When a
warrant was issued for his arrest, he fled to Japan but was deported, whereup-
on he went to Seattle in 1906. Working at various odd jobs, he drifted south to
California. In 1907 he was hired as an interpreter by the United States immigration agency and was assigned to Vancouver to help process Indians entering the
United States from British Columbia. He began organizing Indians in that city,
became secretary of the newly founded Hindustani Association, and started
publishing *Free Hindusthan*, a forum for criticizing British colonialism and
urging Indians in Canada and the United States to resist exclusion. Because of
such activities, British agents began to keep him under surveillance. Das enrolled in a Vermont military academy in 1908. When he was joined by ten
Indian students the following year, the agents became alarmed and asked the
school authorities to pressure him to leave. He moved to New York, where
the editor of the *Gaelic American* helped him to resume publication of *Free
Hindusthan*. But because the largest number of Indian students with nationalist leanings was on the West Coast, Das soon returned there to organize
them. Those spying on him repeatedly asked the United States government to
deport him and to foil his application for naturalization, arguing that Das
desired U.S. citizenship only so he could engage in anti-British activities with
impunity. To their chagrin, after many petitions, he was finally granted citizenship in 1914.

During much of World War I, Das worked among Indians in China, Japan,
and elsewhere to undermine British colonial rule in India. He returned to the
United States and volunteered himself for arrest when the United States government began prosecuting dozens of Indians (who allegedly had been in contact with German officials prior to U.S. entry into the war) for violation of
neutrality laws in 1917. Freed on bail, he continued to work for Indian independence. He was arrested once again, but the U.S. immigration agency failed
in its efforts to deport him. Despite continual harassment, Das received a
Ph.D. degree from Georgetown University in 1924 and later taught occasionally at Columbia University and New York University.

Unlike Das, who became an American, Har Dayal spent only three years in
the United States. Dayal studied first in Lahore and then went to Oxford
University on a scholarship, which he soon renounced in protest of British
educational policies in India. He returned home, but his stay was short-lived.
When police curtailed his political activities, he went back to London, and then
traveled to Paris, Martinique, and Puerto Rico, searching for ways to promote
Indian independence. Landing on the East Coast of the United States in 1911,
he made his way to California, taught as an unpaid lecturer at Stanford Univer-

sity, became secretary of the San Francisco Radical Club, and founded two organizations: the anarchist Bakunin Institute and the revolutionary Gadar party (*Gadar* means mutiny or revolt in Urdu).[38] Arrested by U.S. immigration officials who tried to deport him in 1914, he jumped bail and went first to Switzerland and then to Germany to work with the Berlin India Committee, which during World War I channeled funds from the German government to Indian nationalists for the purchase of arms and munitions to be smuggled into India. After a year he broke with the committee and went to Sweden, where he lived frugally for a decade, lecturing on Indian civilization. In 1919 he publicly recanted his radicalism and declared that he now believed the British Empire was a "fundamentally beneficent and necessary institution." After repeated inquiries from Dayal, the British government finally allowed him to go to England (but not India); however, it never granted him amnesty. Dayal received a Ph.D. degree from the London School of Oriental and African Studies in 1930, published three books on religion and philosophy, and died suddenly in 1939 while on a lecture tour in the United States.

After Dayal's departure from California in 1914, Ram Chandra, the editor of the Gadar newspaper, became the party's leader. During its existence, the newspaper, first published in Urdu in November 1913, and later printed in several languages and distributed in the United States, Canada, Hong Kong, Japan, the Philippines, Malaysia, Singapore, British Guiana, Trinidad, Honduras, South and East Africa, and India itself, served as a medium for spreading revolutionary ideas to Indian patriots. The party, however, never became a disciplined organization and relied on "spontaneous" uprisings to achieve its goals. After Germany and Great Britain went to war, an estimated two thousand Indians from around the world made their way, in small groups and at their own expense, back to India to foment revolution. In August 1914 several hundred Gadarites from North America sailed home, but British intelligence knew of their plans; when their ship docked, they were arrested, disarmed, and court-martialed. More than a dozen were executed.

What was left of the party in California fell into disarray as a result of factional struggles, spurred on partly by infiltrators and informers paid by the British. British agents had kept Indian nationalists under surveillance since 1908; their activities ceased only temporarily after Mewa Singh assassinated W. C. Hopkinson, the key British agent, in 1914. At his trial, in words strikingly reminiscent of those used by the Korean assassin of Durham Stevens, Singh said he had shot Hopkinson "to lay bare the oppression exercised upon my innocent people."[39] Singh was hanged for his deed. The British eventually resumed surveillance and concentrated on breaking up the Gadar party. During the U.S. government's prosecution of Indian radicals in 1917, and 1918, Ram Chandra was shot and killed by another Indian. According to his daughter, his family managed to survive in San Francisco with help from Irish Americans who were involved in anti-British activities.[40]

In retrospect, the significance of the Gadar party lies in its members' ability ✓ to transcend religious, caste, and class barriers—at least for a time—as they worked for a common cause. Among its leaders were Hindus (Har Dayal,

Tarak Nath Das, and Ram Chandra, all intellectuals), Sikhs (Sohan Singh Bhakna, a mill laborer; Santokh Singh, a farmer; Bhagwan Singh, a priest; and Kartar Singh Sarabha, a student), and Muslims (most notably Maulvi Barkatullah, at one time on the faculty of Tokyo University, who edited the Urdu version of the Gadar newspaper). Most of its rank and file, though, were Punjabi Sikhs. When the party revived in the 1920s, it became primarily a Sikh organization and continued in existence until 1947.

The aid that the editor of the *Gaelic American* gave Das in New York and the efforts by Irish Americans in San Francisco to shelter Ram Chandra's family are testimony to the bonds that anti-British nationalism created, for Ireland suffered under English domination for longer than any other colony. More so than other students of Irish immigration, Kerby Miller has traced the historical roots of Irish impoverishment — which eventually led to large-scale emigration — to developments since the Norman Conquest in the eleventh century, thus reminding us that it was not just the potato famine that caused the mass outflow of people. He explores in detail why Irish emigrants considered themselves exiles. Although immigration historians have long recognized that the desire for political or religious freedom has often been a strong motivation for emigration, they have seldom attributed such an incentive to those from Ireland.[41]

The English colonization of Ireland saw its most brutal phase in the early years of the eighteenth century, when the Penal Laws effectively eliminated Irish Catholic landownership. Catholics were forbidden to buy land; they were required to bequeath what land they already owned in equal parts to all their heirs (thus fragmenting it into plots too small for viable subsistence) unless the eldest son converted to Anglicanism and was then allowed to inherit it all. They could not lease land for longer than thirty-one years, and the profits they were permitted to make from rented land could not exceed a third of the rent. Consequently, most Irish Catholics who tilled the soil were tenants or landless laborers. In time, virtually all of Ireland's arable land was owned by alien — often absentee — landlords. Ireland's role was to serve as a breadbasket for an industrializing England, while industrial development in Ireland itself was suppressed. The only industry the Irish were allowed to engage in was linen manufacturing, for which the country became famous. Outside agriculture, Irish Catholics were prohibited from practicing the professions or engaging in certain forms of commerce. Those who lived in towns had to pay special fees. As part of their Anglicization program, the English colonial authorities banished Catholic bishops and priests, forbade children to be sent to Catholic schools, and required orphans to be raised as Protestants. They denied Irish Catholics the franchise and the right to hold office or serve the militia.

As more and more of their land was expropriated for export agriculture, the Irish relied increasingly on the potato for subsistence. When the potato crop failed in the mid-1840s, widespread famine stalked, but the suffering was greatly exacerbated by Ireland's colonial status. Parliament was lackadaisical in providing relief. Even as millions starved to death, Irish grain and meat continued to be exported to England for sale, and heartless landlords evicted thousands upon thousands of destitute tenants to consolidate their landholdings. An amended Poor Law in 1847 made it mandatory for any household that owned more than one-quarter acre of land to give it up before its members could receive public relief. Little wonder that most Irish emigrants perceived departure from their homeland to be bitter, involuntary exile.

Even post-famine emigrants, who actually outnumbered those departing during the famine years, left for reasons related to the economic exploitation and political subjugation in Ireland. In the words of Miller, "post-Famine Ireland was little more than an inferior appendage of British capitalism and imperialism." An increasing portion of the land was used for grazing (which was far less labor-intensive than tillage) as Irish-grown cereals were undercut by U.S. and Argentine wheat in the international market. Thus, craftsmen, factory workers, small farmers, and farm laborers all found it more and more difficult to survive. As the traditional resistance to emigration declined, not only men but an increasing number of women, left to earn a living abroad. In time they came to see departure as an escape or even an opportunity as much as exile. Such a realization led them to set down roots more firmly in American soil and to participate more wholeheartedly in American social and political life.

Even before the massive influx of Irish "famine" immigrants, old-stock Protestant Americans exhibited considerable anti-Catholicism, which found its most visible expression in the burning of the Ursuline Convent in Charlestown, Massachusetts, in 1834.[42] Because a vast majority of the Irish and about half of the German immigrants from the 1840s onward were Catholic, nativists became increasingly paranoid and alarmed, perceiving them as agents of the pope, a "foreign despot." Moreover, because German immigrants often established breweries and Irish immigrants congregated in saloons, they were accused of corrupting the nation's morals. In response to anti-Catholic expressions, Irish immigrants organized to defend themselves. Seeing a connection between their lowly standing and Ireland's colonized status, they found the desire to recover Ireland's independence as powerful a force as Catholicism.

Irish-American nationalism took a particularly romantic form in the Fenian movement.[43] Originally called the Irish Republican Brotherhood, the Fenian Brotherhood was founded in 1857 by John O'Mahoney of New York and James Stephens of Dublin, who were dedicated to the military liberation of Ireland from colonial rule. When the Civil War broke out in the United States, some 150,000 Irish Americans answered the call to colors, partly for the chance to acquire military training. The Fenians operated quite openly in the Union army during the war, and numbered an estimated 50,000 at its end. In 1867 several hundred of them returned to Ireland to participate in an abortive uprising; in 1866 and 1870 other members led ill-fated invasions of Canada as part of an overall attempt to topple the British Empire. But factional disputes soon dissipated their strength, and by the early 1870s the Fenians were no longer a significant force. They were succeeded by several other organizations, such as the Clan na Gael, which linked up with the Irish Republican Brotherhood in

Great Britain to foment anti-British activities, and the New Departure, which relied on political action to gain Irish independence.

In the words of Thomas N. Brown, "The springs of Irish-American nationalism . . . are to be found in the realities of loneliness and alienation, and of poverty and prejudice . . . but it was from life in America that it derived its most distinctive attitudes: a pervasive sense of inferiority, intense longing for acceptance and respectability, and an acute sensitivity to criticism."[44] This statement could just as easily be applied to Korean and Asian Indian immigrants, and doubtless to members of other groups living under the same circumstances.

The creation of the Irish Free State in 1921 finally dampened the nationalist favor of many Irish people, including those in the United States. Long before this happened, however, Irish-American political activism had found an outlet in the machine politics of the Democratic party. By the 1880s Irish-American bosses were well entrenched in the political machines of numerous cities, most notably New York. The link between nationalist support for Ireland's independence and U.S. party politics is demonstrated by the vote in the presidential election of 1920: although they had always been overwhelmingly Democratic, that year large numbers of Irish turned against the Democratic incumbent, Woodrow Wilson, and contributed to the landslide victory of Republican Warren Harding because they had been incensed by Wilson's pro-British stance and his failure to include Ireland as one of the countries to be granted self-determination in the Treaty of Versailles at the end of World War I.

The Irish experience is but the most telling example among European immigrants of how the status of their homelands influenced the settlers' consciousness and action. Among others, Polish immigrants also worked energetically for a reunited and liberated Poland until an independent nation was reestablished under the Treaty of Versailles in 1919. The histories of Czech, Slovak, southern Slavic, Greek, and Armenian immigrants in the United States, when examined in detail, are likely to be replete with similar themes. However, of the various groups of immigrants who were deeply concerned about the fate of their homelands, only the Irish successfully transferred the political skills they had learned in their anticolonial struggles to the U.S. political arena. Edward Kantowicz has explained that Poles never enjoyed the same influence that the Irish did in politics because, unlike the Irish, they had to overcome a language barrier before they could participate actively in American institutional life; furthermore, they came in large numbers at the same time that millions of other immigrants entered, which meant that no single group could dominate politics in any locality. In such a situation, Irish-American politicians, who had already staked out key positions in urban political machines, skillfully retained their preeminence by performing broker functions and catering to the needs of the other ethnic groups.[45] Kantowicz's analysis also holds for other European immigrants, but it cannot be applied fully to Asian immigrants, who were denied the right of naturalization and the franchise, and for whom exclusion from political participation was but one aspect of a complex web of discrimination that circumscribed every aspect of their lives.

Discrimination

All immigrants have encountered danger or hostility of one kind or another. In defending themselves, immigrants have often drawn on skills developed in their "Old World" societies, which were more hierarchical and more rigidly bound by age-old status prescriptions. Although the *nature* of the restrictions in the "New World" differed, the existence of limitations per se was something with which immigrants were quite familiar. That is why regardless of where they might have come from, immigrants could so quickly establish organizations to insure their own survival in an unfamiliar environment. The associations they formed have been quite similar and fall into three broad kinds: economic institutions that provide material goods and services; mutual aid organizations that maintain group and individual well-being; and social and cultural (including religious) institutions that meet the needs of their members for fellowship, recreation, and spiritual comfort. In addition, whenever necessary, immigrants have formed political associations to adjudicate quarrels among themselves and to defend their interests vis-à-vis the outside world.[46]

No immigrant community is entirely self-contained, and in interacting with the larger society, immigrants have been both succored and exploited. Irishmen, Jews, Italians, Slavs of various kinds, as well as Chinese, Japanese, Koreans, Asian Indians, and Filipinos, have all tasted their share of prejudice and violence. Ethnic slurs and jokes are familiar aspects of American culture. As for violence, we need to remind ourselves of only a few incidents. Italians were killed in the Armstrong Coal Works in western Pennsylvania in 1874 and lynched in West Virginia and New Orleans in 1891 and in southern Colorado in 1895. Slavic coal miners on strike were attacked, shot at, and killed in western Pennsylvania in 1886 and 1897.[47] Chinese gold miners were repeatedly harassed and killed in many mining regions from the 1850s through the 1870s, and in the West attempts were made to expel Chinese residents from some forty localities in the 1880s.[48] The best-known incidents include massacres of Chinese in Los Angeles in 1871; Rock Springs, Wyoming, in 1885; Eureka, California, in 1885; Seattle and Tacoma, Washington, in 1885; and along the Snake River in Oregon, in 1887.[49] Asian Indians were expelled from Bellingham and Everett, Washington, in 1907, and Live Oak, California, in 1908.[50] Japanese farm laborers were driven out of various places in California: Turlock and Livingston in 1921; Delano, Porterville, and Los Angeles in 1922; Hopland and again Los Angeles in 1924; and Woodlake in 1926.[51] They were ousted from Toledo, Oregon, in 1925.[52] California mobs attacked Filipinos in Stockton in 1926, Dinuba in 1928, Exeter in 1919, and Watsonville in 1930.[53] In many of these instances, law enforcement agents stood aside during the violence or helped to perpetrate it themselves. Because such incidents were condoned by the public and by the very persons sworn to uphold the law, they helped maintain a tradition of using physical coercion to keep aliens and other minorities in their place.

In the end, however, what set Asian immigrants apart was not the prejudice and violence they encountered but the discriminatory laws that aimed to deprive them of their means of livelihood, restrict their social mobility, and deny them political power. When the coercive powers of the state are used to determine what is acceptable and unacceptable, then individuals who are the targets of codified prejudice have few means with which to counteract such overwhelming moral and physical power. Asian immigrants remained subjugated minorities for so long because all units of the state apparatus—the executive, legislative, and judicial branches of the federal, state, and municipal governments—have at one time or another been used against them. Limitations of space preclude a full discussion of the *causes* of white prejudice; I can only show how, although all the Asian immigrant groups encountered similar discrimination, the federal government treated Japanese immigrants in a far more gingerly way than it did Chinese, Koreans, Indians, and Filipinos, by comparing the diverse ways that exclusion was achieved and the methods used to deprive Asians of means of livelihood.

Except for the sedition laws passed in the early years of the republic, the United States had no immigration laws until 1875, when prostitutes and convicts were excluded. Seven years later, "lunatics," "idiots," and persons unable to care for themselves were added to the list. The Chinese Exclusion Law of 1882, which prohibited the entry of Chinese laborers for ten years, was the first congressional attempt to bar would-be immigrants on the basis of race or color.[54] An Act of September 13, 1888, denied reentry to any Chinese laborer who had returned to China for a visit unless they had a wife, child, or parent in the United States, or owned property valued at one thousand dollars or more. The Scott Act, passed three weeks later, curtailed the reentry of laborers altogether. Over 20,000 Chinese who were visiting China with certificates permitting their return were stranded, including 600 on board ships en route to the United States who were not allowed to land upon their arrival. Congress renewed the 1882 law in 1892 and again in 1902, in the latter instance extending exclusion to the newly acquired territories of Hawaii, the Philippines, and Puerto Rico, as well as to Cuba, then under U.S. administration. In 1904 Chinese exclusion was made permanent. (It was repealed only in 1943 as a gesture of goodwill toward China, a U.S. ally during World War II.) But Chinese received an annual quota of only 105 persons, and all ethnic Chinese (including those with only partial Chinese "blood"), regardless of their citizenship, were charged to this minuscule token quota. Chinese protested their maltreatment through diplomatic channels, by challenging the laws in court, and finally in 1905, by a boycott (in China) of American goods.[55] Although in several instances their actions resulted in some relief, the federal government, for the most part, ignored them because it knew that neither China—a country by then weakened by treaties wresting countless concessions that undermined its sovereignty—nor the Chinese in the United States had any real power to retaliate.

In contrast, attempts to exclude Japanese immigrants were more subtle and complicated.[56] The movement began indirectly in 1905, as a compromise between some of San Francisco's officials and President Theodore Roosevelt. When the San Francisco School Board decided to place Japanese students in the segregated "Oriental School" reserved for Chinese-American children, Tokyo protested. Roosevelt sent his secretary of commerce and labor, Victor Metcalf, a Californian, to investigate. Metcalf found that only ninety-three Japanese students were enrolled in the public schools of the city and that only a handful were overage. Roosevelt understood that the real concern of the San Franciscans was not school segregation but increasing Japanese immigration. However, he was wary of antagonizing Japan because he was very impressed by that country's growing military prowess: during the 1904–1905 Russo-Japanese War, Japan had destroyed the entire Russian Pacific fleet — an accomplishment that Western observers had not thought possible. So he deemed it prudent to be very diplomatic in dealing with the thorny issue of Japanese immigration. Summoning San Francisco's officials to Washington, D.C., he persuaded them to allow Japanese children to attend the regular public schools, and he would work out an unwritten, informal understanding — later dubbed the "Gentlemen's Agreement" — with Japan to curb voluntarily the further issuance of passports to laborers. Japan accepted this face-saving device, which went into effect in 1907, partly because it was concerned with its national honor but also because it had reached an understanding with the United States whereby Japan would recognize U.S. interests in the Philippines in exchange for noninterference by Americans in Japanese actions in Korea.[57] To seal off secondary immigration, Roosevelt signed Executive Order 589 on March 14, 1907, to prohibit Japanese in Hawaii, Canada, and Mexico from entering the United States.

Though laborers could no longer come, Japanese women began to enter in increasing numbers as "picture brides." Many of the Japanese immigrants were young, unmarried men, who, when they realized that their movement across the Pacific would thenceforth be more difficult, decided to start families in the United States. Because it was expensive for them to return to Japan just to get married, many sent home photographs of themselves and requested pictures of potential brides in return. Arranged marriages were a common practice in Japan in those days, so the men did not think their act unusual. Americans, however, who resented their presence, found the practice reprehensible. Exclusionists accused the Japanese of violating the "Gentlemen's Agreement," particularly after Japanese-American children started appearing. To mollify the exclusionists the Japanese government once again voluntarily stopped issuing passports to individuals whom white Americans found unacceptable — in this instance, picture brides. Exclusionists won their final victory when Congress passed the 1924 Immigration Act, which greatly reduced the number of immigrants from central, southern, and eastern Europe and excluded Japanese altogether.[58] However, unlike the Chinese, who were named, the Japanese were never mentioned overtly in any of these measures.

As for the other Asian immigrant groups, the United States did not have to worry about Korean immigration because Japan had already cut it off. Indians were kept out by the "barred zone" provision of the 1917 Immigration Act, in which a geographic rather than ethnographic criterion was used because Indians are technically Aryans or Caucasians.[59] As we have seen, Indian immigrants received no protection from the British colonial government and were, in fact, victimized by the pressure exerted by that government on the United States to prosecute and deport them. Filipinos presented a special dilemma to exclusionists. After the United States acquired their homeland — a colony of Spain for more than three centuries — Filipinos became U.S. "nationals" and carried U.S. passports but enjoyed none of the other rights of citizenship. Hawaiian sugar plantation owners started recruiting Filipinos in the first decade of this century, but large numbers arrived only in the 1920s. By the early 1930s, when racial prejudice was heightened by the economic difficulties of the Great Depression, efforts were made to curb their coming. However, as U.S. nationals, and not foreigners, they could not be subjected to restrictive immigration laws.[60] Realizing this, a strange coalition developed between anti-Filipino exclusionists who wanted the "little brown brothers" to be kept out of the United States and Filipino nationalists who desired independence for their country. The aims of both groups were met by the Tydings-McDuffie Act of 1934, which promised eventual full independence for the Philippines and limited Filipino immigration to fifty persons a year.

The concern of the U.S. executive branch for maintaining amicable relations with Japan while ignoring the ineffectual protests of other Asian nations is also evident in the differing pattern of federal intervention as local and state governments enacted laws to obstruct Asian immigrants' ability to earn a living. The earliest economic discrimination was directed against the Chinese. No sooner had the gold rush started than the California state legislature imposed the Foreign Miners' Tax, which in theory applied to all foreign miners but in fact was collected only from the Chinese. Additional statutes and ordinances outlawed certain kinds of fishing nets that only Chinese used and prohibited laundries in wooden buildings.[61] (Almost all Chinese-operated laundries in San Francisco at that time were in wooden buildings, and white laundries were in brick buildings.) Municipalities and states that enacted such measures were not hindered by the federal government, the judicial branch of which became involved only when Chinese challenged the constitutionality of some of these laws all the way to the U.S. Supreme Court.[62]

When state legislators attempted to pass discriminatory laws against the Japanese, however, the president himself took note. Japanese immigrants had gained a toehold in western agriculture by the first decade of this century, to the dismay of many local citizens. Beginning in 1907, anti-Japanese bills were introduced into every session of the California state legislature, but partly due to federal intervention, none passed until the 1913 Alien Land Law, which prohibited "aliens ineligible to citizenship" from buying agricultural land or leasing it for more than three years. President Woodrow Wilson sent William Jennings Bryan, his secretary of state, as his personal emissary to California to prevent its passage. But Bryan's mission failed because California Governor Hiram Johnson, a Progressive Republican, did not appreciate the Democratic president's meddling.[63] However, the Japanese were not named explicitly in the law, which only stated what "aliens eligible to citizenship" could do with regard to agricultural land, and by implication, what "aliens ineligible to citizenship" could *not* do.

California's leaders asserted that their law was not discriminatory, for it merely followed a distinction made in federal statutes between persons eligible for naturalization and those who were not. Congress had in 1790 reserved the right of citizenship to "free, white persons." After the Civil War, persons of African ancestry were also granted this right. Being neither white nor black, Asian immigrants had an uncertain status. At first, each local court that received a petition from an Asian made its own decision, and dozens of Chinese and then Japanese and Asian Indians were naturalized. But the 1882 Chinese Exclusion Law denied naturalization to the Chinese; forty years later, the U.S. Supreme Court ruled in *Takao Ozawa v. U.S.* (1922) that Japanese were not eligible; the year after that, the justices declared in *U.S. v. Bhagat Singh Thind* (1923) that though Indians were Caucasians, they were not white Europeans, in the eyes of the "common man," and hence were ineligible.[64]

Meanwhile, the 1913 Alien Land Law had little effect because many landowners preferred Japanese tenants, who skillfully turned marginal land into productive fields and orchards and who harvested larger crops than white tenants. The Japanese themselves found they could continue to purchase land either in the names of their American-born children or through corporations in which they held stock. Furthermore, local district attorneys were lax in enforcing the law, given the nation's increased need for food during World War I. After the war was over, however, a campaign was launched to close the loopholes in the 1913 law. Acts passed in 1920 and 1923 prohibited "aliens ineligible to citizenship" from leasing land under any guise.

More than half a dozen other states followed California's example with similar laws, with the result that, along with the Japanese, whatever ambition Chinese, Koreans, and Asian Indians might have had to become tenant farmers and owner-operators was stifled throughout the western United States. By the time that Filipinos came in large numbers, all the avenues for upward mobility in agriculture had been closed, so land leasing and ownership never became an issue with them, but their ethnicity came under attack in another way. Those who found the tendency of Filipino young men to socialize with white women offensive won a victory when the courts broadened antimiscegenation laws outlawing marriages between whites and Negroes and "Mongolians" to include persons of the Malay race, to which Filipinos belonged.[65]

Several additional factors perpetuated the subordinate status of Asian immigrants: the kind of work they did, the nature of the economy in the section of the country in which they first settled, and the slow appearance among them of a second generation. Recent research has shown how the emerging American labor movement used the fear of cheap immigrant labor in its attempt to gain improvements for its native-born constituents.[66] Eastern and southern European and Asian immigrants, as well as blacks and Mexican immigrants, have all suffered from organized labor's hostility to them. Quite apart from the effects of simple prejudice, the economy and labor market in the western and southern

United States have adversely affected Asians, blacks, and Mexican Americans. Where commercial agriculture, logging, and the extraction of metals, minerals, and natural gas predominate, many jobs have traditionally been seasonal. Large-scale commercial agriculture, in particular, has relied on migrant or semimigrant laborers, who have always been the hardest to unionize. So, even when the labor movement finally recognized the importance of including farm workers, the task was by no means easy. In contrast, eastern and southern Europeans worked mainly in the factories and mines of the East and Midwest, where even unskilled workers eventually picked up "industrial" work habits and were drawn into unions, which gave them a modicum of power vis-à-vis employers.

A less obvious barrier that confronted Asian immigrants was the slow development of a native-born second generation. For many immigrant groups, upward mobility has been an intergenerational phenomenon: the sooner an American-born generation appears on the scene, the faster will the overall occupational status of the ethnic group as a whole improve. Asian immigrants did not benefit from such a development until a very late stage, because before exclusion was imposed, no more than an estimated 5 percent of the Chinese, 10 percent of the Japanese, and 10 percent of the Korean immigrants were women.[67] (Because the Philippines was a U.S. territory between 1900 and 1945, there are no immigration statistics for Filipinos and Filipinas.) Virtually no Indian women came between 1904 and 1917. There are many reasons for the small number of Asian immigrant women: Asian cultural proscriptions against women's leaving home; the desire of employers in Hawaii and on the Pacific Coast for male workers; the cost of passage; the hostile reception the menfolk received, which must have given them pause when they desired to send for wives; and the imposition of exclusion at precisely that point in the immigrant communities' development when women might have come. With antimiscegenation laws on the books, Asian men could not marry white women, and nonwhite women were not particularly available either. Thus, a second generation did not become visible among the Chinese until the 1920s — three-quarters of a century after their initial arrival — though small numbers of children had been born since the early 1850s. The Japanese-American second generation also appeared in the 1920s. The consequences of such a demographic pattern have been profound, for it has usually been the American-born children among other immigrant groups who have provided the entering wedge into American society through their citizenship status, proficiency in English, schooling, and easier social intercourse with mainstream society.

In this essay, I have tried to show the utility of looking at these stages in the migration process: conditions leading to departure from the emigrant regions; the relative political standing of the emigrant versus the immigrant countries (which helps to mold the emigrants'/immigrants' behavior); and conditions in the receiving country (in this case the United States) that sort different groups of immigrants into a hierarchical order. Whereas there was a great deal of similarity between Asian and European immigrants in terms of the ecological and economic conditions that motivated them to leave their homelands, after their arrival they were discriminated against in a different manner, with the result that it took Asian immigrants far longer to overcome the barriers placed in their path. Because many of the emigrant nations, both Asian and European, were under foreign domination at the time that large numbers of their people emigrated, they were able to protect the latter from mistreatment. Beyond that, however, legally sanctioned racism made the Asian immigrants' ordeal a much longer one than that endured by their European counterparts.

NOTES

1. Although European and Asian immigration histories are usually treated as separate subfields, a few works do attempt to discuss Asian immigration as part of U.S. immigration history: Roger Daniels, "Westerners from the East: Oriental Immigrants Reappraised," *Pacific Historical Review* 35 (1966): 373–83; Roger Daniels, "American Historians and East Asian Immigrants," *Pacific Historical Review* 45 (1974): 447–72; Shirley Hune, *Pacific Migration to the United States: Trends and Themes in Historical and Sociological Literature* (Washington, D.C.: Smithsonian Institution, Research Institute on Immigration and Ethnic Studies, 1977); Franklin Ng, "The Sojourner, Return Migration, and Immigration History," in *Chinese America: History and Perspectives, 1987*, no editor (San Francisco: Chinese Historical Society of America, 1987), pp. 53–72.

2. The most up-to-date collection of essays on contemporary Asian immigration into the United States is James T. Fawcett and Benjamin V. Cariño, eds., *Pacific Bridges: The New Immigration from Asia and the Pacific Islands* (Staten Island, N.Y.: Center for Migration Studies, 1987).

3. Three major differences are worth noting. First, relatively cheap and fast air travel has minimized the physical trauma of passage. Second, Western cultural values—especially the desire for modern consumption goods—are now widely disseminated through films, broadcast television, and videocassettes that project images of the "good life" in the United States, creating a strong desire among people in many parts of the world to emigrate. Third, many Third World countries, by following an export-based path of development, are now so closely tied to the capitalist world economy that they are deeply affected by even small fluctuations in it. For workers employed in such export industries, wages are low, employment is uncertain, working conditions are harsh, and any form of organizing is outlawed. Under such circumstances, those who can afford to emigrate often do so.

4. John Bodnar, *The Transplanted: A History of Immigrants in Urban America* (Bloomington: Indiana University Press, 1985), synthesizes the existing literature on European immigrants and touches briefly on a few groups of Asians; Thomas J. Archdeacon, "Problems and Possibilities in the Study of American Immigration and Ethnic History," *International Migration Review* 19 (1985): 112–34, looks at why immigration history is such a marginal part of U.S. history, despite the platitude that the United States is a nation of immigrants; John Higham, "Current Trends in the Study of Ethnicity in the United States," *Journal of American Ethnic History* 2 (1982): 5–15, discusses assimilationist versus "hard" and "soft" pluralist approaches to the study of ethnicity; Alejandro Portes, "One Field, Many Views: Competing Theories of International Migration," in *Pacific Bridges: The New Immigration from Asia and the Pacific Islands,*

ed. James T. Fawcett and Benjamin V. Cariño (Staten Island, N.Y.: Center for Migration Studies, 1987), pp. 53–70, identifies four kinds of theory, based on the main issue each addresses: the origins of labor migration, the stability of migration, the uses of labor migration, and patterns of immigrant adaptation; and Ewa Morawska, "The Sociology and Historiography of Immigration," in this volume, outlines four common themes that sociologists and historians have addressed recently: the structural determinants of migration, the collectivist strategies that immigrants have used to facilitate their adaptation to life in the receiving country, the enduring nature of ethnicity, and the interrelation of class and ethnicity in influencing the immigrants' position in the new society.

5. The term *sojourner*, as it has been applied to the Chinese who came to North America, has a complex and controversial history. Sociologist Paul C. P. Siu first used it to characterize the Chinese in America in "The Sojourner," *American Journal of Sociology* 58 (1952): 34–36. Rose Hum Lee, *The Chinese in the U.S.A.* (Hong Kong: Hong Kong University Press, 1960), used it to explain the structure of Chinatowns. Gunther Barth, *Bitter Strength: A History of the Chinese in the United States, 1850–1870* (Cambridge: Harvard University Press, 1964), by attributing anti-Chinese hostility to the sojourning mentality of the Chinese, implies that it was their own behavior, rather than white racism, that was responsible for their maltreatment. Though Barth's thesis has been roundly criticized by Chinese Americans and Chinese Canadians, it has also been widely quoted and accepted by writers who are unfamiliar with Chinese-American history. Stanford Lyman, "The Chinese Diaspora in America, 1850–1943," in *The Life, Influence and the Role of the Chinese in the United States, 1776–1960*, no editor (San Francisco: Chinese Historical Society of America, 1976), pp. 128–46, on the other hand, who also calls Chinese sojourners, has not aroused the same antagonism because he discusses the impact of institutional racism *as well as* the effects of sojourning on the structure of Chinese-American communities. Lyman sees sojourning as a mechanism that the Chinese used "to *adapt* America and its ways to their own purposes rather than *adopt* it to the exclusion and surrender of their own values." Anthony B. Chan, "The Myth of the Chinese Sojourner in Canada," in *Visible Minorities and Multiculturalism: Asians in Canada*, ed. K. Victor Ujimoto and Gordon Hirabayashi (Toronto: Butterworth, 1980), pp. 33–42, argues that it was Canadian immigration laws, which embodied institutional racism, and not the sojourning status of the Chinese that determined the pattern of Chinese immigration into that country. Yuen-fong Woon, "The Voluntary Sojourner among the Overseas Chinese: Myth or Reality?" *Pacific Affairs* 56 (1983–1984): 673–90, by comparing Chinese behavior in Canada and Thailand, shows that the argument made by Chan (and by Peter S. Li, "Immigration Laws and Family Patterns: Some Demographic Changes among Chinese Families in Canada, 1885–1971," *Canadian Ethnic Studies* 12 [1980]: 58–73) is overdrawn. Ng, "The Sojourner," by comparing Chinese and European immigration return-migration rates, provides the most balanced assessment of the issue.

6. Dino Cinel, *From Italy to San Francisco: The Immigrant Experience* (Stanford: Stanford University Press, 1982), pp. 46ff.

7. Stephan Thernstrom, Ann Orlav, and Oscar Handlin, eds., *Harvard Encyclopedia of American Ethnic Groups* (Cambridge: Harvard University Press, 1980), pp. 1036–37. See also Rowland T. Berthoff, *British Immigrants in Industrial America, 1790–1950* (Cambridge: Harvard University Press, 1953), passim, for a discussion of re-emigration among British immigrants.

8. Computed from Mary R. Coolidge, *Chinese Immigration* (New York: Holt, 1909), table, p. 498.

9. Computed from Yamato Ichihashi, *Japanese in the United States* (Stanford: Stanford University Press, 1932), tables, pp. 401–8.

10. Thernstrom et al., eds., *Harvard Encyclopedia of American Ethnic Groups*, pp. 1036–37.

11. Summarized from Josef J. Barton, *Peasants and Strangers: Italians, Rumanians, and Slovaks in an American City, 1890–1950* (Cambridge: Harvard University Press, 1975), pp. 1–10, 27–47.

12. Cinel, *From Italy to San Francisco*, p. 48.

13. The following three paragraphs are drawn from Jon Gjerde, *From Peasants to Farmers: The Migration from Balestrand, Norway, to the Upper Middle West* (Cambridge: Cambridge University Press, 1985), especially pp. 1–24 and 116–36.

14. There is no thorough study of Chinese emigration, but the following works provide scattered information: Robert G. Lee, "The Origins of Chinese Immigration to the United States," in *The Life, Influence and the Role of the Chinese*, no editor (San Francisco: Chinese Historical Society of America, 1976), pp. 183–93; Sing-wu Wang, *The Organization of Chinese Emigration, 1848–1888* (San Francisco: Chinese Materials Center, 1978); June Mei, "Socioeconomic Origins of Emigration: Guangdong to California, 1859–1882," *Modern China* 5 (1979): 463–501; Kil Young Zo, *Chinese Emigration into the United States, 1850–1880* (New York: Arno Press, 1979); Sucheng Chan, *This Bittersweet Soil: The Chinese in California Agriculture, 1860–1910* (Berkeley: University of California Press, 1986), pp. 7–31. Although Robert Irick, *Ch'ing Policy toward the Coolie Trade, 1847–1878* (San Francisco: Chinese Materials Center, 1982), and Arnold J. Meagher, *The Introduction of Chinese Laborers to Latin America: The Coolie Trade, 1847–1874* (San Francisco: Chinese Materials Center, 1975), focus on the traffic in contract laborers to Latin America, they provide more details on how Chinese government officials tried to deal with emigration (during a period when it was prohibited by the Chinese central government) than do the works on Chinese emigration to the United States.

15. Chen Ta, "Chinese Migrations, with Special Reference to Labor Conditions," *Bulletin of the United States Bureau of Labor Statistics*, no. 340 (Washington, D.C.: Government Printing Office, 1923), p. 17.

16. Much of the antagonism against Chinese immigrants came from the mistaken notion that they were "coolies," that is, contract laborers. The confusion arose because during the period when Chinese were coming to the United States—usually through the credit-ticket system, whereby they purchased tickets on credit, with the debt to be paid off by deductions from wages earned after arrival—there was in fact a "coolie trade" to Latin America (mostly Peru and Cuba). See the works by Irick and Meagher for details. For the American role in the trade, see Shih-shan Henry Tsai, "American Involvement in the Coolie Trade," *American Studies* (Taiwan) 6 (1976): 49–66.

17. Sucheta Mazumdar, "A History of the Sugar Industry in China: The Political Economy of a Cash Crop in the Guangdong Delta, 1644–1833" (Ph.D. diss., University of California, Los Angeles, 1984), contains the only detailed discussion in English of land-use patterns in the region.

18. Eve Armentrout Ma, "The Big Business Ventures of Chinese in North America, 1850–1930," in *The Chinese American Experience*, Genny Lim, ed. (San Francisco: Chinese Historical Society of America and the Chinese Culture Foundation, 1984), p. 103.

19. Alexander McLeod, *Pigtails and Gold Dust: A Panorama of Chinese Life in Early California* (Caldwell, Idaho: Caxton Printers, 1947), pp. 86–92.

20. Lucie Cheng and Liu Yuzun with Zheng Dehua, "Chinese Emigration, the Sunning Railroad and the Development of Toisan," *Amerasia Journal* 9, no. 1 (1982):

59-74; Renqiu Yu, "Chinese American Contributions to the Educational Development of Toisan, 1910-1940," *Amerasia Journal* 10, no. 1 (1983): 47-72.

21. Cinel, *From Italy to San Francisco*, pp. 74-75.

22. On Japanese emigration, see Ichihashi, *Japanese in the United States*, pp. 1-15; Hilary F. Conroy, *The Japanese Frontier in Hawaii, 1868-1898* (Berkeley: University of California Press, 1953); Yasui Wakatsuki, "Japanese Emigration to the United States, 1866-1924," *Perspectives in American History* 12 (1979): 389-516; Alan Takeo Moriyama, *Imingaisha: Japanese Emigration Companies and Hawaii, 1894-1908* (Honolulu: University of Hawaii Press, 1985).

23. Yukoko Irwin and Hilary Conroy, "R. W. Irwin and Systematic Immigration to Hawaii," in *East across the Pacific: Historical and Sociological Studies of Japanese Immigration and Assimilation*, ed. Hilary Conroy and T. Scott Miyakawa (Santa Barbara, Calif.: ABC-Clio Press, 1972) pp. 40-55.

24. Moriyama, *Imingaisha*, pp. 20-22.

25. Albert M. Craig, *Choshu in the Meiji Restoration* (Cambridge: Harvard University Press, 1961), pp. 17-23. See also Franklin Shoichiro Odo, "Saga Han: The Feudal Domain in Tokugawa Japan" (Ph.D. diss., Princeton University, 1975).

26. Yuji Ichioka, "Recent Japanese Scholarship on the Origins and Causes of Japanese Immigration," *Immigration History Newsletter* 15 (1983): 2-7 (see footnote 11, p. 5, for the Japanese citations).

27. John Modell, "The Japanese American Family: A Perspective for Future Investigation," *Pacific Historical Review* 37 (1968): 67-81, found that an eldest son was "half again more likely than his younger brothers to emigrate to America," although he notes that the 1924 Immigration Act, which excluded all "aliens ineligible to citizenship" (a category to which Japanese belonged) "must have prevented immigration by many young Japanese whose elder brothers had been able to enter before 1924" (p. 74).

28. W. Peter Ward, *White Canada Forever* (Montreal: McGill-Queens University Press, 1978); Edgar Wickberg et al., eds., *From Canton to Canada* (Toronto: McClelland & Stewart, 1982), pp. 42-72, 135-47; Patricia E. Roy, "The Preservation of the Peace in Vancouver: The Aftermath of the Anti-Chinese Riot of 1887," *BC Studies* 31 (1976): 44-59; and Donald Avery and Peter Neary, "Laurie, Borden, and a White British Columbia," *Journal of Canadian Studies* 12 (1977); 24-34, discuss the anti-Chinese movement in Canada. A. T. Yarwood, *Asian Migration to Australia: The Background to Exclusion, 1896-1923* (Melbourne: Melbourne University Press, 1967); A. C. Palfreeman, *The Administration of the White Australia Policy* (Melbourne: Melbourne University Press, 1976); and H. I. London, *Non-White Immigrants and the "White Australia" Policy* (New York: New York University Press, 1970), examine anti-Asian developments in Australia. Charles A. Price, *The Great White Walls Are Built: Restrictive Immigration to North America and Australia, 1836-1888* (Canberra: Australia National University, 1974); Robert Huttenback, *Racism and Empire: White Settlers and Colored Immigrants in the British Self-Governing Colonies, 1830-1910* (Ithaca: Cornell University Press, 1976); and Andrew Markus, *Fear and Hatred: Purifying Australia and California, 1850-1901* (Sydney: Hall and Iremonger, 1979), compare policies in different "white men's countries."

29. The only detailed studies of Korean emigration are Wayne K. Patterson, "The Korean Frontier in America: Immigration to Hawaii, 1896-1910" (Ph.D. diss., University of Pennsylvania, 1977), and Bong-Youn Choy, *Koreans in America* (Chicago: Nelson-Hall, 1979).

30. C. I. Eugene Kim and Han-Kyo Kim, *Korea and the Politics of Imperialism, 1876-1910* (Berkeley: University of California Press, 1967), places the Japanese coloni-

zation of Korea in the broader context of imperialist rivalry in the region; Fred Harvey Harrington, *God, Mammon and the Japanese: Dr. Horace N. Allen and Korean-American Relations, 1884-1905* (Madison: University of Wisconsin Press, 1944), examines the role of the key American player on the scene; and Woo-keun Han, *The History of Korea*, trans. Kyung-shik Lee, ed. Grafton K. Mintz (Honolulu: University Press of Hawaii, 1974), pp. 361ff.; Takashi Hatada, *A History of Korea*, trans. and ed. Warren W. Smith, Jr., and Benjamin H. Hazard (Santa Barbara, Calif.: ABC-Clio Press, 1969); pp. 90ff.; and Choy, *Koreans in America*, pp. 21-66, provide additional details.

31. Kinsley K. Lyu, "Korean Nationalist Activities in Hawaii and the Continental United States, 1900-1945," Part I (1910-1919) and Part II (1919-1945), *Amerasia Journal* 4, no. 1 (1977): 23-90, and 4, no. 2 (1977): 53-100, and Choy, *Koreans in America*, pp. 141-89, analyze Korean émigré politics.

32. Choy, *Koreans in America*, p. 148.

33. As might be expected, there are differing perspectives on British imperial rule in India. Paul Ernest Roberts, *History of British India under the Company and the Crown*, 3d ed. (London: Oxford University Press, 1952), and Percival Joseph Griffiths, *The British Impact on India* (Hamden, Conn.: Archon Books, 1965), are pro-British, and Ram Gopal, *British Rule in India: An Assessment* (New York: Asia Publishing House, 1963), offers an Indian nationalist view. Writings by Indian Marxist historians on the British period are unfortunately not readily available in this country. Alfred C. Lyall, *The Rise and Expansion of the British Dominion in India* (1910; reprint of 5th ed., New York: H. Fertig, 1968), is an old classic; Francis G. Hutchins, *The Illusion of Permanence: British Imperialism in India* (Princeton: Princeton University Press, 1967), and P. J. Marshall, *Problems of Empire: Britain and India 1757-1813* (London: George Allen & Unwin, 1968), are also useful; Michael Edwardes, *British India, 1772-1947: A Survey of the Nature and Effects of Alien Rule* (New York: Taplinger, 1968), is a popular account; and Karl De Schweinitz, *The Rise and Fall of British India: Imperialism as Inequality* (New York: Methuen, 1983), examines the coercive aspects of British imperialism.

34. The study of Indian (in this instance, Punjabi Sikh) emigration is still in its infancy. Sucheta Mazumdar, "Colonial Impact and Punjabi Emigration to the United States," in *Labor Immigration under Capitalism: Asian Workers in the United States before World War II*, ed. Lucie Cheng and Edna Bonacich (Berkeley: University of California Press, 1984), pp. 316-36, and Joan M. Jensen, *Passage from India: Asian Indian Pioneers in America* (New Haven: Yale University Press, 1988), pp. 24-41, sketch the general conditions related to emigration.

35. Jensen, *Passage from India*, pp. 42-56; Gerald N. Hallberg, "Bellingham, Washington's Anti-Hindu Riot," *Journal of the West* 12 (1973): 163-75; Howard H. Sugimoto, "The Vancouver Riots of 1907: A Canadian Episode," in *East across the Pacific, Historical and Sociological Studies of Japanese Immigration and Assimilation*, ed. Hilary Conroy and T. Scott Miyakawa (Santa Barbara, Calif.: ABC-Clio Press, 1972), pp. 92-126.

36. For details, see Jensen, *Passage from India*, pp. 121-38; Hugh Johnston, *The Voyage of the Komagata Maru: The Sikh Challenge to Canada's Colour Bar* (New Delhi: Oxford University Press, 1979); and Sohan Singh Josh, *Tragedy of the Komagata Maru* (New Delhi: People's Publishing House, 1975).

37. Jensen, *Passage from India*, passim.; Emily C. Brown, *Har Dayal: Hindu Revolutionary and Rationalist* (Tucson: University of Arizona Press, 1975).

38. *Gadar* is also transliterated as *Ghadar* and *Ghadr*. The most detailed study of the party's history in Harish K. Puri, *Ghadar Movement: Ideology, Organization*

and Strategy (Amritsar, India: Guru Nanak Dev University Press, 1983). See also Khushwant Singh, *A History of the Sikhs*, 2 vols. (Princeton: Princeton University Press, 1966), 2: 168–92; Sohan Singh Josh, *Hindustan Gadar Party: A Short History* (New Delhi: People's Publishing House, 1977).

39. Jensen, *Passage from India*, p. 191.

40. Personal communication from Mark Juergensmeyer, from an interview with Lila Chandra, Berkeley, 1973, and an interview with Mrs. Ram Chandra by Vidya Chandra Rasmussen and Mark Juergensmeyer, New York, 1972. A tape of the latter is in the Gadar Collection, South and Southeast Asian Studies Library, University of California, Berkeley.

41. Kerby A. Miller, *Emigrants and Exiles: Ireland and the Irish Exodus to North America* (New York: Oxford University Press, 1985). There is a considerable literature on Irish immigration and Irish Americans. See Cormac Ó Gráda, "Irish Emigration to the United States in the Nineteenth Century," in *America and Ireland, 1776–1976: The American Identity and the Irish Connection* ed. David N. Doyle and Owen D. Edwards (Westport, Conn.: Greenwood Press, 1980), pp. 93–103; Deirdre Mageean, "Perspectives on Irish Migration Studies," *Ethnic Forum* 4 (1984): 36–48; and Michael F. Funchion, "Irish-America: An Essay on the Literature since 1970," *Immigration History Newsletter* 17, no. 2 (1985): 1–8, for useful assessments of the available literature. Thomas N. Brown, *Irish-American Nationalism, 1870–1890* (Philadelphia: Lippincott, 1966), is especially pertinent to my discussion here.

42. John Higham, *Strangers in the Land: Patterns of American Nativism, 1860–1925* (New Brunswick: Rutgers University Press, 1955), identified anti-Catholicism as one of the three main strains of nativism in U.S. history.

43. Brown, *Irish-American Nationalism*, discusses the Fenians as well as other groups.

44. Ibid., p. 23.

45. Edward R. Kantowicz, "Politics," in *Harvard Encyclopedia of American Ethnic Groups*, ed. Stephan Thernstrom et al. (Cambridge: Harvard University Press, 1980), pp. 807–9.

46. Bodnar, *The Transplanted*, pp. 185–205, offers a good overview of immigrant organizations.

47. Higham, *Strangers in the Land*, pp. 48, 89, 90–91.

48. Elmer Clarence Sandmeyer, *The Anti-Chinese Movement in California*, Illinois Studies in the Social Sciences, Vol. 24 (1939), pp. 97–98 gives a list of these localities.

49. William R. Locklear, "The Celestials and the Angels: A Study of the Anti-Chinese Movement in Los Angeles to 1882," *Historical Society of Southern California Quarterly* 42 (1960): 239–56; Paul Crane and Alfred Larson, "The Chinese Massacre," *Annals of Wyoming* 12 (1940): 47–55 (for the Rock Springs, Wyoming, massacre); Lynwood Carranco, "Chinese Expulsion from Humboldt County," *Pacific Historical Review* 30 (1961): 329–40; Jules Alexander Karlin, "The Anti-Chinese Outbreaks in Seattle, 1885–1886," *Pacific Northwest Quarterly* 39 (1948): 103–29; Jules Alexander Karlin, "The Anti-Chinese Outbreak in Tacoma, 1885," *Pacific Historical Review* 23 (1954): 271–83; Shih-shan Henry Tsai, *China and the Overseas Chinese in the United States, 1868–1911* (Fayetteville: University of Arkansas Press, 1983), pp. 86–89 (for the massacre near the Snake River in Oregon). Tsai also discusses the reaction of the Chinese government to the anti-Chinese activities in Denver (pp. 60–63), Rock Springs (pp. 72–78), and Seattle (pp. 78–80). To get a flavor of the expulsion attempts in California, see *Truckee Republican*, June 21, July 12 and 22, August 12 and 19, September 30, 1876, and November 16, 1878, for activities in Truckee; *Chico Enterprise*, March

2, 9, 16, and 30, 1877, for Chico; *Sacramento Daily Record Union*, February 3, 1886, for Gold Run; February 12, 1886, for Arroyo Grande; February 25, 1886, for San Diego; and December 30, 1886, for Anaheim; and *Wheatland Graphic*, February 27, 1886, for Nicolaus.

50. Hallberg, "Bellingham," and Mazumdar, "Punjabi Agricultural Workers in California, 1905–1945," p. 563.

51. Yuji Ichioka, "The 1921 Turlock Incident: Forceful Expulsion of Japanese Laborers," in *Counterpoint: Perspectives on Asian America*, ed. Emma Gee (Los Angeles: Asian American Studies Center, University of California, Los Angeles, 1976), pp. 195–99.

52. Stefan Tanaka, "The Toledo Incident: The Deportation of the Nikkei from an Oregon Mill Town," *Pacific Northwest Quarterly* 69 (1978): 116–26.

53. H. Brett Melendy, "California's Discrimination against Filipinos, 1927–1935," in *The Filipino Exclusion Movement, 1927–1935*, ed. J. M. Saniel, Occasional Papers no. 1 (Quezon City, Philippines: University of the Philippines, Institute of Asian Studies, 1967), pp. 3–10, and Emory S. Bogardus, *The Anti-Filipino Race Riots: A Report Made to the Ingram Institute of Social Science of San Diego* (San Diego: Ingram Institute of Social Science, 1930), both reprinted in Jesse Quinsaat, ed., *Letters in Exile: An Introductory Reader on the History of Pilipinos in America* (Los Angeles: University of California, Los Angeles, Asian American Studies Center, 1976), pp. 35–44 and 51–62, respectively. On Watsonville, see Howard A. De Witt, "The Watsonville Anti-Filipino Riot of 1930: A Case Study of the Great Depression and Ethnic Conflict in California," *Southern California Historical Quarterly* 61 (1979): 291–302.

54. The text of the Chinese Exclusion Law is found in 22 Stat. 58 (1882). Coolidge, *Chinese Immigration*, examines the political maneuverings that led to its passage; Milton R. Konvitz, *The Alien and the Asiatic in American Law* (Ithaca: Cornell University Press, 1946), passim, discusses cases of Chinese challenging both exclusion and the denial of the right of naturalization to them. On the repeal of Chinese exclusion in 1943, see Fred W. Riggs, *Pressures on Congress: A Study of the Repeal of Chinese Exclusion* (New York: Columbia University, King's Crown Press, 1950).

55. On protests by Chinese diplomats in the United States, see Tsai, *China and the Overseas Chinese*, pp. 60ff. On the 1905 Chinese boycott, see Shih-shan H. Tsai, "Reaction to Exclusion: The Boycott of 1905 and Chinese National Awakening," *Historian* 39 (1976): 95–110; Delber L. McKee, *Chinese Exclusion versus the Open Door Policy, 1900–1906: Clashes over China Policy in the Roosevelt Era* (Detroit: Wayne State University Press, 1977); Tsai, *China and the Overseas Chinese*, pp. 104–23; and Delber L. McKee, "The Chinese Boycott of 1905–1906 Reconsidered: The Role of Chinese Americans," *Pacific Historical Review* 55 (1986): 165–91. For a discussion of Chinese challenges in the courts, see B. Frank Dake, "The Chinaman before the Supreme Court," *Albany Law Journal* 67 (1905): 258–67; Konvitz, *The Alien and the Asiatic in American Law*, passim; Christian Fritz, "Bitter Strength (k'u-li) and the Constitution: The Chinese before the Federal Courts in California," *Historical Reporter* 1 (1980): 2–3, 8–15; John Gioia, "A Social, Political and Legal Study of *Yick Wo v. Hopkins*," in *The Chinese American Experience*, ed. Genny Lim (San Francisco: Chinese Culture Foundation and Chinese Historical Society of America, 1984), pp. 211–20; Charles J. McClain, Jr., "The Chinese Struggle for Civil Rights in Nineteenth Century America: The First Phase, 1850–1870," *California Law Review* 72 (1984): 529–58; and Charles J. McClain, Jr., "The Chinese Struggle for Civil Rights in 19th-Century America: The Unusual Case of *Baldwin v. Frank*," *Law and History Review* 3 (1985): 349–73.

56. For the anti-Japanese movement, see Roger Daniels, *The Politics of Prejudice: The Anti-Japanese Movement in California and the Struggle for Japanese Exclusion* (Berkeley: University of California Press, 1962).

57. The understanding was reached in a two-hour conversation on July 27, 1905, in Tokyo between William Howard Taft, then secretary of war and formerly the first civilian governor of the Philippines after the United States took over the islands, and Japanese Prime Minister Taro Katsura. See Raymond A. Esthus, *Theodore Roosevelt and Japan* (Seattle: University of Washington Press, 1967), pp. 102–6; Howard K. Beale, *Theodore Roosevelt and the Rise of America to World Power* (Baltimore: Johns Hopkins University Press, 1956), pp. 156–58.

58. 43 Stat. 153 (1924), whose full title is "An Act to Limit the Immigration of Aliens into the United States, and for Other Purposes," has been referred to by all kinds of names: the Immigration Act of 1924 (its correct short title), the National Origins Act, the Quota Immigration Act, and the Japanese Exclusion Act.

59. A section of 39 Stat. 874 (1917) spells out the "barred zone" from which immigrants would be excluded.

60. H. Brett Melendy, *Asians in America: Filipinos, Koreans, and East Indians* (Boston: Twayne, 1977), p. 43.

61. For anti-Chinese ordinances and laws, see Sandmeyer, *The Anti-Chinese Movement in California*, and Lucile Eaves, *A History of California Labor Legislation* (Berkeley: University Press, 1910), pp. 105–96.

62. In addition to the federal cases cited in note 55, three pieces by John R. Wunder, "Law and Chinese in Frontier Montana," *Montana* 30 (1980): 18–31; "The Courts and the Chinese in Frontier Idaho," *Idaho Yesterdays* 25 (1981): 23–32; and "The Chinese and the Courts in the Pacific Northwest: Justice Denied?" *Pacific Historical Review* 52 (1983): 191–211, examine cases in the lower courts.

63. Thomas A. Bailey, "California, Japan, and the Alien Land Legislation of 1913," *Pacific Historical Review* 1 (1932): 36–59; Spencer C. Olin, Jr., "European Immigrant and Oriental Alien: Acceptance and Rejection by the California Legislation of 1913," *Pacific Historical Review* 35 (1966): 202–15; Paolo E. Coletta, "'The Most Thankless Task': Bryan and the California Alien Land Legislation," *Pacific Historical Review* 36 (1967): 163–87; Herbert P. Le Pore, "Prelude to Prejudice: Hiram Johnson, Woodrow Wilson, and the California Alien Land Law Controversy of 1913," *Historical Society of Southern California Quarterly* 61 (1979): 99–110.

64. Yuji Ichioka, "The Early Japanese Immigrant Quest for Citizenship: The Background of the 1922 Ozawa Case," *Amerasia Journal* 4, no. 2 (1977): 1–22, and Frank F. Chuman, *The Bamboo People: The Law and Japanese-Americans* (Del Mar, Calif.: Publisher's, 1976), pp. 70–71 deal with Japanese attempts to gain naturalization. Gary R. Hess, "The 'Hindu' in America: Immigration and Naturalization Policies and India, 1917–1946," *Pacific Historical Review* 38 (1969): 59–79; and Jensen, *Passage from India*, pp. 246–69, review the efforts of Asian Indians to acquire citizenship in the United States.

65. Megumi Dick Osumi, "Asians and California's Anti-Miscegenation Laws," in *Asian and Pacific American Experiences: Women's Perspectives*, ed. Nobuya Tsuchida (Minneapolis: University of Minnesota, Minneapolis, Asian/Pacific American Learning Resource Center, 1982), pp. 1–37.

66. Alexander Saxton, *The Indispensable Enemy: Labor and the Anti-Chinese Movement in California* (Berkeley: University of California Press, 1971); Gwendolyn Mink, *Old Labor and New Immigrants in American Political Development: Union, Party, and State, 1875–1920* (Ithaca: Cornell University Press, 1986).

67. Lucie Cheng, "Chinese Immigrant Women in Nineteenth-Century California," in *Women of America: A History*, ed. Carol Ruth Berkin and Mary Beth Norton (Boston: Houghton Mifflin, 1979), pp. 223–44; Yuji Ichioka, "*Amerika Nadeshiko*: Japanese Immigrant Women in the United States, 1900–1924," *Pacific Historical Review* 44 (1980): 339–57; Harold Hakwon Sunoo and Sonia Shinn Sunoo, "The Heritage of the First Korean Women Immigrants in the United States, 1903–1924," *Korean Christian Scholars Journal* 2 (1977): 142–77; Eun Sik Yang, "Korean Women of America: From Subordination to Partnership, 1903–1930," *Amerasia Journal* 11 (1984): 1–28.

ETHNICITY AND
SOCIAL STRUCTURE

3

Transplanted Networks

Charles Tilly

When Alexis de Tocqueville visited the United States in 1831, he saw a more homogeneous population and one less marked by immigration than we know today.[1] That sense of homogeneity strongly influenced his analysis of American democracy. "All the new European colonies," he wrote of North America, "contained the seed, if not the whole grain, of full democracy."[2] In the early chapters of *Democracy in America*, Tocqueville insisted that the relative poverty of American immigrants made for equality of condition. He also remarked that the difficulty of putting American land into cultivation and the low yields once cultivation had begun formed barriers to the emergence of a landowning aristocracy. Thus, he thought, the United States had the means of establishing a uniquely egalitarian public life.

Toward the end of his first volume, however, Tocqueville recognized the presence of Indians and blacks in the midst of the white-run democracy. The first group he portrayed as fragmented but wild, the second as deracinated but temporarily docile. Tocqueville thought that the advance of Europeans across the continent would essentially wipe out the Indians. But he predicted great struggles issuing from the coexistence of blacks and whites:

> Whatever efforts southerners make to keep slavery, they will not succeed indefinitely. In a world of democratic liberty and enlightenment, slavery, squeezed into one corner of the globe, attacked by Christianity as unjust and by political economy as deleterious, cannot survive as an institution. Either the slave or the master will end it. In either case, we must expect a terrible outcome.[3]

To Tocqueville, writing in the 1830s, the Europeans of North America formed a fairly homogeneous mass, dominated by English-speakers who had created or assimilated to a local variant of English culture. In different ways, he thought, Indians and blacks lived in utter alienation from white Europeans. The United States, for him, faced serious problems that ultimately stemmed from previous migrations. But immigration itself did not seem to pose particular problems.

The next century made a big difference. Interpreting Americans to themselves and to his fellow Britons in 1944, D. W. Brogan conceded that the remarkable physical uniformity of American towns hid a great deal of ethnic (he said "racial") variety, a consequence of vast migrations. In the Swedish settlements of Minnesota, Detroit's Polish enclave of Hamtramck, and similar zones of intense immigration, large blocks of distinctive populations survived. "But more common," he remarked,

> is the town in which a dozen groups have to live together in close contact, in which a street of Germans borders on a street of Irish, in which the Italians and the Greeks are mingled in school and market, in which Jew and Gentile have to learn to get on together. It is in towns like these that the problem of Americanization is most acute, in which the well-meaning efforts of Rotary Clubs and women's organizations fail in face of the facts that seem to suggest that, whatever the legal fiction may be, there are first-class and second-class and even third-class Americans, that there is a scale descending from the "old stocks" down to the Negroes.[4]

By 1944 Tocqueville's dream of homogeneity and equality had little to do with American reality. For Brogan, as for most thoughtful Americans, immigration had created an acute problem, the problem of Americanization. Immigration, furthermore, intertwined with racial division to produce the further problem of stark inequality among racial and ethnic groups.

Some people thought the two problems were one: insufficient Americanization caused inequality, and assimilation would eradicate inequality. They merely disagreed over whether the Americanization in question meant obliterating distinctive ethnic and racial characteristics or extending basic rights and opportunities. By the first line of reasoning, the systems of rights and opportunities worked efficiently, once newcomers had acquired the appropriate skills, attitudes, and cultural traits. By the second, in contrast, the American system had room for a wide range of skills, attitudes, and cultural traits, once the groups in question had found their niches, made their presences known, and acquired their lawful rights.

Brogan had obliteration (or at least strong convergence) of old-country traits in mind, and thought it was happening. His contemporary Gunnar Myrdal, on the other hand, was less sure. He granted the existence of cultural assimilation but then stressed rights and opportunities: the rights of blacks presented white Americans with a dilemma.[5] Black–white relations were an American dilemma because Americans in general held strong commitments to equality of rights and opportunities, but whites had thus far chosen to define blacks out of the competition. The opening up of opportunity to successive immigrant groups, argued Myrdal, established that the United States had the capacity to extend opportunity to blacks as well.

Brogan or Myrdal? In the choice lie some critical historical questions with significant implications for public policy. What impact did the conditions of American immigration—including the forced immigration of blacks—have on inequality within the United States? To what extent did such consequences of immigration as the formation of distinctive ethnic communities sustain or alter

American patterns of inequality? The research reported in this volume indicates that significant features of American inequality did result from the social organization of immigration. But it also establishes that several once-popular conceptions of immigration's impact on inequality apply poorly to the American experience: the idea of a first-come, first-served sequence of nationalities, queuing for assimilation and opportunity; the notion of wholesale importation of cultural traits whose compatibility with dominant American patterns determined the pace and degree of assimilation; the thought that individual competition in a rapidly expanding labor market was the prime determinant of different immigrant groups' relative success or failure.

All these old conceptions stress individualistic competition. The alternatives pursued by this book's authors range widely, from Kerby Miller's Gramscian model of cultural hegemony to Sucheng Chan's portrayal of capitalist labor markets. As compared with the old individualism, nevertheless, the contributors stress collectivism: ways in which common struggle, shared social relations, and group control affected the fates of whole categories of immigrants and their descendants. This essay will not provide a grand synthesis of our authors' varied views, nor will it discuss the individual papers. It will, instead, pursue their joint inquiry into collective aspects of immigration.

Flows and Counterflows

Tocqueville was ordinarily a shrewd observer of social structure, yet he had little to say about immigration as an influence on American inequality. His lack of concern about immigration resulted in part from the fact that he visited the United States at the end of a lull in the flow of persons to there from Europe. The wars that engaged Europe and North America from the 1740s to 1815 had slowed transatlantic population movements. Meanwhile, slaveholders forced the large numbers of Africans who arrived during the same period to anglicize rapidly. The two trends favored the creation of a predominantly anglophone America.

Migration to North America formed only one stream of the great displacements within the populations of Eurasia and Africa that seem to have accelerated after 1500.[6] In discussing the tropical world, Philip Curtin conveys a sense of that acceleration over the world as a whole. He shows that continental North America remained peripheral to the principal paths of tropical migration, including the slave trade. In the Western Hemisphere as a whole, "four times as many Africans as Europeans arrived in the Americas in the 1820s, and allowing for European repatriation, the two flows were of approximately the same strength in the 1830s. Not until 1840 did arrivals from Europe permanently surpass those from Africa."[7] Nevertheless, the flows between Europe and the Americas constituted a major component of world migration from the sixteenth to the nineteenth centuries.

By the time of Tocqueville's visit, North America had been receiving immigrants — forced, voluntary, or in between — for two hundred years. The seventeenth-century arrival of European settlers introduced foreign diseases that devastated the native population; thus the migrants indirectly created the nearly open space into which they expanded.[8] During the seventeenth and eighteenth centuries, white migrants to North America came mainly from three colonizing powers: France, Spain, and Great Britain. The enslavement and importation of Africans by slavers from the three powers continued through much of the warlike era; indeed, at the prevailing rate of importation if the mortality of newly captured slaves had not been enormously higher than that of Europeans, by the 1820s the size of the black population of the United States (1.8 million in 1820 to 7.9 million whites) would have approached that of the white population.[9] American slaveholders, however, broke up homogeneous clusters of slaves and forced their captive Africans to adopt American manners and speech. The formation of the United States then left most of the French- and Spanish-speakers in separate North American colonies. Thus, a chiefly anglophone country came into being.

In the new United States, people of British stock predominated. In 1790 about 61 percent of the U.S. white population sprang from English origins, 10 percent from Irish, and 8 percent from Scots, for a total of almost 80 percent having origins in the British Isles. Yet Germans, Dutch, French, and Swedes also had appreciable percentages of the remainder.[10] Even after the wartime lulls, the white population showed clear signs of its immigrant origins. And enslaved blacks were still arriving in large numbers. Only in retrospect do immigration and its consequences seem to belong peculiarly to the nineteenth and twentieth centuries.

After the wars ended, European immigration resumed at an unprecedented pace. British migrants increased unsteadily from 25,000 in 1821–1830 to 807,000 in 1881–1890, and Irish arrivals rose from 51,000 in 1821–1830 to 914,000 in 1851–1860; after a few slower decades, another peak of 655,000 Irish immigrants arrived between 1881 and 1890. As time passed, the balance shifted successively to Scandinavia, Germany, Austria-Hungary, Russia, and Italy, with Canada, Latin America, the Caribbean, and Asia becoming increasingly important during the twentieth century.[11]

From the end of the slave trade until recently, then, American immigration consisted chiefly of flows back and forth between Europe and North America. Changes in the social organization of nineteenth-century Europe promoted a speeding up of long-established migratory currents. The extension of capitalist property relations greatly expanded the population that was available for long-distance migration. The separation of households from their means of production, the spread of wage labor, the rising labor productivity of agriculture, and the concentration of capital in cities combined to establish long-term, long-distance migration as an increasingly common response of Europeans to contraction at home and expansion elsewhere.

Capitalist growth probably also helps account for the great nineteenth-century acceleration of natural increase in much of Europe, which fundamentally altered the balance between available niches in farms or shops and the population eligible to fill those niches.[12] Constricted opportunity in Europe

and relatively high wages in North America encouraged people who were already seeking work in the growing industrial and commercial towns of Europe
to extend their searches beyond the Atlantic. Eventually, the decline of European fertility, mortality, and natural increase counteracted the effects of proletarianization and turned some European countries toward the importation of
labor. But that shift occurred after the great waves of European migration to
North America.

Not that the smoothly rational operation of an open, competitive, international labor market characterized by wage differentials accounts for the rhythm
and timbre of American immigration. At the very least we need to recognize
two facts about that immigration. First, it was and is extraordinarily selective
by origin and type of migrant. Second, it usually did not draw on isolated
individual decision makers but on clusters of people bound together by acquaintance and common fate. Nor were there clusters mere categories — skilled
or unskilled, Jew or Gentile, Greek or Italian. To be sure, individuals did
migrate to the United States, and sometimes alone. But they did so as participants in social processes that extended far beyond them. Of course, members
of different categories of the European population migrated to the United
States (and, for that matter, returned to Europe) at spectacularly different
rates. But the categories we ordinarily apply to those differences poorly describe the actual groups that lived and organized transatlantic migration.

From the New Deal era to the immediate postwar period, American historians undertook a major revamping of ideas about immigration. Where earlier
chroniclers had seen immigrants as foreign elements injected, and ultimately
absorbed, into American life, the revisionists portrayed immigration as an
indigenous American social process. The academic analysis had political over-
tones, for it argued against nativism and for the maintenance of equal opportunity. As Oscar Handlin, one of the major revisionists, put it, their approach
started

> with the assumption that the entire population of the United States almost
> from the start was a composite, made up of elements from a multitude of
> sources. Among these heterogeneous multitudes those who had actually been
> born in other countries represented only the extreme of a condition that was
> general to the whole society. The differences between them and the native-born
> of various sorts, while real, were differences of degree rather than of kind.[13]

Not long after making the statement, Handlin published a general history of
the United States, cunningly called *The Americans*, based on the premise that
American history was more than anything else the tale of many peoples who
became — or who are still becoming — one: E pluribus unum.

Historical work of the last quarter-century has not so much rejected that
line of argument as expanded and refined it.[14] Where Handlin and his colleagues saw shock and subsequent assimilation, however, recent historians have
commonly seen continuous processes of collective transformation involving
the use of old social networks and categories to produce new ones. Rather than
individual uprooting, disorganization, and adjustment, collective action and

shared struggle. Rather than person-by-person striving, organized migration networks and labor markets. Rather than wholesale importation (and subsequent degradation) of cultural traits, collective fabrication of new cultures from old materials.

Networks and Categories in Migration

To put it simply: networks migrate; categories stay put; and networks create new categories. By and large, the effective units of migration were (and are) neither individuals nor households but sets of people linked by acquaintance, kinship, and work experience who somehow incorporated American destinations into the mobility alternatives they considered when they reached critical decision points in their individual or collective lives. Long-distance migration entails many risks: to personal security, to comfort, to income, to the possibility of satisfying social relations. Where kinsmen, friends, neighbors, and work associates already have good contacts with possible destinations, reliance on established interpersonal networks for information minimizes and spreads the risks.[15] Implicitly recognizing those advantages, the vast majority of potential long-distance migrants anywhere in the world draw their chief information for migration decisions (including the decision to stay put) from members of their interpersonal networks, and rely on those networks for assistance both in moving and in settling at the destination. Their activity then reproduces and extends the networks, especially to the extent that by migrating they acquire the possibility and the obligation to supply information and help to other potential migrants. Constrained by personal networks, potential migrants fail to consider many theoretically available destinations, and concentrate on those few localities with which their place of origin has strong links. The higher the risk and the greater the cost of returning, the more intense the reliance on previously established ties.

These general principles clearly apply to American immigration. Even when migration occurred one person at a time, migrants commonly drew on information from network members who had already gone to America. Virginia Yans-McLaughlin cites a typical report from among Italians in Buffalo:

> A local immigrant who joined his grandfather and cousins in 1906 recalled: "Immigrants almost always came to join others who had preceded them — a husband, or a father, or an uncle, or a friend. In western New York most of the first immigrants from Sicily went to Buffalo, so that from 1900 on, the thousands who followed them to this part of the state also landed in Buffalo. There they joined friends and relatives who in many cases had purchased the tickets for their steerage passage to America."[16]

The frequency of remittances from emigrants to homefolks and of steamship tickets prepaid by people at the American destination reveals the extent of that mutual aid. As Ewa Morawska reminds us, a survey conducted by the U.S. Immigration Commission on 1908–1909 showed 60 percent of new immigrants from southern and eastern Europe arriving with prepaid passage.

Networks also provided other kinds of aid; as John Gjerde reports in his study of migrants from Norway's western coast:

> When immigrants arrived in a settlement, temporary housing was often pro-
> vided for those who needed it. The communities settled by kinsmen also
> offered opportunities to work and accumulate capital at wages that were usual-
> ly higher than those in Europe. Indeed, emigration was often funded by ad-
> vance wages in the form of prepaid tickets. Unmarried men looking for work
> were often found in settlements peopled by former residents of their home
> community. A group of landless immigrants in 1883 used community ties to
> search for work, moving from one community settlement to another; eventual-
> ly, they settled permanently in another Orsta community. Economic aid con-
> tinued. One immigrant remembered that when he arrived in the Echo commu-
> nity in 1892, "we could get all we desired . . . on credit only by showing that
> we were from Hjorundfjord."[17]

Such step-by-step moves eventually transplanted major segments of existing networks from the old country to the new, and modified the networks' structure in the process. Paradoxically, the high rate of return to many European areas had similar effects, for the returnees reinforced the ties between origin and destination, and thus facilitated further migration along the same lines. Like a honeysuckle vine, the network moved, changed shape, and sent down new roots without entirely severing the old ones. In that sense, networks migrated.

Categories, on the other hand, stay put. Although East Europeans retained some awareness of their divisions into Poles, Slovaks, Czechs, Rusyns, Ukrainians, Armenians, Lituanians, Latvians, Hungarians, Croatians, Serbs, Slovenes, and Jews (to quote Ewa Morawska's list), they did not simply carry these collective identities across the Atlantic like so many pieces of luggage. Where those labels did not simply represent outsiders' tags for collections of people who ordinarily identified themselves in quite other ways, they belonged to the situation at the origin and not necessarily at the destination. Which of these categories, and which of their subdivisions, actually survived the voyage depended on the population mix at the destination and on the previously established categories around which the people already at the destination organized their own lives.

Networks create new categories. In the experience of American immigration, sets of connected immigrants who did not have a common identity at the point of origin often acquired a new identification during interaction with others at the destination. In the United States, Piedmontese, Neapolitans, Sicilians, and Romans became Italians. But not always. That depended on the networks' size, density, and relationship to other groups.

Networks also transform existing categories. In his contribution to this volume, Kerby Miller shows how Irish identity, already formed in Ireland through opposition to the conquering English, altered in the United States under the influence of a bourgeoisie that promoted religiosity, nationalism, and political involvement. Although these three enthusiasms had actually been rare in the rural regions from which most Irish immigrants had departed, in the United States their lack came to seem un-Irish. Similarly, other groups of immigrants — Greeks, Zionist Jews, Armenians are examples — committed themselves more strongly to nationalist politics as Americans than had their ancestors in the old country. In none of these cases can we reasonably think of Americanization as straightforward assimilation to a dominant American culture. In each case members of networks whose identities and internal structures were themselves changing continuously negotiated new relations with other networks, including those in the country of origin.

Political identity was by no means the only sphere in which the simultaneous transformation of networks, identities, and relations with other groups occurred. In the world of employment, the prevalence of subcontracting in manufacturing and construction during the later nineteenth and earlier twentieth centuries epitomized the adaptation of networks initially formed by immigration. In subcontracting, the owner of a business delegates to a second party (most often a foreman or a smaller entrepreneur) the responsibility both for hiring workers and for supervising production, and the second partly delivers finished products to the owner. Migrant networks articulate neatly with subcontracting because they give the subcontractor access to flexible supplies of labor about which he or she can easily get information and over which she or he can easily exert control outside the workplace.

As a result of selective recruitment of workers, trades, shops, and divisions of large firms often display remarkable concentrations of particular racial and ethnic groups. Pittsburgh's steel mills at the beginning of the twentieth century provide an extreme example:

> Most departments, according to Joe R., a Polish immigrant, were dominated by particular national groups. "You take in the erection department — it was the hardest and noisiest and everything — It was mostly all Slavs. . . . Not Slovaks, it was Polish. . . . We didn't have Lithuanians there and the Russians were not involved there." Joe R. explained how the process operated. "Now if a Russian got his job in a shear department . . . he's looking for a buddy, a Russian buddy. He's not going to look for a Croatian buddy. And if he see the boss looking for a man he says, 'Look, I have a good man,' and he's picking out his friends. A Ukrainian department, a Russian department, a Polish department. And it was a beautiful thing in a way."[18]

The continuity of migrants' networks created that "beautiful thing."

We need a rough distinction between sending and receiving networks. The connections among people at a given point of origin constitute the sending networks; those among people at the destination, the receiving networks. The knitting together of the two creates new networks that span origin and destination. The distinction can only be rough because many people make multiple moves, and because once a migration system starts operating, the line between "origin" and "destination" begins to blur. Nevertheless, the distinction makes sense because the characteristics of the new networks depend on the pairings that occur at the junction of origin and destination. Because those pairings

vary significantly over time, the "same" kinds of migrants establish very different relations to the populations at their destinations. Jewish immigrants, Ewa
Morawska points out, were much more likely to become manual workers if they
migrated to New York, Boston, Philadelphia, Baltimore, or Chicago than if
they went to smaller towns; outside the major centers of Jewish settlement,
Jews became self-employed much more often.

Similar contrasts appear on an international scale. With respect to wealth,
education, previous work experience, and region of origin, the 2.3 million
Italians who migrated to Argentina between 1860 and 1914 resembled the 4.1
million who migrated to the United States.[19] What is more, the great majority
of both groups seem to have arrived via chain migration, with the idea of
earning enough to return home. Immediately on arrival in the new land, both
groups moved chiefly into unskilled labor. But Italians came to occupy much
more prominent positions in Argentina (and especially Buenos Aires) than in
the United States (and especially New York). Two factors made a large difference: first, investment opportunities for workers who saved money were greater
in Argentina than in the United States; second, it was easier to move from
unskilled to skilled jobs in Argentina. Both factors gave Italian immigrants
who worked hard and saved in Argentina stronger reasons for remaining in
their adopted country.

The network structure of migration makes implausible several standard
ways of analyzing immigration: an assimilation of individuals to a dominant
culture, as individual status-striving, or as the wholesale transplantation of
preexisting groups. "Assimilation" becomes implausible because the paths of
change vary enormously from stream to stream of migration, because the
process is collective rather than individual, and because the network structure,
multiplied, contradicts the idea of a single dominant pattern to which people
might approximate themselves. Individual status-striving, although it surely
occurs, accounts poorly for group changes after immigration because it misses
the centrality of interpersonal connections to the fate of any particular group.
Wholesale transplantation badly describes a process in which people greatly
transform their social relations, and often create new group identities. Instead
of a series of individual transformations in the direction of a dominant American culture, migration involves negotiation of new relationships both within
and across networks. Instead of individual status-striving, collective efforts to
cope. Instead of wholesale transplantation, selective re-creation of social ties.

Once we recognize the network structure of migration, some of the old,
standard questions stop making sense. It is idle, for example, to ask whether in
general migrants are smarter, braver, or more desperate than nonmigrants;
some systems of social ties select in one direction, some in another. It is not
very useful to classify migrants by intentions to stay or to return home, because
intentions and possibilities are always more complex than that — and the migrants themselves often cannot see the possibilities that are shaped by their
networks. Again, generalizations saying that skilled workers migrate longer
distances than unskilled workers or that younger people migrate more frequently than older ones probably hold on the average but suffer enormous

qualifications depending on the social organization of labor markets. In short, we ought to think of migration as we think of community structure: not reducible to individual characteristics and intentions. The decisive, recurrent regularities concern the structure of migration networks themselves.

Contrasting Types of Migration

The importance of social networks becomes clearer when we stop thinking about migration as a single homogeneous experience, and start recognizing its sharply contrasting forms. A rough but useful typology distinguishes colonizing, coerced, circular, chain, and career migration. The distinctions rest on the links between sending and receiving networks. We can usually distinguish two aspects of those links: (1) the extent to which migrants retain positions in the sending networks, and (2) the degree to which the move is definitive. An entirely temporary move in which the mover retains full membership in the sending network does not qualify as migration at all; we call it mobility. At the other extreme, a completely definitive move in which the mover loses all connection with the sending network is quite rare, despite its popularity as an image of the migrant uprooted; it almost never occurs except under extreme coercion.

The five types of migration overlap somewhat, but differ on the average with respect to both retention of positions in sending networks and permanence of the moves involved. _Colonizing_ migration, in its pure form, simply expands the geographic range of a given population by moving intact segments of the population into territories they had not previously occupied; European farmers who moved to the American frontier, for example, often did so en bloc. _Coerced_ migration entails obligatory departure, forced severing of most or all ties at the origin, and little or no personal connection between the migrants and people at the destination; Philip Curtin's description, elsewhere in this book, of the capture and shipping of slaves illustrates coerced migration very well, as does the shipping of convicts to the Caribbean. _Circular_ migration consists of the creation of a regular circuit in which migrants retain their claims and contacts with a home base and routinely return to that base after a period of activity elsewhere in the circuit; many Mexican immigrants to the United States fit the pattern. _Chain_ migration involves sets of related individuals or households who move from one place to another through a set of social arrangements in which people at the destination provide aid, information, and encouragement to the newcomers; Ewa Morawska's immigrants from southern and eastern Europe traveled largely in such chains. _Career_ migration, finally, characterizes individuals and households that move in response to opportunities to change position within or among large structures, such as corporations, states, and professional labor markets.

Clearly the five types overlap. American immigration has taken all five forms, singly and in combination. Colonizing migration characterized the early decades of North America's settlement, and continued in some regions into the twentieth century. Coerced migration, which applies most evidently to the arrival of enslaved Africans, fits the experience of many Southeast Asian, Caribbean, and Central American refugees as well. The bulk of American immigration has fallen somewhere in the range from circular to chain migration. As John Bodnar says, return rates of 25 to 60 percent for major European groups reflect the intention of most immigrants to go back to their origins if and when they could accumulate the capital to reestablish themselves.[20] Even impoverished Ireland had a return rate of 10 percent toward the end of the nineteenth century; young women who emigrated temporarily to earn money for dowry and liquidation of family debts were common enough in County Longford to merit a special name: "redeemers."[21] For many networks, North America simply represented one more extension of circuits that had long served the same purpose within Europe. To that extent, American immigration followed the model of circular migration.

Circular migration has some familiar correlates. Because it commonly rests on the maintenance of households in the area of origin, it rarely moves whole families and often draws disproportionately on one sex — for example, males for common labor, or females for domestic service. Males long predominated in Chinese migration to the United States, with the correlate that the few Chinese women who did migrate were frequently prostitutes; in the San Francisco of 1870, almost three-quarters of the 2,018 Chinese women enumerated in the census were recorded as prostitutes.[22] Circular migration often means some form of inexpensive collective living for the migrants, hard work, rigorous saving of wages, extensive remittances, and relatively little contact with the receiving population.

Within Europe or Asia and across the ocean, however, the networks of circular migration often transformed themselves into chains displaying a strong balance of movement in one direction. Because capital accumulated at the destination for investment at the point of origin — to buy land, finance a marriage, start a business — could serve similar purposes at the destination, relative opportunities for investment at origin and destination helped determine whether a particular circle became a chain. Likewise, where the initial positions occupied by immigrants at the destination led easily to other, more remunerative, positions, chains grew from circles.

The combination of hard work, extensive savings, and broad commitments to others also facilitated a shift to investment in the opportunities of immigrants' children at the destination. Japanese women of the San Francisco Bay area were often wives of gardeners, and often worked as domestic servants. Older women interviewed by Evelyn Nakano Glenn echoed the report of Mrs. Nishimura: while the present was her easiest time, "my happiest time was then, when my children were small. I was poor and busy then, but that might have been the best time. It was good to think about my children — how they'd go through high school and college and afterwards."[23]

Individual households were not the only ones to reorganize in the transition from circular to chain migration. The brokers and entrepreneurs of circular migration developed longer-term attachments and investments at the destination; helped create local networks of mutual aid in the search for jobs, housing, and sociability; formed patron-client networks that reinforced their own power; and lent money to their compatriots. These forms of mutual aid attached immigrants to American social structure. The immigrants did not necessarily "assimilate"; they did, however, construct social relations that helped assure their survival on a strange terrain. In the process, they built migration machines: sending networks that articulated with particular receiving networks in which new migrants could find jobs, housing, and sociability. The machines worked efficiently, bringing in new labor from overseas when opportunities rose in the particular industries to which they were attached and sending people back when opportunity contracted or when they accumulated enough capital to reenter social life at the origin.

Obviously, similar mechanisms have operated in migration *within* the United States. Migration chains brought workers, both black and white, to Detroit's industry from Kentucky, Tennessee, and other southern states during both world wars, and Jews moved into the small-town retail trade of western Pennsylvania through elaborate chains of kinsmen and *Landsmänner*. Heavy reliance on migration chains in the search for jobs and housing produced the characteristically intense small-scale segregation of nineteenth-century American cities by place of origin.[24]

Compared with the numbers involved in circular and chain migration, career migration has played a relatively small part in American immigration. In our own time, it is true, American medical services have drawn many doctors and nurses from overseas through professional networks, and multinational corporations have set up their own currents of intercontinental migration. But career migration looms much less large in American immigration than it does in migration within the United States. Across the seas, circles and, especially, chains predominate.

Networks and Solidarity

The social networks used and transformed by migration endure far beyond the time of displacement. They provide a setting for life at the destination, a basis for solidarity and mutual aid as well as for division and conflict. In recent years historians and sociologists of American communities have repeatedly shown how migrant groups cluster together as a result of housing searches mainly limited to the local network, job specialization depends largely on the initial contacts of a migrant population with the local labor market, formation of businesses and whole industries is dominated by people from a single origin, social and economic capital accumulates within boundaries set by immigration, and new, compelling identities take shape from the materials deposited by the migration process. Not that all groups huddled together with equal intensity, or maintained their networks with the same solidity; variation in those regards sets one of our major problems of explanation in American social experience.

Josef Barton's study of Italians, Rumanians, and Slovaks in Cleveland makes the variation clear. Migration patterns, he reports,

> had a significant impact on the development of ethnic settlements. The distinctive aspect of Italian migration was the predominance of major village chains. The settlement emerging as a result of this migration pattern formed around a stable core population from ten villages in the Abruzzi and Sicily. Immigrants from these two regions established a hegemony in the settlement, and the marriage choices of the arrivals reinforced the dominant regional groups. The pattern of parochial cultural loyalties that characterized Italian organizations reflected the community's peculiar demographic structure.
>
> The Rumanians and the Slovaks migrated in minor district streams, and village streams were much less important than in Italian migration. In both the Rumanian and Slovak settlements, efforts were made to maximize national rather than local ties, and mixed patterns of settlement and intermarriage across the boundaries of local groups facilitated these efforts. The resulting configuration of cultural loyalties was in sharp contrast to the Italian emphasis on village and regional organizations, for both Rumanian and Slovak societies oriented themselves strongly toward religious and national aims.[25]

Here we watch the initial conditions of migration setting the frame for the creation of a new social structure.

So long as they formed and reformed mainly within the limits set by the migration process, social networks also provided the basis for ethnic identity. Concentrating on the Irish in America, Kerby Miller shows how ethnicity — far from being a form of consciousness carried over from Ireland and gradually dissipated in the new environment — arose from the experience of living in the United States. Miller emphasizes the place of associational activities and institutional affiliations in transforming people's perceptions of themselves, of their collective histories, and of their relations to others.

Susan Olzak has generalized a parallel line of argument into a general model of ethnic conflict. "The central argument," she writes,

> is that increased levels of competition between two or more ethnic groups cause increases in ethnic collective action. This happens because two processes coincide. First, strongly bounded ethnic enclaves encourage high levels of ethnic identification and reaffirmation to cultural values, language, and other characteristics [that] set members apart from others. Second, growth causes enclave communities to expand into job, housing and other markets monopolized by the majority, causing levels of ethnic competition to rise. That is, levels of mobilization rise due to the fact that ethnic solidarity and competition are both high. It is the shifting dynamic of ethnic enclave solidarity coupled with rising levels of ethnic competition that raises the potential for ethnic conflict.[26]

Evidence from American cities between 1877 and 1914 confirms Olzak's general line of argument.[27] The perceptions that immigrant groups form of themselves and others vary considerably with their locations in the social structure.

Those perceptions, and the social practices that complement them, emerge from interaction with other groups, especially competitors and enemies. But they also develop through struggle within the group, as different sets of leaders and interpreters seek to impose their own definitions of the group's origins, character, interests, and destiny. External discrimination and conflict reinforce both processes. Thus, ethnicity acquires its Janus face, looking inward and outward at the same time.

Networks and Inequality

Networks brought into being by immigration serve to create and perpetuate inequality. Lest anyone think that solidarity and mutual aid have nothing but gratifying results, we should recognize two things: (1) members of immigrant groups often exploited one another as they would not have dared to exploit the native-born, and (2) every inclusion also constitutes an exclusion. American immigration produced a remarkable specialization of work by origin, although the precise specializations varied from one locality and migrant stream to another. John Bodnar provides a representative list:

> In Indiana oil refineries, Croatians held jobs in only three categories: stillman helper, firemen, and still cleaners. In the ready-made clothing industry, Jews predominated in small firms with minimal mechanization and segmentation of labor while Italians concentrated in large factories which tended to require less individual skills. Serbs and Croats in New York City were heavily involved in freighthandling. Italians dominated construction gangs and barber shops in Buffalo, Philadelphia, and Pittsburgh. By 1918, Italians represented 75 percent of the women in the men's and boy's clothing industry and 93 percent of the females doing hand embroidery in New York City. Nearly all of the 3,000 employees in Peninsular Car Company in Detroit by 1900 were Polish. Polish women dominated restaurant and kitchen jobs in Chicago by 1909, which they preferred to domestic employment. By 1920, one study found an incredible 69 percent of Slovak males in coal mining and about one-half of all Mexicans working as blastfurnace laborers.[28]

Any student of migration can supply further tales of occupational specialization by regional or national origin.

If we tune our categories finely enough, furthermore, we always find that the specialization goes beyond occupation to include such matters as who owns what kinds of firms, and which people work for others. Looking closely at Jews, Italians, and blacks in New York since 1910, Suzanne Model demonstrates not only that Jews more often owned their own firms but also that Jews more often worked for other people of the same origin.[29] Coethnic employment, as she calls it, was less common among Italians than among Jews, and least common among blacks. Model also provides evidence that coethnic employment, on the whole, contributed to higher incomes and better jobs.

Longer-term effects, although more difficult to detect, probably mattered as well. Coethnic employment most likely fostered capital accumulation within an ethnic group, and thus facilitated investment in the occupational and educational chances of the next generation. The self-exploiting Mama and Papa, with their eyes on the kids' future, could carry out their self-exploitation more easily where they ran their own businesses. They could also use — and underpay — the labor of women and children within their households and kin groups. That happened especially when many people from the same migrant origins moved into the same business.

Every one of these specializations, however, excluded someone else from a particular occupation, trade, or business. In New York and elsewhere, part of the tragedy of black life is that different groups of blacks lost control of the few trades, such as barbering, in which they occupied strong positions during the nineteenth century. For reasons no one seems to understand, they were unable to establish new monopolies. Elsewhere in this volume, Model suggests that black families suffered most, in the long run, from the increasing inability of breadwinners to place their children and kinsmen in sheltered, relatively desirable occupational niches. That inability diminished parental authority, speculates Model, and encouraged an individualistic self-reliance that may have corresponded to American ideals but served blacks badly in the world of work.

Despite occasional exceptions such as Pullman-car portering, blacks differed from most other poor migrants in spreading across a wide range of jobs and industries, almost always in subordinate, insecure, and poorly paid positions. As a consequence, blacks have often found themselves competing unsuccessfully with the latest, poorest immigrants. This structural reality lies behind the ambivalent positions on immigration policy Lawrence Fuchs shows black leaders to have adopted.

The dialectic of inclusion and exclusion did not only set off blacks from whites; it also distinguished ethnic groups from one another, and established a rough hierarchy of advantage and opportunity. Stanley Lieberson, among others, has traced that hierarchy in great detail.[30] The hierarchy depended, to be sure, on the skills and resources different immigrant groups brought with them from their homelands, and on more general routines of discrimination by color, language, and religion in American life.

But initial advantage and discrimination tell only part of the story. The most important teaching of recent work on immigration and ethnic experience concerns the ways in which the social organization of migration itself, the highly variable knitting together of sending and receiving networks, shaped the aspirations, opportunities, strategies, fortunes, and accomplishments of most Americans. That shaping continues today.

The history of American immigration therefore combines the general and the particular in a compelling way. On one side, it is everyone's history, a history in which chains of migrants formed over and over again to link distant places to the United States. On the other, its precise form differs from group to group, even from person to person; each of us has his own tale of migration to tell. ending networks and receiving networks could hardly be more specific, yet their junction and transformation follow well-defined general rules. Connections among persons established by nineteenth-century immigration still affect inequality today. In examining the history of immigration as individual experience or collective phenomenon, we are probing the roots, and the broken branches, of American democracy.

NOTES

1. This is a revised, expanded version of "Transplanted Networks," Working Paper 35 (October 1986), Center for Studies of Social Change, New School for Social Research. I am grateful to members of the New School's proseminar on inequality for criticism of the previous draft.

2. Alexis de Tocqueville, *De la démocratie en Amérique*, 2 vols. (Paris: Galimard, 1961), 1:28.

3. Ibid., 1:379.

4. D. W. Brogan, *The American Character* (New York: Knopf, 1944), p. 98.

5. Gunnar Myrdal, *An American Dilemma: The Negro Problem and American Democracy* (New York: Harper, 1944).

6. See William H. McNeill, "Human Migration in Historical Perspective," *Population and Development Review* 10 (1984): 1–18; William H. McNeill and Ruth S. Adams, eds., *Human Migration: Patterns and Policies* (Bloomington: Indiana University Press, 1978).

7. David Eltis, "Free and Coerced Migrations: Some Comparisons," *American Historical Review* 88 (1983): 255; similarly, in her contribution to this book Sucheng Chan points out that North America figured only as a fringe area for the vast Chinese emigration. Healthy correctives to American megalomania in migration studies!

8. McNeill, "Human Migration," pp. 16–17.

9. Eltis, "Free and Forced Migrations," p. 278.

10. Stephan Thernstrom, Ann Orlov, and Oscar Handlin, eds., *Harvard Encyclopedia of American Ethnic Groups* (Cambridge: Harvard University Press, 1980), p. 479.

11. Ibid., p. 480.

12. See David Levine, ed., *Proletarianization and Family History* (Orlando, Fl: Academic Press, 1984).

13. Oscar Handlin, "Immigration in American Life: A Reappraisal," in *Immigration and American History. Essays in Honor of Theodore C. Blegen*, ed. Henry Steele Commager (Minneapolis: University of Minnesota Press, 1961), p. 11; see also Handlin, *The Americans: A New History of the People of the United States* (Boston: Little, Brown, 1963).

14. For a recent synthesis, see John Bodnar, *The Transplanted: A History of Immigrants in Urban America* (Bloomington: Indiana University Press, 1985).

15. See J. Edward Taylor, "Differential Migration, Networks, Information and Risk," *Research in Human Capital and Development* 4 (1986): 147–71.

16. Virginia Yans-McLaughlin, *Family and Community: Italian Immigrants in Buffalo, 1880–1930* (Ithaca: Cornell University Press, 1977), p. 58.

17. Jon Gjerde, "The Chain Migrations from the West Coast of Norway: A Comparative Study" (Unpublished paper, Department of History, University of California, Berkeley, 1986), p. 22.

18. John Bodnar, Roger Simon, and Michael P. Weber, *Lives of Their Own: Blacks, Italians, and Poles in Pittsburgh, 1900–1960* (Urbana: University of Illinois Press, 1982), p. 62. See also Ewa Morawska, *For Bread with Butter: Life-Worlds of East*

Central Europeans in Johnstown, Pennsylvania, 1890-1940 (Cambridge: Cambridge University Press, 1985).

19. Samuel L. Baily, "The Adjustment of Italian Immigrants in Buenos Aires and New York, 1870-1914," *American Historical Review* 88 (1983): 303. For the general comparison, see also Herbert S. Klein, "The Integration of Italian Immigrants into the United States and Argentina: A Comparative Analysis," *American Historical Review* 88 (1983): 306-29.

20. Bodnar, *The Transplanted*, p. 53.

21. Marjolein 't Hart, "Irish Return Migration in the Nineteenth Century," *Tijdschrift voor Econ. en Soc. Geografie* 76 (1985): 223-31.

22. Lucie Cheng, "Free, Indentured, Enslaved: Chinese Prostitutes in Nineteenth-Century America," in *Labor Immigration under Capitalism: Asian Workers in the United States before World War II*, ed. Lucie Cheng and Edna Bonacich (Berkeley: University of California Press, 1984), p. 421.

23. Evelyn Nakano Glenn, "The Dialectics of Wage Work: Japanese American Women and Domestic Service, 1905-1940," in *Labor Immigration under Capitalism: Asian Workers in the United States before World War II*, ed. Lucie Cheng and Edna Bonacich (Berkeley: University of California Press, 1984), p. 502.

24. See, e.g., Kathleen Nels Conzen, *Immigrant Milwaukee, 1836-1860* (Cambridge: Harvard University Press, 1976), and Olivier Zunz, *The Changing Face of Inequality: Urbanization, Industrial Development, and Immigrants in Detroit, 1880-1920* (Chicago: University of Chicago Press, 1982).

25. Josef J. Barton, *Peasants and Strangers: Italians, Rumanians, and Slovaks in an American City, 1890-1950* (Cambridge: Harvard University Press, 1975), p. 63.

26. Susan Olzak, "Ethnic Collective Action and the Dynamics of Ethnic Enclaves" (Unpublished paper, Department of Sociology, Cornell University, 1985), p. 3.

27. Susan Olzak, "Have the Causes of Ethnic Collective Action Changed over a Hundred Years? Evidence from the 1870s and 1880s and the 1970s," Technical Report 87-6 (Department of Sociology, Cornell University, 1987); "Labor Unrest, Immigration, and Ethnic Conflict in Urban America, 1880 through 1914," Technical Report 87-9 (Department of Sociology, Cornell University, 1987).

28. Bodnar, *The Transplanted*, p. 65. See also Alejandro Portes and Robert D. Manning, "The Immigrant Enclave: Theory and Empirical Examples," in *Competitive Ethnic Relations*, ed. Susan Olzak and Joane Nagel (Orlando, Fl.: Academic Press, 1986), pp. 47-68; Roger D. Waldinger, *Through the Eye of the Needle: Immigrants and Enterprise in New York's Garment Trades* (New York: New York University Press, 1986); Waldinger, "Immigrant Enterprise: A Critique and Reformulation," *Theory and Society* 15 (1986): 249-85.

29. Suzanne Model, "Ethnic Bonds in the Work Place: Blacks, Italians, and Jews in New York City" (Ph.D. dissertation, University of Michigan, 1985).

30. Stanley Lieberson, *A Piece of the Pie: Blacks and White Immigrants since 1880* (Berkeley: University of California Press, 1980).

4

Class, Culture, and Immigrant Group Identity in the United States: The Case of Irish-American Ethnicity

Kerby A. Miller

On July 4, 1805, William James Macneven, scion of an old Irish gentry family, exiled himself to the United States after serving a term of British imprisonment, which he had suffered for helping lead the conspiracy of the Society of United Irishmen that produced the abortive Irish revolution of 1798.[1] Despite his clouded past, Macneven quickly became one of New York City's most eminent physicians and citizens. More than a half century later, Frank Roney left his native Belfast to avoid prosecution for his involvement in the Fenian movement.[2] After landing in New York in 1866, Roney worked his way across the continent before settling permanently in San Francisco, where he found employment in a local iron foundry. Both Macneven and Roney were Irish by birth and Catholic by religion, a part of what contemporary Americans and later historians regarded as the Irish-American ethnic community. However, the associational ties and perceptions that shaped and expressed the ethnic identities of these and other immigrants were remarkably diverse. For example, although Macneven mixed confidently in upper-class American society, he took a strong, paternalistic interest in the welfare of his poorer fellow immigrants and remained loyal to the ideal of an independent Ireland. He assumed a leading role in establishing Irish immigrant charitable organizations and employment bureaus, as well as the first Irish-American nationalist movements. By contrast, the brutal realities of industrial change and of exploitation in San Francisco persuaded Roney to jettison both his religious and his Irish nationalist faiths, and to submerge ethnicity almost entirely in an inclusive working-class struggle against corporate capitalism. These two instances, of an estimated five million Irish Catholics who settled in North America during the nineteenth century, demonstrate the great variety of that immigration and of

Irish-American society, and also suggest the diversity and complexity of ethnic associations and identities even within a single immigrant group.

In this chapter I examine ethnicity, its origins, development, and consequences, with specific reference to Irish immigration and Irish America, although I hope that my theoretical framework and conclusions may be useful to students of other immigrant groups and ethnic communities. Traditionally, most historians and historical sociologists have interpreted the immigration experience in terms of assimilation and acculturation or ethnic resilience.[3] The assimilation interpretation implies that as immigrants experience greater degrees of socioeconomic and cultural integration into their adopted country, they shed Old World social customs and cultural traits for those prevailing in the host society. The existence of ethnically distinctive sociocultural patterns in American society reflects a transitional or arrested stage in the assimilation process; moreover, such patterns are viewed primarily as products of that process, owing more to the American environment than to transplanted institutions and values. By contrast, the ethnic resilience interpretation stresses the persistence if not permanence of at least some imported social patterns and beliefs that provide structure, continuity, and meaning in an alien and alienating New World. Thus, whereas in the former scenario mutable traits encounter an inexorable and ultimately consensual process, in the latter, highly resilient characteristics contend and create an ethnically pluralistic society.

Each model oversimplifies the social and cultural systems of the donor and host societies. Assimilation theory implies the interaction of individual immigrants with American society, although, as Charles Tilly points out in this volume, it is certainly necessary to examine social groups or networks that migrate and interact collectively with new socioeconomic structures and cultural norms.[4] Historians focusing on ethnic persistence sometimes pay insufficient attention to the sociocultural complexity of the donor societies and to the diversity of their emigrants. Some scholars imply that ethnic subsocieties and cultures are relatively homogeneous and "unmeltable" transplants from the Old World, not fundamentally transformed by conditions in the New. Conversely, the assimilationists describe ethnicity as dynamic and situational, though their overriding stress on American determinants tends to downgrade or even deny the importance of overseas origins. Most historians, at least implicitly, have analyzed assimilation in the context of transatlantic modernization or "progress" from rural-preindustrial to urban-industrial society. Such an approach, however, often obscures the socioeconomic and political (and consequent ethnic) stratification of American society and tends to assume that assimilation to bourgeois-capitalist institutions and norms is the only historical possibility.

There is yet a third approach, offered recently by historians of American labor, which sees immigrant assimilation in the context of an ethnically distinct working-class subculture.[5] This model, put forth by David Montgomery, Eric Foner, Michael Gordon, and others, blurs important social and cultural distinctions and interactions, as I will contend in the final section of this paper.

   Despite the efforts of the acculturation and ethnic resilience schools, or
those of recent labor historians, we still lack a means of analyzing ethnicity
that takes account of the fluid social structures and cultural patterns in the
donor society, the immigrant stream, the host society, and the ethnic subsociety, and that explores the complex dialectical relationships between and within those groups. In seeking this more dynamic approach we might start with the
observation of Charles Tilly that "identity" — ethnic or otherwise — is a shared
cultural construction, a set of usages, that people adopt in their relationships
with one another.[6] In the process of immigration, those relationships or networks, on which identities are based, change and generate new explanations
and expressions or reinforce old ones. Whether these social constructions are
residual, ethnic, or assimilationist depends on the nature of the interaction
among both the various elements of the immigrant group and the host society.
Ethnic identity is the result of the dynamic conjunctions of social structures,
class conflicts, and cultural patterns in the old country and the new. Ethnicity
evolves from a complex dialectic that exists between an immigrant group and a
host society but also among the immigrants themselves and among members of
the host society. These interactions must be interpreted within the context of a
vast international development: the growth of a transatlantic capitalism that
shaped the social structures and cultures of both donor and host societies in
ways that impelled, encouraged, and accommodated the enormous nineteenth-
century immigration.

   To understand Irish immigration to North America and the nature of the
Irish-American community within the world-capitalist context requires a me-
diating analytical tool that can explain how ideologies are created that may
deflect or transcend profound social and economic conflicts, such as the tension between capital and labor. That tool exists in the theory of "cultural
hegemony" of Antonio Gramsci, as elaborated by Raymond Williams.[7]

   According to Gramsci, every individual has a "spontaneous philosophy,"
embodied in language, religion, conventional wisdom, and empirical knowledge, that usually contains profound discrepancies between inherited or externally received notions and those that are implicit in one's everyday actions,
experiences, and social position. This "contradictory consciousness," often
producing political passivity or paralysis, is the result of the processes of
"cultural hegemony," by which a ruling class disseminates its values; it does this
through a variety of institutional means and through pervasive cultural expressions that reflect the society's economic "base" or governing social processes:
for example, industrial capitalism. Although the ruling class could exercise
authority through "political" coercion, in a capitalist society it more commonly
creates a hegemony ("intellectual and moral leadership") through the agencies
of "civil" society's "ideological superstructure": instruments of socialization,
such as religion, selective historical tradition, formal education, the organization of work and family life, political parties, trade unions, and other ostensibly "voluntary" organizations.

   Of course, the "political" and "civil" realms are analytically rather than actually distinct. Gramsci defined the nature of power in contemporary society as "hegemony armoured by coercion"; however, the function of hegemony is to produce among the masses a *spontaneous* consent to what another observer calls "the values, norms, perceptions, beliefs, sentiments, and prejudices that support and define the existing distribution of goods, the institutions that decide how this distribution occurs, and the permissible range of disagreement about those processes."[8] In other words, what Raymond Williams has termed the "dominant" culture so saturates a given society that its norms and values seem to be "commonsensical"—organized, experienced, and ratified through popular participation in the processes that generate them. Williams also points out that the dominant or hegemonic culture is neither static nor monolithic. It reflects the dynamism, fluidity, and diversity of society's governing processes, institutions, and classes (which can themselves exhibit contradictory consciousness). Furthermore, it also interacts with potential "counter-hegemonies"—that is, with "alternative" or "oppositional" cultures that reflect "deviant" practices, experiences, and norms. Williams defines these other cultures as either "residual" or "emergent." Residual values are holdovers from previously dominant social formations (for example, feudal or preindustrial); emergent cultures express new meanings that are rooted in actual, contemporary experiences and that reflect the embryonic self-consciousness of new classes (such as the proletariat) and social realities and practices not yet recognized by the dominant culture. The dominant culture usually incorporates certain aspects of the residual and emergent alternatives, thereby reducing their potential opposition. This means that the process of cultural hegemony is "open at both ends."[9]

According to Gramsci, it is primarily society's intellectuals who perform the historic task or function of articulating the hegemonic culture and incorporating or reconciling its potential oppositions. In Gramsci's view, every ruling class, as it advances to power, creates its own "organic" intellectuals. Hence, the needs of the capitalist entrepreneur give rise to the engineer, the scientist, the economist, the journalist, and others who "explain" and express those needs—"hegemonic imperatives"—in contemporary and "materialistic" ways. Also, before a class can exercise hegemony over its rivals and subordinates, it must confront and assimilate what Gramsci calls the "traditional" intellectuals—for example, ecclesiastics and lawyers—that is, the organic intellectuals of *previously* dominant social formations, whose "residual" wisdom, adapted to contemporary conditions, can invest the new hegemonic culture with an apparently timeless and even "spiritual" authority in the consciousness of the subordinate classes. Although Gramsci's distinction between organic and traditional intellectuals is somewhat artificial and vague, the point is that, together, they articulate the ideology of the ruling classes in ways that not only incorporate elements of residual and emergent cultures but in the process facilitate the creation of ideological "blocs" or transcendent political alliances (for example, between the bourgeoisie and, say, the church, skilled trade unions, or farmers, *versus* the industrial proletariat), which themselves serve to disseminate the dominant culture and generate popular consent.

The Irish Background

Nineteenth-century Catholic Ireland was an overwhelmingly rural society.[10] In 1841 only one-seventh and in 1881 only one-fourth of the island's population lived in towns containing more than two thousand inhabitants. Few rural-dwellers engaged exclusively or primarily in commercial agriculture: in 1841 only 17 percent of all farmers held more than thirty acres, while over half the rural population consisted of landless laborers or cottiers renting less than two acres; in 1911 the comparable figures were 33 percent and 30 percent, respectively. Although Catholics constituted about 80 percent of Ireland's inhabitants, until 1829 they were subject to a variety of politically and economically disabling Penal Laws, and until 1869 the Anglican "Church of Ireland" was the legally established religion. Even after those dates, Ireland's so-called Protestant Ascendancy remained disproportionately powerful, led by a handful of landlords — imposed by English conquests — who owned 90 percent of Irish soil, and sustained until 1921 by the island's colonial status under British rule. The socioeconomic and cultural gap between the ascendancy and the Catholic masses helps explain why, in the early nineteenth century, less than half the Catholic population was literate and about the same proportion still spoke Irish, rather than English, as their primary or only language.

Despite Catholic Ireland's relative "backwardness," from the late eighteenth century it was moving rapidly to agrarian capitalism and cultural modernization. After about 1750, British demands for Irish foodstuffs generated greater profits for farmers from market production and greater financial pressures by landlords through higher rents and estate rationalization, to which tenants and subtenants responded by producing more for British consumption.

Meanwhile, Ireland's population doubled, from about four million in 1780 to over eight million in 1841. After the Napoleonic Wars, economic depression, English competition, and mechanization devastated the cottage industries that formerly employed nearly one million peasants and small farmers. Markets for cattle and sheep remained relatively buoyant, but the consequent emphasis on grazing livestock further reduced rural employment and meant the expropriation for pastureland of the tillage farms and potato plots held by subtenants, smallholders, cottiers, and laborers. One result was a tremendous upsurge in Irish emigration between 1814 and 1844 as about one million Irish crossed the Atlantic. Approximately half were Catholic, mostly from northern and eastern Ireland, and representing primarily social groups on the margin between commercial and subsistence farming: artisans, middling and small farmers, better-paid laborers, and the landless children of the tenants who practiced impartible inheritance. A second, more dramatic result was the outbreak of violent struggles over land use and occupancy between the commercial and subsistence farmers as the peasants formed a variety of secret agrarian societies to resist evictions and protest low wages, unemployment, and the commercialization of agriculture. The death of one million people and the emigration of nearly two million others during the Great Famine and its immediate aftermath (1845–1855) nearly eradicated the poorer peasants, thereby eliminating the power of the secret agrarian societies and enabling the Catholic middle class and the Catholic church to gain greater influence over a relatively more affluent, literate, and shrunken populace. During the postfamine period, the ranks of small farmers and, especially, cottiers and farm laborers continued to shrink, largely through emigration (over four million departures 1865 through 1921) as industrial and rural employment steadily declined and as middling and small farmers abandoned the once-common custom of partible inheritance in favor of impartible inheritance, which consigned most farmers' children to the emigrant ships.

Despite these changes, during the nineteenth century nearly all Ireland's Catholics shared certain beliefs. They all hungered for the land that they believed had been stolen from their ancestors by English "upstarts," and they shared an identity based on religion (whether practiced regularly or not) and a legacy of defeat and proscription at the hands of British and Irish Protestants. In addition, I have argued elsewhere,[11] a general worldview—expressed through proverbs, the organization of work, family relationships, archaic landholding patterns, religious beliefs, and even linguistic categories—united most Catholics in emphasizing passive, communal, and precapitalist norms, such as continuity, conformity, and mutuality, while devaluing individual action, ambition, and the assumption of personal responsibility—especially when actions, such as emigration, seemed innovative and threatening to customary patterns of thought and behavior. Indeed, traditional attitudes toward leaving Ireland reflected these cultural biases. The most common way for an Irish-speaker to describe emigration was "*dob éigan dom imeacht go Meirice*": "I had to go to America," or, more precisely, "going to America was a necessity for me." This resigned or fatalistic interpretation was consistent with the ancient but equally common use of the Irish word *deoraí* (literally, exile) to designate *emigrant*, as one subject to imposed pressures. It was also consistent with historic traditions of Catholic Irish rebellion, defeat, and banishment—and, by analogy, with the vague, popular notion that all subsequent Catholic emigration was involuntary exile, somehow caused by British tyranny.[12]

Despite many superficially shared beliefs and symbols, during the nineteenth century socioeconomic changes and conflicts within Catholic Irish society engendered a parallel struggle for cultural hegemony—over the meanings and applications of those norms—and the question of how to interpret the great lower-class emigration and "explain" its causes was at the center of that contest. The position of the Irish Catholic middle class was greatly complicated by Ireland's colonial status. Looking at the United Kingdom as a whole, the Irish middle classes could be seen as merely a regional component of a ruling British middle class, instead of a dominant or potentially dominant class in its own right. In that view, what might be called the Catholic middle class's hegemonic imperatives toward its subordinate classes (the peasantry, the rural and urban proletariat) would be virtually identical to the imperatives of the British governing classes. From an all-United Kingdom perspective, the dominant Irish Catholic subculture could be classed as a regional variant of the dominant British culture, especially with respect to values reinforcing capitalist institutions and processes, such as private property, free competition and individual acquisitiveness, as well as in regard to certain notions of style or taste emanating from the British metropolis. Indeed, in some respects Catholic Ireland's dominant culture was extremely emulative or, as critics charged, "West British."

However, the unequal development of southern Ireland's agrarian economy in its dependent relationship to British industrial and finance capitalism, coupled with Catholic resentment against Irish political inferiority at Westminster and the Protestant Ascendancy at home, inspired much of the Catholic middle class to seek regional self-government or even total independence as a means of becoming a "national" rather than a colonial ruling class. The Catholic middle class had to supplant British Protestant hegemony over Irish civil society before it could challenge British domination; it had to generate what was, to use Gramsci's terms, an emergent, nationalist counterhegemony in order to achieve autonomy from its British Protestant opponents and to secure support from allies, primarily within Irish Catholic society but also among the emigrants. The success or failure of these external and internal "projects" of the Catholic middle class were inextricably related.[13] The attainment of political independence from Britain was contingent on the achievement of internal hegemony and the mobilization of the Irish masses behind the nationalists' program — despite the fact that that program entailed the creation of an Irish polity governed by the same processes and classes primarily responsible for lower-class immiseration and emigration. Conversely, as long as Ireland remained a political colony, the Catholic middle class lacked the authority to order Irish society and incorporate its values through the ideological superstructure.

The processes through which the Catholic middle class "made itself" were necessarily complex and subtle. That class began to emerge as a self-conscious entity in the relatively prosperous late eighteenth century, led by urban merchants and professionals whose ideals and ambitions, shaped by capitalism, were distinct from those of the old Catholic gentry and of the Gaelic peasantry alike. Initially, in the 1770s and 1780s the Catholic middle class desired only the creation of economic and political conditions that would promote the goal of individual "independence" under the British constitution: repeal of the Penal Laws, equal economic opportunities, and equal political rights for propertied Catholics.[14] Inspired by the success of the French Revolution, some middle-class Catholics joined with like-minded Protestants in the Society of United Irishmen, whose efforts to create an independent, nonsectarian Irish republic were crushed in 1798. Most members of the Catholic middle class, however, distrusted the radical egalitarianism and anticlericalism of French republicanism and welcomed both the defeat of the United Irishmen and the subsequent Act of Union in 1800, which seemed to presage the granting of full Catholic rights by the British government. Unfortunately, the Westminster parliament disappointed Catholic hopes. Moreover, the effects of the post-Napoleonic Wars depression not only gave added urgency to the desire for economic and political equality but also convinced many that only repeal of the Act of Union and creation of a new, popularly elected (hence, Catholic-dominated) Irish legislature would enable them to protect and promote their interests. During the pre-Famine period (1814–1844) what Gramsci would call the organic intellectuals of the Catholic bourgeoisie, especially lawyers like Daniel O'Connell, borrowed the theories of Adam Smith, William Godwin, and other British political economists to explain their economic position and political ambitions and to justify successive political campaigns for Catholic emancipation and repeal of the union.

The political notions shared by most Catholics differed greatly from the liberal ideals of their putative leaders. Imperfectly literate at best, artisans, smallholders, and, especially, cottiers and laborers were often intensely provincial, their sense of Irish identity bound to specific localities or to tribal traditions and hatreds rather than to bourgeois concepts of nationalism. For leaders, Irish-speaking peasants and the members of the secret agrarian societies generally preferred men of their own class or even paternalistic landlords, not middle-class townsmen and wealthy graziers whom they regarded as half-Anglicized snobs who eulogized capitalist progress and ignored its consequences for the exploited masses. When such men thought in political terms, they oscillated between visions of a pastoral Gaelic commonwealth and the radical, half-assimilated ideals of the French Revolution and the United Irishmen. Thus, to mobilize and control their potential allies, the Catholic middle class had to broaden its ideological appeal.

The fragmented and transitional nature of Catholic society and the precarious social position of the middle class itself demanded that the nationalist counterhegemony incorporate a range of values and symbols that in more "advanced" capitalist societies would be characterized as residual or premodern. It did so in at least three major ways. First, early in the nineteenth century, under the leadership of Daniel O'Connell, the secular middle class formed a nationalist alliance with the Catholic church. It assimilated the church's traditional intellectuals, who gave a "spiritual" substance and legitimacy to the political goals of the middle class, and gained access to Catholic society's most elaborate and pervasive institutional infrastructure—including temperance societies and confraternities, as well as parish churches. In return, the church assumed a "patriotic" stature in popular opinion, and also gained influence over the course and content of Catholic nationalism, plus the opportunity to assume predominance in future governmental educational and social policies. Because the Catholic clergy's ideal Irish society was organic and authoritarian, guided by religion instead of the marketplace or popular opinion, the alliance between middle-class nationalists and the church created an uneasy synthesis of ideals that historians have termed "Catholic liberalism."

Second, the Catholic bourgeoisie mobilized the land hunger of the lower classes in the nationalist crusade. This was a delicate and complicated process, because middle-class graziers and other "strong farmers," although sharing the resentments of the peasants against landlordism, high rents, and evictions, held divergent attitudes toward agrarian capitalism and the sanctity of private property. It was no wonder that the Catholic bourgeoisie was unwilling to raise the rallying cry "The land for the people" until after the Great Famine, mass emigration, and the Catholic church's increasing influence had reduced and tamed the lower classes. The so-called Land War of 1879–1882 initiated political changes that abolished landlordism by 1920 and enabled Irish tenants to become farm owners, but those developments only ratified the inequitable distribution of Irish soil. The Catholic bourgeoisie vehemently rejected more radical schemes for the redistribution or the nationalization of Irish land, as proposed by the peasant-born leader of the Land War, Michael Davitt, or by the Dublin socialist James Connolly. In a sense, the Catholic middle class's alliances with the church and the peasants' desire for land only incorporated within the nationalist bloc the social and cultural tensions caused by rapid commercialization. And so, third, to resolve or obscure those tensions the Catholic middle class had to generate a hegemonic culture that would assimilate and express the passive, communal, and precapitalist norms of the traditional Irish Catholic worldview, and that would portray the actual or, at least, the ideal structures and processes of Catholic society as in conformity to those norms. This task was especially pressing, though extremely complicated, regarding emigration and its causes. Although many Irish men and women viewed emigration primarily as an economic opportunity for "independence," many others saw it as involuntary exile, glaring evidence that something was profoundly amiss in Irish society.

The dilemma of the Catholic bourgeoisie lay in the fact that its own hegemonic imperatives held a sharp contradiction about emigration. On the one hand, the rural middle class and, to a lesser degree, the Catholic church, shared major responsibility for lower-class emigration: the former through the processes of agrarian capitalism, including impartible inheritance; and the latter, some critics charged, through the clergy's stifling impact on social life and personal expression. The Catholic bourgeoisie had no inclination to adopt the radical measures necessary to halt emigration by restructuring a society whose very shape, stability, and class and family systems obliged and depended on emigration's continuance. On the other hand, however, middle-class politicians and clerics had to oppose emigration publicly, both because wholesale departures threatened ultimate depopulation and vitiated nationalist movements and Catholic congregations, and, more important, because emigration and its socioeconomic causes were the issues that most concerned the disadvantaged sectors of Irish society, whose support the nationalists needed even *after* many members of those sectors emigrated to the New World.

Because middle-class nationalists, churchmen, and farmers, generally, could not justify emigration in "rational," secular terms, they generated obscurantist "explanations" that incorporated widespread popular notions of emigration as a "fated" process. The most important and frequently employed explanation was the centuries-old belief that emigration was tantamount to political exile, caused by British oppression; therefore, nationalists argued, departures would cease only when Ireland achieved self-government or independence, through the efforts of her vengeful "exiles" overseas as well as through nationalist activities at home.

Nationalists and clerics incorporated beliefs of this sort into a broader assertion that Catholic Irish society itself was static, organic, paternalistic, and nonmaterialistic—or would be so, once British Protestant influences were expunged.[15] During the late nineteenth century the church's own crusade against modernity further reinforced increasingly strident reactions against pervasive "Anglo-Saxon" influences on Irish society. Lay and clerical spokesmen alike evoked a traditional and timeless "holy Ireland": an organic, devout, familial, and peasant-based community whose benign institutions and spiritual values could nurture all Ireland's children at home were it not for British misgovernment and the corroding effects of Anglicization. In that ideological context, emigration could result only from political oppression because neither "holy Ireland's" guardians and champions—the Catholic bourgeoisie—nor its selfless, pious products—the involuntary exiles—could be held responsible, save for their fealty to the concept itself.

The notion of "holy Ireland"—demanding loyalty to family, church, and "sacred cause"—was the central element of the Catholic bourgeoisie's hegemonic culture. Its force lay both in its incorporation "from above" and also in its embodying of residual beliefs and values still current among the Irish lower and middle classes. These comforting and customary "explanations" of Ireland's social discontinuities and inequities served the hegemonic imperatives of the Catholic bourgeoisie at the same time as they helped reduce social and psychological tensions between traditional ideals and contemporary exigencies among the poorest sectors and on the most intimate levels of Irish society—for example, within the families of farmers who adopted impartible inheritance.[16] The residual notions of the Catholic masses, their needs for continuity and reassurance, and the hegemonic imperatives of the Catholic bourgeoisie and its clerical allies all converged to create a dominant culture and a contradictory popular consciousness that controlled the conflicts within Catholic society, obscured the real causes of emigration, and united Irish men and women in identification with bourgeois institutions, traditionally conceived.

By its very nature, hegemony could never be complete, especially when the prospect of emigration posed alternatives to the "holy Ireland" ideal. Some of the most ambitious and business-minded young Irishmen found Catholic society's traditional norms stifling to personal initiative and enterprise. To be sure, the process of chain migration—Catholic Ireland's predominant mode of emigration—linked the departed to the society left behind, its demands and norms. However, as Charles Tilly points out in this book,[17] chain migration implied the transportation of social networks or groups, many of which had been imperfectly assimilated to Catholic Ireland's dominant culture and institutions before their departure. In other words, even prior to emigration the contradictions between the dominant Catholic culture and the norms or experiences of the most traditional-minded or oppressed members of Irish society were often too blatant to ignore. Consequently, the emigrants' resentment frequently informed their attitudes toward emigration and, especially after residence in the United States, toward both their adopted and abandoned homelands.[18]

Because Catholic Irish emigration to the United States—unlike Polish or Italian—lasted for more than a century, the formation and incorporation of the ultimately dominant Catholic culture was a long, slow process, affecting disproportionately the successive waves of emigrants to American shores according to their regional origins, social composition, and cultural backgrounds. Although in general the late post-Famine emigrants were far more culturally homogeneous, politically and religiously engaged, and assimilated to middle-class norms than the members of any previous wave, they still included large numbers of proletarianized laborers, provincial Irish-speakers from the Far West, and female fugitives from an oppressive patriarchy. The pre-Famine emigrants were socially and culturally diverse, and at midcentury the impoverished hordes of Famine refugees contained many lower-class, illiterate, unchurched, and Irish-speaking emigrants. These various groups, carrying different kinds of sociocultural baggage, adapted to American environments and interacted with native Americans and one another in diverse ways. Although these tremendous migrations helped ensure bourgeois hegemony in Ireland, middle-class Irish Americans met difficulties in exerting a like influence in the United States. Nevertheless, given the not dissimilar impacts of nineteenth-century capitalism on Irish, American, and Irish-American societies — regional variants of a transatlantic bourgeoisie — it is not surprising that by 1900 the dominant cultures and group identities of Irish Catholics on both sides of the ocean were remarkably similar.

The Host Country

Irish Catholics who immigrated to the United States during the nineteenth century exchanged a society in demographic and economic decline for another characterized by explosive growth. Between 1800 and 1840 the United States population more than tripled, from 5.3 million to 17.1 million, and between 1840 and 1900 — while Ireland's population shrank from 8.2 million to only 4.5 million — that of the United States soared to 76 million. While urban growth in Catholic Ireland stagnated, the proportion of Americans living in cities and towns rose from 11 percent in 1840 to 40 percent in 1900. This urbanization resulted from immigration and industrialization, as well as from the commercialization of agriculture and internal migration. In 1850 the United States officially contained 1.2 million white, foreign-born inhabitants (about 1 million of them Irish), and in 1900 the comparable figure was 5.5 million (including 1.6 million Irish-born, plus another 3.4 million native-born children of Irish immigrants). Between 1820 and 1900 the proportion of the American work force in nonagricultural occupations increased from 28 percent to 62 percent, and the percentage employed in manufacturing and construction grew from 12 percent to 28 percent. Irish Catholic immigrants were on the cutting edge of this urban-industrial growth. For example, in 1870 nearly 95 percent of the Irish-born population was concentrated in just twenty states, mostly in the heavily urbanized and industrialized New England, Middle Atlantic, and Upper Midwest regions. The 1870 census also reveals that less than 15 percent of the nation's Irish-born work force engaged in agriculture (compared to 54 percent of the native-born and 27 percent and 26 percent of German and English immigrants, respectively).[19]

The Irish concentration in U.S. cities and in many of the most dynamic economic sectors—especially construction, transportation, and heavy manufacturing—eventually paid off; by 1900 the Irish-born and their children had achieved relative occupational parity with native-born Americans in all fields except agriculture. At the century's end, roughly the same proportions of male Irish Americans were engaged in white-collar (35 percent), skilled (50 percent), and unskilled (15 percent) jobs as were white Americans of native birth and parentage. In addition, by 1900 skilled Irish-American workers were disproportionately concentrated in the best-paid, most highly unionized trades.[20] Nevertheless, such an overview obscures the terrible poverty and insecurity that most Irish—especially the Famine immigrants—endured at midcentury, when from 60 to 80 percent were semiskilled or unskilled laborers, as well as the crippling setbacks experienced during the severe economic depressions of 1873-1878, 1883-1885, and 1893-1897.

The nineteenth century's earliest Irish Catholic immigrants experienced little difficulty in adapting to Jeffersonian society and its dominant culture. During this era Catholics were only a small minority of a relatively few Irish immigrants, and—like their Irish Protestant peers—a large proportion were of middle-class or at least artisanal origins.[21] Their talents and skills were in great demand, and the goals they sought through immigration—"independence" as either upward mobility or comfortable self-sufficiency—complemented the still-undifferentiated emphases of the new American nation's broad and optimistic republican culture.[22] Additionally, the Catholic church in the United States was so small and uninfluential that most Americans regarded it as merely a curiosity rather than a threat to Protestantism or to republican ideals and institutions. The ideals of the United Irishmen united most early immigrants across both class and sectarian lines, and those norms were reciprocated by their hosts. As one Ulster immigrant reported, "The Irish in America are particularly well recvd. and looked upon as Patriotic republicans, and if you were to tell an American you had flyd your country or you would have been hung for treason against the Government, they would think ten times more of you and it would be the highest trumpet sounded in your praise."[23] Men such as William James Macneven could play widely varying but complementary roles—as Republican politicians and journalists, as employers of both Irish and non-Irish labor, as founders and trustees of Catholic churches, and as leaders and patrons of both ethnic and inclusive benevolent and nationalist associations—without endangering their status in either native- or Irish-American societies.

That happy period was brief and anomalous. After the Panic of 1819, and especially from the 1830s through the 1850s, the position of the Irish in the United States became much more complex and controversial, and, in consequence, the role of the Irish-American middle class became much more precarious. After about 1820, the American society to which Catholic Irish immigrants were obliged to adapt changed rapidly and radically as the old republican concensus fragmented. Manufacturers and ambitious artisans responded to widening markets for industrial goods by abandoning the old household method of production for new systems of subcontracting, putting-out, and factory production. Only about one-third of artisans and journeymen commanded sufficient capital to become employers under the new order; the remainder fell to the ranks of pieceworkers or wage-laborers, forced to compete with semiskilled and unskilled migrants from the American and European countrysides.

Organized workers were unable to create an effective counterhegemony to the bourgeois-capitalist norms evoked by the employer classes, at least not before the rise of the Knights of Labor in the 1880s. Their producer ideology was primarily a petty-capitalist version of the old republican culture, and, consequently, both employers and employees shared similar terms of reference — such as individual freedom, faith in progress and private property, opposition to monopolies, and contempt for the unskilled, "undeserving" poor — which the former could manipulate to their advantage. The entrepreneurial and producer ideologies of employers and native-born workers alike were permeated by religious beliefs that obscured social differences. Although organized workers frequently united around dissenting visions of a Christian commonwealth, the middle class advanced its ideals through a series of religious revivals that convulsed Protestant America from the 1830s on. Evangelical ministers perfectly complemented bourgeois norms, suffusing them with a timeless, spiritual authority, and providing the moral imperative around which the new middle class could coalesce. Evangelical religion, like republican political rhetoric and institutions, created a cultural cohesion for an otherwise fragmenting society, providing Protestant workers with new avenues to success, security, or at least symbolic affinity with the governing classes through "proper" behavior and shared notions of respectability.[24]

The Irish-American Middle Class

During the very periods when economic dislocations, Protestant revivalism, and political tensions were at their height, Irish Catholic immigration turned from a trickle into a flood tide. Even prior to the Great Famine, in the 1830s and early 1840s, Irish immigration to the United States was increasingly dominated by rural Catholics who lacked capital, education, and marketable skills. During the late 1840s and the 1850s, American cities were inundated by waves of impoverished peasants, many of them from the most "backward," least Anglicized regions of southern and western Ireland.[25]

These arrivals clashed with American society and culture in a variety of complementary ways. Even before 1820 anti-Catholic and anti-Irish prejudice was an important component of Anglo-American Protestantism, though obscured by an optimistic, secular republicanism. After that date convictions that the Irish belonged to "a race of savages"[26] — lazy, superstitious, drunken, and violent — became widespread as the new influx of immigrants and the growth of the Catholic church exacerbated and epitomized growing fears for the social stability, political purity, and cultural homogeneity of the new republic. Skilled and unskilled Irish laborers competed increasingly with native workers at precisely the moment when the latter felt least secure. Although skilled Irish Catholic immigrants often shared the same independent-producer ideology as native craftsmen, and sometimes helped organize trade unions and labor federations, as in Philadelphia during the 1830s, fierce competition for jobs and housing and frequent economic depressions converged with Protestant revivalism to aggravate ethnic and religious tensions and forestall working-class solidarity. Philadelphia's General Trades Union collapsed after the Panic of 1837; by 1844 native-Protestant and Irish Catholic workers were engaged in pitched battles on the city's streets; and during the 1850s hostility toward Irish Catholics assumed national proportions, formalized in the so-called Know-Nothing party and, after its collapse, incorporated in the new Republican party coalition.

For their part, many Irish Catholic immigrants were equally at odds with American society and culture. An imported worldview emphasizing communal, anti-individualistic, and even precapitalist values permeated Irish Catholic society, even shaping the outlooks and strategies of the middle class. Such traditional norms became more important when middle-class immigrants encountered a far more ruthlessly competitive environment than anticipated. Although emphases on mutuality and craft integrity may temporarily have united Irish Catholic artisans in trade unions with their Protestant peers, that very unity and its institutional expressions exacerbated class and ethnic differences between the native middle class and skilled-worker Catholics, the latter already concentrated in rapidly mechanizing and downwardly mobile occupations, such as handloom weaving and shoemaking. The involvement of Irish Catholics in trade unions gave employers additional opportunities to stigmatize such organizations as "un-American," which encouraged Protestant workers to abandon such alliances. The poorest, unskilled immigrants were often bewildered and hostile before an American capitalism that barely provided subsistence wages and violated peasant norms of communal justice and interdependence. Under such circumstances, while many Irish Catholics favorably contrasted American opportunity and freedom to Irish poverty and British oppression, large numbers of others became disillusioned and fell back "into the circle of [their] fellow countrymen,"[27] retaining boisterous and sodden peasant customs, forming secret societies like those they had known in Ireland, and reverting to the traditional explanation of emigration as involuntary "exile" to explain their homesickness and alienation. These defenses reified and homogenized Irish immigrant identity, even as they widened the gulf between the immigrants and middle-class Americans.

By the early 1840s, and especially during and after the Famine immigrations, the Irish-American Catholic bourgeoisie was marginal with respect to both Protestant America and the general Irish immigrant population. Although its absolute numbers had grown through immigration and, to a lesser degree, upward mobility, it composed at midcentury an increasingly small minority within a peasant-proletarian mass that was feared and stigmatized by the native middle classes. As the Irish immigrant lawyer John Blake Dillon discovered in the early 1850s, "Although in this country all religions enjoy perfect equality *before* the *law*, in society it is far otherwise. In this latter respect," he concluded, "this country may be said to be eminently Protestant, and the inconveniences to which persons of strong Catholic convictions are subjected are neither few nor inconsiderable."[28] Similar complaints were voiced throughout the late nineteenth century and well into the twentieth century.

Middle-class Irish Catholics were well aware of the major cause of the opprobrium they shared with their poorer countrymen. After all, one bourgeois immigrant admitted at midcentury, "to judge of Ireland and Irishmen from the *enchantillon* which the United States presents, one would be forced to regard the former as the fruitful home of incorrigible ignorance and incurable superstition."[29] Some residual aspects of Irish peasant culture experienced renewed vigor in Irish-American slums, mining camps, and construction sites. For example, Irish "party fights" and secret societies temporarily flourished in the United States, the latter epitomized by Pennsylvania's Molly Maguires during the 1870s, although both had been virtually eradicated in Ireland itself by midcentury. Middle-class Irish immigrants felt disgraced by such activities. The group's overwhelmingly lower-class composition not only lowered the status of the middle-class minority but, equally important, made it extremely difficult for that minority to exercise even the fragile hegemony over the Catholic Irish masses that the Irish bourgeoisie was creating in the old country. In their roles as employers and tenement owners, middle-class Irish Americans often found themselves attacked by their own resentful countrymen. Until recently, historians have paid little attention to class conflicts *within* the Irish-American community. Such conflicts were frequent and often violent, as in Philadelphia's Kensington district in 1842–1843, when organized Irish weavers conducted bloody strikes against Irish Catholic bosses and landlords; in Worcester during the same decade, when railroad laborers and recent Famine refugees assaulted Irish contractors and merchants; and in Denver and Butte during the late nineteenth and early twentieth centuries, when strife between Irish miners and mine owners wracked those communities. "An Irishman was the worst boss you could have" in the United States, reported one Irish immigrant, "slave-driving all the time."[30]

Thus, in the eyes of the native-born, middle-class Irish immigrants were not "good Americans," but in the opinion of many of their transplanted countrymen, they were not "good Irishmen" either. A solution to their dilemma was for the immigrant middle class to create and lead a new ethnic society that would include all Irish Catholic immigrants and their offspring, and that would embody a new, dominant ethnic culture. The new culture would adapt some transplanted norms and symbols to both the Irish immigrant experience and the institutions and ideals of middle-class America, creating in the process a new but doubly derivative identity that would transcend the divisions within Irish America and between that subsociety and native-born America.

The Reconstitution of Hegemony

In the attempt to surmount its dually marginal status, the Irish-American middle class, like its counterpart in Ireland, had to pursue two separate but complementary projects. Because in the New World the Irish nationalist goal of group autonomy was unattainable and, from a middle-class perspective, undesirable, the Irish-American bourgeoisie had to gain acceptance from and access to the classes and institutions that governed native society; more immediately, it also had to assert a social and cultural hegemony over its own lower classes. As in Ireland, the success or failure of the twin projects was highly interdependent. Middle-class immigrants could not gain status in American society until they had both mobilized the Irish-American masses, to demonstrate their political leverage, and imposed bourgeois norms on them, to reassure the host society's governing classes that the group was sufficiently "civilized." Only the prospect of such assimilation would enable the Irish bourgeoisie to provide "successful" models for lower-class immigrant emulation and so exercise effective hegemony.

The process of reconstructing hegemony in the New World was fraught with perils and contradictions. The erosion of immigrant provincialism was a necessary precondition for group mobilization, but ethnic identities shaped by poverty, exclusion, and proletarianization—and expressed through labor unions and secret societies, violent strikes and mob actions, or homesickness for Ireland and alienation from the United States—were hardly compatible with the norms of the Irish-American bourgeoisie. Although many middle-class immigrants became saloonkeepers in Irish-American neighborhoods, their social authority and political patronage were offset partly by the fact that communal whiskey drinking—and Irish bourgeois complicity in group intemperance—only reinforced native Americans' negative image of all Irish Catholics as thriftless, drunken, and undisciplined. Yet, if middle-class Irish Americans sought to appear as censorious as native Protestants, unsympathetic to the problems, yearnings, and customs of the immigrant masses, they stood to forfeit their fellow countrymen's respect and allegiance. Although Irish-American newspaper editors often urged their readers to "take pattern by the Yankee . . . [and] imitate the energy, patience, and prudence of his character," they also realized that most of their potential audience was unable or unwilling to "flow into" what one middle-class immigrant eulogized as "the great current of American life."[31] Consequently, until the very end of the nineteenth century, Irish-American periodicals generally "left the impression that the United States was a suburb of Ireland" because their owners and editors understood that the Irish-Catholic road to respectability would have to follow its own track.[32]

Constitutional and demographic considerations determined that in the United States, unlike Ireland, the Irish middle class could not create an effective political party of its own. The Democratic party of Andrew Jackson and his successors became the principal native-American institution through which middle-class Irish Americans gained access to power, expressed their values, and engaged their adherents. To some extent, the Democracy merely inherited Irish Catholic fealty to the Jeffersonian Republicans — from which the Democrats claimed direct descent — with Andrew Jackson's Irish parentage and his military victories over the hated English easing the transition. In the fierce party competition of the Jacksonian era, Democratic politicians offered patronage in return for votes; in their roles as employers, subcontractors, and saloonkeepers, middle-class and ambitious working-class Irish Americans happily reciprocated. Democratic politicians championed a pluralistic vision of American society that could accommodate Irish Catholics' needs for protection against native-Protestant hostility. The rhetoric of party spokesmen tended to incorporate the ideals and grievances of small producers and disadvantaged workers. Thus, the Democrats could appeal to Irish voters as immigrants, Catholics, and laborers, whereas the Whig party and its Republican successor tended to attract the new urban middle classes and native-born workers and farmers "burned over" by Protestant evangelicalism. The Democracy's support for slavery and its inveterate racism also appealed to most Irish immigrants: while the Whig, Know-Nothing, and Republican parties promised to shelter native-Protestant workers and institutions from Irish Catholic competition and subversion, the Democrats pledged to protect Irish immigrants from Abolitionists and evangelicals who would free the slaves and force the Irish to compete with "degraded" black labor.[33]

Through integration into the Democratic party, middle-class Irish gained perquisites for themselves, patronage for their followers, and a forum for raising ethnic, religious, and cultural issues, such as those over restrictive liquor laws or Protestant influence in the public schools, that engaged Irish immigrants and obscured intraethnic class conflicts. Thus, in the textile weavers' strikes of 1842–1843, Philadelphia's Irish Catholic manufacturers lost control over their immigrant workers, but after two more years of Protestant revivalism, nativist agitation, and mob violence against Irish Catholics and their churches, they emerged as Democratic champions and protectors of an embattled ethnic community, commanding their employees' political allegiance while simultaneously slashing their piece rates to prestrike levels. The coincidence of Irish urban and neighborhood concentrations with the territorially fragmented nature of American urban government, particularly with the ward system, facilitated Irish entry into the Democratic party en bloc, and aided the Irish-American middle class's dual strategies: individual and middle-class access to native society's governing institutions *and* ethnic integrity and solidarity across class lines. For a recently naturalized immigrant such as Patrick Dunny, membership in the Democracy enabled him to be both a "good American" and a "good Irishman" — the two identities conflated as "loyal [Irish-American] Democrat." Dunny, like thousands of other Irish immigrants, found in the Democratic party a communal bulwark and a real and symbolic source of pride and acceptance in native society. "James Buchannon is Elected President on the Democratic ticket by an overwhelming Majority," Dunny exulted in 1856; "there neverr was [such] excitement . . . before at an Elections nor the [native] Americans never got a home blow before the Irish Came out victorious and now Clame as good right here as americans themselves."[34] Of course, as one bourgeois immigrant admitted, Democratic party politics was often "a filthy pool of shabbiness, falsehood, and corruption,"[35] and Irish immigrants' identification with the party of Tammany Hall and Southern secession did little to enhance their reputations among Northern Protestant Whigs and Republicans. Indeed, the fears evinced by many middle-class immigrants of the Democracy's moral deficiencies and working-class biases, plus the disproportionately small size of the Irish-American middle class, determined that the latter would also pursue the same obligatory strategy in the United States as in Ireland: heavy reliance on the Catholic church's "traditional" intellectuals to disseminate the principles of respectability, deference, and group cohesion.

In the nineteenth century's earliest decades, Catholicism was merely one facet of Irish-American identity in a society where the church was institutionally insignificant.[36] When new Catholic parishes were created and churches built, it was often at the initiative of affluent Irish-American laymen, who retained a large measure of control over priests and church finances through the so-called trustee system, which restricted lay influence to middle-class pew renters. Irish-American Catholics successfully demanded their own ethnic parishes and Irish-born priests from early on, but they could contend that their congregations' semidemocratic organization and relative freedom from hierarchical authority made the American church fully compatible with republican norms. During the Jacksonian era, however, the relationship between the Irish-American bourgeoisie and the church began to change radically. The Catholic immigrations of the 1830s and, especially, the 1840s and 1850s contained large numbers of lower-middle- and working-class Irish who, thanks to Daniel O'Connell's alliance with the Irish church, were more amenable to clerical leadership and whose identities had been shaped by a militant Catholicism. The new Irish arrivals also included a substantial majority of unchurched peasants who presented the American hierarchy and the Irish-American bourgeoisie alike with tremendous problems of social control but also enormous opportunities for mobilization in an all-class ethnic *and* religious alliance. To meet this challenge, Rome appointed more American bishops of Irish birth or descent, who imported thousands of priests and teaching nuns from Ireland. Soon American Catholicism was rapidly expanding its institutional infrastructure under a largely Irish hierarchy and clergy. The church's growth and new ethnic complexion increased clerical influence over the immigrants and the Irish-American middle class, whose trustee system was dismantled by an alliance of aggressive bishops and docile new parishioners. The nativist assault on Irish immigrants and their church further conflated secular and religious identities, enabling militant Irish bishops, like New York's Archbishop John Hughes, to rally Irish-American Catholics around issues, such as education, that were church centered but of community-wide symbolic importance. In circumstances that demanded abandonment of so many aspects of communal identity, such as the Irish language, Catholicism became the primary expression of Irish-American consciousness, a development parallel to that taking place in Anglicizing Ireland.

The Irish-American bourgeoisie had no choice but to form an unequal alliance with an Irish-dominated American Catholic church. Irish-American bishops and priests, themselves of middle-class origins, pursued strategies that complemented and furthered those of their secular allies. They labored to transform an inchoate mass of Irish immigrants into "good Catholics," who, they sought to prove, were by virtue of their very Irish Catholicity "good Americans."

Through sermons, parochial schools, moral-uplift societies, and other means, Catholic clerics accommodated middle-class norms, peasant ideals, and the diverse realities of Irish immigrant experience to the church's own institutional goals and traditional teachings. Like its Irish counterpart, the American church preached the twin gospels of respectability and resignation. Through the former they commanded ambitious Irish Americans to industry, thrift, sobriety, self-control, and domestic purity, habits that would prevent spiritual ruin and also shape good citizens and successful entrepreneurs. Through resignation they offered religious consolation to the impoverished and the alienated by expressing the church's own deep suspicions of materialism, progress, and individual ambition, associating the latter with selfishness and potential treason to creed and community. Like the eulogists of "holy Ireland" across the water, Irish-American churchmen offered a morally controlled capitalism in an idealized, organic, and hierarchical society congenial to transplanted peasant parishioners: poverty, part of God's plan, was to be accepted with patience and resignation. Convinced that "Irishness" (as clerically defined) was an essential bulwark of religious faith, the Irish-American clergy homogenized and reinforced immigrant-group identity and integrity, for instance, through ethnic parishes and clerically dominated Saint Patrick's Day celebrations, by disowning "mixed" marriages, and by teaching pride in a sanitized version of Irish history in parochial schools, which were themselves designed to insulate Irish-American and other Catholic children from pernicious "Anglo-Saxon" influences. Simultaneously, however, the church assiduously cultivated American patriotism and countered nativist criticisms by proclaiming that "good Irish Catholics" made the very *best* American citizens because they came to the New World seeking the same civil and religious liberty that had inspired the American Revolution; because church teachings either conformed parishioners to respectability and uplift or commanded their obedience to the laws and their social superiors; or because conservative Catholic values protected an inherently unstable American society from social fragmentation and political radicalism.

In short, the ideals and strategies of Irish-American churchmen broadly coincided with those of the ethnic middle class. On the one hand, the clergy lauded and demanded religious freedom and civil equality in a pluralistic and voluntaristic society, but on the other hand, they exercised that freedom to create an ethnic and religious state within a state — an Irish-American Catholic "ghetto" — whose solidarity and collective purpose could give its middle-class representatives access to American power structures. Irish-American churchmen staunchly defended the capitalist system while incorporating and defusing the resentments of frustrated and impoverished immigrants by criticizing the materialistic, individualistic values that informed that system. It is no wonder that in the 1880s and 1890s, the inherent contradictions in these outlooks engendered heated controversies between liberal ("Americanist") and conservative bishops over the church's proper relationship to American society. Although many members of the Irish-American upper middle class embraced the liberals' more assimilationist thrust, by the end of the century the conservatives were victorious, partly because of Rome's condemnation of modernist ideas, but primarily because their ethnocentric and traditionalist emphases best suited Irish-American society and the dualities of its dominant culture. After 1880 Irish America was composed primarily of the native-born and upwardly mobile, but the coincidence of economic depressions, renewed nativist attacks, and job competition from waves of new immigrants from southern and eastern Europe again placed Irish Americans on the defensive and increased the attractiveness of ethnic solidarity. This was particularly true for the Irish Catholic immigrants who arrived during those decades. All were shaped by the Irish church's pervasive "devotional revolution," and many were impoverished peasants — often Irish-speakers — from the western counties. Their piety or their lack of skills, education, and prior urban-industrial experience made them especially susceptible to the influence of conservative Irish-American churchmen. Confronted by these new arrivals, as well as by an upsurge of national and intraethnic class conflict, most middle-class Irish Americans relied on a traditionalist church to assert hegemony over the masses. "If the priest has no influence, what would guide the people?" wondered one middle-class immigrant.[37] Well before the end of the century, Irish America's hegemonic culture had become a constraining force, and although in the middle class some might chafe at traditional Catholicism's moral restraints, few could forgo regular attendance at mass, membership in religious societies, or other church-centered indices of respectability and ethnicity that justified bourgeois authority over their social inferiors. By the century's later decades most members of the Irish-American bourgeoisie had themselves internalized the spiritual values and contradictory impulses that informed their dominant culture and shaped their communal identity. A highly successful businessman like the Irish Californian Michael Flanagan could lament that in the United States secular concerns "monopolize a man . . . body and soul, to the banishment of what every Christian man should be"; and even John Boyle O'Reilly, Yankee Boston's "token Irishman" and a fervent apostle of immigrant entrepreneurialism and assimilation, poured out his private doubts in poems that longed for "holy Ireland's" imagined purities and critiqued the American notion that the "only meaning of life is to barter and buy."[38]

Irish-American nationalism was the final means through which the immigrant middle classes inculcated their values and forged a united ethnic community. In the early nineteenth century, Irish-American nationalist organizations had been small and ephemeral, confined largely to the upper middle class, and heavily dependent on native American support. Although middle-class Irish Americans rallied in support of Young Ireland's prospects for Irish revolution in the mid-1840s, that movement also collapsed under the impacts of heavy Famine immigration, public embarrassment over the pathetic failure of Young Ireland's 1848 "rising," and Irish-American clerical condemnations of the "red republicanism" and infidelity that purportedly characterized Young Ireland's exiled leaders in the United States. In the latter half of the nineteenth century, however, Irish-American nationalism experienced a great resurgence. During the 1860s the Fenian movement — which aimed to overthrow British rule with Irish-American military aid — gained some fifty thousand members, many of them Irish soldiers in the Civil War, plus hundreds of thousands of ardent sympathizers. Although Irish-American nationalism was moribund for a decade after Fenianism's failure, it revived again in 1879 and the early 1880s, when over half a million Irish Americans joined the Irish National Land League of America to support the contemporary Land War against Irish landlordism. From 1883 through 1916 smaller but still substantial numbers joined organizations and donated money to aid the constitutional-nationalist campaign for Irish provincial self-government (home rule), while some ten thousand more were members of the Clan na Gael, which supported revolution and total Irish independence. Finally, in 1916 Irish Americans responded so negatively to British policies in Ireland that between that date and 1921 some eight hundred thousand joined nationalist organizations and remitted over $10 million to assist Sinn Féin and the Irish Republican Army in their largely successful war for Irish freedom. All these organizations were led by bourgeois Irish Americans, and although working-class immigrants predominated among the rank and file, middle-class membership was disproportionately large.

    In some respects it was natural that middle- as well as lower-class Irish immigrants and their children should identify with Ireland's political struggles. Before emigration their sense of group consciousness had already been shaped either by the mass political mobilizations that characterized Catholic Ireland from the 1820s on, or by peasant traditions of resentment and rebellion. The Famine immigrants and evicted farmers were especially likely to perceive themselves as victims of British and landlord tyranny, and, as noted earlier, peasant traditions and bourgeois strategies converged to reinforce the common notion that essentially all Irish emigration was political exile. Finally, not only were nationalist ideas already internalized by many arrivals — and kept fresh in the New World through contacts with Ireland via letters, chain migration, and newspapers — but in addition poverty, frustration, alienation, and homesickness among many Irish in the United States strengthened their emotional identification with the old country and their allegiance to those who promised to liberate Ireland and abolish emigration's purported causes.

    Although middle-class immigrants benefited from the cultivation of nationalist sensibilities, they also incurred risks. Irish nationalism was frequently associated with violent assaults on life, property, and constituted authority, with various forms of social radicalism, and paradoxically, with both anticlericalism and sectarian massacres, as in 1798. Irish-American support for even peaceful, constitutional nationalism offended many Protestant Americans, who were increasingly Anglophile and forgetful of their own country's past struggle against British rule. In addition, organized immigrant devotion to Ireland inevitably brought nativist charges that Irish Americans were less than fully loyal to the United States: "There can be no such thing as a divided national allegiance," warned an American judge at mid-century,[39] presaging Woodrow Wilson's later attacks on Irish-American "hyphenates" who impeded Anglo-American rapprochement. By implying that the Irish were immigrants by compulsion rather than by choice, the nationalists' interpretation of emigration as forced exile seemed to epitomize the group's ambiguous status in the New World.

Except for some extreme Irish-American nationalists, most nationalist leaders made tortuous efforts to reconcile Irish and American patriotism and to reassure the American middle class, as well as hesitant middle-class immigrants and Catholic clergy, that Irish-American nationalism was fully compatible with aspirations to respectability and assimilation. Irish-American politicians and journalists continued to insist that common political ideals and a shared history of struggle against "English tyranny" still united Irish and native traditions. As one editor put it, "The strongest and best hater of England is sure to prove the best American."[40] Perhaps the most contrived and tragic attempt at such self-serving synthesis occurred in the Civil War's early years, when ingenious Irish-American spokesmen — eager to prove the group's patriotism — urged their countrymen to enlist and join the slaughter to gain military training for subsequent use against England. The Fenian attempt to conquer Canada in 1866 reflected desires to merge Irish animosity against the British Empire with the long-standing American aspiration to annex that valuable "speculation" in northern "real estate."[41] Similarly, in 1916–1921 Irish-American leaders justified agitation for Irish independence in light of their adopted country's contemporary wartime crusade for democracy and self-determination for small nations.

Middle-class Irish Americans explained nationalist aspirations in bourgeois and assimilationist terms. They asserted, for example, that the creation of a free and prosperous Ireland was a necessary precondition for Irish Americans to achieve respect in the New World — an argument that appealed to ambitious entrepreneurs and respectable craftsmen such as New York's Patrick Taggart, who hoped "that ere long Irish men will have a flag of their own to shelter and protect them" from nativist aspersions.[42] The mobilization of Irish immigrants in nationalist movements dissolved parochial loyalties in a common consciousness and united the group in ways conducive to their leaders' domestic goals. For instance, Fenian spokesmen such as Patrick Collins, future mayor of Boston, used the reputations and followings created through their championship of Ireland's "sacred cause" to advance their own political careers. Local nationalist clubs were merely stepping-stones to power for ambitious ward heelers like James Michael Curley. Irish-American entrepreneurs and politicians alike realized that their "patriotic" leadership of nationalist movements could deflect and obscure intraethnic class conflict; sometimes, as in Denver in 1879–1881, they won support even from formerly militant Irish workers. From the perspective of conservative Irish Americans, even extreme Irish-American nationalist societies like the Clan na Gael inadvertently performed the valuable function of diverting the radical resentments of immigrant workers from more dangerous domestic channels. Nationalist movements would be successful, middle-class leaders admonished, only if Irish Americans took care to "be faithful, be Catholic, be practical, be temperate, be industrious, [and] be obedient to the laws";[43] and the nationalist rhetoric of emigration-as-exile itself obscured internal differences by implying that all Irish Americans shared similar, externally imposed reasons for immigration. Conversely, the demands of Irish-American nationalists that the immigrants remain loyal to the "*mother*land" — like clerical injunctions to fidelity to "mother church" — coincided with the needs of the Irish and the Irish immigrant family and imposed strong communal pressures for ethnic solidarity and conformity on ambitious or assimilation-minded individuals.

The success in employing nationalism as a medium for cultural hegemony was demonstrated by its thorough integration with the other means of incorporation: the Democratic party and the Catholic church. Democratic politicians quickly learned to "twist the British lion's tail" for Irish-American voters; Ireland's cause gained few practical benefits from such rhetorical exercises, but the symbolic assimilation of Irish and native-American political traditions both legitimated the former and opened up the latter for middle-class Irish Americans. Irish-American churchmen soon understood that a clerically recognized and tamed Irish-American nationalism could strengthen religious faith, that clerical expressions of "sympathy with the national aspirations of the race" helped cement Irish loyalties to the church in the United States as in Ireland.[44] Irish-American nationalism was conflated with American patriotism, loyalty to the Democracy, and fidelity to Catholicism in a synthetic ethnic identity. The success of that synthesis largely explains both the last, remarkable resurgence of nationalism in 1916–1921 — when the group was composed overwhelmingly of second- and third-generation Irish Americans — and the fact that Irish America retained its ethnic identity despite the nearly total disintegration and disappearance of organized Irish-American nationalism after the creation of the Irish Free State in 1922.

Hegemony and Working-Class Subculture

David Montgomery, Eric Foner, and other labor historians have argued that Irish-American ethnicity derived primarily from the stratification and segmentation of Irish immigrant laborers.[45] Most Irish immigrants adapted not to bourgeois models of individual respectability and upward mobility, they argue, but to an American working-class subculture; and the preindustrial or artisanal traditions of Irish immigrants merged with the ideals of native and other immigrant workers to forge a militant American working-class consciousness that incorporated and transcended ethnic identities. During the late 1860s, the 1870s, and especially the 1880s, there emerged a "symbiotic relationship"[46] between Irish immigrants' traditional oppositions to landlordism and British imperialism, and American labor leaders' contemporary crusades against plutocracy and wage slavery. The two were conflated by spokesmen such as the Irish-American newspaper editor Patrick Ford, whose *Irish World and Industrial Liberator*—the nation's most popular Irish weekly in the 1870s and 1880s—offered a working-class road to assimilation via a radical brand of Irish-American nationalism that demanded fundamental socioeconomic reforms on both sides of the Atlantic. Once his readers realized, as Ford put it, that "the cause of the poor in Donegal is the cause of the factory slave in Fall River,"[47] then Irish-American nationalism broadened and prepared its working-class Irish adherents for their increasingly prominent position in militant trade unions, the Knights of Labor, and the third-party efforts—such as Henry George's 1886 campaign for mayor of New York—that characterized the 1880s.

In assessing this interpretation we should begin by acknowledging that mass participation by Irish immigrants and their sons in the late-nineteenth-century American labor movement is incontrovertible, as is their disproportionately large membership in the Knights of Labor. Indeed, Terence Powderly, the Knights' national leader, was an Irish-American Catholic, and in 1890–1920 workers of Irish stock were "incredibly dominant" among both the leadership and the rank and file in most of the craft unions affiliated with the American Federation of Labor, which then accounted for 75 percent of all organized laborers.[48] Nor is there any doubt that the bonds forged among Irish immigrant workers in iron mills, construction sites, mining camps, and working-class neighborhoods simultaneously heightened a consciousness of class as well as of ethnicity, at least insofar as the two coincided. Nevertheless, I contend that the emphasis of Foner, Montgomery, and others has been misplaced and that the symbiotic relationship between Irish Catholic immigrants and working-class organizations served to diminish proletarian consciousness among both, assimilating them instead to the "quasi-middle-class" values that characterized the dominant cultures of Irish America and native America alike.[49]

With few and extremely transitory exceptions, Irish-American working-class neighborhoods were not the crucibles of proletarianization that some scholars have hypothesized. In cities such as Fall River, where the work force was distinctly segmented and residentially segregated on ethnic lines, job competition and the sociocultural and territorial divisions between Irish and other neighborhoods only intensified ethnic consciousness and insularity.[50] In most instances it is only superficially accurate to speak of Irish *working-class* neighborhoods, as if that phrase indicated either social or cultural homogeneity. Most such districts were dominated, socially and politically, by the presence of saloonkeepers, grocers, contractors, and other small entrepreneurs and employers, and although such men were often former factory or even unskilled laborers, and although they often supported strikes by local residents and customers, their functions and life-styles oriented their neighborhoods toward "broader," bourgeois-dominated associations and values that undermined both parochial and proletarian identities.

Studies such as one of Worcester at midcentury demonstrate that after a brief period of severe social dislocation precipitated by the Famine influx, the actual working-class populations of Irish neighborhoods were dominated—socially, culturally, and eventually demographically—by families that a historian of a later period, Roy Rosenzweig, characterizes as "working-class respect-ables" or "settled livers."[51] Unlike other groups from southern and eastern Europe, the central importance of the Irish-American family was ensured early on by an unusually high proportion of female Irish immigrants (about 50 percent in 1850–1900). Family ties and responsibilities alone tended both to encourage ethnic insularity and discourage proletarian militancy. The segrega-tion of workers' lives between home and workplace (and saloon) tended to foster a cult of domesticity that converged with middle-class norms and found physical expression in the stereotypical lace curtains adorning the windows of "respectable" working-class Irish homes.[52] The peculiar role of the Irish immi-grant woman may have been particularly significant.[53] In the great majority of cases, immigrant Irish women, mostly young and single, had experienced prior to their embarkations rather severe degrees of social and personal repression in an overtly male-dominated society. Their best avenue to status or expression in Ireland was through the Catholic church, and so most became extremely atten-tive to religious devotions. Because their experiences at home also tended to make them highly "independent" and ambitious, however, most regarded emi-gration to the United States as opportunity or even escape, and once abroad they tended to embrace American consumerism and its underlying norms. Before marrying (almost exclusively to other Irish Americans), most of the women labored as domestic servants in middle-class American households, where they gained further exposure to bourgeois values. Their experiences, ambitions, and intense religiosity — as well as the fact that in the United States they married by choice rather then under the rural Irish dowry system — allowed Irish immigrant women to play crucial roles in working-class Irish-American families as disseminators of middle-class norms and aspirations for respectabil-ity and uplift among husbands and children.

These factors, combined with the desire of transplanted peasants for securi-ty, may help explain why working-class Irish families seem to have been espe-cially assiduous and successful in acquiring property and, particularly, in be-coming home owners. As an index of status and permanence, home ownership itself inculcated conservative attitudes. In addition, although the overall expan-sion of the American economy in 1850–1900 was most important, the central-ity of the Irish-American family and, especially, of the mother's role also may help explain the occupational mobility and diversity that the group had at-tained by the century's end, when "most Irish American families were fluid in their kinship and communal status relationships." The result, as the historian David Doyle has recorded, was that "the railroad worker, switchman or mainte-nance worker, would have a cousin a grocer, a brother a small official, a son a teacher or a traindriver."[54] Consequently, he would not identify with a "closed" socioeconomic community but, rather, with associations and formal institutions that transcended those fluid relationships and that were the very media through which the Irish-American bourgeoisie disseminated its hegemonic culture.

From the late 1860s on, nearly all Irish-American neighborhoods not only were dominated by Catholic churches and Democratic party organizations but also were saturated by branches of national ethnic and religious benevolent and fraternal societies, such as the Irish Catholic Benevolent Union, the Catholic Total Abstinence Union, the Ancient Order of Hibernians, and, by the century's end, the Knights of Columbus.[55] These societies' leadership cadres and membership lists often overlapped on both national and local levels, and, most important, their leaders were predominantly middle-class, often second-generation Irish Americans, and the bulk of their members were either of petty bourgeois or skilled-worker status. Consequently, although these associations expressed the full range of emphases allowed by the dominant ethnic culture — from "Irish Chauvinism" to "Catholic Americanism," to employ the terms of historian Timothy Meagher[56] — they all espoused an ostentatious American patriotism and preached a gospel of progress and individual uplift through self-discipline, industry, thrift, and, especially, sobriety.

Like the Democratic party, the Catholic church, and organized Irish-American nationalism, these supplemental media also served the hegemonic imperatives of the Irish-American bourgeoisie, forging group solidarity across class divisions and incorporating middle-class norms with working-class sensibilities in a synthetic ethnic culture. Irish immigrant workers who joined these societies recognized that self-discipline and temperance were as necessary for conducting successful strikes as they were likely to enhance their chances for job stability or promotion. Nevertheless, even in the late 1860s the future of the Irish-American working class already belonged to devout, aspiring laborers such as Patrick Taggart, who proudly avowed his "abstinence from those mixtures which . . . debases man lower than the beast"; after all, he concluded, "a man cannot have a good reputation without soberiety [*sic*]."[57]

In light of the above, how can we reassess the relationship between Irish America and organized labor? There is no doubt that ethnoreligious affinities informed and solidified Irish workers' efforts to organize and protest. However, the very bases of such "class" alliances tended to separate Irish from native-American and other immigrant workers. This was especially true by the 1880s and 1890s, when class and ethnicity were *dis*-integrating for various reasons. First, as we have seen, Irish-American workers were increasingly drawn into formal, bourgeois-dominated ethnic associations that transcended class divisions and disseminated middle-class outlooks. As a result, organized Irish workers had competing allegiances to political, religious, and social institutions that in practice were often hostile to organized labor but whose rhetoric appealed to proletarian as well as ethnic sensibilities. This helps to explain why, in the 1880s, Irish-American Democratic politicians were successful in co-opting or, on occasion, crushing Irish and other workers' third-party challenges, and also why Terence Powderly was obliged to expend a disproportionate amount of time and energy protecting the Knights of Labor from reactionary Irish-American bishops and priests, whose powers of excommunication threatened to force Irish workers to quit the organization.[58] Both Tammany patronage and hierarchical condemnations were instrumental in defeating Henry George's bid for New York's mayoralty in 1886, as the secular and clerical wings of the Irish-American bourgeoisie united publicly to stamp out oppositional interpretations of Irish ethnicity. These connections, both coer-

cive and co-optational, between the Democracy, the church, and the Knights of
Labor alienated many of the latter's native-American, Protestant-Republican
members and facilitated their incorporation into another manifestation of all-
class nativism, the American Protective Association, which emerged in the late
1880s and peaked during the economic crisis of the next decade. Likewise,
despite Patrick Ford's efforts, in the long run the connection between Irish
labor and Irish-American nationalism also may have diminished working-class
consciousness, both by heightening Irish workers' ethnic awareness and incorporating them into alliances with bourgeois Irish employers, and also by providing native businessmen and workers with additional opportunities to denounce or perceive Irish laborers as disloyal to American institutions and
values. In the areas where Irish ethnicity and class consciousness coincided
most closely — for example, in the Pennsylvania anthracite fields and in Troy's
iron industry — militant labor's identification with Irish Catholics enabled native employers and their legal, clerical, and editorial allies to stigmatize strikes,
boycotts, and other forms of labor protest as stereotypically Irish and "un-
American."[59]

Second, the early Irish dominance of the urban-industrial work force
meant that by the 1880s and 1890s the increasing stratification of American
labor, coupled with Irish mobility from the unskilled ranks, had placed the
organized vanguard (by 1900 a large majority) of Irish-American workers in a
relatively privileged but highly tenuous position. On one hand, skilled Irish
workers were threatened by employers' efforts to reduce production costs
through wage cuts and mechanization, and on the other hand, those workers
faced new sources of job competition from waves of unskilled immigrants from
southern and eastern Europe, from the so-called Black Belt of the U.S. South,
and even — in California — from China. According to Irish workers, these newcomers "work cheaper & are more submissive than the English-speaking working man,"[60] and, indeed, employers often used the new arrivals to defeat strikes
and break Irish-dominated trade unions. The point is that the defensive posture
of the heavily Irish craft unions made their leaders and members job or craft,
not class, conscious, and to the extent that skilled jobs as machinists, bricklay-
ers, and so on were monopolized by the Irish, that coincidence reinforced
ethnic consciousness as well. Many trade unions became Irish-American bas-
tions, perpetuating their ethnic complexion through exclusive aprenticeship
programs and other forms of nepotism — by such media incorporating not only
their members' sons and nephews but also recent arrivals from Ireland. As
Richard Oestreicher and other historians have pointed out, Irish "craft conservatives" ultimately rejected the Knights of Labor's utopian reformism and
sabotaged its efforts to create an all-inclusive working-class movement, instead
embracing (and shaping) the job- (and ethnic-) conscious strategies of the
American Federation of Labor.[61]

Finally and ironically, the assimilation of Irish-American workers into the
American labor movement only made them more exposed and vulnerable to
middle-class ideals. For example, to the extent that strikes were successful in
raising wages or shortening work hours, such material improvements facilitated

Irish families' incorporation to a culture of respectability and consumerism. As in the early nineteenth century, the ideologies of American labor organizations were at least implicitly conservative in many respects. Both the Knights and the AFL fostered a belief in American exceptionalism and an abhorrence of degraded, "servile" labor that reinforced Irish immigrants' imported but sorely tested faith in American institutions and that converged with their economic resentments and cultural prejudices against new-immigrant, black, and Chinese competitors. The Knights' efforts to create a nearly all-inclusive cooperative commonwealth blurred class distinctions between workers and "good" employers, while AFL leaders explicitly disavowed both reformism and independent labor politics, striving instead to form pragmatic coalitions with those sectors of the bourgeoisie sympathetic to Samuel Gompers's argument that higher wages would produce increased consumerism, larger corporate profits, and industrial harmony.

Most important, the increasing coincidence of Irish ethnicity and the boundaries of organized labor not only reinforced the former but also brought the trade unions themselves into intimate contact—and, eventually, tacit alliances—with those bourgeois-dominated institutions that defined Irish-American ethnicity. Marc Karson has demonstrated the extensive influence in the late nineteenth and early twentieth centuries of the Catholic church on the American Federation of Labor, shaping the conservative policies of its predominantly Irish-stock leaders.[62] Gwendolyn Mink has argued recently that racist opposition to new immigrants, Chinese laborers, and black migrants united Irish-American labor leaders and politicians, and facilitated the incorporation of the AFL into an all-class, nativist coalition under the Democratic party of Bryan and Wilson.[63] Ironically, although Irish Americans were themselves still subject and morbidly sensitive to Yankee prejudices, both their middle- and working-class spokesmen embraced a fashionable racism through which they could both emphasize their ethnic distinctiveness and simultaneously claim affinity with, and preferential treatment from, the governing native classes. In many cities unorganized semiskilled and unskilled Irish laborers were even more dependent on the Democratic party, specifically on Irish-dominated political machines, to provide jobs as street pavers, gas workers, and so on in the face of competition from Italians, French Canadians, and blacks. In many urban parishes the links between Irish-American contractors, politicians, city employees, priests, and trade-union leaders were so intimate and inextricable that members of other immigrant groups turned to Yankee-Protestant, business-Republican leadership—which in turn only further reinforced Irish workers' multiple ethnic allegiances. The relationship between Irish-American nationalism and organized labor was less close and important, but AFL conventions regularly issued statements supporting Irish freedom, and on occasion, as in the 1894 convention, Irish craft-union leaders cynically manipulated nationalist issues to defeat socialist motions emanating from the federation's German- or native-American constituents.

Through both direct and indirect influence on Irish workers and their organizations, the Irish-American bourgeoisie was able to incorporate many of its key values and implement its hegemonic strategies even via an ostensibly "proletarian" institution, the AFL. To be sure, such an incorporation (like Irish nationalists' embrace of peasant land hunger) inevitably broadened the dualities of the dominant subculture, but it both solidified the ethnic ideological bloc across class lines and opened new avenues for collective and individual access to influence and power—strengthening, for example, the positions of both Irish-American politicians and bishops in their relationships with native Americans and new immigrants, as well as their own Irish constituents.

Thus, a complex, multifaceted, but virtually all-inclusive Irish-American ethnicity was now complete, adapting Irish traditions and American experiences to both the hegemonic imperatives of the Irish-American bourgeoisie and the assimilable needs and notions of their social inferiors. By 1900 Irish ethnic identity had achieved ultimate synthesis: a "good Irish American" was at least one if not all of the following: a good Democrat, a practicing Catholic, a good family man (or devoted wife and mother), in most cases a loyal union member, and nearly always at least a passive supporter of Ireland's "sacred cause." Most important, whereas identifications with Catholicism, nationalism, transatlantic family ties, and middle-class values, generally, still linked Irish Americans—symbolically if not tangibly—to Ireland and *its* hegemonic culture, all the bourgeois-defined traits and associations that characterized "good Irish Americans" also enabled them to assert that they were "good Americans" as well; indeed, so much so that cultural affinity with the governing classes legitimated the group's intermediate position and allowed its leaders to play "Americanizing" roles for the new immigrants. Ironically, whether as foremen, politicians, union leaders, bishops, or merely as fellow guardians of American capitalism and cultural or racial "purity," by the early twentieth century Irish Americans had earned Henry Cabot Lodge's designation of "honorary Anglo-Saxons" through the very process of creating a bourgeois-defined Irish ethnic identity.

NOTES

1. The bulk of this chapter is condensed from my book, *Emigrants and Exiles: Ireland and the Irish Exodus to North America* (New York: Oxford University Press, 1985). Consequently, to save space below I will cite only quotations and those books, articles, etc. read specifically for this essay.

I would like to thank Charles Tilly for his help in revising this paper for publication, and also William Zeisel for his excellent editorial work.

On Macneven, see Victor R. Greene, *American Immigrant Leaders, 1800-1910: Marginality and Identity* (Baltimore: Johns Hopkins University Press, 1983), pp. 25–27; Jane M. Macneven, "Memoir of William James Macneven," in R. R. Madden Papers (Ms. 873; Trinity College, Dublin).

2. Ira B. Cross, ed., *Frank Roney: Irish Rebel and California Labor Leader: An Autobiography* (Berkeley: University of California Press, 1931); Neil L. Shumsky, "Frank Roney's San Francisco—His Diary: April 1875-March 1876," *Labor History* 17 (Spring 1976): 245–64.

3. The literature on assimilation and ethnicity is enormous, but see Nathan Glazer, "Ethnic Groups in America: From National Culture to Ideology," in *Freedom and Control in Modern Society,* ed. Morroe Berger et al. (New York: Octagon Books, 1964); Nathan Glazer and Daniel P. Moynihan, *Beyond the Melting Pot: The Negroes, Puerto Ricans, Jews, Italians, and Irish of New York City,* 2nd ed. (Cambridge: MIT Press, 1970); Nathan Glazer and Daniel P. Moynihan, eds., *Ethnicity: Theory and Experience* (Cambridge: Harvard University Press, 1975); Andrew Greeley, *Ethnicity in the United States* (New York: Wiley, 1974); Milton Gordon, *Assimilation in American Life* (New York: Oxford University Press, 1964); John Higham, "Current Trends in the Study of Ethnicity in the United States," *Journal of American Ethnic History* 2 (Fall 1982): 5–15; Fred Matthews, "Cultural Pluralism in Context: External History, Philosophic Premise, and the Theories of Ethnicity in Modern America," *Journal of Ethnic Studies* 12 (Summer 1984): 63–79; Howard F. Stein and Robert F. Hill, *The Ethnic Imperative* (University Park: Pennsylvania State University Press, 1977); Werner Sollors, "Theory of American Ethnicity," *American Quarterly* 33 (Fall 1981): 257–83; Stephen Steinberg, *The Ethnic Myth: Race, Ethnicity, and Class in America* (New York: Atheneum, 1981); Robert P. Swierenga, "Ethnicity in Historical Perspective," *Social Science* 52 (Winter 1977): 31–44.

4. See pp. 84ff.

5. David Brundage, "Irish Land and American Workers: Class and Ethnicity in Denver, Colorado," in *"Struggle a Hard Battle": Essays on Working-Class Immigrants,* ed. Dirk Hoerder (DeKalb: Northern Illinois University Press, 1986), pp. 46–67; Eric Foner, "Class, Ethnicity, and Radicalism in the Gilded Age: The Land League and Irish America," *Marxist Perspectives* 1 (Summer 1978): 7–55; Michael Gordon, "Studies in Irish and Irish-American Thought and Behavior in Gilded Age New York City" (Ph.D. diss., University of Rochester, 1977); Herbert Gutman, "Work, Culture, and Society in Industrializing America, 1815–1919," *American Historical Review* 78 (June 1973): 531–87; David Montgomery, *Beyond Equality: Labor and the Radical Republicans, 1862–72* (New York: Knopf, 1967); David Montgomery, "The Irish and the American Labor Movement," in *America and Ireland, 1776–1976: The American Identity and the Irish Connection,* ed. David N. Doyle and Owen Dudley Edwards (Westport, Conn.: Greenwood Press, 1980), pp. 205–18.

6. Charles Tilly, "Transplanted Networks," Working Paper 35 (October 1986), Center for Studies of Social Change, New School for Social Research, pp. 1–11; Charles Tilley, letter to author, December 2, 1986.

7. Unless otherwise cited, the two following paragraphs are from Antonio Gramsci, *The Modern Prince and Other Writings* (New York: International Publishers, 1957); Quentin Hoare and Geoffrey Nowell Smith, eds., *Selections from the Prison Notebooks of Antonio Gramsci* (New York: International Publishers, 1971); and Raymond Williams, "Base and Superstructure in Marxist Cultural Theory," *New Left Review* 82 (November-December, 1983): 3–16.

8. Joseph V. Femia, *Gramsci's Political Thought: Hegemony, Consciousness, and the Revolutionary Process* (Oxford: Clarendon Press, 1981), p. 28; T. J. Jackson Lears, "The Concept of Cultural Hegemony: Problems and Possibilities," *American Historical Review* 90 (June 1985): 569.

9. Lears, "The Concept of Cultural Hegemony," 571–73.

10. For a more detailed exposition of the material in this section, see the author's "Emigration as Exile: Cultural Hegemony in Post-Famine Ireland" (Conference paper, St. Paul, Minnesota, November 1986), to be published in a collection of essays, edited by Rudolph J. Vecoli. In this paper I exclude consideration of the Protestant-dominated,

urban-industrial counties of northeastern Ireland (Ulster), considered as a sociocultural system distinct from that of Catholic Ireland.

11. Kerby A. Miller, with Bruce Boling and David N. Doyle, "Emigrants and Exiles: Irish Cultures and Irish Emigration to North America, 1790–1922," *Irish Historical Studies* 22 (September 1980): 97–125; also, Miller, *Emigrants and Exiles,* pp. 102–30.

12. Ibid. For contrasting interpretations of Irish emigration and of the United States as "promised land," see the author's essay, "Golden Streets, Bitter Tears: The Irish Image of America During the Era of Mass Migration," in the *Journal of American Ethnic History* (Fall 1990).

13. Terminology borrowed from Michael Peillon, *Contemporary Irish Society: An Introduction* (Dublin: Gill & Macmillan, 1982).

14. In their letters, Irish immigrants from business, professional, and affluent farming backgrounds employed the term *independence* in reference to ambitions for individual upward mobility, whereas small farmers, artisans, and laborers used the term to signify their desire for comfortable self-sufficiency through farm ownership or steady employment.

15. This ideal took shape in the early nineteenth century, primarily under clerical auspices, but its outlines were sharpened in the 1840s by the impact of romantic nationalism, imported from the Continent, on middle-class, urban Catholics, some of whom formed the Young Ireland movement and staged an abortive revolution in 1848. Although O'Connell, conservative lay Catholics, and the bishops disliked Young Ireland's secular republicanism and belief in cathartic violence, in subsequent decades middle-class nationalists drew heavily on the movement's sentimental literature.

16. On emigration and the Irish family, see the author's "Paddy's Paradox: Emigration and America in Irish Imagination and Rhetoric" in *The Image of America,* ed. Dirk Hoerder and Horst Ruessler (New York: Holmes & Meier, forthcoming).

17. See pp. 84ff.

18. Even the successful assimilation of intending immigrants into the Irish nationalist bloc meant that they would "see" and expect resolution of their ideals and grievances through specific political programs. When pragmatic or conservative middle-class leaders failed those expectations, one possible result was apostasy from nationalism or even from Catholicism (not uncommon in the United States), but more frequent were "purist" schisms that resulted in new, more extreme varieties of Irish and Irish-American nationalism, such as Fenianism in 1858–1867 and Sinn Féin in 1916–1921.

19. *Historical Statistics of the United States: Colonial Times to 1970* (Washington, D.C.: U.S. Census Bureau, 1975), pp. 8–14, 116–18; *United States Census, 1870,* 1:698–702. Information on Irish-American concentration, courtesy of Dr. David N. Doyle, University College, Dublin. Doyle's research also shows that almost 70 percent of Irish immigrants in 1870 resided in merely 146 out of the 1,090 counties in those twenty states (the counties characterized by urbanization or mining); nearly 45 percent lived in the nation's fifty largest cities, 34 percent in the largest fifteen.

20. David N. Doyle, *Irish Americans, Native Rights, and National Empires: The Structure, Divisions, and Attitudes of the Catholic Minority in the Decade of Expansion, 1890–1901* (New York: Arno Press, 1976), pp. 48–49, 59–63.

21. During the century's earliest decades, Irish immigrants from professional, entrepreneurial, and commercial farming backgrounds may have composed 25 percent of the exodus, in addition to perhaps 40 percent more who were artisans. Most of these early immigrants were Protestants, primarily from Ulster.

22. The recent historical literature on republican culture and the American working class is large and growing, but see especially, Sean Wilentz, *Chants Democratic: New*

York City and the Rise of the American Working Class, 1788–1850 (New York: Oxford University Press, 1984).

23. James Richey, September 26, 1826 (courtesy of Professor E.R.R. Green, Queen's University, Belfast).

24. Mike Davis, *Prisoners of the American Dream: Politics and Economy in the History of the US Working Class* (London: Verso, 1986), pp. 7–21 and passim.

25. By the 1830s and early 1840s, only about one-third of an increasingly Catholic Irish immigration was composed of migrants who possessed significant degrees of capital, education, business experience, or marketable skills. This proportion continued to decline during the periods of Famine and post-Famine immigration, when middle-class arrivals probably never exceeded 5–6 percent annually, plus another 10–12 percent of skilled workers.

26. John Chambers, February 12, 1822 (D.1739/3B; Public Record Office of Northern Ireland, Belfast).

27. Thomas C. Grattan, *Civilized America* (1859; reprint, New York: Russell, 1969), 2:8–9.

28. John Blake Dillon, December 12, 1852, in William Smith O'Brien Papers (Ms. 445; National Library of Ireland, Dublin).

Theoretically, Victorian America's dominant culture promoted acceptance of middle-class Irish Catholics on meritocratic grounds, but the fact that its liberal values were viewed as both inseparable from Protestantism and threatened by Irish Catholic immigration guaranteed that even men such as Dillon would encounter prejudice and proscription. Irish Protestant immigrants encountered no such barriers. During the nineteenth century perhaps one million Irish Presbyterians and Anglicans settled in the United States. Not only did they share the evangelical religion and anti-Irish Catholicism that colored the dominant culture but they were also disproportionately well educated or skilled and came primarily from urban-industrial or commercial farming backgrounds. Consequently, most adapted rapidly to American society, largely through membership in native Protestant churches and fraternal organizations, such as the Masons. Indeed, their social and religious identities conflated so readily with those of the host society that they often played prominent roles in American nativist movements. The sole designation — "Scotch-Irish" — cultivated by the group's spokesmen was intended to distinguish the group from the Catholic Irish, not from native Americans.

29. Anonymous immigrant's letter, in *Cork Constitution,* March 12, 1857 (courtesy of Professor Arnold Schrier, University of Cincinnati).

30. Ms. 1409, p. 327 (Collections of the Department of Irish Folklore, University College, Dublin).

31. George Potter, *To the Golden Door: The Story of the Irish in Ireland and America* (Boston: Little, Brown, 1960), p. 282; J. Fitzgerald, August 21, 1860 (courtesy of Alan Kennedy, Castletroy, County Limerick).

32. Robert Ernst, *Immigrant Life in New York City, 1825–1863* (Port Washington, N.Y.: Ira J. Friedman, 1965 ed.), pp. 150–53.

33. Davis, *Prisoners of the American Dream,* pp. 25–29.

34. Patrick, Dunny, December 30, 1856 (courtesy of Professor Arnold Schrier, University of Cincinnati).

35. Richard O'Gorman, January 1, 1859 (Ms. 445; William Smith O'Brien Papers, National Library of Ireland, Dublin).

36. The best recent history of the American church is Jay P. Dolan, *The American Catholic Experience: A History from Colonial Times to the Present* (Garden City, N.Y.: Doubleday, 1985).

37. P. Flanagan, August 16, 1891 (courtesy of Peter and Mary Flanagan, Tubberto-by, Clogherhead, County Louth).

38. Michael Flanagan, April 14, 1877 (Courtesy of Peter and Mary Flanagan, Tubbertoby, Clogherhead, County Louth). On O'Reilly, see John Duffy Ibsen, "Will the World Break Your Heart? An Historical Analysis of the Dimensions and Consequences of Irish-American Assimilation" (Ph.D. diss., Brandeis University, 1976), pp. 106–20.

39. Oliver MacDonagh, "Irish Emigration to the United States of America and the British Colonies during the Famine," in *The Great Famine: Studies in Irish History,* ed. R. Dudley Edwards and T. Desmond Williams (New York: New York University Press, 1957), p. 382.

40. William L. Joyce, *Editors and Ethnicity: A History of the Irish-American Press, 1848–1883* (New York: Arno Press, 1976), p. 77.

41. Montgomery, *Beyond Equality*, p. 133.

42. Patrick Taggart, June 14, 1869 (Robert Humphreys Papers, Cornell University Archives).

Some historians, most notably Thomas N. Brown in *Irish-American Nationalism, 1870–1890* (Philadelphia: Lippincott, 1966), contend that the primary, if not only, purpose of Irish-American nationalism was to promote its middle-class adherents' goals of acceptance and upward mobility in American society. That interpretation is too one-sided, for the most loyal followers of nationalist movements were usually alienated laborers and homesick peasants, recently arrived; likewise, many of the most dedicated leaders—especially of extreme, revolutionary organizations like the Clan na Gael—were totally indifferent to their personal prospects in the native society. However, although Irish-American nationalism was a multifaceted phenomenon, it was precisely through its incorporation of Irish America's socioeconomic and ideological dualities that its predominantly middle-class leaders were able to employ it to exercise hegemony.

43. Thomas N. Burke, *Lectures on Faith and Fatherland* (London: Burns, Oates, & Washburne, n.d.), p. 235. Burke, an Irish priest, was a popular lecturer among the American Irish.

44. J. P. Gaffey, *Citizen of No Mean City: Archbishop Patrick Riordan of San Francisco* (Hawthorne, Calif., 1976), p. 144.

45. See note 5.

46. Foner, "Class, Ethnicity, and Radicalism," pp. 26–27.

47. Brown, Irish-American Nationalism, p. 108.

48. David N. Doyle, "The Irish and American Labour, 1880–1920," *Saothar: Journal of the Irish Labour History Society* 1 (1975): 42–53.

49. Ibid., pp. 50–51.

50. On the Irish in Fall River, see John Cumbler, *Working Class Community in Industrial America: Work, Leisure, and Struggle in Two Industrial Cities, 1880–1930* (Westport, Conn.: Greenwood Press, 1979).

51. Vincent E. Powers, "Invisible Immigrants': The Pre-Famine Irish Community in Worcester, Massachusetts, from 1826 to 1860" (Ph.D. diss., Clark University, 1976); Roy Rosenzweig, *Eight Hours for What We Will: Workers and Leisure in an Industrial City, 1870–1920* (Cambridge: Cambridge University Press, 1983), especially pp. 65–90.

52. On the privatization of workers' lives, see Susan E. Hirsch, *Roots of the American Working Class: The Industrialization of Crafts in Newark, 1800–1860* (Philadelphia: University of Pennsylvania Press, 1978).

53. On Irish immigrant women, see Carol Groneman, "Working-Class Immigrant Women in Mid-Nineteenth Century New York: The Irish Woman's Experience," *Journal of Urban History* 4 (May 1978): 255–73; and Hasia R. Diner, *Erin's Daughters in*

America: Irish Immigrant Women in the Nineteenth Century (Baltimore: Johns Hopkins University Press, 1983).

54. Doyle, "The Irish and American Labour," pp. 50–51.

55. There was a brief period during and after the famine immigration when many Irish immigrant neighborhoods were bereft of formal, middle-class political, religious and social institutions, which may help explain the 1860s phenomenon of Fenianism, with its unique promise to *return* large numbers of alienated, unattached Irish-American males to Irish soil. However, by the 1870s and 1880s a typical working-class immigrant in Philadelphia could observe that "Irishmen are pretty well organized here. . . . This is a great place for societies." Owen O'Callaghan, December 12, 1884 (courtesy of Eugene O'Callaghan, Fallagh, Kilmacthomas, County Waterford).

56. Timothy J. Meagher, "'The Lord Is Not Dead': Cultural and Social Change among the Irish in Worcester, Massachusetts" (Ph.D. diss., Brown University, 1982).

57. Patrick Taggart, June 14, 1869 (Robert Humphreys Papers, Cornell University).

58. See Davis, *Prisoners of the American Dream,* pp. 29–40; Leon Fink, *Workingmen's Democracy: The Knights of Labor and American Politics* (Urbana: University of Illinois Press, 1983); Henry J. Browne, *The Catholic Church and the Knights of Labor* (New York: Arno Press, 1976 ed.).

59. On the Irish in Troy, see Daniel J. Walkowitz, *Worker City, Company Town: Iron and Cotton-Worker Protest in Troy and Cohoes, New York, 1855-84* (Urbana: University of Illinois Press, 1978), especially pp. 219–44.

60. Patrick McKeown, September 11, 1904 (courtesy of Professor Arnold Schrier, University of Cincinnati).

61. Richard J. Oestreicher, *Solidarity and Fragmentation: Working People and Class Consciousness in Detroit, 1875-1900* (Urbana: University of Illinois Press, 1986), especially pp. 30–67, 172–214; Davis, *Prisoners of the American Dream,* pp. 40–45.

62. Marc Karson, *American Labor Unions and Politics, 1900-1918* (Boston: Beacon Press, 1965 ed.), pp. 212–84.

63. Gwendolyn Mink, *Old Labor and New Immigrants in American Political Development: Union, Party, and State, 1875-1920* (Ithaca: Cornell University Press, 1986).

5

Work and Family:
Blacks and Immigrants from
South and East Europe

Suzanne W. Model

Differences in the living standards and life-styles of the many racial and ethnic groups that have immigrated to the United States have long been a subject for intense study and debate. Among the most glaring discrepancies is the gap that emerges in comparisons of Afro-Americans and Europeans. The forced migrations that brought most blacks to the United States actually preceded the vast European inflows of the late nineteenth and early twentieth centuries. By the time that blacks began entering northern labor markets, they were only slightly less educated, skilled, or familiar with urban life than many of their European counterparts. Yet, by the late twentieth century, the socioeconomic gulf separating these migrant streams had widened in a myriad of ways that command the attention of policymakers and scholars.

Nowhere is the discrepancy between blacks and European ethnics more evident than with respect to family structure. By 1985 over 40 percent of all black families were headed by women. Analogous figures for later-generation European ethnics are not available, but a variety of investigators concur that family structure among these groups increasingly resembles that of the larger white community, in which, at last count, less than one-fifth of families were female headed.[1] Although blacks have always displayed a higher incidence of female headedness than whites, racial differences have grown steadily in recent years. Such differences invite investigation not only because they are interesting in the abstract but because there is evidence that in a capitalist system, members of female-headed families face substantial disadvantage. The most obvious manifestation of this disadvantage is the low wages that women workers receive. The median earnings of women employed full time typically have averaged about 60 percent of the earnings for similarly employed men. When children are involved, economic hardship is exacerbated by the failure of more than half of divorced fathers to contribute any support toward the care of their children.[2] Not surprisingly, then, racial differences in family structure deserve consideration in any careful investigation of the relative economic well-being of blacks and whites.

Early explanations for racial disparities in family structure emphasized that the institution of slavery exposed black women to independence and work in a manner never experienced by white women. According to sociologist E. Franklin Frazier, writing in the 1930s, slavery both reduced the prerogatives of most black men and enhanced the responsibilities of most black women — with the result that the black mother tended to hold the preeminent position in the slave family. At the same time, Frazier believed that when blacks entered the impersonal environment of the urban wage economy, financial instability and the declining influence of kin, neighbors, and church further eroded the black male's position as head of the family.[3]

More recent research has questioned Frazier's interpretation that slavery left a legacy of female dominance, while acknowledging the detrimental effects of urbanization on the black conjugal (husband-wife) family. Most scholars concur that a significant rise in the incidence of female headedness among black families was associated with their initial relocation out of the rural South. Thereafter, female headedness among urban black families advanced but slightly, only to increase sharply among all segments of the black community during the past two and a half decades. Today, fewer and fewer blacks have been marrying or remarrying, while the vitality and significance of the extended family (a broader unit of consanguinal and fictive kin) remains strong.[4]

The notion that migration and urbanization weakened the conjugal families of European immigrants was also a popular view among social scientists of the 1920s and 1930s. Since that time, however, a broad range of studies has refuted this interpretation, showing instead that conjugal — and to a lesser degree, extended — families prospered under immigrant conditions.[5] To be sure, as time passed, the descendants of immigrants displayed weaker family bonds and stronger individualism and independence than before, but these shifts did not undermine their commitment to the conjugal family, even if they entered into more than one marriage in a lifetime.

Thus, one is left wondering why migration and urbanization had such divergent short- and long-term consequences for blacks and white ethnics. Even if blacks and immigrants entered urban environments with slightly different cultural legacies, the variations appear insufficient to explain why city life reinforced the conjugal family form among immigrants but not among blacks. This chapter takes another look at the urbanization process in an effort to explain this result. A central assumption is that economic needs influence the ways that individuals will form and maintain family relationships. Such an assumption is compatible with a wide range of theories about human behavior, including Marxism, human-capital theory, and social-exchange theory.[6] In all these perspectives, the relationship among family members is a function of their relative share of resources, particularly economic resources. Because job opportunities provide the primary means for such resources, work and family are inexorably intertwined.

The effort to uncover the most salient differences between urbanizing blacks and immigrants could proceed using a variety of immigrant groups for comparison, but space does not permit the pursuit of multiple comparisons; hence, some group or subset of similar groups must provide the required contrast. The groups chosen for this task are the immigrants from southern and eastern Europe, exclusive of the Jews or the residents of the Iberian peninsula. There are several reasons for this choice. First, these immigrants, like blacks, were primarily unskilled proletarians of rural origins. Second, they were relative latecomers to the industrial scene, arriving for the most part after 1880. As a result, they competed more directly with blacks, whose numbers in the North increased after that date. The comparison is made easier by the large amount of research that has accumulated on southern and eastern Europeans in the past few years.

Although the analysis below proceeds as if these immigrant groups were relatively homogeneous, this approach is a simplification for reasons of pedagogy and space. Similarly, in the compass of a short chapter, it will often be necessary to speak in broad generalizations and to limit the discussion to the aspects of the migration and urbanization process that bear most directly on family structure. The reader should look elsewhere in this book for a discussion of the rise and development of capitalism as the driving force of the global migrations of the past two centuries. The extensive literature on labor history and on organizational life is also relatively neglected. This chapter offers a description and explanation of the family patterns of blacks and immigrants that emphasizes the intersection of work and family.

Immigration from Southern and Eastern Europe: 1880–1924

During the second half of the nineteenth century, the rapid industrialization of the United States required an increasing number of hands. Improvements in technology provided entrepreneurs with the means to replace relatively high priced, increasingly recalcitrant native labor with less-demanding foreign workers. To secure their cheap labor, most employers initially relied on the combination of urban employment bureaus and labor agents, the latter often compatriots of the desired nationality and fluent enough in English to handle both sides of the bargain. Some employment bureaus were large, publicly operated clearinghouses, such as New York's Castle Garden. Others were run for profit and would place workers in exchange for considerable fees. Employment was also negotiated in immigrant-owned saloons, banks, and restaurants.[7]

Despite growing labor demand in a variety of endeavors, workers could hardly be described as moving randomly into industries. A combination of employers' stereotypes and workers' preemigration skills and preferences resulted in the channeling of particular nationalities into particular endeavors. Italians, familiar with construction jobs in Europe, pursued similar tasks in the

United States, often under the supervision of the notorious Italian padrone or labor boss. Some Poles transferred their affiliation with Germany's steel industry to that of Western Pennsylvania.[8]

Once a given nationality had established an industrial beachhead, the need for formal intermediaries in the hiring process evaporated. Each worker was actually and potentially in touch with a reservoir of untapped labor in his homeland, a fact that it did not take long for employers to appreciate. Thus, foremen, supervisors, and other gatekeeping figures turned increasingly to their existing labor force in the search for additional labor.

Reliance on worker intermediaries was a cheap way of procuring labor; it was also more efficient than recruiting outsiders. When existing employees sponsored new workers, the ties between the two simplified on-the-job training and socialization. Even though skill demands were low, some orientation remained necessary and was facilitated by a shared linguistic background between sponsor and protégé. Employers likely also noticed that when newcomers entered the workplace via personal sponsorship, they felt an obligation not to let the sponsor down, an obligation that motivated them to greater diligence than they might otherwise display.[9] For these reasons, employers' eagerness to engage the relatives and friends of their workers was an inexpensive way of obtaining valuable workers.

The willingness of the employers of immigrants to hire the relatives and friends of their workers constituted a strong inducement to brave the voyage, as can be seen in the following letter:

> Dear Brother Waclaw: . . . I inform you about an offer from which you will perhaps profit. My old boss told me today that he had much work, so perhaps I knew some carpenters, and if so I should send them to him. I told him that I had a brother carpenter (i.e. you) who was working, but if the work would be steady, I could bring him. He answered that he hoped to have steady work. So, I advise you to come dear brother . . . we could live here in the foreign land together. . . .[10]

By the end of the nineteenth century, the human movement across the Atlantic could be characterized as a chain migration, involving "sets of related individuals or households who move from one place to another through a set of social arrangements in which people at the destination provide aid, information, and encouragement to newcomers. . . . "[11] The typical southern or eastern European immigrant was not an uninformed, rootless adventurer but a man with a sponsor, a destination, and not infrequently a job. Once settled in his new home, usually in a heavily coethnic neighborhood, he would reactivate the chain by encouraging members of his own kin network to follow his path.

Chain migration surrounded the migrant with people who both saddled him with obligations and supplied the mechanisms through which he could fulfill those obligations. The departing migrant felt obliged to repay any contributions his kinsmen may have made toward his expenses and to underwrite their efforts for upward mobility at home. He was also indebted to the seasoned immigrant who so readily extended a hand of assistance.[12]

Southern and eastern Europeans arrived in the United States with specific economic goals: to earn enough money to buy a small plot in the mother country, open a business there, or otherwise improve themselves at home. The overwhelmingly male composition of these early migrant streams and the enormous amounts of money they sent to their hometowns are just two indicators of the fact that they did not intend to stay. Journeying to the United States was an extension of an already well-established pattern of short-distance migration into wage labor to enrich the family budget; for example, Italian migration to France, Germany, and northern Africa was common in the nineteenth century. But the transatlantic voyage was farther and more expensive. A longer sojourn was required to justify the greater investment.[13]

Just how this sojourn became permanent and for whom remains an untold story. The proportion of eastern and southern Europeans who went back varied by country and time period, running from as low as 30 to as high as 60 percent. Many of those who remained only gradually extended their stays, perhaps disappointed that they could not yet return rich, perhaps encouraged that they had fared so well. Ultimately, the passage of the National Origins Act in 1924, legislation that effectively barred southern and eastern Europeans from entering this country, discouraged many of these nationals from risking a journey home. But already by the turn of the century, wives and sweethearts were receiving encouragement to travel, and families were forming in the new land. Although sex ratios continued disproportionately male, many immigrant men were shifting from "target" earners who spent a bare minimum in order to remit every possible penny to their dear ones, into heads of households who struggled to support a growing family on a proletarian's wage.[14]

The decision to establish a family in the United States brought a dilemma. Newcomers sought only to support themselves at a bare minimum, scrupulously saving their meager surplus for their families abroad. Their low wage demands were precisely what made them attractive to employers. Families, however, required greater solvency. How could more money be secured? Two strategies that immigrants brought to bear on this problem were collective action for better wages and the family economy.

Whether collective action proved helpful or not varied with industry, ethnicity, location, and time. In crafts, success was considerable; in industry, mining and the garment trades were among the few arenas where workers enjoyed any noteworthy gains before the 1930s. The seemingly endless supply of cheaper recruits and the government's willingness to tolerate extreme repression tipped the balance of power squarely into the hands of employers.[15]

A second, more consistently successful way that immigrants advanced their livelihoods was the practice of a family economy, a strategy in which all family members pooled the fruits of their labors to maximize their common welfare. For immigrants, this practice had its roots in the old country, where family members were already used to thinking little about personal aggrandizement and much about family welfare. The family economy remained a valuable adaptation in the American environment because, by pooling their efforts, family members could maximize their financial well-being. Indeed, not only

immigrants but most white working-class Americans relied on family economies in the nineteenth and early twentieth centuries.

Wives, whose cultural heritage usually forbade employment outside the
home, contributed by caring for boarders, engaging in home-based manufacture, or helping in a family business. Children, as soon as they were of sufficient age, left school and entered the work force. Girls usually turned over
nearly all their wages to their mothers, who served as family bankers and
accountants. Boys were more likely to keep at least some modest amount for
their own needs.[16]

Implementation of this strategy meant that a family's economic position
fluctuated across the life cycle. Poverty was often greatest when children were
small and dependent, or after they left the nest, though this danger could be
offset by housing boarders. Because children were associated with economic
gain, fertility remained relatively high.[17] In the old country, spiraling population growth and declining land holdings had begun to spell disaster. American
industry absorbed extra hands more readily.

One difference among immigrants and natives, though, was that the former
were less likely to discontinue the practice of child labor once the family had
achieved a modicum of financial security. Among immigrants especially, an
important motivation for sending children to work was to accumulate a sufficient nest egg to purchase a home, usually near compatriots. Yans-McLaughlin
writes: "The desire to own a home can be seen as the wish of former peasants to
possess — even at great sacrifice — something which had been denied to so many
for generations. Land was an important symbol of wealth, security, and status
in the old country."[18] A home was also an investment. Once an immigrant
family owned a home, rooms could be rented for cash or used by adult children
after they married.[19]

The kinds of employment pursued by the expanding second generation
varied considerably. When fathers were able to sponsor their sons' employment, and sons were willing, the two generations might toil side by side. Slavic
fathers, for instance, frequently smoothed the way for their sons' entrance into
the mines and steel mills of Pennsylvania. Both the building trades and the
entrepreneurial occupations enjoyed above-average rates of familial succession.
Sons of artisans whose skills were becoming obsolete, however, such as shoemakers or tailors, had little choice but to try their luck elsewhere.[20]

Of course, even the son who moved into an occupation different from that
of his father might receive job assistance from other kin: brothers, uncles, or
cousins. When the task was too great for the kin group alone, a host of other
personal ties might fill the gap. In the big cities, the political machines survived
mainly by dispensing job favors. Ethnic associations and unions were also
valuable sources of job information and personal contacts. Thus, even when
the circles of influence widened to include nonkin, job-search strategies were
rarely individualistic.[21]

Daughters were somewhat less likely to work outside the home than sons,
perhaps for cultural reasons but also on account of their lower wages. Yet, as
early as 1890, first- and second-generation immigrant women were nearly twice

as likely to work as were native women of native parentage, partly because of the more precarious economic circumstances of their parents. The difference was very pronounced among young single women.[22] Because few women worked in durable manufacture, mining, or construction, most southern and eastern European fathers could not directly assist daughters in finding employment. But women had their own employment spheres: jobs in clothing manufacture or personal service and occasionally in other light industries such as candy, cigars, or textiles. Word of mouth was again the key mode of entry in finding such jobs. Because immigrant women were even more concentrated in their employment than were men, older sisters, as well as neighbors and friends of the same sex, were often able to help.[23]

In sum, most transatlantic migrants experienced dislocation but not disruption. The fact that migrants and their children so often secured job opportunities through the intercession of kin and other coethnics created strong interpersonal obligations. Indeed, the success of the family economy brought its members closer to the peasant ideal of the interdependent family unit than had been possible in the old country. Contrary to popular belief, adjustment to the United States did not require the sacrifice of familism to the indulgence of individualism but rather the compromise of personal goals for the greater good of the kinship group.[24] Early in marriage, couples struggled to make ends meet on the husband's wage and on whatever supplementary earnings the wife could produce without sacrificing her commitment to home and children. Once those children were of working age, their contributions to the family budget lessened economic pressures, and not a few immigrant families achieved their dream of owning their own modest home.

Black Migration: The Postbellum Era to World War I

At the beginning of the Civil War, just over 5 percent of the nation's blacks lived in the North as "free colored." In the South, 7 percent of blacks were free, having obtained their liberty through purchase or manumission, but the remaining 93 percent were in bondage as field hands, servants, or occasionally as artisans.[25] The end of the war brought forth a great deal of population movement as former slaves sought to unify their families and to establish a livelihood. Most chose to remain in agriculture, hopeful that Reconstruction would bring freedom and prosperity. In fact, however, the political gains of Reconstruction were short-lived and the economic gains were minimal. Most blacks did not have the resources to become landowners, and even those who did increasingly dropped to the status of tenants. Cotton production engaged the great majority of farmers, and dependency on that one crop meant a precarious existence. For many, tenancy came to mean debt peonage because tenants were kept perpetually obligated to the planter or merchant who provided seed, fertilizer, and tools.[26]

Life on the land encouraged the pooling of family labor and resources, but the southern black conjugal family was somewhat less common than its European counterpart. Black families were also more likely to house consanguinal and fictive kin, a practice that had flourished both in Africa and in slave times. Still, most postbellum black farm families were conjugal in form, and many family members relied upon other relatives in the immediate vicinity as well.[27]

Studies report considerable regional and temporal variation in the proportion of black rural families that were headed by women, uncovering rates as low as 10 percent and as high as 24 percent between 1870 and 1900. One study indicates that over one-third of black rural families had identifiable kin nearby, and probably a much larger proportion were involved in meaningful extended and fictive kin networks. Sharing of resources, laboring assistance, adoption, and fosterage were common between households, though an individual's primary responsibility was to contribute to the conjugal family. Within that domain, older children took care of younger or worked in the fields. Wives also worked at farm labor, but only rarely in the white planter's home, perhaps because husbands found this practice too reminiscent of slavery.[28]

Throughout the late nineteenth and early twentieth centuries, southern blacks (and whites) turned to migration as a solution to their poverty. As in Europe, circular migration was common among men, who worked temporarily for wages in agriculture, lumber, mining, or construction. Young women occasionally went into service for periods of time in nearby towns. When land became available in the Southwest, whole families relocated to Kansas, Texas, and Oklahoma.[29] In addition, some black families and individuals pulled up stakes and moved to southern cities, though they seldom did so to accumulate funds to buy farms, as Europeans had done. Although these new black urbanites frequently made visits home and often remitted sums to those remaining on the land, they did not romanticize rural life.[30] For most, the break with the land was consciously permanent.

In the postbellum southern city, blacks already displayed conjugal patterns that deviated from those of either rural blacks or urban immigrants. Female-headed families increased, ranging from 20 to 40 percent of all black households, a trend that reflected changed circumstances.[31] First, unfavorable sex ratios forced many black women to live without mates. This pattern was already evident in 1860, by which time a redistribution of slaves based on more pressing rural needs reduced the population of black males in southern cities.[32] After the war, this imbalance was heightened because the two sexes did not always entertain the same migration destinations. Areas with job opportunities for women were not necessarily areas of job opportunities for men. In addition, overwork, exposure, and violence meant that urban black men were somewhat more vulnerable to an early death than their female counterparts.[33] Second, marital instability likely also contributed. In the urban South, black women, wives included, began to enter wage labor; demand for servants and laundresses was strong and competition from white women minimal. Black men's wages were so low that economic necessity now occasionally overruled black husbands' distaste for their wives' employment in the homes of whites. Likely too, the inability of women to avoid arduous labor under slavery made paid employment more acceptable. At the time of the 1890 census, approximately 40 percent of all black women in southern cities worked, and 22.5 percent of black wives reported gainful employment.[34] A considerable amount of research supports the hypothesis that wives' employment has an effect on marital outcomes. In particular, the smaller the wage gap between the sexes, the weaker the commitment to marriage. According to one investigator, wage rates between black males and females were nearly equal in turn-of-the-century southern cities, thus increasing the likelihood of illegitimacy and marital dissolution.[35]

A final factor that may have weakened marital bonds was the small number of children in black urban families. In southern cities, overcrowding, poor sanitation, and inadequate medical care encouraged the transmission of tuberculosis and venereal disease, ailments that caused low fertility and high infant mortality. Moreover, children who did survive seem to have left the parental home early, perhaps to work as migrant laborers or live-in servants. To the extent that offspring hold a couple together, black spouses were deprived of this motivation more frequently than their white counterparts.[36] Nevertheless, the conjugal family was the predominant family form, while at the same time the extended family remained an important source of strength and assistance for southern black urban dwellers. New arrivals frequently boarded with kin who had resettled earlier, and grandmothers looked after youngsters while their mothers worked.

Because the economic conditions that blacks encountered in the urban South were unattractive and disappointing, many chose to relocate again, this time in the North. Poor North–South rail linkages and the plentiful supply of immigrant labor had previously limited the number of blacks heading north. By the late nineteenth century, however, a pattern had developed in which rural blacks moved to southern cities to fill opportunities vacated by their predecessors who were settling in the North.[37] In the 1890s the number of black northern migrants reached 312,000, triple the previous decade, and another 267,000 made the trip in the first ten years of the twentieth century. This migration would likely have been even greater had it not been for the bountiful supply of cheap immigrant labor already available to northern labor markets.[38]

The condition of the northern black population varied considerably from place to place, with living standards somewhat higher in the smaller, newer cities of the West and Midwest than in the older, commercial cities of the eastern seaboard. But as blacks became a larger and more visible proportion of the northern labor force, racial discrimination intensified even in formerly more tolerant locations. In the crafts, blacks found themselves increasingly excluded from union membership or apprenticeships. In manufacturing, good industrial jobs were hard to secure. Black migrants, like other newcomers, occasionally entered industry as strikebreakers, only to find that once their employers had won, their welcome waned. Finally, in business, blacks found that even those services that were once their province, such as barbering and bootblacking, fell into the hands of immigrants. White customers seemed to prefer dealing with their own race. Blacks increasingly had to take up service jobs: janitor, elevator operator, porter, dishwasher, and the like. W.E.B. Dubois's landmark study of black Philadelphia in 1896 revealed that in the Seventh Ward, the section holding the largest number of black residents in the city, 45 percent of black men over age twenty-one were laborers and another 34 percent worked in service jobs. Although unemployment in service work was relatively low, wages in no way compensated for the steadier work.[39]

Given these conditions, it is not surprising that the black family patterns associated with southern cities persisted in northern urban areas. Some eastern locales had unbalanced sex ratios, again a result of both high male death rates and the tendency for men and women to settle in different places. The low earning potential of black husbands motivated wives to work outside the home, and health problems depressed fertility and sent children to the grave.[40]

In addition to a smaller proportion of husband-wife couples, black families differed from immigrant families in the adaptations typical of their teenaged children. These youngsters were more likely to remain in school than were immigrant children, perhaps because black youth could not easily find work, perhaps because few of their families could expect to own homes, or perhaps because of cultural commitments to education. If they did work and resided at home, black teens were rather more likely to keep their wages than surrender large proportions to parents in the way of immigrant teens. Finally, black offspring continued to leave their parents' households at younger ages than immigrant children, which reduced the size of black households in the process.[41]

Within the urban North, the proportion of black female-headed families varied by locale, generally running higher than among immigrants but not as high as among southern black urban dwellers. Some investigators have also noted intriguing distinctions by place of birth. For example, in Boston, black women born in the North exhibited higher rates of female headedness (31 percent) than those born in the South (21 percent). This pattern is significant because it suggests that later generations in the city would have more difficulty maintaining the conjugal family than did their migrant forbears.[42] At the same time many writers stress the continued importance of the extended family to migrants in the North. Family members could count upon one another in times of grief and joy. Migrants also received support from relatives in the South. Children were cared for by kin as young black women ventured north in search of work, visits home were frequent, and the exchange of funds continued.[43]

In searching for explanations for black-immigrant differences in family strategies, this chapter has so far emphasized sex ratios and economic opportunities, the most commonly cited scholarly contributions. But an additional distinctive feature of the black experience was uncovered by historian John Bodnar and his colleagues in interviews with black, Polish, and Italian men who entered Pittsburgh before World War I: black migrants and white immigrants found jobs differently.

Researchers had long recognized the importance of personal contacts for the immigrant job search, but the data collected by Bodnar and his associates revealed that black men were not easily able to assist one another in finding work. Employers in Pittsburgh's expanding steel mills and construction industry hired few if any blacks. When they did, they assigned black men the most arduous and disagreeable jobs, and when these ranks were filled, no more were wanted. Black men, therefore, were forced to find jobs as individuals, frequently going from workplace to workplace in the search for openings.[44]

Bodnar and his co-workers speculate that the situation encouraged black men to display more individualistic strategies for survival than their immigrant counterparts. Differences in methods of job procurement could have repercussions on family strategies as well. If black fathers were less able to assist their sons in finding jobs, these sons might prefer to remain in school or they might choose to leave home in the search for work. Either way, it is likely that ties of mutual obligation between black sons and their families were weaker than among their immigrant counterparts. If this hypothesis is correct, it may have significance for the structure of black family life.[45] Before taking up this question, two issues demand attention: Did the Pittsburgh situation typify the experience of black men, and was the individualized job search equally the lot for black women?

On the first matter, the Pittsburgh study represents one of the few detailed investigations of the early job-search behavior of black men. Unfortunately, none of the many studies in black communities devote systematic attention to this subject. Data on ethnic and racial employment patterns are also informative, however, because they permit the researcher to locate group niches, arenas in which a particular background enjoyed dominance. Particularly if such niches were expanding, interpersonal means of job access would become likely because, as already pointed out, hiring through contacts brings employers quality labor at low cost.

During the pre-World War I period, northern black men were disproportionately occupied in two arenas: service work and transportation.[46] In some service industries, black concentrations may have been large enough to support interpersonal recruitment. Hotels, for example, utilized primarily black bellboys and waiters. Katzman found that black headwaiters controlled access to subordinate jobs in Detroit.[47] Most service jobs, however, were situated in nonservice industries and formed a relatively inconsequencial proportion of the work force within a firm. In such instances it is doubtful that recruitment by insiders proceeded on a large scale. Although some black men worked as domestic servants, a form of employment in which, as discussed below, informal recruitment was considerable, women became an increasing proportion of such workers as time passed.

In transportation, the opportunities may have been somewhat greater. Though hostelry and stabling were essentially small operations, railroads absorbed large numbers of black males as sleeping-car porters and in track maintenance. These jobs represented the nonunionized portion of the railroad industry, hence blacks were not excluded. The segregated nature and popularity of black occupations in railroading suggests that sufficient opportunities existed to make personal referral a likely mode of entry.

At the same time, immigrants and their children experienced much higher levels of segregation in the sorts of job environments conducive to contact hiring. Disagreeable as many immigrant jobs may have been, those open to blacks were even worse, and that reality may have offered an additional incentive for black job seekers to search for work on their own. In sum, the available materials on black male employment patterns suggest that the Pittsburgh experience, with its heavy reliance on only a few industries, may have translated into especially individualistic job searches, but that in general, black men could not offer one another as much assistance in job procurement as immigrants did.

The experience of black women was very different. The demand for their services as domestics was probably greater than any specific demand for the labor of black males. As a result, black women were overwhelmingly segregated into employment as household workers, a situation that enabled them to assist one another to obtain jobs. Even when a given employer did not wish to engage another hired woman herself, she frequently knew someone who did. Black women shared with immigrant men the likelihood of migrating with foreknowledge of a job, as well as the chance of obtaining assistance from kin and friends when changing positions. Both groups occasionally found employment through agencies or advertisements, but personal recommendation remained the preferred method.[48]

Though household work was less well paying than most other forms of employment, between 1870 and 1910 the total number of women in such jobs grew steadily and the proportion of nonfarm black women employed in domestic service ran close to 80 percent. A gradual shift from live-in to day work brought improvements in working conditions, but few black women could escape the long hours, capricious working conditions, or demeaning status of the servant's life. Nevertheless, wage studies suggest that the earnings of household workers were at least as high as, sometimes higher than, those paid in other "feminine occupations" of the period.[49]

The implication for family life of female- rather than male-dominated "chain occupations" is open to conjecture. Goldin, whose study of 1880 Philadelphia reveals that black daughters were more likely to work if their mothers were employed, speculates that this finding was due to the ability of mothers to assist their daughters in locating work.[50] Moreover, the low fertility of black urban women suggests that their mutual assistance might extend beyond the conjugal family into the extended family. If, as is likely, black women found their services in great demand, and if the organization of their employment made them especially successful in assisting their near and distant kin in finding jobs, then black women would enjoy corresponding influence and authority in their associated kin groupings. This interpretation implies that urban structural conditions, rather than rural cultural legacies, provided a very early basis for differences in the relative power of the sexes and in the composition of the meaningful family unit among immigrants and blacks.

The Impact of War and Depression

The period between 1910 and 1920 brought a net gain of nearly seven hundred thousand blacks to the North, over half as a result of the great migration of the World War I era. Several factors "pushed" blacks out of the South, especially the eastward spread of the dreaded boll weevil, which devastated crops and prevented many tenant farmers from meeting their bills. On the "pull" side, the needs of wartime industry stimulated labor demand at a time when steamship travel was too perilous to transport the desired immigrant workers. Many northern industries had little choice but to send labor recruiters south in the hopes of securing extra hands.[51]

Although southern planters fought the seduction of their labor force, they could not stem the tide that increasingly flowed directly out of the countryside. The influential Chicago newspaper *Defender* exhorted relocation in its editorials, advertisements, and correspondence page. Moreover, most migrants remained in touch with a corps of kin and friends via letters, remittances, and visits home. Exposure to such experiences created many individuals who, like their European counterparts, formed a mass of potential migrants. When circumstances permitted, they too would go north, relying on those who went before to ease their way. One comparative study of male newcomers, however, indicates that although relatives readily opened their homes to black arrivals, they were less able to assist these migrants in finding jobs than were their European counterparts. One reason for this lower assistance was that black male migrants more frequently joined households composed entirely of females than did Europeans. The sexual division of labor made it difficult for these women to obtain useful information on job opportunities for their newly arrived male kin.[52]

The industrial nature of the new labor demand meant that many companies sought large numbers of male workers, and in some midwestern cities sex ratios favored males. At the same time, the proportion of black women in domestic service dropped between 1910 and 1920 as they welcomed the chance to exchange the drudgery of the household for the bustle of the factory. Several industries opened their doors to black workers, including steel in Pittsburgh, automobiles in Detroit, and slaughtering and meat-packing in Chicago. At the same time blacks invariably received the most arduous jobs in the factory, a situation they sometimes responded to with erratic work habits and sudden departures.[53]

With the end of the war came economic contraction, and returning white workers competed with blacks for employment. Black women were actively pushed out of industrial jobs and their proportions in service work climbed again. The willingness of some black men to work as strikebreakers, or for wages that were lower than those of whites, stirred racial hatred. Blacks and whites competed as well for scarce housing, and residential segregation intensified.[54]

The racial antagonisms, employment difficulties, and residential overcrowding of northern cities could not but exact a toll on black conjugal families. Sex ratios remained unbalanced and fertility continued low. In 1930 the U.S. census found that 22.7 percent of black families in the State of New York were headed by a woman, compared to only 12.0 percent in rural Georgia.[55]

The effect of the global economic downturn of the 1930s was even more pernicious. As industry after industry cut back on labor, black men lost their jobs more quickly and more completely than other American males. Already in 1929 the Chicago Urban League noted, "Every week we receive information regarding the discharge of additional race workers who are being replaced by workers of other races." The small but prospering black business sector that had begun to serve the new black ghettoes fell into bankruptcy. And, when the earnings of black women were needed more than ever before, this group endured the highest unemployment rates in the nation. The surplus of domestic workers resulted in "slave markets" on many city street corners, where women would congregate in the hopes of negotiating a day's work from housewives driving by.[56]

Major unemployment and poverty, not only for blacks but for the nation as a whole, compelled the federal government to introduce two new policy initiatives: the federally subsidized (though often locally implemented) welfare state, and the legitimation of industrial labor unions. Prima facie, it could be expected that these changes would benefit blacks, whose disproportionate poverty made them appropriate candidates for financial assistance. Racism and lack of skill had prevented their profiting from the earlier successes of craft unions, but in the new industrial organization of the Congress of Industrial Organizations (CIO), the needs of black workers were at last formally addressed.[57]

Evidence of the Depression's impact on the urban conjugal family appears in the first perceptible rise in the proportion of black female-headed families. In 1940, 28 percent of nonwhite families in the northeastern states had a female head. White urbanites also experienced slightly higher rates during this period; rural folk of both races did not. Another sign of the deteriorating urban condition was the decline in black departures from the South; more than half of all black migration in the 1930s occurred between cities.[58] The necessity to search a wide area for jobs probably motivated this behavior, which further strained black conjugal families. Blacks coped by relying more on relatives, neighbors, and friends. As one black domestic worker remarked, "You got to have somebody that cares."[59]

While the fortunes of blacks seesawed through the 1920s and plunged in the 1930s, several developments combined to assure that by 1940 immigrants and their children were on their way to a better life. Following World War I, the U.S. labor force became increasingly white collar in character, providing new jobs for more educated whites, generally of native-born stock. This change created vacancies in upper reaches of the blue-collar ranks, opportunities that some southern and eastern Europeans were able to obtain. For example, during the 1920s, supervisors and foremen in the packinghouses and steel plants of Bethlehem, Pennsylvania, were usually Poles, Austrians, and Lithuanians.[60] At the same time changes in U.S. policy made immigration difficult for new arrivals from Europe, and their admission was almost wholly restricted after 1924. As access to the United States became limited, immigrants confronted the irreversibility of return migration. Sojourners turned into settlers, a growing proportion of whom had considerable experience in American industry.

Together, occupational shifts, a dearth of unsophisticated European newcomers, and racist sentiments combined to assure that the new black migrants received the least desirable jobs while many immigrants and their children moved up.[61] But immigrant workers found corresponding progress in wages and working conditions impeded by the continuing availability of black strike-breakers and the growth of corporate welfare paternalism. Union membership plummeted and organized labor struggled to survive.

The Depression, however, changed the balance of power between management and unions. Although immigrant men experienced lower unemployment rates than blacks or women, their family economies were pushed to the limit. Immigrant children, and less frequently wives, sought any kind of paid employment. As entire industries slowed down, workers skilled and unskilled were thrown out of work and national disorder became endemic. Industrial workers became impatient with the moderate policies of the American Federation of Labor (AFL) and launched new, industry-wide initiatives under the CIO. The government's legitimation of unions in the Wagner Act of 1935 and the Fair Labor Standards Act of 1938 forced employers to listen.[62] The success of the unionization drive placed the immigrant industrial worker on firmer footing than ever before. Labor had improved its position without changing jobs or the qualifications associated with those jobs.[63] For many southern and eastern European men, a wage that could support a family was available at last.

World War II and Beyond

In the postwar era, working-class southern and eastern Europeans and their children held good jobs in the unionized industries, such as steel and autos, that most benefited from the new prosperity. During economic downswings they usually had enough seniority to avoid a layoff, or to be rehired quickly when they did not. Financial security often permitted a father to support the entire family; if his wages were low, or if the family experienced unusual expenses, daughters might help out, and wives began to enter the labor market as well.[64]

By the 1950s second-generation eastern and southern Europeans began to make considerable gains in education, with the maturing cohorts of most groups pushing further ahead of northern-born blacks and even ahead of native whites of native parentage. In his complex attempt to explain this development, Stanley Lieberson holds shifts in unemployment patterns most responsible: between 1930 and 1950, northern black unemployment fell somewhat, but that of eastern and southern European immigrants dropped sharply.[65] Probably the major cause of the educational changes was that eastern and southern European immigrant parents were concentrated in unionized jobs, which provided both the security and the income necessary for the prolonged education of offspring.

How much education sons pursued became the largest single determinant of their eventual occupational status. Additional schooling might improve opportunities even in traditional realms, as a Croatian miner explained: "When they started to mechanize mining, it came to the point where they needed more foremen. That's about the time our people started educating themselves a bit more. Our boys would go out to high school and then take night courses in mining. Slowly they moved in there and took everything over."[66]

Some groups, such as Italians, were slower to seize educational opportunities and concentrated in fields like construction, where parental intercession continued to be the admission ticket to the union and to jobs. Indeed, a study of four northern labor markets (Chicago, Detroit, Philadelphia, and New York) showed that as recently as 1970, eastern and southern Europeans remained overconcentrated in their traditional industries.[67]

Extended education exposed students to the individualistic values of ambition and self-fulfillment. Job sponsors were less often kin than colleagues or acquaintances encountered at school or in other nonfamily settings. Greater educational and occupational opportunities, in turn, led to new friends, intermarriage, ethnically mixed neighborhoods, and smaller families. Today, if children work, they keep their own earnings. Wives increasingly leave home to supplement the family income or to find self-fulfillment. Divorce has appeared, frequently followed by remarriage. The family has become an emotional link between distinct individuals with different, sometimes conflicting, agendas. The descendants of southern and eastern Europeans have assimilated.[68]

Blacks have had a very different experience. In the immediate postwar period, a number of factors continued to depress black opportunities, particularly unimpeded migration from the South, racism, and union policies. The large influx of low-wage labor from the South dampened the opportunities of established northern blacks by stimulating discriminatory behavior among higher-paid white workers. The influx also had a draining effect on the energies and resources of their earlier settled kin. Early in this century policies such as the "Gentlemen's Agreement" with Japan (1907) and the National Origins Act (1924), although racist in intent, caused a decline in immigration that permitted those already here to expend more of their resources on themselves. Such laws could not apply to blacks, who were internal migrants. Ironically, it was New Deal legislation that provided subsidies for leaving land fallow and for the mechanization of agriculture that pushed more and more blacks out of southern rural livelihoods. Not until the late 1960s did black movement out of the South begin to abate.[69]

Northern whites exhibited increasing racism toward the large influx of relatively unschooled and unskilled blacks, confining them to central cities and inferior public services whenever possible. Because later-generation urban blacks, unlike descendants of white immigrants, wore their group membership on their skin, they were as likely to experience discrimination as their country cousins.

The discrimination operated not only on a personal level but in an institutional fashion. Institutional racism was especially obvious in the formalization of seniority rights in union agreements. Unions, long concerned about man-

agement's discretion over hirings, firings, and promotions, introduced seniority rights that protected more-experienced workers from random or unanticipat-
ed employer decisions. By the same token, seniority rules hindered the promotion and job security of workers with the least experience, a group
disproportionately black. As a result, black unemployment rates have been
running roughly twice those of whites since 1954. According to Lieberson, the
large difference in the unemployment rates of blacks and immigrants was a
major explanatory factor in the far greater levels of college attendance reported
by the latter group in the early postwar period. The higher the group unemployment rate, the greater the possibility that parental resources are insufficient
for a long extension of children's educations.[70]

In her insightful analysis of the causes of high black unemployment, Edna
Bonacich also faults organized labor, although with a different emphasis. She
argues that rising labor costs, particularly for unskilled and semiskilled labor,
have induced employers to cut costs in ways that have disproportionately
harmed black workers. Among management's most pernicious responses have
been automation and plant relocations overseas or to the U.S. South, where
labor is cheap and unions are weak.[71]

Indeed, over the past twenty years, foreign competition, as well as a host of
factors too complex to delineate here, reduced the manufacturing sector as
output of services strengthened. Opportunities for industrial labor have vastly
declined, while openings in low-paying service jobs and high-tech professions
remain strong. These changes have combined with government initiatives that
flowed out of the civil rights movement to create a situation that William
Wilson describes as a polarization of the black community. By this he means
that civil rights laws and affirmative action demands have assured a market for
well-trained middle-class black men who can meet the continuing need for
upper-white-collar workers, and that manufacturing contractions and relocations out of central cities have left poorly educated, marginal black males
without meaningful work.[72]

A recent study of the income-determination process among young male
household heads illustrates the polarization process. Young black men with
college degrees are earning incomes roughly comparable to their white counterparts; those without a high school diploma receive substantially less than similarly qualified whites.[73] The labor force participation rate of young black males
in central cities has dropped drastically. Some observers believe that these
statistics reflect a rejection of dead-end, menial employment by these young,
urban-reared blacks, who, like their ethnic counterparts of the 1930s, seek
more attractive jobs than their migrant forebears required. But the possibility
of upgrading job rewards without changing the tasks and skill requirements
associated with those jobs no longer exists. As a result, increasing numbers of
poorly educated ghetto youth reject the work ethnic and find the "irregular
economy" of crime hard to resist.[74]

The recent economic experience of black women has been somewhat different. Across occupational levels, they now face very small disadvantages in

earnings when compared to similarly qualified white women. Their proportions in domestic service have dropped sharply, and their representation in white-collar fields has enlarged. Employment figures for 1986 revealed, for the first time, a slight excess in the numbers of employed black women compared to employed black men, a sign of the increasing decline in the economic resources of men relative to women. Women with children who lack jobs and husbands qualify for a variety of welfare benefits, though the extent and value of these outlays has dropped in recent years.[75]

From this chapter's perspective, the essential issue is: What are the implications of these trends for the black family? Already in the mid-1960s, Daniel Patrick Moynihan focused public attention on a decline in the proportion of black conjugal families, noting that about one-quarter of urban black families were female-headed. Black fertility had overtaken white, and the proportion of illegimate births was rising.[76] In fact, while the shift in urban fertility represented a historical reversal, the proportion of female-headed families had not yet reached depression levels. Moynihan was correct, however; a new trend was under way.

In the ensuing years the black conjugal family has become even less prevalent, particularly as a result of changing family patterns among young black women, who compose a growing proportion of the black community. Out-of-wedlock births have skyrocketed, particularly among teens, although the fertility rate of these young women has actually declined. The illegitimacy crisis reflects the growing reluctance of pregnant teens to marry the fathers of their children, especially in the central city. Not only are large proportions of black women remaining single but divorce and separation rates are high, and remarriage is considerably less common than among whites.[77]

Statistics make clear that the conjugal family is far more prevalent among middle-class than among poor blacks, though racial differences still remain within the more affluent group.[78] Potential causes of these differences include the large proportion of educated, white-collar black women relative to their male counterparts and the social mores that still encourage a woman's marrying her economic equal or superior. There are simply not enough high-status black men available to satisfy demand, a situation that leads some educated black women to forgo marriage. Middle-class black men have less incentive to remain unhappily married in so favorable a marriage market. But those least likely to marry are poor black teens. The males have little desire to accept a responsibility they cannot meet, and the females cannot locate a desirable partner. According to one estimate in 1982, as many as 46 percent of working-age black men were either unemployed or out of the labor force, and this proportion was increasingly unfavorable the younger the age.[79] High incarceration rates and the risk of death by homicide pose serious problems for young black men. Many have argued that welfare programs, particularly those that provide benefits only when a male is not present in the household, have contributed to this situation, but evidence on this point is mixed. Welfare rolls increased most dramatically in the late 1960s and 1970s, particularly in the

North, but declined in the 1980s. The proportion of black families headed by women, on the other hand, rose steadily from the 1960s through the 1980s in both the South and the North.[80]

One development that welfare has accomplished, however, is to give poor black women, rather than poor black men, economic resources. Some writers see job prospects, welfare, and extended kin networks as combined factors that reduce the attractiveness of marriage for poor black women. Carol Stack states:

> The emptiness and hopelessness of the job experience for black men and women, the control over meager [AFDC] resources by women, and the security of the kin network, militate against successful marriage or long term relationships. . . . The life histories of adults show that the attempts by women to set up separate households with their children and husbands, or boyfriends, are short-lived. Lovers fight, jobs are scarce, houses are condemned, and needs for services among kin arise. . . . Calamities and crises contribute to the constant shifts in residence. Newly formed households are successive recombinations of the same domestic network of adults and children, quite often in the same dwellings.[81]

But, the extended kin network remains important for blacks. The 1980 census reports that 30 percent of all black households contain extended kin, compared to 18 percent of white households.[82] Moreover, even when black family members do not have the same domicile, they extend significant help to one another. One important, underresearched area concerns the quantity and quality of extended family linkages between poor blacks and those who are better off. Studies have demonstrated that the extended family is important to the black middle class, though the scope of mutual assistance is probably more limited than among the poor. From her study of 178 middle-income black families in a mid-Atlantic coast city, three-quarters of whom were married, Harriette McAdoo concluded that the extended family remained a meaningful locus of emotion and exchange in the overwhelming majority of cases.[83] Interestingly, the amount of exchange reported did not vary with marital condition. But the literature to date reflects disagreement on how frequently extended kinship ties cross class lines. Some researchers maintain that the needs of the impoverished extended family are so great that upwardly mobile blacks must distance themselves from their less successful relatives or be completely drained by the latter's expectations.[84] One small study, however, finds evidence that class boundaries do not sever extended kin ties, especially if the more successful remain geographically proximate to their kin.[85]

Even if extended kinship groups do contain members of varying social classes, the crucial issue is the sorts of assistance that can be rendered. Help in locating work was a central dynamic of the immigrant family economy. Clearly, such assistance would be invaluable for blacks today. Among the few commentators on this subject, Elmer and Joanne Martin explain: "Most extended families can do little to help a family member become better-off economically or attain middle class status. They can only assure that the basic necessities are met. The family member who 'makes it' does so largely on his own initiative, though with encouragement from family members."[86]

In an increasingly credentialist society, there is little a white-collar worker can do for a high school dropout. And within that white-collar world, as suggested above, relationships between schoolmates and co-workers are more successful ways of finding jobs than family connections. Thus, even as many blacks move ahead, there is little the successful ones can do for the less fortunate. Progress has come too late to invoke the sorts of family mechanisms that southern and eastern Europeans used to secure employment for themselves and their sons. Ironically, when these immigrants were unskilled and suffered discrimination, they did not have to go it alone. But their black counterparts in today's labor market do not enjoy the same advantages.

Conclusion

This chapter has traced the historical experience of immigrants and Afro-Americans from the time that they entered urban labor markets to the present in an effort to capture the most salient differences in work and family relationships. The analysis reveals an initial precariousness in the employment experience of working-class black men unknown to their immigrant counterparts. Immigrant wives rarely worked for wages; black wives had less choice in the matter. This situation placed them on a more equal footing with their spouses but weakened their marriages in the process. Factors such as black women's ability to help one another in the job market, as well as the small size of black families, and the threat of premature widowhood added stresses to the black marriage rarely faced by immigrants.

In the ensuing decades, immigrants and their children enjoyed considerable economic progress. White wives, ethnic or not, began to enter the work force in large numbers and their greater independence heightened their propensity to dissolve an unhappy marriage. But because the economic opportunities of white men remain promising, remarriage is an attractive option and the conjugal family has not lost popularity. Some blacks, too, moved up the economic ladder. One might therefore expect that among the black middle class, marital patterns would mirror those of whites. That they do not reflects the lower proportion of middle-class black men relative to demand and the favorable remarriage chances these men enjoy. Among the black poor, the situation is far more serious because the relative resources between the sexes now favor women even more than in the past. The drastic reduction in the job opportunities of uneducated young black males, the greater wage discrimination experienced by these men relative to their female counterparts, their high death and incarceration rates, and the availability of welfare (soon to be workfare) combine to give poor black women little incentive to marry.

Were it the case that unmarried women could enjoy the same standard of living as their married counterparts or that their children would enjoy the same educational and economic opportunities that are open to the offspring of two-parent families, concern over the rise in black female-headed households would simply reflect normative preferences in life-styles. But such is not the case. Indeed, the dual-earner family has become an increasingly popular mechanism for coping with the inflation and stagnation that have alternately plagued the U.S. economy of the late twentieth century. The absence of a male earner handicaps any family, black or white. Yet, in both past and the present, this form of handicap has fallen disproportionately on black Americans.

The conclusion of this chapter must be that the demands of the economy were the prime movers of black family organization in the nineteenth century and remain so today. Unless the economic position of lower-class black males is improved, it is difficult to see how the conjugal family among poor blacks can be strengthened. Benjamin Hooks, executive director of the NAACP, has argued that the black community has the institutional and voluntary resources to be effective in this task, a position that at best seems unduly optimistic.[87] In the absence of drastic structural change, the extended family may become the primary refuge for increasing numbers of disadvantaged Afro-Americans.

NOTES

1. U.S. Bureau of the Census, *Statistical Abstract of the United States: 1986* (Washington, D.C., 1985), p. 40.

2. For data on the economic disadvantage of female-headed families, see Reynolds Farley and Walter R. Allen, *The Color Line and the Quality of Life in America* (New York: Russell Sage Foundation, 1987), p. 167; and Paula England and George Farkas, *Households, Employment, and Gender: A Social, Economic, and Demographic View* (New York: Aldine De Gruyter, 1986), pp. 149, 163. England and Farkas also provide information about the economic effects of divorce on the family; see p. 66.

3. E. Franklin Frazier, *On Race Relations*, ed. G. Franklin Edwards (Chicago: University of Chicago Press, 1968), pp. 191–95, 202–8.

4. For a useful summary of historical research on black families, as well as data regarding their current plight, see Marian Wright Edelman, *Families in Peril: An Agenda for Social Change* (Cambridge: Harvard University Press, 1987), chap. 1. Additional useful discussion can be found in Andrew Hacker, "American Apartheid," *New York Review of Books* December 3, 1987, pp. 26–31.

5. William I. Thomas and Florian Znaniecki, *The Polish Peasant in Europe and America*, ed. Eli Zaretsky (Urbana: University of Illinois Press, 1984), pp. 272–80, epitomizes the old view; John Bodnar, *The Transplanted: A History of Immigrants in Urban America* (Bloomington: Indiana University Press, 1985), chap. 2, well represents the new.

6. Frederick Engels, *The Origin of the Family, Private Property, and the State* (New York: International Publishers, 1972), pp. 137–38; Gary Becker, *A Treatise on the Family* (Cambridge: Harvard University Press, 1981), pp. 242–43; Robert Staples, "Changes in Black Family Structure: The Conflict Between Family Ideology and Structural Conditions," in *The Black Family: Essays and Studies*, 3d ed., ed. Robert Staples (Belmont, Calif.: Wadsworth, 1986), pp. 23–25.

7. Charlotte Erickson, *American Industry and the European Immigrant, 1860–1885* (New York: Russell & Russell, 1957), p. vii, chaps. 5, 7; D. Georgevitch, N. Maric, and N. Moravcevich, *Serbian Americans and Their Communities of Cleveland* (Cleveland: Cleveland State University, 1977), pp. 103–4; Gerd Korman, *Industrialization, Immigrants, and Americanizers* (Madison: State Historical Society of Wisconsin, 1967), p. 29. On formal methods of recruitment, see also Ivan Cizmic, "Yugoslav Immigrants in the U.S. Labor Movement, 1880–1929," in *American Labor and Immigration History, 1877–1929*, ed. D. Hoerder (Urbana: University of Illinois Press, 1983), p. 180; Grace Abbott, "The Chicago Employment Agency and the Immigrant Worker," *American Journal of Sociology* 14 (1908): 289–308; Shelby M. Harrison, *Public Employment Offices: Their Purpose, Structure, and Methods* (New York: Russel Sage Foundation, 1924), pp. 593–97.

8. Richard Alba, *Italian Americans: Into the Twilight of Ethnicity* (Englewood, N.J.: Prentice-Hall, 1985), pp. 51–55; Caroline Golab, "The Polish Experience in Philadelphia: The Migrant Laborers Who Did Not Come," in *The Ethnic Experience in Pennsylvania*, ed. J. Bodnar (Lewisburg, Pa.: Bucknell University Press, 1979), p. 52. On employer stereotypes, see Niles Carpenter, *Nationality, Color, and Economic Opportunity in Buffalo* (Westport, Conn.: Negro Universities Press, 1970), pp. 108–11; Caroline Golab, *Immigrant Destinations* (Philadelphia: Temple University Press, 1977), p. 61; Virginia Yans-McLaughlin, *Family and Community: Italian Immigrants in Buffalo, 1880–1939* (Ithaca: Cornell University Press, 1977), pp. 37–38. On the padrone system, see especially Edwin Fenton, *Immigrants and Unions, A Case Study: Italians and American Labor, 1870–1920* (New York: Arno Press, 1975), chaps. 3, 4.

9. Although many scholars have believed that personalistic methods of job recruitment are incompatible with a modern, industrial order (see, for example, David Katzman, *Seven Days a Week: Women and Domestic Service in Industrializing America* [New York: Oxford University Press, 1978], p. 99), research on methods of job procurement does not support this interpretation. For a discussion of these issues, see Mark Granovetter, *Getting a Job* (Cambridge: Harvard University Press, 1974), and M. S. Grieco, "Family Structure and Industrial Employment: The Role of Information and Migration," *Journal of Marriage and the Family* 44 (1982):701–7. For explanations from an economic point of view, see Albert Rees, "Information Networks in Labor Markets," in *Readings in Labor Market Analysis*, ed. J. Burton, L. Benham, W. Vaughn, and R. Flanagan (New York: Holt, Rinehart, & Winston, 1971), pp. 245–52, and George Stigler, "Information in the Labor Market," in *Readings in Labor Market Analysis*, ed. J. Burton, L. Benham, W. Vaughn, and R. Flanagan (New York: Holt, Rinehart, & Winston, 1971), pp. 233–43.

10. Quoted in Thomas and Znaniecki, *The Polish Peasant in Europe and America*, p. 133.

11. Charles Tilly, "Transplanted Networks," this volume.

12. J. S. MacDonald and L. D. MacDonald, "Chain Migration, Ethnic Neighborhood Formation, and Social Networks." *Milbank Memorial Fund Quarterly* 52 (1964): 84–90; Donna Gabaccia, *From Sicily to Elizabeth Street* (Albany: SUNY Press, 1983), pp. 59–61; John Briggs, *An Italian Passage: Immigrants to Three American Cities, 1890–1930* (New Haven: Yale University Press, 1978), pp. 69–73; Josef Barton, *Peasants and Strangers: Italians, Rumanians, and Slovaks in an American City, 1890–1950* (Cambridge: Harvard University Press, 1975), pp. 49–57; Ewa Morawska, "Sociological Ambivalence: The Case of East European Peasant Immigrant Workers in America, 1890s–1930s," *Qualitative Sociology* 10 (1987): 225–50.

13. Dino Cinel, *From Italy to San Francisco: The Immigrant Experience* (Stanford:

Stanford University Press, 1982), pp. 1, 64–65; Golab, "The Polish Experience in Phila-delphia." pp. 50–51; Ewa Morawska, *For Bread with Butter: Life Worlds of East Central Europeans in Johnstown, Pennsylvania, 1890–1940* (New York: Cambridge University Press, 1985), pp. 69–70.

14. Michael Piore, *Birds of Passage: Migrant Labor and Industrial Societies* (New York: Cambridge University Press, 1979), pp. 149–54; Bodnar, *The Transplanted*, pp. 53–54; Donald Tricarico, *The Italians of Greenwich Village* (Staten Island, N.Y.: Center for Migration Studies, 1984), p. 4; Ewa Morawska, "The Sociology and Historiography of Immigration," this volume.

15. David Gordon, Richard Edwards, and Michael Reich, *Segmented Work, Divided Workers: The Historical Transformation of Labor in the United States* (New York: Cambridge University Press, 1982), pp. 157–60; Robert M. Jackson, *The Formation of Craft Labor Markets* (New York: Academic Press, 1984), pp. 29, 318–19; David Montgomery, "Nationalism, American Patriotism, and Class Consciousness among Immigrant Workers in the U.S. in the Epoch of World War I," in *Struggle a Hard Battle*, ed. D. Hoerder (DeKalb: Northern Illinois University Press, 1986), p. 345.

16. Christine Bose, "Household Resources and U.S. Women's Work: Factors Affecting Gainful Employment at the Turn of the Century," *American Sociological Review* 49 (1984): 488–89; John Sharpless and Joan Rury, "The Political Economy of Women's Work, 1900–1920," *Social Science History* 4 (1980): 323; Judith Smith, *Family Connections* (Albany: SUNY Press, 1985), pp. 23–24; Elizabeth Ewen, *Immigrant Women in the Land of Dollars: Life and Culture on the Lower East Side, 1890–1925* (New York: Monthly Review Press, 1985), pp. 104–6.

17. John Bodnar, Roger Simon, and Michael Weber, *Lives of Their Own: Blacks, Italians, and Poles in Pittsburgh, 1900–1960* (Urbana: University of Illinois Press, 1982), pp. 102–8; Morawska, *For Bread with Butter*, pp. 127–33; Bodnar, *The Transplanted*, pp. 77–78.

18. Yans-McLaughlin, *Family and Community*, p. 177. Morawska, in *For Bread with Butter*, pp. 144–45, argues that home ownership satisfied needs both for achievement and security.

19. On the relationship between home owning and education, see David Hogan, "Education and the Making of the Chicago Working Class, 1880–1930," *History of Education Quarterly*, 1978, pp. 232–36. On the frequency and purposes of homeowning among immigrants, see especially Bodnar, Simon, and Weber, *Lives of Their Own*, pp. 153–55, 179–80; and Olivier Zunz, *The Changing Face of Inequality: Urbanization, Industrial Development, and Immigrants in Detroit, 1880–1920* (Chicago: University of Chicago Press, 1982), pp. 152–61.

20. John Bodnar, "Immigration and Modernization: The Case of Slavic Peasants in Industrial America," *Journal of Social History* 10 (1976): 57; Morawska, *For Bread with Butter*, pp. 194–95; Joseph Lopreato, *Italian Americans* (New York: Random House, 1970), p. 145; Smith, *Family Connections*, pp. 65–66; Cinel, *From Italy to San Francisco*, p. 144.

21. Bodnar, Simon, and Weber, *Lives of Their Own*, pp. 245–45; Cinel, *From Italy to San Francisco*, p. 204; Herbert Hill, "Race and Ethnicity in Organized Labor: The Historical Sources of Resistance to Affirmative Action," in *Ethnicity and the Work Force*, ed. W. Van Horne and T. Tonnesen (Madison: University of Wisconsin Press, 1985), pp. 44–45; Ira Katznelson, *Black Men, White Cities* (London: Oxford University Press, 1973), pp. 111–13.

22. Among married women in 1890, the census reported that 2.2 percent of native white women of native parentage worked, compared to 2.7 percent of native white

women of foreign parentage, and 3.0 percent of foreign-born women. For single women, the analogous statistics were 18.1 percent, 30.5 percent, and 58.4 percent. Department of Interior, Census Office, *Report of the Population of the United States at the Eleventh Census: 1890, Part II* (Washington, D.C.: Government Printing Office, 1897), p. cxxix. However, scholars have long believed that early censuses underestimated women's employment. When Judith Smith compared oral history data with census manuscripts on identical individuals, she found this to be the case. See Smith, *Family Connections*, p. 191.

23. Leslie Woodcock Tentler, *Wage-Earning Women: Industrial Work and Family Life in the United States, 1900–1930* (New York: Oxford University Press, 1979), pp. 105–7; Bodnar, *The Transplanted*, p. 62; Yans-McLaughlin, *Family and Community*, p. 173; Smith *Family Connections*, p. 59. On occupational segregation among women, see Christine Bose, "Employment of Black and Ethnic Women in 1900" (Paper delivered at the Annual Meeting of the American Sociological Association, August 1984), San Antonio, pp. 6–7 and tables 1, 2.

24. John Bodnar, Michael Weber, and Roger Simon, "Migration, Kinship, and Urban Adjustment: Blacks and Poles in Pittsburgh, 1900–1930," *Journal of American History* 66 (1979): 565; Bodnar, "Immigration and Modernization," p. 45; Yans-McLaughlin, *Family and Community*, pp. 262–63; Francis Ianni, *A Family Business: Kinship and Social Control in Organized Crime* (New York: Russell Sage Foundation, 1972), p. 156; Donna Gabaccia, "Kinship, Culture, and Migration: A Sicilian Example," *Journal of American Ethnic History* 3 (1984): 48.

Although familism was a dominant value for the second generation, conformity to parents' expectations did not proceed without conflict, especially among more recent cohorts. See Irvin L. Child, *Italian or American? The Second Generation in Conflict* (New York: Russell & Russell, 1970), pp. 76, 93–94, 179; Cinel, *From Italy to San Francisco*, pp. 127–29; Robert Orsi, *The Madonna of 115th Street: Family and Community in Italian Harlem, 1880–1950* (New Haven: Yale University Press, 1985), chap. 5.

25. Secretary of the Interior, *Population of the United States in 1860* (Washington, D.C.: Government Printing Office, 1864), p. xii.

26. On family reunification, see Joel Williamson, *The Crucible of Race* (New York: Oxford University Press, 1984), pp. 44–45. On Reconstruction, see William Wilson, *The Declining Significance of Race* (Chicago: University of Chicago Press, 1978), pp. 52–60. On Southern agriculture and debt peonage, see Neil Fligstein, *Going North: Migration of Blacks and Whites from the South, 1900–1950* (New York: Academic Press, 1981), chap. 2; and Michael Reich, *Racial Inequality: A Political-Economic Analysis* (Princeton: Princeton University Press, 1981), pp. 226–33. For a vivid personal description of how peonage operated, see David Katzman and William Tuttle, Jr., eds., *Plain Folk: The Life Stories of Undistinguished Americans* (Urbana: University of Illinois Press, 1982), pp. 151–63.

27. Herbert Gutman, *The Black Family in Slavery and Freedom, 1750–1925* (New York: Pantheon, 1976), p. 211; Demitri Shimkin and Victor Uchendu, "Persistence, Borrowing, and Adaptive Changes in Black Kinship Systems: Some Issues and Their Significance," in *The Extended Family in Black Societies*, ed. D. Shimkin, E. Shimkin, and D. Frate (The Hague: Mouton, 1978), pp. 392–95.

28. Jacqueline Jones, *Labor of Love, Labor of Sorrow* (New York: Basic Books, 1985), pp. 84, 92, 333, 336–37; Gutman, *The Black Family in Slavery and Freedom*, p. 489; Elizabeth Pleck, *Black Migration and Poverty: Boston, 1865–1900* (New York: Academic Press, 1979), p. 184. The cited study is by Jones, *Labor of Love, Labor of Sorrow*, pp. 84–85. On the employment patterns of female former slaves and their

reluctance to work in the fields, see Jones, *Labor of Love, Labor of Sorrow*, p. 90; Gutman, *The Black Family in Slavery and Freedom*, pp. 167–68, 443; and Williamson, *The Crucible of Race*, p. 47.

29. Jones, *Labor of Love, Labor of Sorrow*, p. 92; Clyde Kiser, *Sea Island to City* (New York: AMS Press, 1967), p. 93; Elizabeth Bethel, *Promiseland: A Century of Life in a Negro Community* (Philadelphia: Temple University Press, 1981), pp. 124–27; Nell Irvin Painter, *Exodusters: Black Migration to Kansas after Reconstruction* (Lawrence: University Press of Kansas, 1986), pp. 184–87, 194.

30. Elizabeth Clark-Lewis, "This Work Had A' End: The Transition from Live-In to Day Work," Working Paper 2 (Memphis: Memphis State University, Center for Research on Women, July 1985), pp. 32–33.

31. Pleck, *Black Migration and Poverty*, pp. 183–84.

32. Claudia Dale Goldin, "Urbanization and Slavery: The Issue of Compatibility," in *The New Urban History: Quantitative Explorations by American Historians*, ed. Leo Schnore (Princeton: Princeton University Press, 1975), p. 234.

33. Zane L. Miller, "Urban Blacks in the South, 1865–1920: An Analysis of Some Quantitative Data on Richmond, Savannah, New Orleans, Louisville, and Birmingham," in *The New Urban History: Quantitative Explorations by American Historians*, ed. Leo Schnore (Princeton: Princeton University Press, 1975), p. 193.

34. Miller, "Urban Blacks in the South, 1865–1920," p. 187; Jones, *Labor of Love, Labor of Sorrow*, pp. 112–24; Claudia Dale Goldin, "Female Labor Force Participation: The Origins of Black and White Differences, 1870 and 1880," *Journal of Economic History* 37 (1977): 101; Goldin, "Urbanization and Slavery," p. 95.

35. Warren Sanderson, "Herbert Gutman's *The Black Family in Slavery and Freedom, 1750–1925*: A Cliometric Reconsideration," *Social Science History* 3 (1979): 79–80. See also Becker, *A Treatise on the Family*, pp. 76, 231–32.

36. Stanley Engerman, "Black Fertility and Family Structure in the U.S., 1880–1940," *Journal of Family History* 2 (1977), tables 2, 5; Herman Lantz and Lewellyn Hendrix, "Black Fertility and the Black Family in the Nineteenth Century: A Reexamination of the Past," *Journal of Family History* 3 (1978): 255–58; Jones, *Labor of Love, Labor of Sorrow*, p. 123; Miller, "Urban Blacks in the South," p. 193; Farley and Allen, *The Color Line and the Quality of Life in America*, pp. 20–23.

37. Golab, *Immigrant Destinations*, p. 20; Miller, "Urban Blacks in the South," pp. 190–92; W.E.B. DuBois, *The Philadelphia Negro: A Social Study* (New York: Schocken Books, 1971). p. 76.

38. Carter Woodson, *A Century of Negro Migration* (New York: AMS Press, 1970), pp. 91–95; Michael Banton, *Racial and Ethnic Competition* (Cambridge: Cambridge University Press, 1983), p. 261; Daniel Johnson and Rex Campbell, *Black Migration in America: A Social Demographic History* (Durham: Duke University Press, 1981), p. 69.

39. David Gerber, *Black Ohio and the Color Line, 1860–1915* (Urbana: University of Illinois Press, 1976), chaps. 4, 11; Kenneth Kusmer, *A Ghetto Takes Shape: Black Cleveland, 1870–1930* (Urbana: University of Illinois Press, 1976); David Brody, *Steelworkers in America: The Nonunion Era* (Cambridge: Harvard University Press, 1960), pp. 184–85 and chap. 4; David Katzman, *Before the Ghetto: Black Detroit in the Nineteenth Century* (Urbana: University of Illinois Press, 1973), pp. 115–17; St. Claire Drake and Horace Cayton, *Black Metropolis* (New York: Harcourt, Brace, 1945), pp. 302–3; DuBois, *The Philadelphia Negro*, pp. 100–101.

Regarding unemployment, Suzanne Model finds that in 1910 New York City blacks averaged 2.33 weeks unemployment, compared to 4.51 weeks for Italians and 5.35 weeks for Jews. See Suzanne Model, "Ethnic Bonds in the Work Place: Blacks, Italians, and Jews in New York City" (Ph.D. Diss., University of Michigan, 1985), p. 184. A similar interpretation appears in Alexander Keyssar, *Out of Work: The First Century of Unemployment in Massachusetts* (New York: Cambridge University Press, 1986), pp. 88–89.

40. Claudia Goldin, "Family Strategies and the Family Economy in the Late Nineteenth Century: The Role of Secondary Workers," in *Philadelphia: Work, Space, Family, and Group Experience in the Nineteenth Century*, ed. T. Hershberg (New York: Oxford University Press, 1981), pp. 298, 287; DuBois, *The Philadelphia Negro*, p. 165; Model, "Ethnic Bonds in the Work Place," p. 455.

41. Goldin, "Family Strategies and the Family Economy in the Late Nineteenth Century," p. 298; Bodnar, Weber, and Simon, "Migration, Kinship, and Urban Adjustment," pp. 559–60, 563, 565.

42. Pleck, *Black Migration and Poverty*, pp. 166, 182–85. See also Frank F. Furstenberg, Jr., Theodore Hershberg, and John Modell, "The Origin of the Female-Headed Black Family: The Impact of the Urban Experience," in *Philadelphia: Work, Space, Family, and Group Experience in the Nineteenth Century*, ed. T. Hershberg (New York: Oxford University Press, 1981), pp. 441, 443.

43. James DeVries, *Race and Kinship in a Midwestern Town: The Black Experience in Monroe, Michigan, 1900–1915* (Urbana: University of Illinois Press, 1984), pp. 29, 147, 153–54; Kiser, *Sea Island to City*, p. 96; Jones, *Labor of Love, Labor of Sorrow*, p. 156; Bethel, *Promiseland*, p. 124.

44. Bodnar, Simon, and Weber, *Lives of Their Own*, pp. 56–63; Bodnar, Weber, and Simon, "Migration, Kinship, and Urban Adjustment," pp. 554–57.

45. For a discussion of the relationship between family bonds and paternal economic assistance, see William Goode, *World Revolution and Family Patterns* (New York: Free Press, 1970), chap. 1.

46. Published tabulations of industrial affiliations by race and ethnicity are woefully inadequate. An analysis of data obtained from male family heads in Philadelphia and New York City by the U.S. Immigration Commission in 1909 indicates that among blacks, about one-quarter were employed in personal service industries and another one-quarter in transportation. See Suzanne Model, "Competitive Individualism and the Persistence of Minority Disadvantage," CRSO Working Paper 320 (Ann Arbor: University of Michigan, 1984), table 1. The argument below draws on these data and on pp. 5–17 of this paper.

47. Katzman, *Before the Ghetto*, pp. 111–12.

48. For examples of personal recruitment of household workers, see Kiser, *Sea Island to City*, p. 95; and Clark-Lewis, "This Work Had A' End," pp. 13, 20. Katzman maintains that household workers usually used formal intermediaries to secure jobs, a conclusion partly due to his reliance on published studies of employment agencies. (See Katzman, *Seven Days a Week*, pp. 98–104.) Research based on employment agency data is an efficient method of securing information, but it does not provide a basis for generalization about job-getting strategies. For an excellent example of the agency-based approach that is devoted to black household workers in a somewhat later period, see Elizabeth Ross Haynes, "Negroes in Domestic Service in the U.S.," *Journal of Negro History* 4 (1923).

49. Katzman, *Seven Days A Week*, tables A-3 and A-11, and appendix 3; Gerber, *Black Ohio and the Color Line*, p. 305.

50. Goldin, "Family Strategies and the Family Economy in the Late Nineteenth Century," p. 302.

51. Johnson and Campbell, *Black Migration in America*, pp. 72–74; Fligstein,

Going North, pp. 101–4, 127–31; Florette Henri, *Black Migration: Movement North, 1900–1920* (Garden City, N.Y.: Anchor Books, 1976), pp. 60–62.

52. Dewey Palmer, "Moving North: Migration of Negroes During World War I," *Phylon* 28 (1967):58–60; Henri, *Black Migration*, pp. 62–66; Banton, *Racial and Ethnic Competition*, p. 259; Carol Marks, "Lines of Communication, Recruitment Mechanisms, and the Great Migration of 1916–1918," *Social Problems* 31 (1983): 76–77; Louise V. Kennedy, *The Negro Peasant Turns Cityward* (New York, AMS Press, 1968), p. 41. For examples of the thousands of letters written by migrants, see Emmett Scott, "Letters of Negro Migrants of 1916–1918," and "Additional Letters of Negro Migrants of 1916–1918," both in *Journal of Negro History* 4 (1919). On group differences in job assistance, see Suzanne Model, "Mode of job Entry and the Ethnic Composition of Firms: Early Twentieth Century Migrants to New York City," *Sociological Forum* 3 (1988):110–127.

53. On sex ratios, see Kennedy, *The Negro Peasant Turns Cityward*, pp. 139–40; and Joe William Trotter, Jr., *Black Milwaukee* (Urbana: University of Illinois Press, 1985), p. 45. On women's employment see Henri, *Black Migration*, pp. 142–43; and Katzman, *Seven Days a Week*, table A-11. On the demand of specific industries for largely unskilled black workers, see Dennis C. Dickerson, *Out of the Crucible: Black Steelworkers in Western Pennsylvania, 1875–1980* (Albany: SUNY Press, 1986), pp. 48–60; Alma Herbst, *The Negro in the Slaughtering and Meat Packing Industries in Chicago* (New York: Arno Press, 1971), pp. xxi–xxii, 109; and Zunz, *The Changing Face of Inequality*, pp. 396–97.

54. Kenneth Kusmer, *A Ghetto Takes Shape*, pp. 203–4; Katzman, *Seven Days a Week*, table A-3; Allan H. Spear, *Black Chicago: The Making of a Negro Ghetto, 1890–1920* (Chicago: University of Chicago Press, 1967). pp. 160–66; Robert B. Grant, *The Black Man Comes to the City* (Chicago: Nelson-Hall, 1972), p. 83.

55. Bureau of the Census, *Fifteenth Census of the U.S.: 1930, Population, vol. 6, Families* (Washington, D.C.: Government Printing Office, 1933), pp. 303, 920.

56. Stanley Lieberson, *A Piece of the Pie* (Berkeley: University of California Press, 1980), pp. 239–52. The Urban League statement is quoted in Drake and Cayton, *Black Metropolis*, p. 83. On slave markets, see Jones, *Labor of Love, Labor of Sorrow*, p. 205.

57. On the development of the social programs of the 1930s, see Frances Fox Piven and Richard A. Cloward, *Regulating the Poor: The Functions of Public Welfare* (New York: Vintage, 1971), chap. 3. On CIO success and its ambivalent commitment to black workers, see Reich, *Racial Inequality*, pp. 256–60.

58. The U.S. census does not provide strictly comparable figures on family structure for 1930 and 1940; patterns are discernible, nonetheless. For example, the rate of female-headedness among white residents of New York State in 1930 was 14 percent; among black residents, 22.7 percent. In rural Georgia in the same year, the white rate was 7.2 percent; the black rate, 12 percent (Bureau of the Census, *Fifteenth Census of the U.S.: 1930, Population*, vol. 6, *Families*, pp. 303, 920). In 1940 the rate among white residents of the northeastern states was 16 percent, among blacks 28 percent. Among white residents of the rural South, 7.6 percent of white families were headed by a woman; 11.7 percent among black residents. (Bureau of the Census, *Sixteenth Census of the U.S.: 1940, Population, Families, Types of Families* [Washington, D.C.: Government Printing Office, 1943], pp. 94–95, 99–100.)

On black migration patterns, see Johnson and Campbell, *Black Migration in America*, p. 95.

59. Jones, *Labor of Love, Labor of Sorrow*, p. 198.

60. Paul Taylor, *Mexican Labor in the U.S.: Bethlehem, Pennsylvania* (Berkeley:

University of California Press, 1931), p. 92, quoted in Mark Reisler, *By the Sweat of Their Brow: Mexican Immigrant Labor in the U.S., 1900-1940* (Westport, Conn.: Greenwood Press, 1976), p. 105.

61. Piore, *Birds of Passage*, p. 154; Peter Blau and Otis Dudley Duncan, *The American Occupational Structure* (New York: Free Press, 1967), pp. 107-11; Lieberson, *A Piece of the Pie*, p. 378.

62. Piven and Cloward, *Regulating the Poor*, pp. 61-66; James Green, *The World of the Worker* (New York: Hill & Wang, 1980), chap. 5; Gordon, Edwards, and Reich, *Segmented Work, Divided Workers*, pp. 176-82.

63. Piore, *Birds of Passage*, p. 162.

64. On Italian girls' entry into white-collar work to assist the family, see Miriam Cohen, *From Workshop to Office: Employment, School, and Family in the Lives of New York Italian Women, 1900-1950*, (Urbana: University of Illinois Press, forthcoming), chap. 5. Analysis of the 1940 and 1950 Public Use Microdata Sample data of the U.S. census indicates that among single, native-born daughters of foreign parents, 56.9 percent were in the labor force in 1940, and 60.6 percent in 1950. But among similar married women with spouse present, only 12.9 percent were in the labor force in 1940, though that proportion jumped to 21.1 percent in 1950 (Ellen Kraly, Samuel Fridman, and Keiko Yamanaka, "Ethnic Women in the U.S. Economy: 1940 and 1950" [Paper presented at the Annual Meeting of the American Sociological Association, 1986], table 2). This growth in the employment of wives signaled an eventual shift in the distribution of financial responsibilities within white ethnic families.

65. Lieberson, *A Piece of the Pie*, chap. 8. For a cultural interpretation of the same phenomenon, see Andrew Greeley, *Ethnicity, Denomination, and Inequality* (Beverly Hills, Calif.: Sage Publications, 1976), pp. 71-76.

66. John Bodnar, *Workers' World: Kinship, Community, and Protest in an Industrial Society, 1900-1940* (Baltimore: Johns Hopkins University Press, 1982), p. 102.

67. Herbert Applebaum, *Royal Blue: The Culture of Construction Workers* (New York: Holt, Rinehart, & Winston, 1981), pp. 18-19; Jules Herbert Lichtenstein, "White Ethnic and Black Economic Assimilation and Mobility: A Study of Employment Patterns and Determinants in Selected SMSA's" (Ph.D. diss., Cornell University, 1975), chap. 6 and appendix J. See also Scott Cummings, "Collectivism: The Unique Legacy of Immigrant Economic Development," in *Self-Help in Urban America*, ed. Scott Cummings (Port Washington, N.Y.: Kennikat Press, 1980), table 1-1.

68. On some thoughts about the changes that higher education bring to Italians, see Herbert J. Gans, *The Urban Villagers: Group and Class in the Life of Italian Americans* (New York: Free Press, 1962), pp. 214-17. On job finding and social class, see Mark Granovetter, "The Strength of Weak Ties: A Network Theory Revisited," in *Sociological Theory, 1983*, ed. R. Collins (San Francisco: Jossey-Bass, 1983), pp. 201-09. On intermarriage, see Richard D. Alba, "Interethnic Marriage in the 1980 Census" (Paper presented at the Annual Meeting of the American Sociological Association, 1985), pp. 6-17. On Italian assimilation, see Alba, *Italian Americans*, pp. 134-40, 145-50. On Poles, see Helena Znaniecka Lopata "The Polish Immigrants and Their Descendants in the American Labor Force," in *Ethnicity and the Work Force*, ed. W. Van Horne and T. Tonnesen (Madison: University of Wisconsin Press, 1985), pp. 132-40.

69. On sociopolitical changes pushing blacks out of the South, see Fligstein, *Going North*, chap. 7; and Piven and Cloward, *Regulating the Poor*, pp. 200-205. On the gradual reversal in the direction of black migration, see Johnson and Campbell, *Black Migration in America*, pp. 155-59; and Farley and Allen, *The Color Line and the Quality of Life in America*, pp. 117-19.

70. Reich, *Racial Inequality*, p. 261; Gordon, Edwards, and Reich, *Segmented Work, Divided Workers*, p. 180; Ray Marshall, *The Negro and Organized Labor* (New York: Wiley, 1965), p. 41; Wilson, *The Declining Significance of Race*. pp. 89–90; Lieberson, *A Piece of the Pie*, chap. 8.

71. Edna Bonacich, "Advanced Capitalism and Black/White Relations in the United States: A Split Labor Market Interpretation," *American Sociological Review* 41 (1976): 47–49.

72. For a more complete discussion of the polarization of black Americans, see Wilson, *The Declining Significance of Race*. chaps. 6, 7.

73. In Soo Son, Suzanne Model, Gene Fisher, "Occupational Mobility of Young Black Males in the Late 1970s: A Test of William J. Wilson's Hypothesis," *Sociological Forum* 4 (1989): 309–27.

74. Piore, *Birds of Passage*, pp. 160–63; Gordon, Edwards, and Reich, *Segmented Work, Divided Workers*, pp. 206–10. In these pages, the same writers also argue that blacks are disproportionately concentrated in low-paying, labor-intensive, insecure jobs, jobs the writers equate with a peripheral or secondary labor market. Recent empirical research, however, has suggested that blacks are rather evenly distributed across the economy. See, for example, Randy Hodson, *Workers' Earnings and Corporate Economic Structure* (New York: Academic Press, 1983), pp. 107–8.

75. Farley and Allen, *The Color Line and the Quality of Life in America*, pp. 262–66; Wilson, *The Declining Significance of Race*, pp. 177–78; Edelman, *Families in Peril*, p. 13.

76. Lee Rainwater and William Yancey, *The Moynihan Report and the Politics of Controversy* (Cambridge: MIT Press, 1967), pp. 51–60. On trends in black family size and illegitimacy, see Bureau of the Census, *Statistical Abstract of the United States: 1986* (Washington, D.C.: Government Printing Office, 1985), pp. 44, 62.

77. Hacker, "American Apartheid," pp. 26–27; Edelman, *Families in Peril*, chap. 1. In the 1980 census, 21 percent of black female household heads gave their marital status as separated, compared to 13 percent of white female household heads. The proportion of black female household heads who were divorced, however, was only 25 percent, compared to 43 percent of comparable whites. See Farley and Allen, *The Color Line and the Quality of Life in America*, p. 165.

78. Wilson, *The Declining Significance of Race*, tables 15, 16; Farley and Allen, *The Color Line and the Quality of Life in America*, p. 173.

79. For a discussion of the problems black women face in the marriage market, see Graham Spanier and Paul C. Glick, "Mate Selection Differentials between Whites and Blacks in the United States," in *The Black Family: Essays and Studies*, 3d ed., ed. Robert Staples (Belmont, Calif.: Wadsworth, 1986), pp. 114–28. The statistics on black employment status come from Staples, "Changes in Black Family Structure," p. 22.

80. In 1980, for example 43.2 percent of black families in New York State were female headed, compared to 13.5 percent of white families. In Georgia, 36.2 percent of black families had a female head, compared to 10.6 percent among whites. (Bureau of the Census, *1980 Census of Population and Housing, Provisional Estimates of Social, Economic, and Housing Characteristics* (Washington, D.C.: Government Printing Office, 1982), pp. 49, 55. The rise in female-headedness among southern blacks suggests new erosion in the position of the rural black male, perhaps because of changes in the organization of agriculture.

81. Carol Stack, *All Our Kin: Strategies for Survival in the Black Community* (New York: Harper & Row, 1974), pp. 108, 122.

82. Farley and Allen, *The Color Line and the Quality of Life in America*, p. 168.

83. See Harriette P. McAdoo, "Factors Related to Stability in Upwardly Mobile Black Families," *Journal of Marriage and the Family* 40 (1978): 761–78; and Harriette P. McAdoo, "Black Mothers and the Extended Family Support Network," in *The Black Woman*, ed. L. Rodgers-Rose (Beverly Hills, Calif.: Sage Publications, 1980), pp. 125–44.

84. Stack, *All Our Kin*, pp. 24, 105–7; Elmer Martin and Joanne Martin, *The Black Extended Family* (Chicago: University of Chicago Press, 1978), pp. 74–75.

85. Ann C. Zollar, *A Member of the Family; Strategies for Black Family Continuity* (Chicago: Nelson-Hall, 1985), pp. 153–54.

86. Martin and Martin, *The Black Extended Family*, p. 74.

87. *Proceedings of the Black Family Summit* (New York: National Urban League, 1985, Mimeographed), p. 101.

6

From South of the Border: Hispanic Minorities in the United States

Alejandro Portes

Hispanics are those individuals whose birth or declared ancestry locates their origin in Spain or in the Latin American countries. Until recently, this rubric did not exist as a self-designation for most of the groups so labeled, being essentially a term of convenience for administrative agencies and scholarly research. Thus, the first thing of note to be said about this population is that it is not a consolidated minority but, rather, a group-in-formation whose boundaries and self-definitions are in flux. The emergence of a Hispanic "minority" has depended more on the actions of government and the collective perceptions of Anglo-American society than on the initiative of the individuals so designated. The increasing attention gained by this category of people derives mainly from their rapid population growth during the past two decades, a consequence of high fertility rates among some national groups, and, more important, of accelerated immigration. The heavy concentration of this population in certain regions of the country has added to its visibility. Over 75 percent of the 14.5 million people identified by the 1980 census as Hispanics are concentrated in just four states: California, New York, Texas, and Florida; California alone absorbed almost one-third.[1]

The absence of a firm collective self-identity among this population is an outcome of its great diversity, despite the apparent "commonness" of language and culture that figures so prominently in official writings. Under the same label, we find individuals whose ancestors lived in the country since at least the time of independence and others who arrived last year; substantial numbers of professionals and entrepreneurs along with humble farm laborers and unskilled factory workers; whites, blacks, mulattoes, and mestizos; full-fledged citizens and unauthorized aliens; and finally, among the immigrants, those who came in search of employment and a better economic future and those who arrived escaping death squads and political persecution at home. Aside from divisions between the "foreign" and the native-born, no difference is more significant than that of national origin. Nationality not only stands for different geographic places of birth but serves as a code word for the very distinct histories of each major immigrant flow, which molded the patterns of entry and adaptation to American society. For this reason the literature produced by "Hispanic" scholars has tended until recently to focus on the origins and evolution of their own national groups rather than encompassing the diverse histories of all those falling under the official rubric.

Most members of the Spanish-origin population—at least 60 percent—are of Mexican origin, divided between native-born Americans and immigrants; another 14 percent come from Puerto Rico and are U.S. citizens by birth, whether they were born in the island or the mainland; the third group in size is Cubans, who represent about 5 percent and are, overwhelmingly, recent immigrants coming after the consolidation of a communist regime in their country. In addition to these major groups, there are sizable contingents of Dominicans, Colombians, Salvadorans, Guatemalans, and other Central and South Americans, with their own distinct histories, characteristics, and patterns of adaptation.[2]

The complexity of Hispanic ethnicity is a consequence, first of all, of these diverse national origins, which often lead to more differences than similarities among the various groups. Lumping them together is not too dissimilar from attempting to combine turn-of-the-century northern Italian, Hungarian, Serbian, and Bohemian immigrants in a unit based on their "common" origin in various patches of the Austro-Hungarian Empire. A second difficulty is that most Spanish-origin groups are not yet "settled"; they continue to expand and change in response to uninterrupted immigration and close contact with events in the home countries. This dense traffic of people, news, and events between U.S.-based immigrant communities and their not-too-remote places of origin offers a far more challenging landscape than, for example, the condition of European ethnic groups, whose boundaries are generally well defined and whose bonds with the original countries are becoming increasingly remote.[3]

Migration and Settlement Patterns

Ethnic groups come into being in one of three ways: conquest, immigration, or political settlements. The third way is exceptional and is based on the agreement of spatially contiguous nationalities to cooperate in the creation of a common nation-state. Through such settlements, countries like Switzerland, Belgium, and Yugoslavia have emerged, and individual nationalities within each—especially the less numerous ones—have become ethnic minorities.[4] U.S. history does not register a single significant instance of this pattern of "negotiated" ethnicity, and thus ethnic groups have generally emerged through the other alternatives: conquest or immigration.[5]

Spanish-origin groups are well represented under each rubric because the historical events that created today's largest communities involved a mix of both conquest and immigration. To anticipate the argument: the migration flows that consolidated these communities reflect, almost mirrorlike, the expansion of the United States into its immediate periphery. The countries that supplied the major Spanish-origin groups in the United States today were, each in its time, targets of this expansionist pattern. U.S. intervention undermined the social and economic fabric constructed under Spanish colonial domination and reoriented it toward the new hegemonic power. This internal imbalancing of postcolonial societies, which preceded the onset of migration, has created today's ethnic communities. In a sense, the sending populations were Americanized before their members actually became immigrants to the United States.

Mexicans

Mexico is the prime example of the creation of a Spanish-origin community through conquest and immigration. As Mexican-American scholars have frequently noted, their ancestors were already here before a war of conquest converted them into foreigners in their own land.[6] Like native Indians, Mexicans represent a classic example of ethnic-group formation through military conquest and occupation. Things did not stop there, however, because the rapid expansion of the U.S. economy into what had been northern Mexico reclaimed labor from the portion of the country south of the Rio Grande. Growers and railroad companies sent paid recruiters into the reduced Mexican republic to offer free rail travel and advances on wages as incentives for local workers to come north. Mexican immigration thus had its immediate origins in deliberate recruitment by North American companies, and was not a spontaneous movement.[7] Economic penetration followed political intervention in shaping what eventually became the largest Spanish-origin minority in the United States.

At the time of the labor-recruitment waves in the nineteenth and early twentieth centuries, the border was scarcely enforced. As original settlers of the land, Mexicans came with the territory, and the arrival of new contract laborers and the movement back and forth across the Rio Grande met with little official resistance. Hence, Mexicans were an integral part of the Southwest's population before they became immigrants and much before they became "illegal" immigrants. The latter term made its appearance after passage of the National Origins Immigration Act of 1924 and the creation of the Border Patrol (established to prevent the inflow of Asians and other elements deemed undesirable, rather than the crossing of Mexicans). In 1929, for example, the U.S. Supreme Court upheld an earlier administrative decree declaring individuals who commuted between residences in Mexico and their work in the United States to be legal immigrants.[8] It was only in the post-Depression era and especially after World War II that crossing the border became a formally regulated event leading to the criminalization of the traditional inflow.[9]

Thus, contrary to the conventional portrait of Mexican immigration as a self-propelled movement of foreigners across a well-defined border, the process had its origins in North American geopolitical and economic interests that first restructured the neighboring nation and then proceeded to organize dependable labor ouflows out of it. Such movements across the new border were a well-established routine in the Southwest before they became redefined as immigration, and then "illegal" immigration.

Puerto Ricans

Puerto Rico, a long-neglected outpost of the Spanish Empire, came into U.S. hands as an outcome of the Spanish-American War. North American influence, which had a profound effect on this mostly rural society dedicated to coffee exports and simple subsistence agriculture, began shortly after the military occupation, when U.S. capital started pouring into new sugarcane plantations and mill construction. The land requirements of the new industry and the political power of its promoters led to the rapid displacement of subsistence peasants. Because the labor requirements of sugar growing fall mainly during the harvest season, an increasing number of dispossessed peasants were forced into the cities, where urban unemployment, previously unknown, became an established feature of Puerto Rican society.[10]

In 1917 the Jones Act gave the islanders U.S. citizenship along with the obligation of serving in the armed forces. Despite the absence of legal restrictions on immigration and the new economic conditions in Puerto Rico, migration to the mainland began slowly. In 1920 Puerto Ricans in the United States were estimated at only twelve thousand, and twenty-five years later, they were still fewer than one hundred thousand.[11] The inflow accelerated after World War II, owing to three principal causes. The first was the continuing industrialization and urbanization of the island under U.S. auspices, especially after initiation of "Operation Bootstrap" in the late 1940s. Touted as a comprehensive solution to underdevelopment, the new policy industrialized the country and brought the majority of its population into the cities, but the capital-intensive industries did not generate enough jobs to keep up with the urban inflow and with rapid population growth. Unemployment became acute at a time when modern consumption expectations from the mainland were being diffused widely among the urban population.[12] Second, the barrier of a long and expensive sea journey disappeared with the advent of inexpensive air travel. Just as new products and fashions were pouring in from the North, the means to travel there in order to acquire them became available to the mass of the population. Third, the increasing economic reasons to leave the island and facilities for doing so were directly activated by labor recruiters, a practice that began at the turn of the century but became widespread only during and after World War II.[13]

These were years of rapid expansion in the U.S. economy, which generated a strong demand for low-wage unskilled labor. Just as Mexicans coming under the Bracero program helped meet that demand in the Southwest and Midwest, Puerto Rican contract labor filled the gap in the East. Job opportunities available to members of both migrant groups were similar, except that the Puerto

Rican inflow had a stronger urban bent, which accelerated rapidly during the 1950s and 1960s. Puerto Rican men became employed in increasing numbers as unskilled factory operatives and as menial help in hotels and restaurants; Puerto Rican women worked as domestics and were hired by the thousands as seamstresses in the garment industry.[14]

From their places of destination Puerto Rican migrants moved gradually west, finally meeting the outposts of the Mexican inflow. Chicago, in particular, became a major point of confluence of the two Spanish-speaking labor streams. It was in the East and primarily in New York City, however, that the largest Puerto Rican concentrations emerged. Settling in dilapidated neighborhoods left behind by older immigrants, Puerto Ricans added a new flavor to the city's ethnic mix. East Harlem became Spanish Harlem; the South Bronx, the Lower East Side of Manhattan (redubbed *Loisaida*), and other urban districts were also rapidly Hispanicized.[15]

The consolidation of these ethnic communities represented the end point of a process that began with the acquisition and economic colonization of Puerto Rico. Just as in Mexico, the migrations that gave rise to today's ethnic minority did not occur spontaneously but had their beginnings in political decisions and economic initiatives on the receiving side. The rise of Spanish-speaking working-class communities in the Southwest and Northeast may thus be seen as a dialectical consequence of past expansion of the United States into its immediate periphery. The process of internal restructuring after intervention was more thorough in Puerto Rico than in Mexico, given direct political control by the United States and the weakness of the prior political and economic structures, a difference that stands at the core of the diverging paths of economic adaptation followed by immigrants from the two places.

Cubans

Cuban immigration, which also had its roots in the history of relations with the United States, took a different and more dramatic form. One effect of the Cuban War of Independence in the late nineteenth century was to create sizable émigré communities on the mainland, especially in New York, Key West, and Tampa. With the economic support of these three communities, the Cuban Revolutionary party launched the last and successful war of independence against Spain.[16] After three years of conflict, the United States intervened, and when the Spanish-American War ended, Cuba formally became a republic. However, the island was occupied by U.S. troops and governed by military authority from 1900 to 1902 and again in 1908–1909. The Platt Amendment, approved by the U.S. Congress as an addendum to the Cuban constitution, guaranteed the United States the right to intervene in Cuban internal affairs. Politically and economically, the island became a protectorate. North American capital flowed into the sugar industry and into iron and nickel mining shortly after the first occupation, although the growing of tobacco, coffee, and other agricultural exports remained in Cuban hands.[17] Despite domination by North American interests, Cuba never became a recruiting ground for cheap agricultural labor, mainly because of the somewhat higher level of development of the island's economy, relative to its neighbors, and the division of the rural labor force into small commercial farmers in tobacco, fruits, and coffee, and an organized rural proletariat in the cane fields. Both factors reduced the size of the subsistence peasantry and hence the pool of readily available workers. In addition, Cuba did not share a land border with the United States, as did Mexico, and was not a full U.S. possession, as was Puerto Rico.[18]

The Platt Amendment was formally abolished in the 1930s, but the heavy tutelage over Cuban internal and foreign affairs continued. In 1941, for example, Cuba declared war against the Axis powers on the same day as the United States, and voted consistently on the U.S. side in all international meetings during and after World War II. The North American hegemony shaped a local bourgeoisie that was profoundly Americanized in its outlook and behavior. The Cuban upper class relied on the North for political guidance and imitated American ways of doing business and patterns of consumption. This hegemony also promoted strong feelings of anti-imperialism in other segments of the population, especially among young intellectuals, whose desire to escape U.S. tutelage grew with the years.[19]

These contradictory trends were to culminate in the revolution against Fulgencio Batista. All segments of the nation participated in this struggle, but their visions of the future were quite different. For the Cuban bourgeoisie, Batista represented a throwback to a primitive era, which had to be overcome in order to consolidate liberal democracy. For the young intellectuals who led the fight, however, Batista was a U.S. puppet whose defeat would mark the beginnings of a genuine struggle of national liberation.[20] Opposition to imperialism became a rallying cry of the triumphant revolution as it pressured the Cuban upper and middle classes into submission. Deprived of political power and suffering wave after wave of confiscations, these groups saw their only escape in moving north to secure U.S. help for reconquering the island. True to their origins and past, the Cuban bourgeoisie relied on U.S. leadership and firmly believed that a communist regime so close to U.S. shores was an impossibility.[21]

The waves of exiles drastically transformed the character of the U.S. Cuban community. From a small group of descendants of the nineteenth-century émigrés and some occasional immigrants, Cubans became one of the most rapidly growing and most concentrated foreign minorities in the country. The political origins of this inflow gave it quite distinct characteristics compared to those initiated by labor recruitment. The first waves of Cuban refugees were strongly committed to return after the overthrow of Castro's regime, and were supported in this goal by the U.S. government.[22] The commitment waned after the Bay of Pigs defeat, especially after resolution of the Missile Crisis of 1962, which committed the U.S. government to restrain exile organizations in exchange for removal of Soviet missiles from the island. An adaptation process then began, which saw subsequent refugee cohorts become progressively less oriented toward immediate return and more toward family reunification and a new life in the United States.

The Kennedy and Johnson administrations attempted to resettle the Cubans away from Miami but met stubborn resistance. Gradually, resettled refugees drifted back to Miami, making Cubans one of the most spatially concentrated immigrant groups. Proximity to the island and climate may have something to do with this behavior, but the principal reason appears to have been the framework for daily life and economic opportunity created by the earlier cohorts of exiles, which generated a context of incorporation quite different from that awaiting other Latin immigrants.[23] Consequences of these patterns will be examined below.

Despite its unique history, Cuban immigration was also influenced decisively by the earlier hegemony exercised by the United States over the island. In this case, it was not deliberate recruitment that triggered large-scale migration but a major political upheaval that confronted the classes adapted to and prospering under U.S. hegemony with groups irreconcilably opposed to it. The victory of the latter led to an exodus of formerly dominant classes in the only direction that, given past history, they could possibly take.

Nonimmigrants

More recent migrations also illustrate the same general pattern of U.S. political and economic intervention. For instance, the present sizable inflow from the Dominican Republic did not start until the 1960s, in the wake of direct U.S. intervention to stem a leftist military uprising. The country had been occupied by U.S. troops earlier in the century but, during the decades of the Trujillo dictatorship, it remained an isolated backwater. The assassination of Trujillo and reassertion of U.S. hegemony in the country coincided with rapid increases in out-migration, as a consequence of which Dominicans represent today the seventh-largest immigration contingent to the United States and one of the most concentrated.[24] Unlike Cubans, they have chosen not south Florida but the New York metropolitan area as their principal place of settlement, where in 1985, they were the single largest immigrant nationality, accounting for 17 percent of the New York-bound inflow.[25]

The absolute and relative sizes of immigrant national cohorts drop rapidly as we leave the immediate periphery of the United States and the countries that experienced its intervention most directly. Despite its size, for example, Brazil has been a minor contributor to U.S.-bound immigration. In 1980 there were slightly more than forty thousand Brazilian-born persons in the United States, who represented only 0.3 percent of the foreign-born and less than one-tenth of 1 percent of the Brazilian population. The same is true of immigrants from Argentina, who amounted to 0.5 percent of the foreign-born, and whose weight relative to the Argentine population was less than one-third of 1 percent.[26] Geographical distance alone does not account for these patterns, however. For example, Costa Rica is a small country relatively close to the United States, yet in 1980 there were only 29,639 Costa Ricans in the United States. Unlike other Caribbean nations and several of its Central American neighbors, Costa Rica has been able to avoid, at least until recently, direct U.S. intervention and thus retain a measure of national autonomy. Neighboring El Salvador, however, which has experienced such intervention in its domestic life, has seen an accelerated process of out-migration, mainly to the United States.[27]

Charles Tilly argues in his chapter for the importance of networks in the process of immigration. There is little doubt that immigration is a network-mediated process and that networks account for the continuity of these flows, even when the original conditions have changed,[28] but questions remain as to what forces initiate the process, why it originates in certain countries and locations and not in others, and what accounts for the different compositions and patterns of incorporation of various groups. Attempts to explain specific outflows must therefore rest on the identification of broader structural determinants. In this respect the contrasting experiences of Latin American countries offer a valuable clue because they show that contrary to much journalistic lore, the flows do not arise spontaneously out of poverty. Equally undeveloped countries and regions may have different migration histories, and sizable outflows may originate in more-developed areas rather than less-developed areas. The reason is that the beginnings of these movements are rooted in the history of prior economic and political relationships between sending and receiving countries. In particular, contemporary migration patterns tend to reflect precisely the character of past hegemonic actions by regional and global powers.

Labor Market Trends

The literature on labor-market performance and the socioeconomic condition of the major Spanish-origin groups in the United States has sought to answer three questions: Are there significant differences in the condition of these groups both in comparison with the U.S. population and among themselves? Are there significant differences in the *process* by which education, occupation, and income are achieved? If there are differences in this process, what are their principal causes?

Table 6–1 presents a summary of descriptive statistics drawn from the 1980 census. Aside from age and nativity, included as background information, the rest of the figures indicate that the socioeconomic performance of Spanish-origin minorities is generally inferior to that of the U.S. population as a whole and, by extension, of the white non-Hispanic majority. This is true of education, occupation, income, and entrepreneurship (measured by rates of self-employment), although less so of labor force participation, especially among females.

The same figures also indicate major disparities among Spanish-origin groups. In general, Puerto Ricans are in the worst socioeconomic situation, as manifested by high levels of unemployment, female-headed families, and poverty, and correspondingly low levels of education, occupation, and income. Mexicans occupy an intermediate position, although consistently below the U.S. population. Note that Mexicans are the majority of all Hispanics and have a disproportionate weight in aggregate figures that purport to describe the Spanish-origin population as a whole. Cubans are in a better situation, as the "Other Spanish." Both groups have rates of occupation, family income, and

TABLE 6-1. Selected Characteristics of Spanish-origin Groups, 1980

Variable	Mexicans	Puerto Ricans	Cubans	Other Spanish	Total U.S.
Number (in millions)	8.7	2.0	0.8	3.1	226.5
Median age	21.9	22.3	37.7	25.5	30.0
Percentage native born	74.0	96.9	22.1	60.5	93.8
Percentage female-headed families	16.4	35.3	14.9	20.5	14.3
Median years of school completed[a]	9.6	10.5	12.2	12.3	12.5
Percentage high school graduates[a]	37.6	40.1	55.3	57.4	66.5
Percentage with 4+ years of college[a]	4.9	5.6	16.2	12.4	16.2
Percentage in labor force[b]	64.6	54.9	66.0	64.6	62.0
Percentage females in labor force[b]	49.0	40.1	55.4	53.4	49.9
Percentage married women in labor force[c]	42.5	38.9	50.5	45.7	43.9
Percentage self-employed[d]	3.5	2.2	5.8	4.5	6.8
Percentage unemployed	9.1	11.7	6.0	8.0	6.5
Percentage professional specialty, executive, and managerial occupations:					
males	11.4	14.1	22.0	19.0	25.8
females[d]	12.6	15.5	17.9	17.2	24.7
Percentage operators and laborers:					
males	30.4	30.9	23.1	23.8	18.3
females[d]	22.0	25.5	24.2	19.9	11.7
Median family income	14,765	10,734	18,245	16,230	19,917
Median income of married couples with own children	14,855	13,428	20,334	16,708	19,630
Percentage of families with incomes of $50,000+	1.8	1.0	5.2	3.6	5.6
Percentage of all families below poverty level	20.6	34.9	11.7	16.7	9.6

Sources: Bureau of the Census, *General Population Characteristics, United States Summary*, 1983a: tables 39, 48, 70; Bureau of the Census, *General Social and Economic Characteristics, United States Summary*, 1983b: tables 141, 166–71.

[a]Persons twenty-five years of age or older.
[b]Persons sixteen years of age or older.
[c]Women sixteen years of age or older; husband present and own children under six years of age.
[d]Employed persons sixteen years of age or older.

self-employment closer to the U.S. average. ("Other Spanish" consists of immigrant groups too small to be counted individually plus those that declared Spanish-origin ancestry without further specification. The conflation of groups make it difficult to provide a meaningful interpretation of the absolute condition of the category or the processes that have led to its creation.)

The existence of differences in the socioeconomic position of the Spanish-origin population, a phenomenon well known to researchers in the field, must have some cause or causes.[29] As framed in current research efforts, the issue is whether the condition of a specific minority is explainable entirely on the basis of its background characteristics or, rather, derives from other factors. If members of a given group attain socioeconomic positions comparable to those of native-born Americans with similar human-capital endowments, the observed differences can be imputed to the group's current average levels of education, work experience, and other significant causal variables. If, on the other hand, differences persist after statistically equalizing the minority's background, other factors must come into play. If the gap is disadvantageous, discrimination is generally assumed to play a role; if the gap is advantageous, collective characteristics of the group are explored in search of a possible explanation.

Several analyses, especially those of educational attainment, tend to support the "no-difference, no-discrimination" hypothesis. This is the conclusion reached, for example, by Hirschman and Falcón after a broad-gauged study of educational levels among "religio-ethnic" groups in the United States.[30] However, these authors also report that after controlling for all possible relevant predictors, the Mexican educational attainment still falls 1.4 years below the norm. Similarly, in a study of occupational attainment based on the 1976 Survey of Income and Education (SEI), Stolzenberg concludes that the causal process is essentially the same among all Spanish-origin groups and that, after standardizing individual background characteristics, no evidence of discrimination remains. However, Stolzenberg includes in the analysis a series of state dummy variables in order to control for the possible confounding of geographic location and ethnicity. What he does, of course, is to insure a priori that ethnic differences would be insignificant because of the high concentration of particular groups in certain states. Including "Florida" as a causal predictor, for example, pretty much eliminates the distinct effect of Cuban ethnicity because this group is highly concentrated in that state; the same is true for New York and the Puerto Ricans. Even with state dummies included, significant ethnic effects on occupational attainment remain in Stolzenberg's analysis of the Mexican and Cuban groups. The Mexican coefficient is negative, indicating lower occupational levels than those expected on the basis of the group's average characteristics; the Cuban effect is positive, however, indicating above-average attainment, and becomes stronger when state controls are deleted.

A subsequent and more carefully specified analysis of SEI wage data by Reimers yields conclusions similar to Stolzenberg's. After controlling for selection bias and human-capital predictors, Reimers finds that male Puerto Rican wage levels fall 18 percent below the average for white non-Hispanic men; those of Mexicans and other Hispanics are 6 and 12 percent below, respectively. These sizable differences are interpreted as evidence of labor-market discrimination. Cuban men, however, receive wages 6 percent above white non-Hispanics of similar human-capital endowment. These differences lead Reimers to conclude that "the major Hispanic-American groups differ so much among themselves . . . that it makes little sense to lump them under a single 'Hispanic' or 'minority' rubric for either analysis or policy treatment."[31] Studies based on different and more recent data sets also tend to replicate the finding of significant disadvantages in occupational and earnings attainment for Mexicans and, in particular, Puerto Ricans, and a small but consistent advantage for Cubans relative to their human-capital levels.[32]

In attempting to explain the differences, we are not helped by arguing that there is discrimination in the labor market because that does not clarify why discrimination operates differentially among culturally similar groups and sometimes not at all. The only course is to examine the particular characteristics and history of each group. To do this, we must not only abandon the general label "Hispanic" but also leave behind the residual category "Other Spanish," which is too heterogeneous to permit a valid summary explanation. Left are the three major Spanish-origin minorities: Mexicans, Puerto Ricans, and Cubans.

When the socioeconomic performances of these groups are compared, two major riddles emerge. First, why do Mexicans and Puerto Ricans differ so significantly in such characteristics as labor force participation, family structure, and poverty, as well as in levels of wage discrimination; and second, why do Cubans register above-average occupations and family incomes relative to their levels of human capital? The below-average socioeconomic condition of the first two groups is *not* itself a riddle because their migration and settlement histories reveal the roots of exploitation and discrimination. What historical accounts do not explain is why the present condition of these groups should differ so markedly. Similarly, the absolute advantage of Cubans relative to other Spanish-origin groups is not mysterious because, as seen above, this minority was formed largely by upper- and middle-class persons who left Cuba after the revolution. The puzzle is rather why the collective attainment of Cubans should sometimes exceed what can be expected on the basis of their average human-capital endowment. A fairly common explanation is that Cubans were welcomed in the United States as refugees from a communist regime, receiving significant government aid denied to other groups. This explanation, mentioned in passing by Jasso and Rosenzweig, and vigorously defended by Pedraza-Bailey[33] in her comparative study of Cuban and Mexican immigrants, runs against evidence from other refugee groups that have received substantial federal benefits but remain in a precarious socioeconomic condition. Southeast Asian refugees, for example, benefited from the extensive aid provisions mandated by the 1980 Refugee Act, more comprehensive and generous than those made available to Cubans during the 1960s, yet levels of unemployment, poverty, and welfare dependence among most Southeast Asian groups continue to exceed those of almost every other ethnic minority.[34]

Although the favorable governmental reception of Cubans in the United States certainly contributed to their adaptation, it must be seen as part of their distinct mode of incorporation. This interpretation calls attention to the social and economic context in which successive immigrant cohorts are received. A sociological explanation to the above riddles can be found in the distinct modes of incorporation of the three major Spanish-origin groups. Mexican immigrants and new Mexican-American entrants into the labor force tend to come from modest socioeconomic origins and have low average levels of education. In addition, however, they enter labor markets in the Southwest and Midwest, where Mexican laborers have traditionally supplied the bulk of unskilled labor. As noted by Tilly, social networks within the ethnic community tend to direct new workers toward jobs similar to those of their coethnics, a pattern reinforced by the orientation of employers. Lacking a coherent entrepreneurial community or effective political representation, Mexican wage workers must fall back on their own individual resources, "discounted" by past history and present discrimination against their group. Because many Mexican workers are immigrants and a substantial proportion are undocumented, employers continue to view them as a valuable source of pliable low-wage labor, a "preference" that may account for the relatively low average rates of Mexican unemployment, yet it also creates barriers for those who seek upward mobility.[35]

Puerto Rican migrants fulfilled a similar function for industry and agriculture in the Northeast during an earlier period, but with two significant differences. First, Puerto Ricans often entered labor markets that were highly unionized, unlike those of the Southwest; second, they were U.S. citizens by birth and thus entitled to legal protection and not subject to ready deportation. These two factors combined over time to make Puerto Rican workers a less pliable, more costly, and better organized source of labor. When employers in the Northeast began gradually to shift to other immigrant groups — West Indian contract workers in agriculture, and Dominican, Colombian, and other mostly undocumented immigrants in urban industry and services — Puerto Ricans on the mainland were shunted aside in the labor market but lacked an entrepreneurial community to generate their own jobs.[36] During the past two decades they have migrated back to the island in record numbers, and those remaining in the Northeast have experienced levels of unemployment and poverty comparable only to those of the black population.[37]

The Cuban pattern of adaptation is different because the first exile cohorts created an economically favorable context of reception for subsequent arrivals. The bulk of early Cuban migration, composed of displaced members of the native bourgeoisie rather than laborers, brought the capital and entrepreneurial skills with which to start new businesses; later arrivals followed a similar course, leading eventually to the consolidation of an ethnic enclave economy in south Florida.[38] The strong entrepreneurial orientation of the earlier Cuban cohorts is illustrated by census figures on minority-business ownership in Table 6–2. In 1977, when these data were collected, black- and Mexican-owned businesses were the most numerous in absolute terms, reflecting the size of the

TABLE 6-2.   Spanish-origin and Black-owned Firms in the United States

Variable	Mexicans	Puerto Ricans	Cubans	All Spanish	Black
Number of firms, 1977	116,419	13,491	30,336	219,355	231,203
Firms per 100,000 population	1,468	740	3,651	1,890	873
Average gross receipts per firm (thousands of dollars)	44.4	43.9	61.6	47.5	37.4
Firms with paid employees, 1977	22,718	1,767	5,588	41,298	39,968
Firms with employees per 100,000 population	286	97	672	356	151
Average employees per firm	4.9	3.9	6.6	5.0	4.1
Average gross receipts per firm with employees (thousands of dollars)	150.4	191.9	254.9	172.9	160.1
Ten largest Hispanic industrial firms, 1984:					
Percentage located in area of group's concentration[a]	40	10	50	100	
Estimated sales (millions of dollars)	402	273	821	2,317	
Number of employees	5,800	1,100	3,175	10,075	
Ten largest Hispanic-owned banks and savings banks, 1984:					
Percentage in area of group's concentration[a]	40	20	40	100	
Total assets (millions of dollars)	1,204	489	934	2,627	
Total deposits (millions of dollars)	1,102	434	844	2,380	

Sources: Bureau of the Census, *1977 Survey of Minority-Owned Business Enterprises*, 1980; Hispanic Review of Business, *Annual Survey of Hispanic Business*, 1984, 1985.

[a]Southwest locations for Mexicans; New York and vicinity for Puerto Ricans; Miami metropolitan area for Cubans.

respective populations. In per capita terms, however, Cuban-owned firms were by far the most numerous and the largest in gross receipts and number of employees. Figures in the bottom rows of Table 6-2 suggest that the relative weight of Miami Cuban firms among Hispanic-owned businesses has continued to grow since 1977. By 1984 five of ten largest Hispanic-owned firms in the country and four of the ten largest banks were in Miami, at a time when the

Spanish-origin population of the area represented barely 5 percent of the national total.

This helps explain how successive cohorts of Cuban immigrants have been able to make use of past human-capital endowments and exceed their expected level of attainment. Employment in enclave firms allows new arrivals to use their occupational skills and experience without having them "discounted" by discrimination or unfamiliarity with the receiving culture, and it creates opportunities for upward mobility within existing firms or through self-employment. The bond between co-national employers and employees helps fledgling immigrant enterprises survive by taking advantage of the cheap and generally disciplined labor of the new arrivals; the latter may benefit over the long term, however, by availing themselves of mobility opportunities within the enclave that are generally absent elsewhere.

A longitudinal study of Cuban and Mexican immigrants conducted during the 1970s illustrates different patterns of adaptation, conditioned by the presence or absence of an enclave mode of incorporation. By the early 1970s the middle-class immigration from Cuba had ceased and new arrivals came from more modest socioeconomic origins, comparable to those of Mexican legal immigrants. The study interviewed samples of Cuban refugees and Mexican legal immigrants at the time of their arrival during 1973–1974, and followed both samples for six years, interviewing respondents twice during that interval.[39] Table 6–3 presents data from the last follow-up survey, which took place in 1979–1980. The first finding of note is the degree of concentration of Cuban respondents, 97 percent of whom remained in the Miami metropolitan area. By

TABLE 6–3.   The Socioeconomic Position of Cuban and Mexican Immigrants after Six Years in the United States

Variable	Mexicans (N=455)	Cubans (N=413)
Percentage in city of principal concentration	23.7	97.2
Percentage speaking English well	27.4	23.7
Percentage home owners	40.2	40.0
Percentage self-employed	5.4	21.2
Percentage employed by other Mexicans/Cubans	14.6	36.3
Average monthly income[a]	912	1057
Average monthly income of employees in large Anglo-owned firms[a]	$1,003	$1,016
Average monthly income in small nonenclave firms[a]	$ 880	$ 952
Average monthly income in enclave firms[a]	–	$1,111
Average monthly income of the self-employed, Cubans[a]	–	$1,495

Source: A. Portes and R. Bach, *Latin Journey: Cuban and Mexican Immigrants in the United States* (Berkeley: University of California Press, 1985), chaps. 6, 7.

[a]1979 dollars.

comparison, the Mexican sample dispersed throughout the Southwest and Midwest, with the largest concentration — 24 percent — settling in the border city of El Paso.

Otherwise, samples were similar in their knowledge of English — low for both groups after six years — and their rates of home ownership. They differed sharply, however, in variables relating to their labor-market position. More than one-third of 1973 Cuban arrivals were employed by Cuban firms in 1979, and one-fifth had become self-employed by that time; these figures double and quadruple the respective proportions in the Mexican sample. Despite their concentration in a low-wage region of the United States, after six years the Cubans had an average monthly income significantly greater than that of Mexicans. However, a closer look at the data shows no major differences among either Mexicans or Cubans employed in large Anglo-owned firms, commonly identified as part of the "primary" labor market. Nor are there significant differences among those employed in the smaller firms identified with the "secondary" sector; Mexicans and Cubans in both samples received lower wages than primary-sector employees. The significant difference between Cuban and Mexican immigrants lies with the large proportion of the former employed in enclave firms, whose average income was actually the highest in both samples. In addition, self-employed Cuban immigrants exceeded the combined monthly incomes of both samples by approximately $500, or one-half of the total average.

Regarding Mexicans and Puerto Ricans, there is no comparable empirical evidence to support the mode of incorporation hypothesis as an explanation of observed occupational and income differences. Few studies compare Puerto Rican patterns of attainment and those of other minorities, but the available information points to the gradual supplanting of Puerto Ricans by newer immigrant groups as sources of low-wage labor in the Northeast.[40] This evidence is congruent with the interpretation of the current situation of one group — Mexicans — as an outcome of its continued incorporation as a preferred source of low-wage labor in the Southwest and Midwest and that of the other — Puerto Ricans — as a consequence of its increasing redundancy for the same labor market in its principal area of concentration.

Political Behavior and Citizenship

Differences among Spanish-origin groups are again highlighted by their political concerns, organizations, and effectiveness. Regardless of national origin, a major gap separates the native-born, whose interests are always tied to their situation in the United States, and immigrants, whose political allegiance and organized actions often relate to events in the country of origin. The political sociology of Hispanic-Americans can thus be conveniently summarized under two main categories: first, the goals and actions of established groups, including the native-born and naturalized citizens; and second, the political orientations, particularly the problematic shift of citizenship, among immigrants.

Ethnic Politics

The political history of Mexican-Americans bears considerable resemblance to that of American blacks. Both groups endured subordination and disenfranchisement and then attempts to dilute their electoral power through such devices as literacy tests, gerrymandering, and co-optation of ethnic leaders, and both groups have had similar reactions to past discrimination. Mexican-Americans differ from black Americans, however, in one crucial respect, namely, their proximity to and strong identification with the country of origin. Attachment to Mexico and Mexican culture correlates strongly with a sense of "foreignness," even among the native-born and, hence, with lower rates of political participation.[41] The reluctance to shift national allegiances appears to have presented a major obstacle in the path of effective organizing by Mexican-American leaders.

Despite these difficulties, a number of organizations have emerged that articulate the interests of one or another segment of the minority. These range from the earlier *mutualistas* and the Orden de Hijos de America to the subsequent League of United Latin American Citizens (LULAC) and the G.I. Forum, created to defend the interests of Mexican-American World War II veterans.[42] The 1960s marked a turning point in Mexican-American politics. Inspired in large part by the black example, a number of militant organizations emerged that attempted to redress past grievances by means other than participation in the established parties. Many radical student and youth organizations were created, and a third party, La Raza Unida, won a series of significant electoral victories in Texas. Although the more militant demands of these organizations were never met and most of them have ceased to exist, they succeeded in mobilizing the Mexican-American population and creating a cadre of politicians who could forcefully defend its interests before national leaders and institutions. Today, LULAC and the Mexican-American Legal Defense Fund (MALDEF) are among the most powerful and active Hispanic organizations. In 1984 ten of the eleven members of the Hispanic Caucus in Congress represented districts with a heavy Mexican-American population.[43]

Unlike Mexicans, Puerto Ricans are U.S. citizens by birth and do not face the obstacle that naturalization proceedings pose to political participation. In addition, the Puerto Rican migrant population is concentrated in New York, where both the city and state have a long tradition of ethnic politics. A number of factors have conspired, however, to reduce the political weight of this population over the years; these include lack of knowledge of English, generally low levels of education and occupation, and the resistance of established political "clubs" led by Jews, Italians, and other older immigrants. The strong sojourner orientation of many migrants has also reduced their interest and attention to local politics. For many years, Puerto Rican activism on the mainland aimed at improvements in the economic and political status of the island rather than of the New York community.[44]

Although concern for the welfare of Puerto Rico has not diminished, the needs of the mainland communities have gradually gained attention since World War II. During the 1960s Puerto Rican politics paralleled the course followed by Mexicans and blacks, with the appearance of militant youth organizations like the Young Lords and the Puerto Rican Revolutionary Workers' Organization. There were also significant advances in mainstream politics as a number of Puerto Ricans won local and state offices; like Mexicans, Puerto Ricans have voted overwhelmingly Democratic. By 1982, when the joint Black and Puerto Rican Caucus had been established, there were six Puerto Rican state legislators. During the 1970s Puerto Ricans also elected their first state senator and first congressman. At present Robert Garcia (the Bronx, 18th District) is the eleventh member of the Hispanic Caucus in the U.S. House and the sole Puerto Rican representative. Two other congressional districts in New York City and two in the New Jersey suburbs have concentrations of Hispanic population that might make possible the election of additional Puerto Rican legislators.[45] This will depend, however, on increasing the levels of registration and voting among Puerto Ricans and on securing the support of naturalized immigrants from other Latin American countries, such as Colombians and Dominicans, who compose an increasing proportion of the area's population.

Like Mexicans, first-generation Cuban immigrants face the riddle of naturalization, and like Puerto Ricans, they tend to remain preoccupied with events in their country. Cubans, like both Mexicans and Puerto Ricans, usually speak little English on arrival, which also conspires against effective participation. Despite these obstacles, Cuban-Americans have become a potent political force in south Florida, and now hold mayoral offices in the largest cities in the area, Miami and Hialeah, and in several smaller municipalities. Cuban-Americans are influential in the local Republican party and have elected a substantial delegation to the state legislature. Observers agree that in time they will send their first representatives to Congress from Florida's 17th and 18th districts. Meanwhile, a political action group funded by exile businessmen—the Cuban-American National Foundation—has lobbied effectively in Washington for such causes as the creation of Radio Martí and the appointment of Cubans to federal offices.[46] The loyalty of Cuban-Americans to the Republican party dates from two events of the Kennedy administration: the defeat of the Bay of Pigs invasion in 1961 and the Soviet-American agreement of 1962 that reined in the exiles and prevented their launching new military attacks. Cubans have blamed the Democrats for these two events, which destroyed chances for a victorious return to the island. As hopes for return became dimmer and the refugee community turned inward, Cubans naturalized in record number and lined up solidly behind the Republican party, which has become an increasingly serious contender in Florida politics.[47] The trend culminated in the election of the Spanish-origin Republican mayor of Tampa as the new governor in 1986.

There are recent indications, however, that the monolithic conservatism of the Cuban vote may be more apparent than real. It is true that Cubans overwhelmingly supported Ronald Reagan and other Republican candidates for national office in 1980 and 1984, and that they continue to oppose any foreign policy initiative perceived as "soft" on communism. Nevertheless, the vote in local elections has become more progressive and guided by local concerns and issues. During the last mayoral election in Miami, for example, the Republican candidate finished a distant last. The final race was between two Cuban-Americans, a conservative banker supported by the Latin and Anglo business communities and a more progressive, Harvard-trained lawyer. The latter won handily, primarily because of a heavy Cuban grass-roots vote. Similarly, indications are that Cuban representatives in the state legislature are more likely than their Republican colleagues to be concerned with populist issues, especially those involving ethnic minorities.

An important topic for future research is the apparent convergence of the political organizations representing major Spanish-origin groups. Although, as noted earlier, there is little similarity in the historical origins or present socio-economic situation of these groups, political leaders see a basic community of interests on such issues as the defense of bilingualism and a common cultural image. If the term *Hispanic* means anything of substance at present, it is at the political level. An indication of this trend is the emergence of the National Association of Latin Elected Officials (NALEO), a strong organization consisting of Mexican, Puerto Rican, and Cuban congressmen, state legislators, and mayors.[48] So far, this organization has managed to function smoothly and effectively, despite major differences among its disparate constituents.

Citizenship

The first step for effective political participation by any foreign group is citizenship acquisition. Table 6-4 presents data showing the different rates of naturalization among the foreign-born in recent years. During the 1970s, naturalized Mexican immigrants represented only 6 percent of the total, even though they were the most numerous of all nationalities and represented close to 20 percent of all legal admissions during the preceding decade. By contrast, the much smaller number of Cuban immigrants contributed 12 percent of all naturalizations, exceeding the figure for Canada despite the much larger number of eligible Canadian immigrants. The rest of Latin America contributed only 3 percent, owing to the relatively small size of the cohorts of legal immigrants from the region before the 1970s.

The remaining columns of the table present data for the 1970 immigrant cohort that is representative of trends during recent years. The highest rates of naturalization are for Asian immigrants — mostly Chinese, Indians, South Koreans, and Filipinos — and Cubans. Citizenship acquisition among these groups represented close to one-half of the 1970 immigrant cohorts from the respective source countries. Intermediate rates — close to one-fifth of the 1970 immigrant cohort — are found among western Europeans and Central and South Americans. The lowest rates, less than 7 percent, are for immigrants from the two countries contiguous to the United States: Mexico and Canada. Mexican immigrants are also the slowest to naturalize, as indicated by their peak year of naturalizations during the decade — the ninth, two full years behind the norm for all countries.[49]

The analytical literature on determinants of these differences contains two separate strands: first, studies that attempt to explain variation among nation-

TABLE 6-4. U.S. Citizenship Acquisition for Selected Countries and Regions, 1970–80

	Naturalized 1971–80	Percentage of total	Cohort of 1970[b]	Naturalized during next decade	Percentage of cohort	Peak year during decade[c]
Cuba	178,374	12	16,334	7,621	47	8th (2,444)
Mexico	68,152	5	44,469	1,475	3	9th (404)
Central and South America	40,843	3	31,316	6,161	20	9th (1,480)
Canada	130,380	9	13,804	856	6	8th (182)
Western Europe	371,683	25	92,433	17,965	19	7th (5,103)
Asia	473,754	32	92,816	44,554	48	7th (15,129)
Totals[a]	1,464,772		373,326	94,532	25	7th (27,681)

Source: Immigration and Naturalization Service, Annual Reports, various years.

[a]All countries; column figures do not add up to row total because of exclusion of other world regions (Africa, Eastern Europe, and Oceania).
[b]Number of immigrants admitted for legal permanent residence.
[c]Year of most numerous naturalizations during the decade after legal entry; actual number naturalized in parentheses.

alities, and second, those that focus on proximate causes within a particular group. A pioneer contribution to the first or comparative literature is the study by sociologist W. Bernard, who identified literacy, educational attainment, and occupational prestige as major causes of differences in the rates of naturalization between "old" and "new" European immigrants, as defined in his time. Subsequent studies have generally supported Bernard's hypothesis.[50]

In addition, more recent quantitative studies have identified other variables, such as the political origin of migration and the geographical proximity of the country of origin. Refugees from communist-controlled countries naturalize in greater numbers, all things being equal, than other immigrants. Those from nearby countries, especially nations that share land borders with the United States, tend to resist citizenship change more than others. Both results seem to reflect the operation of a general factor, which may be labeled the potential "reversibility" of migration: immigrants for whom it is more difficult to return because of political conditions back home or the high cost and difficulty of the journey tend to naturalize at higher rates than those for whom return is a simple bus ride away.[51]

Studies of the proximate determinants of citizenship have generally focused on minorities with the lowest propensities to naturalize. Mexican immigrants are notorious in this respect, their collective behavior having given rise to a huge gap between the pool of potentially eligible citizens (and voters) and its actual size. Accordingly, several recent studies have sought to identify the principal determinants of both predispositions and behaviors with respect to U.S. citizenship within Mexican immigrant communities. This research includes both quantitative analyses and ethnographic observations.[52] Studies that focus on objective variables have identified such characteristics as length of U.S. residence, level of education, knowledge of English, age, marital status, citizenship of spouse, and place of residence as potentially significant. In general, the decision to naturalize appears to derive from a complex of determinants, including individual needs and motivations and facilitational factors. Mexican immigrants whose stake in the United States is limited to low-wage jobs have little motivation to obtain citizenship. Those, on the other hand, who have acquired property, whose spouses or children are U.S. citizens, and who begin to feel barriers to upward mobility because of their legal status have much greater incentives to begin the process.[53]

Motivation is not enough, however, because citizenship acquisition is not easy. It requires knowledge of English and some knowledge of civics to pass the naturalization test, which favors the better-educated immigrants and those who have lived in the country longer and know more about it. Finally, there is the question of external facilitation. The most significant factors in this respect are social networks and the conduct of official agencies in charge of the process. Networks, as noted earlier, play a variable role in this process because networks consisting solely of Mexican kin and friends tend to be unsupportive of the naturalization process and those that include U.S.-born or naturalized relatives and friends facilitate it.[54] The key governmental agency involved in the process, the U.S. Immigration and Naturalization Service (INS), has a decidedly ambiguous approach toward Mexican applicants. Indeed, ethnographic research has identified "fear of the INS" as a significant deterrent to naturalization among Mexican immigrants, and North, in *The Long Gray Welcome,* an in-depth study of the agency's naturalization procedures, describes the numerous obstacles – from heavy backlogs to arbitrary examiners – often thrown in the way of poor and poorly educated immigrants.[55] Confronted with such barriers, the appropriate question may not be why so few Mexicans naturalize but why so many succeed in doing so.

Conclusion

The history of the major Spanish-origin communities above the Rio Grande reveals a turning point with the expansion and intervention of a rising national power during the nineteenth and early twentieth centuries, and provides context for today's efforts to reach economic and political parity within American society. The success of these efforts depends on the material and educational resources of the different immigrant groups and on the social contexts that receive them. Workers coming to perform low-wage labor in agriculture and industry have faced the greatest obstacles because they lack the resources to move up quickly in the U.S. economy and have been subject to much discrimination. In addition, immigrant workers who see their journeys as temporary maintain strong expectations of return, which adds to their sense of "foreignness" and discourages active participation in mainstream American life.[56]

The contrasting history of the Cuban community is not likely to be repeated any time soon because the circumstances of its origin and initial reception in the United States are unique. Except for professionals migrating legally from several South American countries, whose patterns of adaptation tend to be fairly smooth, the most likely trend for future years is the continuation of manual labor immigration from Mexico, the Dominican Republic, and other countries of the Caribbean Basin. One reason for this trend is noted by Charles Tilly in this book, namely, the resilience of networks of migration over time: migrant flows tend to become self-sustaining through the actions of kin and friends across space. A second reason is the continuing demand for immigrant labor by domestic employers. In the West, demand for Mexican workers remains strong both in agriculture and in industry. In the East, a similar demand exists for Colombians, Dominicans, West Indians, and other Caribbean nationalities.[57] The strength of these market forces is likely to prevent the recently enacted Immigration Reform Act from stopping the inflow of undocumented immigrants.

An exception to this trend is the situation of Puerto Ricans. For reasons discussed above, the condition of "preferred" low-wage labor shifted gradually from this minority to other Caribbean immigrant groups. As a result, the cities of the Northeast face the paradox of unemployment levels among their Puerto Rican communities twice as large as those of native whites, along with the influx of thousands of undocumented immigrants who face little trouble in finding employment. The situation of urban Puerto Ricans thus approaches the bleak one of inner-city blacks, except for the possibility of return migration to the island. Thousands have made use in recent years of this "reverse" escape valve away from the grim conditions of the mainland. In general, the diversity of Spanish-origin communities and the complexity of migration and settlement patterns is likely to continue. Although it is too soon to anticipate the outcome, the growing size of many of these groups, their concentration, and their increasing political and economic presence guarantee them a not insignificant role in American society.

NOTES

1. Bureau of the Census, *Condition of Hispanics in America Today*, Special Release, September 13, 1983.

2. C. Nelson and M. Tienda, "The Structuring of Hispanic Ethnicity: Historical and Contemporary Perspectives," *Ethnic and Racial Studies*, 1985: 49–74; Immigration and Naturalization Service, *Annual Report* (Washington, D.C.: Government Printing Office, 1984).

3. N. Glazer, "Pluralism and the New Immigrants," *Society* 19 (1981): 31–36; R. D. Alba, *Italian Americans: Into the Twilight of Ethnicity* (Englewood Cliffs, N.J.: Prentice-Hall, 1985).

4. F. Nielsen, "Structural Conduciveness and Ethnic Mobilization: The Flemish Movement in Belgium," in *Competitive Ethnic Relations*, ed. S. Olzak and J. Nagel (Orlando, Fla.: Academic Press, 1986), pp. 173–98; K. Hill, "Belgium: Political Change in a Segmented Society," in *Electoral Behavior: A Comparative Handbook,* ed. R. Rose, (New York: Free Press, 1974), pp. 29–107.

5. S. Lieberson, "A Societal Theory of Race and Ethnic Relations," *American Sociological Review* 26 (1961): 902–10.

6. M. Barerra, *Race and Class in the Southwest: A Theory of Racial Inequality* (Notre Dame: Notre Dame University Press, 1980); A. Camarillo, *Chicanos in a Changing Society* (Cambridge: Harvard University Press, 1979).

7. J. Samora, *Los Mojados: The Wetback Story* (Notre Dame: University of Notre Dame Press, 1971); J. A. Bustamante, "The Historical Context of Undocumented Mexican Immigration to the United States," *Aztlán* 3 (1973): 257–81; M. J. Piore, *Birds of Passage: Migrant Labor and Industrial Societies* (New York: Cambridge University Press, 1979).

8. R. L. Bach, "Mexican Immigration and the American State," *International Migration Review* 12 (1978): 536–58.

9. Bustamante, "The Historical Context of Undocumented Mexican Immigration"; Barrera, *Race and Class in the Southwest.*

10. F. A. Bonilla and R. Campos, "A Wealth of Poor: Puerto Ricans in the New Economic Order," *Daedalus* 110 (1981): 133–76.

11. J. Moore and H. Pachón, *Hispanics in the United States* (Englewood Cliffs, N.J.: Prentice-Hall, 1985).

12. C. Rodriguez, *The Ethnic Queue in the U.S.: The Case of Puerto Ricans* (San Francisco: R & E Research Associates, 1976); Bonilla and Campos, "A Wealth of Poor."

13. E. Maldonado, "Contract Labor and the Origin of Puerto Rican Communities in the United States," *International Migration Review* 13 (1979): 103–21; Moore and Pachón, *Hispanics in the United States.*

14. V. Sanchez-Korrol, *From Colonia to Community* (Westport, Conn.: Greenwood Press, 1983); Bonilla and Campos, "A Wealth of Poor."

15. Sanchez-Korrol, *From Colonia to Community*; Bonilla and Campos, "A Wealth of Poor"; J. Fitzpatrick, *Puerto Rican Americans: The Meaning of Migration to the Mainland* (Englewood Cliffs, N.J.: Prentice-Hall, 1971).

16. J. Mañach, *Martí, El Apostol* (Hato Rey, P.R.: El Mirador, 1963).

17. F. Ortiz, *Cuban Counterpoint: Tobacco and Sugar* (New York: Knopf, 1947).

18. H. Thomas, *Cuba, the Pursuit of Freedom,* Book V (New York: Harper & Row, 1971).

19. N. Amaro, "Class and Mass in the Origins of the Cuban Revolution," Washington University Series in Comparative International Development, no. 10 (1969); M. Zeitlin, "Political Generations in the Cuban Working-Class," in *Latin America: Reform or Revolution?*, ed. J. Petras and M. Zeitlin (New York: Fawcett, 1968), pp. 235–48.

20. Thomas, *Cuba, the Pursuit of Freedom*, Book VIII; Amaro, "Class and Mass in the Origins of the Cuban Revolution."

21. S. Pedraza-Bailey, "Cuba's Exiles: Portrait of a Refugee Migration," *International Migration Review* 19 (1985): 4–34; T. D. Boswell and J. R. Curtis, *The Cuban-American Experience* (Totowa, N.J.: Rowman & Allanheld, 1984).

22. Pedraza-Bailey, "Cuba's Exiles"; N. Amaro and A. Portes, "Una Sociología del Exilio: Situación de los Grupos Cubanos en Estados Unidos," *Aportes* 23 (1972): 6–24.

23. S. Diaz-Briquets and L. Perez, "Cuba: The Demography of Revolution," *Population Bulletin* 36 (1981): 2–41; K. L. Wilson and W. A. Martin, "Ethnic Enclaves: A Comparison of the Cuban and Black Economies in Miami," *American Journal of Sociology* 88 (1982): 135–60.

24. S. Grasmuck, "Immigration, Ethnic Stratification, and Native Working-Class Discipline: Comparisons of Documented and Undocumented Dominicans," *International Migration Review* 18 (1984): 692–713; J. A. Moreno, "Intervention and Economic Penetration: The Case of the Dominican Republic," University of Pittsburgh Latin American Occasional Papers, no. 13 (1976).

25. Immigration and Naturalization Service, *Annual Report* (Washington, D.C.: Government Printing Office, 1985).

26. Bureau of the Census, *Annual Report* (1984).

27. P. W. Fagen, "Central Americans and U.S. Refugee Asylum Policies" (Paper presented at the conference on immigration and refugee policies sponsored by the Inter-American Dialogue and the University of California, San Diego, La Jolla, 1986, Mimeographed).

28. A. Portes and J. Walton, *Labor, Class, and the International System* (New York: Academic Press, 1981).

29. Nelson and Tienda, "The Structuring of Hispanic Ethnicity"; L. Perez, "Immigrant Economic Adjustment and Family Organization: The Cuban Success Story Reexamined," *International Migration Review* 20 (1986): 4–20; Pedraza-Bailey, "Cuba's Exiles."

30. C. Hirschman and L. M. Falcón, "The Educational Attainment of Religio-ethnic Groups in the United States," Research in Sociology of Education and Socialization 5 (1985): 83–120.

31. C. W. Reimers, "A Comparative Analysis of the Wages of Hispanics, Blacks, and Non-Hispanic Whites," in *Hispanics in the U.S. Economy*, ed. G. J. Borjas and M. Tienda (Orlando, Fla.: Academic Press, 1985), pp. 27–75.

32. Nelson and Tienda, "The Structuring of Hispanic Ethnicity"; L. Perez, "Immigrant Economic Adjustment and Family Organization"; G. Jasso and M. R. Rosenzweig, "What's in a Name? Country-of-Origin Influences on the Earnings of Immi-

grants in the United States," Bulletin 85-4 (Minneapolis: University of Minnesota, Economic Development Center, 1985, Mimeographed), table 4.

33. Jasso and Rosenzweig, "What's in a Name?"; Pedraza-Bailey, "Cuba's Exiles."

34. M. Tienda and L. Jensen, "Immigration and Public Assistance Partcipation: Dispelling the Myth of Dependency," Discussion Paper 777-85 (Madison: University of Wisconsin-Madison, Institute for Research on Poverty, 1985, Mimeographed); R. L. Bach, L. W. Gordon, D. W. Haines, and D. R. Howell, "The Economic Adjustment of Southeast Asian Refugees in the U.S.," in U.N. Commission for Refugees, *World Refugee Survey* (Geneva: United Nations, 1984), pp. 51–56.

35. Barrera, *Race and Class*; Nelson and Tienda, "The Structuring of Hispanic Ethnicity"; J. S. Passel, "Undocumented Immigrants: How Many?" (Paper presented at the annual meeting of the American Statistical Association, Las Vegas, 1985); F. D. Bean, A. G. King, and J. S. Passel, "The Number of Illegal Migrants of Mexican Origin in the United States: Sex Ratio Based Estimates for 1980," *Demography* 20 (1983): 99–109; F. D. Bean, A. G. King, and J. S. Passel, "Estimates of the Size of the Illegal Migrant Population of Mexican Origin in the United States: An Assessment, Review, and Proposal," in *Mexican Immigrants and Mexican Americans: An Evolving Relation*, ed. H. L. Browning and R. de la Garza (Austin: University of Texas, Center for Mexican-American Studies, 1986), pp. 13–26; H. L. Browning and N. Rodriguez, "The Migration of Mexican Indocumentados as a Settlement Process: Implications for Work," in *Hispanics in the U.S. Economy*, ed. G. J. Borjas and M. Tienda (Orlando, Fla.: Academic Press, 1985), pp. 277–97.

36. J. De Wind, T. Seidl, and J. Shenk, "Contract Labor in U.S. Agriculture," *NACLA Report on the Americas* 11 (1977): 4–37; C. H. Wood, "Caribbean Cane Cutters in Florida: A Study of the Relative Cost of Foreign and Domestic Labor," (Paper presented at the annual meetings of the American Sociological Association, San Antonio, 1984); S. Sassen-Koob, "Formal and Informal Associations: Dominicans and Colombians in New York," *International Migration Review* 13 (1979): 314–32; S. Sassen-Koob, "Immigrant and Minority Workers in the Organization of the Labor Process," *Journal of Ethnic Studies* 1 (1980): 1–34; E. Glaessel-Brown, *Colombian Immigrants in the Industries of the Northeast* (Ph.D. diss., Massachusetts Institute of Technology, 1985); R. Waldinger, "Immigration and Industrial Change in the New York City Apparel Industry," in *Hispanics in the U.S. Economy*, ed. G. J. Borjas and M. Tienda (Orlando, Fla.: Academic Press, 1985), pp. 323–49.

37. F. D. Bean and M. Tienda, *The Hispanic Population of the United States* (New York: Russell Sage Foundation, 1987), chap. 1; Centro de Estudios Puertorriqueños, *Labor Migration under Capitalism* (New York: Monthly Review Press, 1979).

38. The characteristics of the Cuban enclave have been described at length in the research literature: K. L. Wilson and A. Portes, "Immigrant Enclaves: An Analysis of the Labor Market Experiences of Cubans in Miami," *American Journal of Sociology* 86 (1980): 295–319; A. Portes and R. D. Manning, "The Immigrant Enclave: Theory and Empirical Examples," in *Competitive Ethnic Relations*, ed. J. Nagel and S. Olzak (Orlando, Fla.: Academic Press, 1986), pp. 47–64; Wilson and Martin, "Ethnic Enclaves."

39. A. Portes and R. L. Bach, *Latin Journey: Cuban and Mexican Immigrants in the United States* (Berkeley: University of California Press, 1985).

40. De Wind et al., "Contract Labor in U.S. Agriculture"; Glaessel-Brown, *Colombian Immigrants*.

41. J. A. Garcia, "Political Integration of Mexican Immigrants: Explorations into the Naturalization Process," *International Migration Review* 15 (1981): 608–25.

42. Moore and Pachón, *Hispanics in the United States*, pp. 176–86.

43. E. R. Roybal, "Welcome Statement," in *Proceedings of the First National Conference on Citizenship and the Hispanic Community* (Washington, D.C.: National Association of Latin Elected Officials, 1984), p. 7.

44. A. Falcón, "Puerto Rican Politics in Urban America: An Introduction to the Literature," *La Red* (1983): 2–9; J. Jennings, *Puerto Rican Politics in New York City* (Washington, D.C.: University Press, 1977).

45. Moore and Pachón, *Hispanics in the United States*, pp. 186–90.

46. L. J. Botifoll, "How Miami's New Image Was Created," Occasional Paper 1985-1 (Coral Gables: University of Miami, Institute of Interamerican Studies, 1984); Boswell and Curtis, *The Cuban-American Experience*, chap. 10; M. F. Petersen and M. A. Maidique, "Success Patterns of the Leading Cuban-American Entrepreneurs" (Coral Gables: University of Miami, Innovation and Entrepreneurship Institute, 1986, Mimeographed).

47. S. Nazario, "After a Long Holdout, Cubans in Miami Take a Role in Politics," *Wall Street Journal*, June 7, 1983.

48. Moore and Pachón, *Hispanics in the United States*, pp. 194–98.

49. R. Warren, "Status Report on Naturalization Rates," Working Paper CO 1326, 6C (Washington, D.C.: Bureau of the Census, 1979, Mimeographed); A. Portes and R. Mozo, "The Political Adaptation Process of Cubans and Other Ethnic Minorities in the United States," *International Migration Review* 19 (1985): 35–63.

50. W. S. Bernard, "Cultural Determinants of Naturalization," *American Sociological Review* 1 (1936): 943–53.

51. Jasso and Rosenzweig, "What's in a Name?"; Portes and Mozo, "The Political Adaptation Process of Cubans."

52. Garcia, "Political Integration of Mexican Immigrants"; L. Grebler, "The Naturalization of the Mexican Immigrant in the U.S.," *International Migration Review* 1 (1966): 17–32; R. R. Alvarez, "A Profile of the Citizenship Process among Hispanics in the United States: An Anthropological Perspective," Special Report to the National Association of Latin Elected Officials (1985, Mimeographed; 34 pp.); C. Fernandez, "The Causes of Naturalization and Non-naturalization for Mexican Immigrants: An Empirical Study Based on Case Studies," Report to Project Participar (1984, Mimeographed); D. S. North, *The Long Gray Welcome: A Study of the American Naturalization Program,* Monograph report to the National Association of Latin Elected Officials (1985, Mimeographed); W. A. Cornelius, "The Future of Mexican Immigrants in California: A New Perspective for Public Policy," Working Paper on Public Policy 6 (La Jolla: Center for U.S.-Mexico Studies of the University of California-San Diego, 1981).

53. Alvarez, "A Profile of the Citizenship Process among Hispanics in the United States"; A. Portes and J. Curtis, "Changing Flags, Naturalization and Its Determinants among Mexican Immigrants," *International Migration Review* (forthcoming).

54. Garcia, "Political Integration of Mexican Immigrants"; Fernandez, "The Causes of Naturalization and Non-naturalization for Mexican Immigrants."

55. Alvarez, "A Profile of the Citizenship Process among Hispanics in the United States"; North, *The Long Gray Welcome.*

56. Garcia, "Political Integration of Mexican Immigrants"; D. S. Massey, "Understanding Mexican Migration to the United States," *American Journal of Sociology* 92 (forthcoming).

57. Sassen-Koob, "Immigrant and Minority Workers"; Glaessel-Brown, *Colombian Immigrants*; C. H. Wood, "Caribbean Cane Cutters in Florida: A Study of the Relative Cost of Foreign and Domestic Labor" (Paper presented at the annual meetings of the American Sociological Association, San Antonio, 1984).

THE STUDY
OF IMMIGRATION

7

The Sociology and Historiography of Immigration

Ewa Morawska

Between 1820 and 1940, nearly forty million people entered the United States. In the four decades since World War II, about fifteen million have arrived. And they keep coming. Who are the immigrants filling U.S. cities? Why do they come? How do they and their families fare in this country? How do they change with time? What makes them successful? How do the achievements of one ethnic group compare with those of another? Three-quarters of a century ago these questions, posed by William Thomas, Florian Znaniecki, and Robert Park, laid the foundations of contemporary American sociology. Half a century ago similar questions raised by Marcus Hansen and Oscar Handlin made the study of immigration part of mainstream U.S. historiography. The answers provided by these scholars served as a model that guided the studies of generations of sociologists and historians. Their research on various aspects of immigration and ethnicity, ranging from national and regional surveys of aggregate data to ethnocultural studies of single ethnic communities, immigrant parishes, and local associations, has produced an immense body of literature, whose number of pages, like the number of immigrants, runs into the millions. Yet, in 1989 fundamental questions remain open about the fate of the immigrants, their children and grandchildren, and the ways and means by which they adapt to this country while at the same time creating it. Not surprisingly, the challenge to search for new and better answers has motivated scholars to continue their probing, for, ultimately, these questions address the nature, the opportunities, and the future of American society.

In recent years, sociologists and historians have shown increasing interest in each other's disciplines—an interest also visible in the immigration and ethnic

I wish to thank Charles Hirschman, Ivan Light, Douglas Massey, Suzanne Model, Alejandro Portes, Jonathan Sarna, and Olivier Zunz for their very helpful suggestions and comments on the original version of this paper.

studies pursued in both fields. For sociologists, this concern is reflected princi-pally in an increased appreciation of the importance of historical contexts of the phenomena studied. For historians, this cross-fertilization is manifested primarily in the adoption of sociological methods of data analysis. Still, de-spite the growing reciprocal awareness of the significance each has for the other, and despite appeals from both sides for mutual incorporation of con-cepts, research strategies, and findings, most of the current work in the sociol-ogy and historiography of immigration continues to flow in two separate streams.[1] Although they ran parallel for considerable stretches, these two intel-lectual movements are not sufficiently aware of each other. Students in one discipline "discover" what has been acknowledged and treated in the other's research for quite some time. Not infrequently, working with one foot in each field, I hear comments like that of an ethnic historian reacting to the latest "vogue" in immigration research among my sociologist colleagues, "But we have known that for a decade!" And an immigration sociologist had a similar response to some new volume put out by ethnic historians: "Well, don't they ever read what we write?" In no small way, this mutual alienation results from the sheer amount of current writing produced within each field, which has to be digested by its practitioners before they can reach out to acquaint themselves with related — and likewise vast — research in the neighboring discipline. And in part, too, it has been academic parochialism, persistent if diminishing, that keeps these two fields apart.

It is not the ambition of this essay to bridge the existing gap. Welcome as it would be, a systematic comparative review of even the standard issues that constitute the traditional research agendas of sociological and historical studies of immigration would call for a team of workers and a separate volume. A more modest purpose, but one useful and appropriate to the occasion, is to illustrate with empirical evidence some convergent themes that have informed recent sociological and historical studies of immigration and ethnicity and that are indicative of the directions current research is taking.

To simplify the discussion, I will limit it to two immigrant waves. The first is the traditional subject of ethnic historiography: the South and East Europeans who made up about three-fourths of all arrivals in the United States during the period of mass immigration between the 1880s and 1914. In historical studies, they are usually called "new" immigrants as distinct from the earlier ones from northern and western Europe. The second wave is the favorite subject of cur-rent sociological research: the successors of South and East Europeans and now the proper contenders for the "new" title — the immigrants from Hispanic America and Asia, whose numbers, limited before World War II, have been rapidly growing in the past decades, and who now constitute over two-thirds of all arrivals in the United States.

Each of these immigrant waves contains several different peoples. Space limitations will permit only occasional references here to some of the differ-ences among them. It should be kept in mind, however, that under the summa-ry label "South Europeans" hide such diverse peoples as the Italians (from the very different North and South of the country), Greeks, Bulgarians, Albanians, and Macedonians. The blanket term "East Europeans" covers no less than fourteen different groups (each keenly aware of its distinctiveness): Poles, Slovaks, Czechs, Rusyns, Ukrainians, Armenians, Lithuanians, Estonians, Latvians, Hungarians, Croatians, Serbs, Slovenes, and Jews (who were further divided into subcultural groupings depending on the territories from which they came). Similarly, "Hispanics" are composed of different peoples with different traits and histories, of whom the Mexicans, Puerto Ricans, Cubans, Dominicans, Colombians, and Hondurans are the most numerous in the United States. The label "Asians" covers the Chinese, Japanese, Filipinos, Koreans, Indians and Pakistanis, Vietnamese, Cambodians, and Laotians, each group possessing separate cultural traditions and economic and social characteristics.[2]

The most visible parallel in the development of the sociology and historiography of immigration over the past fifteen years has been the unsettling of two classical paradigms that dominated American studies of immigration and ethnicity from their inception as an academic subdiscipline until the late 1960s. One has been the assumption that in modern, urban-industrial society the socioeconomic success — "attainment" is the term commonly used in the literature — and the life course in general of the immigrants and their offspring depend mainly on "human capital," that is, on the motivations, values, talents, and skills possessed by individuals. The second general conception, closely affiliated with the first and derived from the same underlying vision of the nature of modern society, has been that of assimilation, that is, of the progressive weakening and ultimate disappearance of the primordial traits and bonds of ethnicity as succeeding generations adopt the general society's unitary system of cultural values and become absorbed into economic, social, and political networks that are blind to ethnicity. These classical conceptualizations, which first appeared in such seminal works as those of William Thomas and Florian Znaniecki, *The Polish Peasant*; Oscar Handlin, *Boston Immigrants* and *The Uprooted*; and Robert Park, *Race and Culture*, among others, have been seriously challenged.[3] Recent sociological and historical research is demonstrating (1) that factors above and beyond individual motives and skills significantly influence actions and achievements of immigrant group members, and (2) that large "ethnic pockets" and intergroup differences persist for several generations in the economic, social, and cultural realms of American life. In both disciplines, new concerns and ideas, basically similar in their interpretative thrust — even if differently phrased and profiled — have been introduced to the study of immigration. They have given a new understanding to the basic concepts structuring this field of inquiry and have considerably shifted its major emphases.

Four such shared themes appear to have had the most impact. One is the emphasis on broadly conceived structural determinants, such as time, location, and the economic and political environments, of the processes involved in the movement of immigrants from the home country and their adaptation to the new society. The second theme focuses on collectivist (that is, socially embedded and group-sustained, rather than "self-made" individualistic) strategies used by the immigrants and their families, starting with the immigration process itself and continuing through the incorporation into the economic and social systems of the receiving society. Closely related to this theme is the third, stressing the resilient character of ethnicity, and the contextual and instrumental, rather than primarily expressive, cultural-psychological genesis and function of ethnic ties and identities. The fourth and final theme is the interrelation of class and ethnicity in influencing the immigrants' position in the host society, and the group identities and associations that they form.[4]

In undertaking their studies, sociologists and historians of immigration usually have different goals in mind, reflecting the different traditional approaches of their respective disciplines. Sociologists want to test competing theoretical models for general applicability, while historians aim at specifying the conditions under which a given interpretation will best account for the phenomena studied. They also usually work with different source materials, and they pursue their studies in response to problem agendas specific to their fields. Naturally, then, within the general framework of their shared thematic concerns, there are obvious differences in the conceptualization of research, its emphases and argumentation. For instance, in a series of recent sociological studies of immigration, the underlying idea has been to demonstrate the primary importance of structural determinants of the origins and processes of labor migrations to the United States, and of the socioeconomic achievement of particular ethnic groups.[5] These studies are usually elegantly conceptualized, tightly argued, and supported by formidable quantitative evidence—a pleasure for a sociologist to read. If their strong emphasis on the "objective" as opposed to the "subjective" factors in influencing the immigrants' actions and their outcomes appears at times overdrawn, at the expense of more complex interpretations with a lighter touch, it is in part because these studies, which are conceptualized within the model-testing framework of the discipline, are vigorously contesting the individualist human-capital, status-attainment paradigm that still has a strong hold on mainstream sociological literature on immigration and ethnicity.[6] In part, too, the type of sources most commonly used in current sociological research—aggregate census and survey data, which permit only a certain kind of analysis—tend to move structurally minded scholars toward "objectivist" interpretations.

On the other hand, in the historiography of immigration, the individualist status-attainment model has never gained such predominance. The fascination with so-called social mobility studies, which applied conventional sociological measurements of intra- and intergenerational socioeconomic attainment to particular ethnic groups by tracing individual movement up and down status ladders, began with Thernstrom's seminal work in Newburyport, Massachusetts (1965), and Boston (1973). A cornucopia of studies conducted in different American cities and time periods followed, but the interest soon waned. Their major contribution was a successful debunking of the "land-of-opportunity" image of industrializing America, at least in relation to large segments of lower-class populations.[7]

A difference in research methods also influences the outcome. Despite some applications of sociological modes of analysis, historians of immigration and ethnicity usually rely on fine-grained investigations of particular localities. (This approach, once highly respected and widely practiced by sociologists, has now given way to highly sophisticated quantitative analyses of large sets of aggregate data. In such studies, sociologists measure ecological variables only crudely, as whole regional units, or at best as standard metropolitan or rural areas, while such elements of the social process as personal networks, communal associations, or collective resources are captured not at all or inadequately.) As the number of thoroughly investigated cases has accumulated, immigration historians have gained solid empirical knowledge about the social and economic opportunities and situations in a wide range of geographically and historically different localities and how these affected the adaptation of immigrants and their families. It is perhaps for these reasons that in comparison with its sociological counterpart, recent historical writing seems less aggressively assertive or more secure in acknowledging the evident importance of structural factors in the entry, position, and socioeconomic success of immigrants in the dominant society. Having established the constraining impact on people and phenomena studied of a particular constellation of structural forces, much of the recent research in ethnic history subsequently "transcends" it, as it were, by focusing on the reconstruction of various ways in which the immigrants and their families creatively coped with these structural limitations by maneuvering within them and playing against the constraints in an effort to bring their environment into closer conformity with their purposes.[8] This emphasis by ethnic historians on "playing within structures" has its close counterpart in works in the historical sociology of immigration that investigate the adaptation of earlier ethnic groups originating from southern and eastern Europe and Asia before World War II; a similar interpretative direction also informs some recent sociological studies of "new" Asian and Hispanic immigrants.[9]

The introduction of new themes into the study of immigration and ethnicity and the accumulation of new findings and interpretations have unsettled the two classical paradigms of "self-made" achievement and assimilation but have not rendered them useless. On the contrary, much in their conceptual framework, research questions, and empirical findings remains worthy of continuing sociological and historical inquiry. Since there is no consensus, in either the sociology or history of immigration, regarding the "appropriate" ways to conduct ethnic studies, this wealth of ideas is somewhat bewildering. What certainly has come out of the past decade and a half of reassessment is the awareness, shared by immigration historians and sociologists alike, of the enormous complexity of the processes involved in peoples' migrations from one place to another, and in their subsequent adaptation to new environments. This complexity should not yield to reductionist explanations.

The remainder of this chapter will illustrate selected themes informing recent sociological and historical research on immigration and ethnicity, as specified earlier, in three sections: (1) origins and process of migration to the United States; (2) incorporation into the American economy; and (3) sociocultural adaptation to American society. The third section will be the shortest, outlining the common themes with only a minimum of illustrations in order to underscore particularly important points. Shortest not because the reader will be getting weary by that point (although that is perhaps a legitimate consideration), and certainly not because of the paucity of empirical material, but because there is simply much too much of it. Of the three areas of research selected for discussion, this one — sociocultural adaptation — has the largest and most fragmented literature. Multiplied by two, this abundance becomes a deluge.

Origins and Process of Migration to the United States

The traditional interpretation of labor migrations explains the international flow of people in terms of "push" and "pull" forces. The demographic and economic conditions in the sending and in the receiving countries prompt individuals to move from places with a surplus of population, little capital, and underemployment to areas where labor is scarce and wages are higher. This classical version focuses on individual decisions and actions, seen as the outcomes of a rational economic calculation of the costs and benefits of migration. A newer, modified version of this model views the role of individual actions as important, but as played out within the context of broader structural forces from both the "pull" and "push" sides of the process. The most recent literature on international migrations has further reconceptualized this problem by moving the unit of analysis from separate nation-states linked by the one-way transfer of emigrants responding to economic cycles and shifting social conditions to an extended, unified system composed of a dominant "center" and a dependent "periphery" — a system that forms a complex network of supranational exchanges involving the back-and-forth flow of technology, capital, and labor. Rather than the individual and his or her decisions, this interpretation places the central emphasis on the broad structural determinants of human movements within the global economic system. Until recently, the global-system and dependency theory have had a greater impact on sociological research about immigration, which focuses on current flows from Third World countries, than on historical studies of past migrations from South and East Europe. Most of the latter are conducted within a modified push-and-pull conceptual framework that acknowledges the impact of broader socioeconomic forces, without denying the autonomous role of individual and local group actions. During the past couple of years, however, some historians of European immigration have begun to apply the global-system–dependency model to the interpretation of labor migrations within and from the southern and eastern parts of the Continent at the turn of the century.[10]

Informed by a shared concern for the importance of structural inducement to human actions, recent historical and sociological analyses of the genesis and content of labor migrations to the United States emphasize the profound imbalances and dislocations that capitalist transformations have caused in the traditional local economies of the "peripheral" societies. The absorption of these societies into the orbit of the expanding capitalist system has been setting millions of people in motion in different parts of the world for over one hundred years: from Russian, Polish, Italian, Magyar, Slovak, Transylvanian, Greek, Mexican, Chinese, Japanese, Korean, and Filipino villages in the later part of the nineteenth century, and from the present-day Dominican, Guatemalan, and Colombian towns and countryside.[11]

While the structural environment delineates the general boundaries of the possible and impossible within which people live, it is at the local level of their immediate surroundings that they make their decisions, define purposes, and undertake actions. In comparison with sociological studies of present-day population movements, more pronouncedly structuralist in their approach and methods, the detailed, microscopic analyses of the historiography of mass migrations at the turn of the century have made headway in elucidating the impact of local conditioning factors on these processes. Patterns of land tenure and local gradations of status and income; access to transportation and distance from other employment sources; the level of literacy and the local taxation system, household composition, and rates of fertility — the interplay of all these and of other factors, historically and geographically variant, significantly affects the course, social characteristics, directions, goals, and intensity of migrations.[12]

Two converging conclusions reached by these studies, of apparent validity across time and space, should be noted here. One is that, contrary to a conventional view of the emigrants as "pushed out" of their homelands and "pulled into" the United States in a two-step, unidirectional movement, both the "old" migrants and their "new" counterparts have been part of extensive migratory flows well before they accomplished their move to America. And two, that contrary to the well-established stereotype of the "huddled masses," most U.S.-bound migrants, while certainly poor by absolute and relative standards, did not originate from the poorest regions and were not members of the lowest economic classes but, rather, came from the lower and lower-middle ranks of their home societies. Post-World War II immigrants are much more heterogeneous in economic background and social composition than were their predecessors a century ago. In the peak decade (1900–1910) of U.S. immigration, about 85 to 90 percent of the entering Italian, Slavic, Hungarian, and Mexican peasants and 65 percent of the Jews were manual workers, and 1 to 2 percent were in the professions.[13] In the same period, 75 percent of the Chinese and Japanese immigrants were also classified as laborers (in agriculture, industry, and domestic services), with no more than 2 percent in professional occupations.[14] Passage of the 1965 amendments to the Immigration and Nationality Act changed U.S. admission policy by giving preference to persons joining their families already in this country, and to highly skilled workers. As a result, today's immigrants consist of either upper-echelon white-collar workers (20 to over 50 percent of the current entries, depending on national group) or industrial workers from the lower strata (from 20 to 65 percent of the total). In addition, an estimated four to six million undocumented immigrants — nearly two-thirds of them from Mexico and about one-third from other Western Hemisphere countries — have entered the United States during the past decade. But even these people, less skilled and less educated than the legal entrants, do not originate from the most impoverished areas or from the bottom ranks of their societies but, like those arriving at the turn of the century, come from the lower and lower-middle economic strata.[15]

In a parallel shift away from the "self-induced"/individualist emphasis that underlay earlier interpretations of past and present movements of people between countries and regions, recent immigration studies emphasize the collectivist nature of the migration process itself. In a radical break from Handlin's once paradigmatic description of the immigrants as "uprooted" from their home backgrounds and venturing alone into the New World, a series of historical studies of migrations from virtually all corners of South and East Europe at the turn of the century have confirmed the socially embedded, family- and community-supported character of these endeavors. The decisions leading to migration as well as the actual transplantation routinely occurred through "chains" of social networks that extended from the place of origin to the destination in the United States. According to a study by the U.S. Immigration Commission, conducted in 1908–1909, about 60 percent of the new immigrants arriving from South and East Europe declared that their passage was arranged for by immigrants already in this country. An even greater number were headed for destinations where they were awaited by relatives or acquaintances from their home towns and villages, with the ten largest cities in the Northeast and Midwest absorbing the greatest share of the arrivals.[16] Similar findings have been reported by students of the nineteenth-century migrations to the United States of the Chinese, Japanese, Filipinos, and Mexicans, who also came in enveloping chains to the cities of the West Coast (Asians) and to the rural Southwest (Mexicans), where clusters of earlier settlers already existed.[17]

Collective migration patterns, originating in the home country and extended through social support networks into the United States, have also been recorded by students of present-day immigration from Mexico, Puerto Rico, Colombia, the Dominican Republic, and other countries of the Caribbean basin, and from Japan, Taiwan, Hong Kong, and Korea. In a recent sociological study of documented Mexican immigrants arriving in the United States in the early 1970s, 90 percent of the respondents said they were awaited by family or friends, and 80 percent knew beforehand their prospective employers. Like their predecessors at the turn of the century, most of today's immigrants are headed to residential locations where their kin, friends, and compatriots are already settled. Seventy-five percent of the Cubans go to Florida and New Jersey; 80 percent of Mexicans to Texas and California; 75 percent of Puerto Ricans to New York; 60 percent of Colombians to New York and New Jersey; 70 percent of Dominicans to New York; 70 percent of Japanese to California and Hawaii; 65 percent of Chinese and Filipinos to California, Hawaii, and New York; and 50 percent of Koreans to California, Hawaii, New York, and Illinois. In these states, eight metropolitan centers — Miami, Los Angeles, San

Francisco, Houston, San Antonio, Honolulu, Chicago, and New York — take in the largest number of immigrants.[18]

The majority of immigrants arriving in the United States at the turn of the century were young men who came as migrant laborers rather than as permanent settlers. They intended their stay to be temporary, and hoped through a few years of hard work to accumulate sufficient capital to return and better their station at home. Most of the original sojourners eventually remained in the United States, but the proportion of those who returned was much higher than was assumed in earlier immigration historiography and in popular images. For instance, no less than 35 percent of the Poles, Serbs, Croatians, and Slovenes, 40 percent of the Greeks, and over 50 percent of the southern Italians and Magyars, and Slovaks from the northeastern part of Austria-Hungary returned to Europe. Even the Jews, whose mass emigration from eastern Europe at the turn of the century was prompted as much by increasing political persecution as by adverse economic conditions, and the majority of whom came with their families intending their move as permanent, returned, during the period between 1880 and 1900, at the considerable rate of over 20 percent.[19] Among the early Asian immigrants on the West Coast and in Hawaii, departures were much higher — two-thirds — caused largely by a series of expulsion acts between 1882 and 1903.[20] The return rate of Mexican immigrants, estimated at about 20 percent during the first two decades of this century, increased to over 80 percent in the interwar period, mainly as a result of deportations during the depression.[21] However, with improved and cheaper transportation, a number of those who went home often came back again. For instance, at the beginning of the century, two-thirds of the Chinese, one-third of the Mexicans, and between 15 and 20 percent of the Italians, Slovaks, Hungarians, and Rusyns investigated by the U.S. Immigration Commission reported previous visits to the United States. Historical studies of American labor migrations of Polish peasants before World War I report multiple entry rates of 20 to 40 percent.[22]

In the postwar period immigration to the United States became more permanent. Still, it is estimated that over 15 percent of all persons admitted into the country after 1960 departed within a decade, with the proportion of return migration for persons thirty years or older even higher, nearly 25 percent.[23] The actual migratory flows are much more intense, however, since this estimate does not include undocumented circular movements between Mexico and other Western Hemisphere countries and the United States. In a recent study of Mexican immigrants, 60 percent of the arrivals reported one or more previous American sojourns, many of which were probably undocumented.[24] Repeated migrations from Puerto Rico are also unmeasured; by the late 1970s it has been estimated that a high 15 percent of the island's population consisted of return migrants from the mainland United States.[25]

The ebb-and-flow character of immigration to the United States, from the nineteenth century to the present, further substantiates the conceptualization of this process as a continuous exchange between interrelated segments of a unified, extended system. It also indicates an additional dimension for the interpretation of the migration process as a collective endeavor. Paralleling the extended two-way system in which it arises, this collectivism works both "forward," from the immigrants' place of origin into the United States, as they prepare to leave and actually arrive, and "backward" in the direction of home when they are in the United States. Both sociological research and historical research demonstrate that as long as they remain sojourners, and even after they settle permanently in this country, "old" and "new" immigrants alike maintain close contact with their families and friends left at home. For a long time, they send home remittances. At the turn of the century, Italian and Slavic laborers were capable of saving 60 to 65 percent of their monthly earnings for transfer home.[26] Today, Mexican migrants save up to 40 percent for the same purpose.[27] Among less-studied groups such as Koreans, some of the immigrants arrange to have capital brought to the United States to establish themselves.[28] In either case, they continue long-distance management of their households left behind, either through repeated visits or via supervision and advice administered through correspondence and other means of communication.[29]

Incorporation into the American Economy

A similar shift away from individualism and toward structuralist and collectivist emphases has also occurred in recent sociological and historical studies regarding interpretations of the socioeconomic position and status attainment in the United States of the immigrants and their offspring. The structural emphasis underscores the importance of factors external to individuals and their human capital; the collectivist one stresses the coping resources of the group of which the immigrants are members: family, ethnic, and class. Since each of these two themes covers a number of issues worth touching upon even briefly, we shall discuss them separately in order.

In taking account of structural factors in shaping the immigrants' opportunities and achievements in the American economic system, sociological and historical research has followed different paths to demonstrate similar points. Historians, partly in reaction to disappointments with the "mobility studies" of the early 1970s, which were conducted without due attention to the structural context, have since amassed a rich documentation of how the socioeconomic position and status achievement of immigrants of similar backgrounds and human capital were affected by the different economic, political, and developmental dynamics of particular regions and localities in which they entered the labor market. At the turn of the century, the American urban economy needed large quantities of manual labor for its rapidly expanding manufacturing and mining industries, and the millions of South and East European immigrants filled this demand. In 1910, among foreign-born Slavic and Hungarian men in active employment, almost three-quarters were concentrated in four major American industries: coal, iron and steel, metals and slaughtering and meat-packing. A similar proportion of foreign-born Italian men were employed in four industries: coal, iron and steel, construction, and clothing. Among 60 percent of East European Jewish immigrants engaged in manufacturing, nine-tenths were concentrated in garment, wool, silk, fur, leather, and other related industries, with the remainder employed in trade and peddling and in lower-white-collar occupations.[30] The analyses of conditions obtaining in particular cities where these immigrants settled — their size, demographic profile, ethnic composition, political organization, and economic development — have demonstrated considerable differences in local opportunity structures and, consequently, in the processes of incorporating particular immigrant groups into the urban economies, such as their dispersion among particular subsegments of the labor markets and different rates of movement up and down occupational ladders. For instance, New York and Chicago, the two wide-open, growing metropolises with highly differentiated occupational structures and, in particular, a white-collar sector already expanding rapidly at the beginning of the century, allowed for substantial shifts of East European Jewish and Italian immigrants between branches of the local economies and within occupations during a short period after their arrival in these cities during the 1880s and 1905–1915.[31] The rapid economic expansion of Detroit during the first two decades of this century loosened up the earlier tight occupational clusters, permitting the new immigrants a wider range of work opportunities in the industrial sector.[32] In comparison, Boston and Philadelphia apparently offered more limited opportunities, but changes in the location and structure of job supplies in the period from 1880 to 1930 helped the immigrants to shift within and directly outside these cities.[33] The multifaceted, nonindustrial economy and the absence of large ethnic concentrations in Washington, D.C., provided a "modest plurality of opportunities" for Italian immigrants, who from the beginning of their settlement there ventured into various kinds of employment.[34] In smaller localities, such as Steelton and Johnstown in Pennsylvania, which were characterized by autocratic political orders and dominated by one major industry and which became economically stagnant during the interwar period, both the entry position and the subsequent socioeconomic attainment of the South and East European immigrants who settled there were more severely circumscribed, with about three-quarters of the men present in 1900 having remained ordinary laborers by 1925–1930.[35] Nearby Pittsburgh, also a steel city, was larger and had more developmental momentum — the white-collar sector expanded by 10 percent between 1900 and the 1920s (compared to about 5 percent in Johnstown) — which permitted a greater dispersion of immigrants within the city's economy. By 1920, 45 percent of Polish and Italian men present since the beginning of the century had shifted their occupational position in some way.[36]

Most East European Jewish families settled in New York, Boston, Philadelphia, Baltimore, and Chicago, and entered the U.S. economy as working class, employed in the garment and other related industries. A sizable minority — 25 to 30 percent — went to places with different economic characteristics, where they entered the economy mostly through commerce. For instance, by World War I, 65 percent of Russian Jewish immigrants in Providence, Rhode Island, were self-employed, mostly in small family businesses or in service occupations, and only 23 percent were manual workers (as compared with nearly 60 percent in New York, 60 percent in Philadelphia, and 40 percent in Chicago during the same period). In Worcester and Fall River, Massachusetts, the proportion of self-employed Jewish immigrants in that same period was nearly 60 percent. My own research on the adaptation of East European Jews in Johnstown, Pennsylvania, a predominantly blue-collar steel town, shows this proportion to have been as high as 75 percent throughout the four decades preceding World War II.[37]

In Los Angeles and San Francisco on the West Coast, and in Atlanta in the South, the loose economic structure, still in the making at the turn of the century, permitted new European immigrants who ventured there to take up job opportunities created by the emerging industries and to circulate between occupations even more easily than in the expanding northeastern and midwestern metropolises. The same social and economic volatility, however, made their economic and social status achievements quite unstable; easy to accomplish, the moves upward were frequently followed by swift declines.[38]

Since social-historical analyses usually focus on a particular locality and cover varying time frames, from limited decadal investigations to large projects encompassing half a century, their findings are not readily comparable, a situation that has caused immigration historians to voice growing concern for the need to bring this research together in a more synchronized and concerted fashion. Two recently published works of a synthetic character, one providing a historical overview of the general direction of urban processes in the United States, the other proposing a typology of economic and political structures of American cities since the nineteenth century, with implications for the varying economic opportunities they offered the immigrants and their offspring, should help to move current research in this direction.[39]

In the field of sociology, voluminous research on the status attainment and social mobility of immigrants and their offspring since World War II indicates that by and large most of them have made visible progress. Still, considerable differences persist in the processes and rates of mobility among particular groups. To a significant degree, these are attributable to differential human-capital skills of the individuals who make up these groups, such as parental background, schooling and occupational training, work experience, and, in the case of the foreign-born, English proficiency and time spent in the United States. But even when all these factors are taken into consideration and "neutralized," considerable differences in socioeconomic achievement remain among certain groups, indicating the operation of factors that transcend individual inputs.[40]

In an attempt to account for this "leftover," recent sociological research on ethnic socioeconomic achievement has applied the concepts of dual economy and segmented labor markets. Developed during the 1970s by political economists, these concepts derive from observations of the progressive bifurcation of capitalist enterprises into two tiers, called primary and secondary sectors.[41] Basically, the present-day primary labor market in the United States corresponds to employment in public and other large-scale institutions, and in the oligopolistic sector of industry (such as coal, metals, oil, chemicals), which are characterized by stability of employment and by union regulations. Employment in the primary sector provides good wages and working conditions, as well as institutionalized internal job ladders with opportunities for advancement in pay and status. Enterprises in the secondary sector, on the other hand, are those in small-scale, competitive branches of the economy, such as light industry, retailing, and services, that are characterized by fluctuating production, lack of union protection, and rapid labor turnover. Employment in this sector lacks stability, requires little or no prior training, offers predominantly menial, dead-end jobs for low wages, and has few if any mobility opportunities within firms. The primary and secondary sectors have little overlap, although the former contains a subordinate subsegment of jobs whose characteristics correspond to those in the secondary sector.

Sociological research on immigrant and ethnic achievements has produced two major theses that take into consideration the impact of the sectoral segmentation of labor. The first is that above and beyond the human capital possessed by individuals, their differential insertion into the labor market means access to unequal opportunities, and therefore plays an important role in determining occupational status and earnings. The second is that in the secondary sector of the economy, workers are hired primarily on the basis of their ethnicity, a fact which significantly affects the rewards they receive for their labor, thereby suppressing the impact of human-capital investments.

Most research using the dual-labor-markets approach deals with the present-day American economy and current labor migrations. In fact, in the sociological literature the segmentation of labor markets has commonly been treated as a post-World War II phenomenon characteristic of advanced capitalism.[42] But the theorists who developed this mode in the 1970s point out that "most of [their initial] hypotheses have not arisen from historical research but have been adduced from [contemporary] local market investigation and cross-sectional analysis," and that since these hypotheses concerning "the dynamics and dialectics of jobs, people and labor market operations . . . are explicitly historical," the dual-labor-market theory "poses a challenge [for historical research] which economists have not yet begun."[43] More recent studies of the historical transformation of labor in the United States trace the origin of labor market segmentation in the U.S. economy to the first decades of this century as it emerged through two overlapped processes: the "middling out" of industrial skills as the result of the mechanization of production, and the introduction of new internal job ladders and the "departmentalization" of specific work in the factories.[44] To the best of my knowledge, however, except for a couple of studies by economists and a somewhat larger number of mainly descriptive analyses in the historical literature, the segmented-labor-markets model has not yet been applied in a systematic and analytical fashion to the situation of the Slavic, Hungarian, and Italian workers in American factories at the beginning of this century.

Eighty years ago, the major industries employing these immigrants—coal and metals, both classified today as belonging to the primary sector—possessed most of the features typical of secondary employment as described by the dual-labor-market theory. They exhibited frequent and intense shifts in the volume of production, with annual turnover of over 65 percent; were still largely nonunionized; and they relied heavily on low-skill labor, which formed up to 50 percent of the workforce. As a result of these characteristics, within the "lower occupational circuits" of the industrial establishments into which South and East European immigrant laborers were incorporated en masse, there existed conditions that the dual-labor-market theory treats as a source and an index of labor market division: employment instability and a large pool of basically unstructured, low-paid, and menial jobs. For the next two decades, the hiring process and the internal allocation of jobs and wages effectively excluded these workers from participation in the more stable, better rewarded, and better structured job tracks reserved for native-born U.S. and West European workers. Perhaps this situation should be described as an ethnically split "secondary internal labor market."[45] Comparative analyses by economic historians of the earnings of "new" immigrants and native-born American workers in the manufacturing industries investigated in 1908–1909 by the U.S. Immigration Commission show that after eliminating the effects of differential human-capital variables, including English proficiency and time spent in the United States, the ethnic origin of the workers accounted for 10 to 25 percent of the difference in remuneration received by these two groups. Another study of the 1901 and 1909 wages received by "new" immigrants and U.S. workers in selected industries in Illinois, Massachusetts, New York, and Pennsylvania indicates that the considerably greater instability of employment experienced by the immigrants was the main cause of their diminished earnings: in comparison with the average of 4.3 weeks of unemployment per annum for native-born American workers, the "new" immigrants went jobless for an average of 7.5 weeks during the year.[46]

The allocation of South and East European laborers among the departments of the Bethlehem Steel Company mills in Johnstown, Pennsylvania, and of the wages they received in comparison with American and West European workers, as reported by the Immigration Commission that visited the city in 1908–1909, indicate that two internal labor markets existed within the local mills, with differential wage rates for similar types of labor, depending on the ethnic composition of the work force. In the less prestigious departments, which paid common laborers daily rates of $1.25 to $1.35, almost 80 percent of the employed were South and East Europeans, while in the "better" shops, where laborers' wages were $1.45 to $1.65, South and East Europeans constituted no more than 20 percent. Ethnicity was also a stronger determinant of earnings than work experience. Among those who had been employed in the company for five years, almost 70 percent of Italian and Slavic day laborers, as compared with only 40 percent of Americans and West Europeans in the same general labor category, earned less than $12.50 a week. Even in the group of pieceworkers with an equal number of years in the company, the ethnic effect on wages persisted: almost 40 percent of the Slavic, as compared with 30 percent of the native-born American and West European laborers who had been employed in the Bethlehem mills for five years still earned less than $12.50 a week.[47]

Unlike the turn-of-the-century immigrants, a numerically significant proportion of those arriving today are directed to the primary sector of the economy (from the standpoint of the sending societies often called the "brain drain"). Nevertheless, a large number of immigrants still enter the U.S. labor market in the secondary sector. They, like their predecessors, are multiply disadvantaged in that they possess little human capital, such as English proficiency and familiarity with the American environment, often represent groups considered inferior in the cultural hierarchy of the dominant society, and — a disadvantage spared the South and East Europeans arriving a century ago — are politically vulnerable if their entry was not legal. These new immigrant laborers fit well the needs of the secondary sector of the American economy.

Current Mexican immigration provides a prototypical example of secondary labor. A disproportionately high number of foreign-born Mexicans (55 percent, as compared with 35 percent of the native born) are employed in the secondary sector, most of them in agriculture and light industry, and the remainder in services.[48] A recent sociological study of Mexican immigrants who (legally) entered the United States in the early 1970s shows their concentration in the secondary labor market to be even higher: 75 percent.[49] Research on the earnings accruing to foreign-born and second-generation Mexicans employed in the primary and secondary sectors indicates that for both groups the returns to human capital are significantly lower in the secondary sector, even after eliminating the effects of regional differences (the cost of living and wages being lower in the rural Southwest, where the majority of Mexican Americans reside). A study comparing earnings of Mexicans with those of Anglos in 1960 and 1970 found the average net "cost" of Mexican ethnicity to represent 13 percent in lost income.[50] A more recent investigation has shown that for Mexican immigrants employed in the secondary sector, human capital (education, English proficiency, work training and experience, and length of U.S. residence) account for no more than 25 percent of the variance in earnings.[51] Employment in the secondary sector of the economy is not only more "costly" in the sense that it brings fewer rewards for similar individual investments but also less stable. A study of Mexican immigrants who arrived in the United States during the early 1970s, three-quarters of whom entered the secondary labor market, showed that by the end of the decade 40 percent had shifted jobs at least once within a six-year period, and that each such job shift cost Mexican immigrants $37.50 a month.[52]

Another Hispanic group concentrated primarily (70 percent) in the secondary labor sector is the Puerto Ricans, most of whom reside in New York.[53] Research on this group indicates that since the 1960s their socioeconomic position has been deteriorating. In 1980, 40 percent of Puerto Rican families (30 percent in 1970) lived below the poverty level, as compared with 20 percent and 11 percent of Mexican and Cuban households respectively.[54] A particularly unfavorable combination of factors accounts for this situation. Not only are most Puerto Ricans employed in the secondary labor market, where they receive less remuneration for similar human-capital investments, and where this remuneration is further depleted by frequent spells of unemployment, but they are also concentrated in a region (the Northeast) and industries (New York garment and textile) that have been experiencing economic decline. In addition, a disproportionately large number of Puerto Rican families (41 percent, as compared with 16 percent of Mexican and 18 percent of Cuban households) are headed by women, whose position in the secondary labor market is even weaker than that of men. As a result, the socioeconomic attainment of Puerto Ricans is constrained by the triple structural disadvantage of geography, industrial location, and household composition.[55]

In the original formulation by political economists, both primary and secondary labor markets belong to the mainstream economy in the sense that they are managed and controlled by representatives of the dominant groups in American society. Recent studies on immigration and ethnicity have pointed to the existence of yet a third variant in labor market segmentation, namely, the "ethnic economic enclave" or "ethnic (sub)economy," consisting of ethnic-owned enterprises employing workers of the same immigrant origins.[56] Some immigrant groups, such as Jews, Greeks, Chinese, and Japanese among the "old" ones, and Cubans, Koreans, and Dominicans among the "new" ones, have a distinct proclivity toward a concentration in economic niches, particularly as self-employed members of certain trades and services and in some branches of light industry, where they also employ their kin and fellow ethnics. The reasons for this pronounced clustering vary historically and for particular groups, and there has been a long-standing and continuing debate in the ethnic literature as to which explanatory models would best account for the structural, cultural, and various situational factors important in the genesis and persistence of this phenomenon. For instance, the "old" Asian immigrants on the West Coast before World War II concentrated in ethnic economic enclaves mainly as a result of discriminatory policies by state and local governments and because of open hostility from dominant groups. For the Jews in the East at the turn of the century, the likely reason for the clustering, at least initially, was a timely matching of demand for particular skills in the expanding garment, leather, and related industries in the major cities in which they settled, combined with a supply of skilled labor — 65 percent of Jewish foreign-born men had been skilled craftsmen in Eastern Europe, and the majority specialized in trades adaptable to light manufacturing.[57] On the other hand, for those who ventured into smaller localities, disproportionate clustering in self-employed occupations probably resulted from a transfer of the old-country entrepreneurial tradition, supported by intragroup social-economic networks. For the Cubans in Florida, it has been the transplantation to the United States of a large segment of the entrepreneurial strata — along with their economic resources — in the wake of Castro's revolution.[58] The case of recent Korean immigrants, about half of whom come from the professional and managerial strata, may represent in miniature a pattern similar to that of the post-1959 Cubans, with the exception that Korean migration to the United States has been voluntary.[59]

Despite the rapid accumulation of historical and sociological research on the differential modes of immigrant groups' absorption into the American economy — or perhaps because of it — the evidence for the advantages and disadvantages of participation in coethnic economies as opposed to mainstream primary and secondary sectors has been far from conclusive. Where these studies do converge is in their shared emphasis on the interpretation of ethnicity, in particular of ethnic bonds and loyalties, as a resource that is situationally activated to cope in the host environment. Closely related to the above issue is the theme of the collective: the family- and social-group-embedded character of these adaptive strategies. However, the question of who takes advantage of these resources, and under what specific conditions, remain open. The internal group tensions and contradictions engendered in the operation of different ethnic enclaves, and of ethnic collectivism in general, also need further study.

Collectivism in general as an adaptive strategy, and ethnic enclaves as a particular form, may help the incorporation of immigrants into the host society in two ways or phases: first, in the initial period of their adaptation, when simple survival and putting down of roots are the primary concern, and later, when progressive incorporation involves socioeconomic advancement for the immigrants and their families. Let us look at these two aspects separately.

The historical and sociological research appears unanimous on the facilitating functions of both collectivism and ethnic enclaves during the first phase of immigrants' entry into the U.S. economic system. Once pioneers have carved out a chunk of the local economy, such as a specific trade or service, the ethnic enclave provides what those following in the chain migratory pattern require most: jobs, as well as the informal networks and organized resources necessary for finding other, possibly better employment. Such was the mode of entry into the U.S. economy a century ago for Japanese and Chinese immigrants on the West Coast, who found economic support in the already established firms run by their countrymen, and in the *hui, ko, tenomoshi, tsu,* and *ken* — an array of institutions for extending loans, credit, and information about employment opportunities in the enclave.[60] On the East Coast, the garment enterprises in New York City, 90 percent of which were owned by (mostly German) Jews at the turn of the century, served as an extensive ethnic enclave that absorbed thousands of Jewish immigrants from eastern Europe, who entered it in a chain pattern based on kin and personal contacts and on complex networks of *Landsmannschaften* and other social-support institutions, which provided loans and information about job openings. (At the beginning of the century, the *Jewish Communal Register* of Jewish organizational resources in the city ran to nearly 1,500 pages.) The put-out system of work in the garment industry paid the immigrant lower wages than the average received by foreign-born workers in the city, but as a trade-off it permitted them to put more family members to work, including children, and to observe Jewish holidays.[61] In smaller cities, where the majority of Jewish immigrants went into retail businesses, they also formed economic enclaves with ethnically homogeneous linkages, vertical (to the wholesalers) and horizontal (to other retail merchants), which served as employment resources to new arrivals. In Johnstown, and in the surrounding towns in western Pennsylvania, practically all my Jewish informants (150) admitted that they or their immigrant parents arrived in the area and either set up family businesses or entered coethnic employment following earlier established ethnic economic connections, or upon the advice of fellow immigrants who knew or heard that it was "a good place." A similar pattern of Jewish economic enclaves being formed by early settlers at the turn of the century and then extending a helping hand to followers by setting them up in business or by employing them in their own enterprises has been reported in Providence, Pittsburgh, Columbus, and Atlanta, as well as in Los Angeles, San Francisco, and other western cities.[62]

Like the immigrants absorbed into ethnic enclave economies, South and East European men who entered the lower subsegments of American factories, mills, and coal mines at the turn of the century, and women, most of whom worked in light industry or in domestic service as cooks, maids, and general helpers in service establishments, obtained their jobs through networks of kin and other social connections with fellow immigrants. In order to secure much needed labor, American employers deliberately relied upon ethnic-based hiring, and so this mode of incorporation, supported from both sides, was self-sustaining. Even before they had left their villages in Europe, the migrants knew not only to what American city they were going but usually—from letters from the United States that circulated widely and from return visits by immigrants—where they would work, with whom, and for what wages. A few days after their arrival, they were usually already at work in the place where their relatives or friends had arranged a job for them. The men who went to the factories commonly worked in "labor gangs" composed of members of the same nationality or even from the same region in Europe, and the same people who helped to procure work also taught the new immigrants how to perform it. When they lost work, or voluntarily decided to seek other employment, it was again arranged through networks of kin and acquaintances extending across the major centers of immigrant settlements in the United States. Also, the immigrant press regularly published reports on current labor conditions in particular cities, describing how many people from which regions in South and East Europe resided there, how they lived and were employed, and what general economic prospects could be expected by potential movers. Relying on these group resources for information and employment, Italian, Slavic, and Hungarian immigrants circulated among basically similar ethnic subsegments that existed within all major industries employing South and East European labor.[63]

As indicated by sociological studies focusing on present-day immigrants, for those such as Cubans, Dominicans, Koreans, or Chinese, who tend to enter the labor market through ethnic enclave subeconomies, as well as those such as Mexicans or Puerto Ricans who usually enter it through the mainstream secondary sector, reliance on collective, familial, and social group resources and on ethnic loyalties similarly facilitates—albeit not without cost—the initial period of adaptation. New arrivals who are introduced by the fellow immigrants into the ethnic niches of the mainstream secondary sector and work there in the company of their countrymen acquire what is most important—

jobs; but their employment is highly unstable, menial, and poorly paid. The situation of those who have access to the established enclave subeconomies seems more advantageous, but not unequivocally so, depending on the position of the immigrants and the type of work that they do. The national data show that ethnic groups possessing their own strong economic enclaves, such as the Cubans, Chinese, Japanese, and Koreans, have lower overall rates of unemployment than those who do not, such as the Mexicans or Puerto Ricans. Obviously, there are many other characteristics of these groups, such as age, sex, household composition, educational and occupational profile, and regional and industrial concentration, that account for this difference, but the existence of ethnic enclave subeconomies may well be one of them.

New immigrants who enter the coethnic subeconomy as employees rather than as employers get jobs that they can perform in a familiar cultural and social environment. As an additional bonus, if mixed blessing, they profit from the paternalistic care of coethnic supervisors. But they are often underpaid (especially female workers), have to work long hours, and are unprotected by union regulations. One the other hand, those new arrivals who become entrepreneurs in the ethnic enclave economy but are overqualified because of their education and occupational skills, and who undertake the work mainly because they lack English proficiency and knowledge of mainstream American society, often, like the Cubans or Koreans, suffer a status loss as the price of their transplantation.[64] Little is known, however, about the role of personal and collective ethnic networks in the incorporation of new immigrants who enter the primary sector of the American economy; it is an interesting question that awaits investigation.

The second, perhaps more important, and certainly much more complicated question related to the role played by kin and social group collectivism, and by the ethnic enclaves, concerns their impact on the socioeconomic advancement of the immigrant families after they have become permanently settled. It is a highly complex matter, involving the interplay between historically changing external structures and the internal group responses to these constraints and opportunities. Probably the most thoroughly researched and the best known in ethnic literature is the case of "old" Asian immigrants—the Chinese and Japanese—who, since their arrival on the West Coast in the nineteenth century, have concentrated in significant proportions in ethnic enclave economies, supported by extensive institutions and resources aimed at promoting the economic performance of members. It has been convincingly argued by students of the social histories of these two groups that, above and beyond their cultural value systems supportive of an "achievement drive," it was primarily their prolonged enforced enclosure in enclave subeconomies, and their efficient utilization of collective resources (such as the involvement of all household members in the family business) that permitted the immigrant generation to build the economic base from which their children could move further upward. The educational attainment of Chinese and Japanese offspring between 1914 and 1925 already equaled that of native-born white Americans, but they remained confined within their ethnic enclaves until after World War II.[65] A peculiar, if not perverse, historical dialectic of the extraordinary present-day success of the Chinese and Japanese, the "model American minorities," is that it was severe exclusionary discrimination, rather than the opportunities presented by an open society that enabled them to accumulate economic and human capital within their enclaves — capital, which, once released by the relaxation of native prejudice, was used by following generations to move into the mainstream society in a spectacular display of accomplishment.[66]

On the other side of the continent, another group — the Jews — has displayed yet another pattern of "model minority" achievement. As early as the late 1920s, the rate of Jewish college attendance already exceeded that of the white American population, and by the 1930s about 12 percent of foreign-stock Jews, as opposed to about 8 percent of the white American population, were employed in professions.[67] This remarkable performance has usually been attributed to Jewish cultural values that placed a high premium on education, foresight, and personal responsibility, and to the carryover from Europe of the traditions of urbanism and entrepreneurship — all predispositions particularly well suited for achievement in modern industrial society.[68] Recent historical and sociological research on Jewish achievement in the United States has found such cultural-psychological explanations insufficient, and has emphasized the underlying importance of economic and social factors.[69] Of these, ethnic collectivism and the ethnic enclave economy have, as in the case of the Chinese and Japanese, constituted significant though not the only facilitators, and were embedded in larger, historically changing contexts of the surrounding environment.

Not surprisingly, considering their greatest concentration there, it is usually New York City and the New York Jews that serve as the basis for generalizations about the performance of this group in the United States. As we have seen, by the 1900s there existed in New York City a large ethnic enclave economy, namely, the garment and related industries, that employed the majority of East European Jewish families. A few recent investigations of the impact of ethnic employment on the status achievement of New York Jewish immigrants and their children during the first two decades of this century indicate that it was positive. Jewish immigrants employed in the coethnic economy, as compared with foreign-born Italians employed otherwise, were found to have held higher and more secure occupational positions. A significantly larger proportion of Jewish "enclave" fathers, as compared with "nonenclave" Italians, were able to transmit their elevated occupational status to their sons. Another study, based on oral history interviews with elderly Jewish immigrants in the city, has also shown a high rate of continuity between the successful entrepreneurial positions of fathers and sons.[70] This early occupational advantage of enclave employment, however, did not translate immediately into the provision of better education for the immigrant children. Recent historical research has demonstrated that, contrary to a popular stereotype of the rapid Jewish ascent to the ranks of the middle class through formal education, this process was not only slower but also much more complex. Prolonged schooling of Jewish children did not precede but, rather, followed the securing of a firmer economic base for the whole family, and was as much a consequence as a means of social mobility. During the first decade of this century, only 45 percent of East European Jewish children who enrolled in the early grades of New York public schools continued through the seventh grade, and of those no more than 25 percent completed their elementary education.[71] Those who dropped out went to work with their parents. Only by the late 1920s and during the 1930s did the increased numbers of second-generation Jews in New York begin to avail themselves of the opportunity of higher education. At that time, a fortuitous intertwining of factors exogenous to individual and group "input" characteristics with the facilitating impact of the ethnic enclave permitted members of the second generation to use extended schooling for socioeconomic advancement. The existence in New York of the (free) City College, a mecca for Jewish youngsters, made it possible for large numbers of even less economically secure but aspiring families to provide their children with a university education. The expanding public sector of the city absorbed a significant number of college graduates. But perhaps more important, the sheer size of the New York Jewish community (30 percent of the city's population), by then permanently settled and well along its way in the Americanization of life-styles and material and cultural aspirations, needed increased quantities of doctors, dentists, lawyers, public accountants, real estate agents, community workers, instructors of all sorts, artistic performers, and others. The existence of this vast ethnic market for various professional services guaranteed economic returns to the educational investments of the second generation, which were built upon the base created by their immigrant parents.[72]

The effects of the participation of Jewish immigrants in the coethnic economic enclaves in smaller U.S. cities before World War II on the socioeconomic attainment of their families have not been systematically studied. My own research in Johnstown, Pennsylvania, indicates that, as in New York, these effects depended upon a constellation of contextual factors specific to the locality. Reliance on vertical and horizontal intragroup economic networks permitted the Johnstown Jews, the majority of whom owned small- and medium-sized retail stores employing family members and fellow ethnics, to establish themselves relatively early and to hold onto their businesses, which in times of industrial prosperity provided decent incomes. But since they served a predominantly working-class clientele from the local mills and coal mines, and because of highly cyclical local industrial production, the economic position of the whole Jewish "enclave," as well as that of individual families, was unstable. The town, whose white-collar sector had hardly expanded during the interwar period, and whose Jewish community never exceeded 1,300 people out of a population of about 60,000, needed only a limited number of doctors, lawyers, dentists, teachers, and other professionals. Hence, even by the 1930s, college education was not the ambition of most second-generation Jews in Johnstown; no more than 15 percent of them went to college (as compared with 30 percent or more in New York in that period), and the majority had joined their parents in family businesses. At the University of Pittsburgh, attended in large part by young residents of surrounding industrial towns similar to Johnstown, only about 14 percent of the student body was Jewish, as compared to nearly 50 percent in New York colleges and universities (the proportion of Jews in the Greater Pittsburgh area was 12 percent; in New York it was 30 percent).[73] Perhaps, then, in addition to structural, situational, and other factors that facilitated or impeded Jewish educational attainment before World War II, it was the eagerness of the children of industrial workers to leave the ranks of the proletariat that functioned as an added incentive for many Jews in New York to attend college, while those from middle-class entrepreneurial backgrounds, particularly in smaller localities, stagnant and rather parochial in their outlook, were less motivated to use this avenue of status elevation.

In the case of "new" postwar immigrants, it is difficult to assess the role that collectivism and participation in the ethnic enclave economy have played in influencing socioeconomic attainment, particularly for the second generation, since many of them are recent arrivals and still in the initial phase of establishing themselves in the United States. (For instance, 90 percent of the half million Koreans living in the United States today arrived after 1970.) Also, because they come from differently conceptualized studies, existing data are not easily comparable. I will, then, briefly summarize only the general findings of some recent sociological studies on the subject that raise interesting questions for future investigation.

In support of the thesis of ethnicity as the organizing principle of the enclave economy serving as a mechanism facilitating socioeconomic achievement, a study of Cuban immigrants in Miami has demonstrated positive effects of enclave employment on their occupational status and income attainment within the six-year period after their arrival in this country in 1973. In particular, participation in the coethnic economy permitted the immigrants to effectively translate their human capital skills into an upgrading of their economic position. Between 1973 and 1979, a substantial one-fifth of them achieved self-employed status in the ethnic enclave. In comparison with immigrants employed in the secondary sector, the incomes of the enclave-employed Cubans were also considerably higher, approaching those obtained in the mainstream primary sector.[74] However, since the three-sector comparison of earnings combined in one ("enclave") category both the self-employed and the employees of the ethnic subeconomy, results indicating higher overall financial returns in the enclave may reflect an interaction between class and ethnicity, rather than the advantage of ethnic employment per se. Six years after immigration, the enclave-employed Cubans did not differ from those employed in the secondary sector in their perceptions of opportunities for further job advancement: both groups were less optimistic than immigrants in the primary sector. The authors interpret this finding as a possible reflection of the already satisfied ambitions of the enclave *employers*. But it may also be that it is the enclave *employees* who see their advancement prospects as restrained.

The position of the employees in ethnic enclave economies in relation to status achievement has attracted more attention from students of contemporary Asian immigrants, perhaps in reaction to the widely held "model-minority" image of this group. Investigators regard this image as not entirely accurate, and they stress the similarity of adverse labor conditions in the mainstream secondary sector and in sweatshop garment, textile, and wig-manufacturing enterprises—the major branches of production in the enclave economies of the Chinatowns and Koreatowns in U.S. cities on both sides of the continent. Employers, finding their own position in the market highly insecure because of intense competition and rapidly fluctuating demand for their products, exploit their coethnic employees, who are usually female and recent immigrants. Employees receive wages that vary with frequent shifts in the volume of sales, and they are alternatively laid off and rehired as contracts come and go. Unfamiliar with labor regulations and union laws that apply in the outside society, the workers in these coethnic enterprises are practically defenseless and have few prospects of significant improvements in their position.[75]

A less depressing situation of the position and prospects of employees in the ethnic enclave economy has been reported in a study of Dominican-run garment enterprises in New York. Although similarly underpaid in comparison with the mainstream sectors, and also at continuous risk of losing employment if the whole firm goes under owing to competition, Dominican enclave workers seem generally satisfied both with their ethnic employment and with coethnic employers. They also appear relatively optimistic about prospects for occupational advancement, seeing their present employment as a first step toward something better in the future, preferably self-employed status in a similar line of business.[76]

Recent research suggests that the extensive organizational networks and intragroup resources that supported the functioning of ethnic enclave economies a century ago are relatively less important today. The Korean, Chinese, and Cuban immigrants do have their mutual help societies, professional clubs, and loan-and-credit associations, but these seem less vital than they had been before to the functioning of ethnic enclaves and to the economic success of their members, who rely increasingly on their own family resources, on loans obtained privately from coethnic friends, or on assistance from mainstream American institutions.[77] A similar shift from traditional ethnic collectivism to individualism in economic behavior has been reported for contemporary Jewish Americans.[78]

These scattered data permit no generalizations, but at least five lines of future inquiry suggest themselves: (1) the differential opportunities for socioeconomic attainment offered by the ethnic enclave economy depending on the class position of its participants; (2) the differential effects on opportunities for socioeconomic attainment depending on the size of the enterprises, and on the branch of production or services (which is the specialty of the enclave economy), in the context of the enclave's relation to both intraethnic and larger markets; (3) the impact of the gender composition of the enclave workforce on the opportunities it offers for socioeconomic advancement; (4) the implications of an apparent shift from traditional collectivist toward more individualistic bases of economic behavior on the part of contemporary ethnic entrepreneurs; and (5) a bonus for those courageous enough to risk the wrath of the "ethnics" threatened in their group public respectability, on a specific variant of ethnic enclave employment as an avenue for upward mobility that was not mentioned above, namely, crime. There exist a few interesting studies of this particular, if marginal, ethnic "success avenue" among the Chinese, Italians, and Jews, but the problem has by and large remained outside the purview of students of immigrants' collective strategies toward economic achievement.[79]

The effects of coethnic employment and of kin and ethnic collectivism as an adaptive strategy on the socioeconomic achievement of the families of immigrants employed in the "ethnicized" subsegments of the mainstream U.S. economy have been more thoroughly investigated in social-historical studies of earlier ethnic groups than in the research on present-day immigrants. The latter documents the negative influence of ethnicity in the secondary sector, as reflected in lower rewards and the subordinate social and economic position of immigrant employees. For instance, the increased number of years spent in the United States makes it considerably easier for Mexican immigrants employed in the secondary and subordinate primary sectors to translate their human-capital skills, initially of negligible effect, into high earnings. But it still takes them between fifteen and twenty years to catch up in earnings with the native-born population.[80] These studies do not tell much, however, about the extent to which friends and relatives with whom Mexicans work in the ethnic subsegment of the secondary sector are able to help them in acquiring better paying jobs in the same workplace or even more remunerative ones elsewhere. A recent sociological investigation of the help extended to newly arrived Mexican immigrants during the initial three years after their arrival in the United States (1973–1976) found no significant impact of such assistance on their earnings and occupational status.[81] Using the same sample of Mexican immigrants who came to this country in 1973, another study found "prior stay in the United States" to have had a positive effect on respondents' incomes by 1979.[82] This could be interpreted as an increase of human-capital skills, meaning that prior sojourns have given the immigrants better general knowledge of American society. It could also mean the augmentation of "social capital," that is, the use of previously established ethnic support networks to obtain better-paying employment. Without elaborating on the importance of familial collectivism as a road to greater economic stability and possibly an improvement in the position of immigrant households, the same study also reports that wives and other household members added significantly to the incomes received by Mexican and Cuban male breadwinners. Among the Cubans, two-thirds of the wives and over one-fourth of the other household members (mostly offspring) were gainfully employed, contributing an additional 50 percent and 39 percent, respectively, to the family income above the average earnings of the male breadwinner. Among the Mexicans, one-third of the wives and one-tenth of the other household members worked for wages, with respective additional contributions of 64 percent and 70 percent of the main breadwinner's average monthly income.[83]

The pooling of household economic resources as a financial attainment strategy, such as the taking in of boarders and the outside employment of wives and children, has also been demonstrated in a recent ethnographic study of

Mexican *indocumentado* (undocumented) families in Texas. While it did not lead to occupational advancement of the workers, whose undocumented status prevented them from moving out of the peripheral job market, familial collectivism helped improve the material standard of the immigrant households.[84]

A similar reliance on familial collectivism in the immigrants' strategies toward improving their economic position has been reported in research on present-day Asian-Americans. About two-thirds of their households have two or more gainfully employed workers, and one-fifth have three. It is most often wives who seek out employment. In 1970, over 50 percent of the immigrant Chinese and Japanese women in the 25 to 64 age group (as compared with 40 percent of "Anglo" females) were gainfully employed. Most of them worked part time, either, like their Hispanic counterparts, in the peripheral sectors of the mainstream economy, or in family-run ethnic businesses, with average contributions to the household income of $4,300 a year.[85]

As noted earlier, at the beginning of this century, in the "lower occupational circuits" of U.S. factories employing Italian, Slavic, and Hungarian laborers, it was also ethnicity and not human-capital skills that was the primary basis for hiring and for the allocation of economic and social rewards. The South and East European immigrants nevertheless actively maneuvered within this constraint, relying on collective resources to carve out as much as possible from the little that was available. Particularly useful in these actions was the interpenetration of kin/ethnic and work/occupational spheres. It was mainly imposed from the outside by the organization of the labor process in the factories, but in part it was also created and sustained by the immigrants themselves, who saw this interpenetration as a resource for coping with the economic environment, first and foremost defensively, against the continuous insecurity of their existence as subordinate lower-skilled foreign laborers, and, whenever circumstances permitted, also more offensively to procure some financial and occupational gains. The same weapon their employers used against them — ethnicity — the immigrants threw back at the employers: a few colleagues managed to moved into a better shop in the mills and "pulled in" others; a neighbor became a turn foreman in a department paying piece rates instead of a fixed daily wage and brought in a group of coethnic workers; a fellow officer from the ethnic society got a position in the employment office and, learning about job openings, in time informed others; a cousin heard about a well-paying contract nearby and took along the whole clan of relatives, together with a score of friends. Outside the workplace, the cooperative household economy became an additional collective resource. Where women had few opportunities for outside employment, they contributed to the family income by taking in boarders. As reported by the Immigration Commission in 1911, about one-half of South and East European households kept lodgers; the average of five per family permitted an addition of over 25 percent to the husband's monthly wages obtained from unskilled labor in the factory. The children regularly took odd jobs after school, on weekends, and during the summer, and their contributions made up from 10 to 30 percent of the family income. The money coming from new boarders, from other sources, such as sewing or weaving, and, in smaller U.S. towns, from selling the produce from small agricultural plots, along with the contributions from wives, combined with those from the children, increased the annual incomes of South and East European families in the first decades of this century by 30 to 40 percent.[86]

All these tactics, however, were efficient mainly to play within the constraining "walls" but could not overcome them. While their situations varied depending on the opportunities offered in the localities in which they settled and on the available ethnic collective resources, before World War II the socioeconomic achievement of Slavic, Italian, and Hungarian immigrants, and of their children born during the first two decades of this century, remained confined mostly to material accumulation and to the upgrading of status within manual occupations. Only the second-generation cohorts born after 1925, who entered the labor market in the postwar era, have moved in significant numbers out of the lower circuits of the industrial sector and the inner-city foreign colonies. This breakout would not have been possible without the major changes that affected the whole of American society.

The U.S. economy was restructured, particularly through the further mechanization of jobs and the upgrading of skills in the manufacturing industries that employed the largest proportions of these groups, and simultaneously the white-collar sector expanded, from 29 percent in 1930 to 45 percent by 1970. Unionization swept through the major industries employing South and East Europeans during the 1930s, which guaranteed job security and institutionalized upward mobility on the internal job ladders. There was a rapid expansion and democratization of higher education, starting in the early 1930s at the high school level and, after 1940, also including colleges and universities, and this came at the beginning of a prolonged period of postwar economic prosperity that lasted through the 1960s. Finally, after the war, there was a relaxation of the previously hostile attitudes of the dominant groups toward the ethnics — the immigrants and their offspring of non-West European backgrounds.[87]

Sociocultural Adaptation to American Society

As indicated at the beginning of this essay, a shift has occurred in recent sociological and historical studies of immigration and ethnicity away from the once-dominant assimilation model of sociocultural adaptation. It is not that assimilation has not been taking place. On the contrary, there exists solid empirical evidence of this process in several areas of life: residential (decreasing ethnic segregation), social (increased intergroup contacts, including intermarriage), cultural (both in outward behavior such as language and customs, and in values and attitudes), and psychological (identification with American national symbols and a sense of civil-political membership).[88]

The reason why the classical assimilation model of linear progression toward a common American amalgamate of lifestyles, cultural values, and social patterns has been abandoned is that it turned out to be much too simplistic, not capacious enough to account for the complexity of processes involved in the sociocultural adaptation of the immigrants and their descendants. As historical and sociological studies have produced more and more evidence of the persistence of "unassimilated" areas in many different domains of people's private lives and in their social and cultural institutions, the focus has shifted, first toward stressing "resilient ethnicity" in opposition to assimilation, and then, more to the left of the middle, so to speak, emphasizing ethnic resilience but acknowledging its coexistence with parallel assimilation processes.[89]

The second shared theme in current research on the incorporation of immigrants and their offspring into the American sociocultural system has been the emphasis on the importance of structural contexts of this process. Several interplaying factors are taken into consideration (as pointed out earlier, historical and sociological studies usually differ in the way these are treated in analyses). Here are the most commonly acknowledged: (1) the general economic, social, and political conditions in the societies from which the immigrants come, and particular aspects of class and cultural milieus from which they originate; (2) the historical timing of their arrival in the United States, implying differences in economic, political, and cultural circumstances of their entry into, and confrontation with, the dominant society; (3) the location of immigrants and their families in particular regions of the country, characterized by different economic profiles, demographic characteristics, and political and cultural traditions; (4) their location within particular urban or rural areas, with different developmental dynamics, economic opportunities, and political and cultural "auras," and with varying residential patterns, ethnic composition, and rates of immigrant concentration, all of which have a differential impact on the development of local ethnic communities and on intergroup contacts; and (5) the insertion of immigrants into particular segments of the labor market, which results in different earnings, working conditions, and prospects for socioeconomic advancement, and in a variety of interactions among members of the same and other ethnic groups. All these factors are historically variant. Their changing constellations ease or impede the incorporation of the immigrants and their families into the American sociocultural system and influence the share in this process of ethnic resilience and assimilation.[90]

Particularly conducive to "emergent ethnicity"—that is, to the crystallization of strong and enduring ethnic identities and cultural bonds, informal social networks, and ethnic institutions—is the concentration of immigrants in segregated residential neighborhoods, combined with their condensation in the same labor segment and (to a significant degree responsible for this) the exclusionary practices and attitudes of the dominant groups. The ethnicization effect of such reinforced enclosure has been abundantly documented in numerous historical studies of "old" immigrants from South and East Europe, China, and Japan, as well as in research on present-day Hispanic and Asian groups.[91]

Demonstration of persisting ethnic loyalties, bonds, and institutions under the conditions of segregation and enclosure is not incompatible with the assimilation model, which predicts that the increased proximity and interaction among members of different ethnic groups weakens and dissolves the distinct ethnic identities and social networks. However, evidence gathered by both historians and sociologists indicates that under some circumstances it may be precisely the participation and contact of immigrants with representatives of the dominant society that produce an intensified "divisive" awareness and the strengthening of ethnic-group bonds. Interactions occurring in the context of prejudice by members of the dominant society against the immigrants and their ethnic group in general seem particularly conducive to such a development. Such was, for instance, the case of South and East Europeans participating in the American labor struggle and socialist movement at the beginning of this century, many of whom became more ethnic in reaction to hostility from native-born workers.[92] Today, and apparently for similar reasons, sharpened ethnic identity and increased ethnic involvement have been reported among recent Cuban immigrants, most of whom came to the United States to join their families, whose higher education and better skills permitted them entrance into the lower-middle or middle echelons of mainstream American society.[93]

The third common theme has been the instrumental character of ethnicity. Activated by external conditions, ethnicity is at the same time created, sustained, and used by the immigrants themselves as a resource to cope with the environment. Seen in this perspective, the ethnicization of personal identities, social bonds, and institutional networks becomes an important, and sometimes preeminent, mechanism of social and cultural adaptation to the host society. During prolonged periods of social and cultural enclosure, such as those experienced by the Asians on the West Coast, or South and East Europeans in large immigrant concentrations in Northeastern cities before World War II, or in today's Chinatowns and Mexican barrios, ethnicity serves as the basis for the formation of sociocultural subsegments (interpenetrating the economic ones discussed in the previous section). These segments consist of formal and informal associations that serve the immigrants' diverse needs — instrumental as well as expressive — and function alongside the dominant American system, and it is through participation in these ethnic networks that the immigrants and their families incorporate themselves into American society.

The historical record of U.S. ethnic groups indicates that for most of them, ethnicization as a means of sociocultural adaptation, even if enforced from the outside, has generally been of an "accommodating" character. It may happen, however, that a particularly adverse structural environment in which the immigrants find themselves, combined with their cultural subjugation (systematic discrimination and prejudice), will result in an ethnic-adaptive response that takes the form of rebellion rather than accommodation. This could involve cognitive and emotional rejection of the dominant society and avoidance of contact with it, or, even more radically, ethnic collective action against the dominant system. In its accommodating version, ethnicization as a mode of cultural adaptation may coexist with parallel processes of assimilation, each taking up somewhat different areas of the immigrants' consciousness and existence, or even partially overlapping; as rebellion, however, it obviously acts against it.[94]

The fourth and last theme is the cross-cutting of class and ethnicity in the sociocultural adaptation of the immigrants and their families to American society. Here the specific concerns and interpretative emphases in studies of particular ethnic groups in different historical periods have shown a wide range of variation. Since most of the immigrants at the turn of the century entered U.S. society at the bottom of the economic ladder, and the majority stayed close to that level for the next half century, ethnic history has been essentially working-class history (the "middleman minorities," Jews and Asians being the exceptions). Hence the major focus in historical studies of the sociocultural adaptation of peasant-immigrants to American urban industrial society has been on the confluence of two developments occurring at the same time: ethnicization and proletarianization. There were, to be sure, regions and localities where, because of the immigrants' residential dispersion, low concentration in the labor segment, or lack of intragroup resources to form enduring communal networks, the proletarianization of immigrant families was not mediated by ethnicity. But in the places where most of them settled, in larger and smaller cities in the Northeast and the Midwest, the South and East Europeans became members of the working class, and they acquired working-class identities, lifestyles, and aspirations as members of ethnic groups with particular social patterns and cultural traditions. Conversely, in this one-in-two process, as they were acquiring their ethnic identities and building their ethnic communities, it was as industrial workers, and with workers' interests, goals and concerns.[95]

For their part, students of the Japanese, Chinese, and Jewish "middleman" groups before World War II, and of the postwar immigrants from Hispanic America and Asia (who are much more diverse in their socioeconomic composition than were the turn-of-the-century immigrants from rural South and East Europe), have been more concerned with the interlocking class and ethnic interests of the "bourgeois" stratum and its ethnic resilience effect.[96]

Just as ethnic networks and loyalties have been found to support the ethnic economy, so, reciprocally, the ethnic economy has provided the basis for sustained ethnic identity and communal participation. Sociological studies have revealed that the members of present-day Asian and Hispanic economic enclaves (including the second generation) are considerably more "ethnic" in their attitudes and behavior than fellow ethnics employed in the mainstream economic sectors, including the ethnicized secondary sector. Evidence of intense ethnic identities and communal participation by ethnic entrepreneurs, the managers of coethnic economies, indicates mutual reinforcement of class and ethnic interests in fostering ethnic resilience.[97] Recently, following the realization that there was considerable internal social differentiation within the prewar South and East European immigrant communities, a concern has emerged in social-historical studies of earlier labor immigration that is more convergent with the preoccupations of students of ethnic groups with large middle-class segments, namely, the role played by the minority petty-bourgeois stratum in basically working-class immigrant communities in the process of their ethnicization and Americanization.[98] Although these studies address somewhat different issues and are not readily comparable with those for the postwar immigrants, they suggest that the immigrant middle class held a complex position involving contradictory interests related to this group's intermediate location between the ethnic enclave and the dominant society. On the one hand, this small group, disproportionately represented in the leadership of ethnic clubs, societies, and associations, and motivated probably by class interests similar to those of today's Asian and Hispanic counterparts, played an important role in promoting ethnic awareness of peasant-immigrants, whose identifications and loyalties usually did not transcend the boundaries of their home village or, at best, of the surrounding region, and whose more encompassing "national" (ethnic) consciousness and solidarities developed only in the United States. On the other hand, however, and perhaps prompted by simultaneous class aspirations directed outside toward the dominant society, the immigrant bourgeoisie was active in fostering the Americanization of their working-class fellow ethnics, leading the campaigns toward this end initiated by the local American establishments, organizing "citizenship drives," and founding "American Citizens' Clubs" in the immigrant neighborhoods.[99] Even when the existing evidence from both sociological and historical studies is combined, it is still insufficient to permit any generalizations. The problem is interesting and clearly deserves more attention in future research, preferably conducted within a broadly comparative framework that includes different ethnic groups in different locations and time periods.

Conclusion

During the past fifteen years a similar shift of paradigms in the sociology and historiography of immigration and ethnicity has redirected the attention of researchers in both disciplines toward new problems and new interpretive emphases. I have illustrated four shared concerns that have informed recent studies of immigration. One theme has been the impact of various structural factors on the immigrants' movement from their home countries to the United States, and on their subsequent economic and social adaptation. The second has been the collectivist, that is, socially embedded and group-sustained, means by which the immigrants confronted the new environment. The third theme has been the resilient character of ethnicity, which the immigrants and their families used as an adaptive tool to cope with the constraints and challenges encountered in their American experience. And the fourth theme has been the modes and functions of the relationship between class and ethnicity in influencing the immigrants' positions in American society and the group identities and interests they have formed in this country. Presented in three thematic sections — the origins and process of migration to the United States, incorporation into American economy, and sociocultural adaptation to American society — the historical and sociological investigations of these four questions have, obviously, not had identical findings. The immigrant groups differ among themselves, as do the conditions of their transplantation and settlement in this country over the past century. Findings concerning "old" and "new" immigrants are often difficult to compare, owing to the discipline-specific ways in which historians and sociologists formulate their research problems, and to the differences in methods they use in gathering and analyzing data. But our review of the evidence that has accumulated in these two fields of scholarship does reveal some interesting and important similarities regarding the general patterns of migration and adaptation of immigrants to American society, apparently common across time and space.

As we have seen, rather than a series of parallel or subsequent one-way population streams, both the "old" and the "new" immigrations to the United States have been part of an ongoing process of back-and-forth exchanges of technology, capital, and labor, structurally linking different parts of the world in an extended transnational macrosystem. The migrants themselves have sustained this process at a microlevel by forming enveloping social-support links to facilitate their movements. These networks of contact and assistance points composed of kin and local group members have served in the past and serve in the present to ease the risks and traumas of the immigrants' transplantation and of their initial encounters with a different world.

Evidence of a multiplicity and of the transformations over time of the economic opportunity structures in different regions and localities in which the immigrant families have settled, and of the segmentation of the labor markets they have entered, indicates that the classical, individual-centered human capital model of socioeconomic achievement is insufficient to explain the process of status attainment of the immigrants and their descendants, whether those from the turn-of-the-century or the new arrivals. A much wider explanatory net must be cast, both in terms of the nature of factors involved (particularly to incorporate those exogenous to the individual and his or her specific skills and motivations), and in terms of the scope of analysis, to include comparisons across space and time of how dynamic conjunctions of various influences have helped or hindered particular immigrant groups.

By the late 1960s, the Horatio Alger legend of "rags to riches" had lost much of its credibility as historical studies began to document the limited social mobility of working-class immigrant families in American industrial centers during the nineteenth and early twentieth centuries, and sociological investigations revealed large pockets of persistent poverty among contemporary "ethnics." Research accumulated in the past fifteen years has further questioned this image, not only the end-goal it implies but also the method. As documented in both historical and sociological studies, the immigrants, "old" and "new," have striven first for subsistence and then, as circumstances permitted, for economic success and social elevation — not individualistically, according to the prescriptions of the classical American creed, but collectively, in family units and relying on extensive formal and informal ethnic support networks. Evidence of the pervasive character of these collective strategies across time and space calls for further modification of the human-capital theoretical model.

Some evidence has been gathered to suggest that as immigrants climb higher on the social ladder and reach an elevated class position, collectivism tends to recede, giving way to more individualist behavior. Could it be that the peculiarity of the American historical experience has been that collectivism is

more the domain of ethnicity, and individualism more that of class? The issue
is quite complex. As shown in this essay, both historical and sociological research indicate different patterns of the relationship between class and ethnicity, with their respective interests and identities reinforcing each other in certain
conditions and conflicting in others.[100]

And finally, assimilation—the theme that for several decades dominated
studies of immigration in both disciplines and that fell into disrepute with the
"ethnic revival" of the 1970s, to be resuscitated again in a modified form.[101]
Moving in circles may not be a bad march as long as it is along an ascending
plane, and recent research on the sociocultural adaptation of the immigrants
and their families to American society seems to have been doing just that.
While stressing ethnic resilience, historical and sociological studies in the past
fifteen years have identified various structural conditions that generate and
sustain this phenomenon. More recent investigations in both disciplines seem
to focus increasingly on analysis of the contiguity of ethnic resilience and
assimilation assessed against the impact of different economic, political, and
cultural factors in the surrounding environment that influence the balance
between these two concurrent processes and shape the particular outcomes.
The assimilation paradigm in its classical version has been abandoned on
account of its excessive simplicity, and the "ethnicity-forever" approach that
replaced it is also passing away. The sociology and historiography of immigration may now be on their way toward formulating a more encompassing conceptual framework for the interpretation of the adaptation to American society
of the immigrants and their offspring that would integrate both the assimilation and ethnicization processes.

NOTES

1. See, for instance, Charles Hirschman, "Theories and Models of Ethnic Inequality," *Research in Race and Ethnic Relations* 2 (1980): 1–20; Thomas Archdeacon, "Problems and Possibilities in the Study of American Immigration and Ethnic History,"
International Migration Review 19 (1985): 112–35.

2. For a summary discussion of U.S. immigration history, U.S. immigration policy,
and the ethnic composition and characteristics of "old" and "new" immigrants, see
Frank Bean and Marta Tienda, *The Hispanic Population of the United States* (New
York: Russell Sage, 1987); William Bernard, "Immigration: History of the U.S. Policy,"
in *Harvard Encyclopedia of American Ethnic Groups*, ed. Stephan Thernstrom, Ann
Orlov, and Oscar Handlin (Cambridge: Harvard University Press, 1980), pp. 486–95;
John Bodnar, *The Transplanted: A History of Immigrants in Urban America* (Bloom-
ington: Indiana University Press, 1985); Pastora Cafferty et al., *The Dilemma of Ameri-
can Immigration* (New Brunswick: Rutgers University Press, 1983); Richard Easterlin,
"Immigration: Economic and Social Characteristics," in *Harvard Encyclopedia of
American Ethnic Groups*, ed. Stephan Thernstrom et al. (Cambridge: Harvard Univer-
sity Press, 1980), pp. 476–86; Robert Gardner et al., "Asian Americans: Growth,
Change and Diversity," *Population Bulletin* 40 (1985): 1–44; Nathan Glazer, ed., *Clam-
or at the Gates* (San Francisco: JCS Press, 1985); Douglas Massey et al., *Return to
Aztlan: The Social Process of International Migration from Western Mexico* (Berkeley:

University of California Press, 1987); William Petersen, "International Migration," *Annual Review of Sociology* 4 (1978): 533–76; Charles Price, "Methods of Estimating the Size of Groups," in *Harvard Encyclopedia of American Ethnic Groups*, ed. Stephan Thernstrom et al. (Cambridge: Harvard University Press, 1980), pp. 1033–76; David Reimers, *Still the Golden Door: The Third World Comes to America* (New York: Columbia University Press, 1985).

3. William I. Thomas and Florian Znaniecki, *The Polish Peasant in Europe and America* (Boston: Knopf, 1927); Oscar Handlin, *Boston Immigrants: A Study of Acculturation* (Cambridge: Harvard University Press, 1941) and *The Uprooted* (Boston: Little, Brown, 1951); Robert Park, *Race and Culture* (Glencoe, Ill.: Free Press, 1950). See also Milton Gordon, *Assimilation in American Life* (New York: Oxford University Press, 1964); Peter Blau and Otis Duncan, *The American Occupational Structure* (New York: Wiley, 1967); Beverly and Otis Duncan, "Minorities and the Process of Stratification," *American Sociological Review* 33 (1986): 356–64; Thomas Sowell, *Ethnic America: A History* (New York: Basic Books, 1981).

4. For a summary exposition, review, and critique of the classical and new approaches to the study of immigration and ethnicity in sociological and historical literature, see Harold Abramson, "Assimilation and Pluralism Theories," in *Harvard Encyclopedia of American Ethnic Groups,* ed. Stephan Thernstrom et al. (Cambridge: Harvard University Press, 1980), pp. 150–60; Archdeacon, "Problems and Possibilities in the Study of American Immigration and Ethnic History"; Bodnar, *The Transplanted*; Edna Bonacich and John Modell, *The Economic Basis of Ethnic Solidarity: Small Business in the Japanese American Community* (Berkeley: University of California Press, 1980); Nathan Glazer and Daniel P. Moynihan, eds., *Ethnicity: Theory and Experience* (Cambridge: MIT Press, 1978); Andrew Greeley, *Why Can't They Be Like Us?* (New York: Dutton, 1971) and *Ethnicity in the United States* (New York: Wiley, 1974); John Higham, "Current Trends in the Study of Ethnicity in the United States," *Journal of American Ethnic History* 1 (1982): 5–16; Charles Hirschman, "American Melting Pot Reconsidered," *Annual Review of Sociology* 9 (1983): 397–423: James McKay, "An Exploratory Synthesis of Primordial and Mobilizationist Approaches to Ethnic Phenomena," *Ethnic and Racial Studies* 5 (1982): 395–421; Michael Novak, "Pluralism: A Humanistic Perspective," in *Harvard Encyclopedia of American Ethnic Groups*, ed. Stephan Thernstrom et al. (Cambridge: Harvard University Press, 1980), pp. 772–81; Petersen, "International Migration"; Michael Walzer, "Pluralism: A Political Perspective," in *Harvard Encyclopedia of American Ethnic Groups*, ed. Stephan Thernstrom et al. (Cambridge: Harvard University Press, 1980), pp. 781–87; William Yancey et al., "Emergent Ethnicity: A Review and Reformulation," *American Sociological Review* 41 (1976): 391–403; Milton Yinger, "Ethnicity," *Annual Review of Sociology* 11 (1985): 151–81; Olivier Zunz, "American History and the Changing Meaning of Assimilation," *American Journal of Ethnic History* 4 (1985): 53–73.

5. See, for instance, Bean and Tienda, *The Hispanic Population of the United States*; Lucie Cheng and Edna Bonacich, eds., *Labor Migration under Capitalism: Asian Workers in the United States before World War II* (Berkeley: University of California Press, 1984); Calvin Goldscheider and Alan Zuckerman, *The Transformation of the Jews* (Chicago: University of Chicago Press, 1984); Sylvia Pedraza-Bailey, *Political and Economic Migrants in America: Cubans and Mexicans* (Austin: University of Texas Press, 1985); Alejandro Portes, "Migration and Underdevelopment," *Politics and Society* 8 (1978): 1–48, and "Modes of Structural Incorporation and Present Theories of Labor Migration," in *Global Trends in Migration*, ed. Mary Kritz et al. (New York: Center for Migration Studies, 1981), pp. 279–88; Alejandro Portes and Robert Bach, *Latin Journey: Cuban and Mexican Immigrants in the United States* (Berkeley: Univer-

sity of California Press, 1985); Saskia Sassen-Koob, "Immigrant and Minority Workers in the Organization of the Labor Process," *Journal of Ethnic Studies* 8 (1980): 1–35.

6. See Richard Alba, "The Twilight of Ethnicity among Americans of European Ancestry," *Ethnic and Racial Studies* 8 (1985): 134–58; Barry Chiswick, "The Effect of Americanization on the Earnings of Foreign-Born Men," *Journal of Political Economy* 51 (1978): 897–921, "The Economic Progress of Immigrants: Some Apparently Universal Patterns," in *Contemporary Economic Problems,* ed. William Fellner (Washington, D.C.: American Enterprise Institute, 1979), pp. 357–99, "Immigrant Earning Patterns by Sex, Race and Ethnic Groupings," *Monthly Labor Review* 103 (1980): 22–25, and (as ed.) *The Gateway: U.S. Immigration Issues and Policies* (Washington, D.C.: American Enterprise Institute, 1982); Greeley, *Ethnicity in the United States* and "Immigration and Religio-Ethnic Groups: A Sociological Reappraisal," in *The Gateway: U.S. Immigration Issues and Policies,* ed. Barry Chiswick (Washington, D.C.: American Enterprise Institute, 1982), pp. 159–93; Gardner et al., "Asian Americans"; Robert Hauser and David Featherman, *The Process of Stratification: Trends and Analyses* (New York: Academic Press, 1977); Charles Hirschman and Morrison Wong, "Trends in Socioeconomic Achievement among Immigrant and Native-born Asian Americans, 1960–1976," *Sociological Quarterly* 22 (1981): 495–513; Douglas Massey, "Dimensions of the New Immigration to the United States and the Prospects for Assimilation," *Annual Review of Sociology* 7 (1981): 57–81, and *Patterns and Effects of Hispanic Immigration to the U.S.,* (Report to the National Commission for Employment Policy, 1982); Victor Nee and Jimmy Sanders, "The Road to Parity: Determinants of the Socioeconomic Achievements of Asian Americans," *Ethnic and Racial Studies* 8 (1985): 75–93; Lisa Neidert and Reynolds Farley, "Assimilation in the U.S.: An Analysis of Ethnic and Generation Differences in Status and Achievement," *American Sociological Review* 50 (1985): 840–50; Sowell, *Ethnic America.*

7. Stephan Thernstrom, *Poverty and Progress: Social Mobility in a Nineteenth-Century City* (Cambridge: Harvard University Press, 1964), and *The Other Bostonians. Poverty and Progress in the American Metropolis, 1880–1970* (Cambridge: Harvard University Press, 1973). For critiques of historical mobility studies, see Clyde Griffen, "Occupational Mobility in Nineteenth-Century America: Problems and Possibilities," *Journal of Social History* 5 (1972): 310–31; James Henretta, "Social History as Lived and Written," *American Historical Review* 84 (1979): 1293–1323; Michael Katz, "Social Class in North American Urban History," *Journal of Interdisciplinary History* 11 (1981): 579–607; Zunz, "American History and the Changing Meaning of Assimilation."

8. See, for instance, John Bodnar, *Workers' World: Kinship, Community and Protest in an Industrial Society* (Baltimore: Johns Hopkins University Press, 1982); John Bodnar, Roger Simon, and Michael Weber, *Lives of Their Own* (Urbana: University of Illinois Press, 1982); John Briggs, *An Italian Passage: Immigrants to Three American Cities, 1890–1930* (New Haven: Yale University Press, 1978); Dino Cinel, *From Italy to San Francisco* (Stanford: Stanford University Press, 1982); Scott Cummings, ed., *Self-Help in Urban America* (Port Washington, N.Y.: Kennikat Press, 1980); Donna Gabaccia, *From Italy to Elisabeth Street* (Albany: SUNY Press, 1983); Victor Greene, *For God and Country: The Rise of Polish and Lithuanian Ethnic Consciousness in America* (Madison: State Historical Society of Wisconsin, 1975); Tamara Hareven, "The Role of Family and Ethnicity in Adjustment to Industrial Life," *Labor History* 16 (1975): 248–65, "The Dynamics of Kin in an Industrial Community," *American Journal of Sociology* 84 (1978): 271–89, and *Family Time and Industrial Time* (New York: Cambridge University Press, 1982); June Mei, "Socioeconomic Origins of Emigration: Guangdong

to California, 1850–1882,"in *Labor Migration under Capitalism*, ed. Lucie Cheng and Edna Bonacich (Berkeley: University of California Press, 1984); pp. 219–48, and in the same volume (pp. 370–402), "Socioeconomic Developments among the Chinese in San Francisco, 1848–1906"; Deborah Moore, *At Home in America: Second Generation New York Jews* (New York: Columbia University Press, 1981); Judith Smith, *Family Connections: A History of Italian and Jewish Lives in Providence, Rhode Island, 1900–1940* (Albany: SUNY Press, 1985); Mark Stolarik and Murray Friedman, eds., *Making It in America: The Role of Ethnicity in Education, Business Enterprise and Work Choices* (London and Toronto: Associated University Press, 1986); Norbuya Tsuchida, "Japanese Gardeners in Southern California, 1900–1941," in *Labor Migration under Capitalism*, ed. Lucie Cheng and Edna Bonacich (Berkeley: University of California Press, 1984), pp. 435–58; Virginia Yans-McLaughlin, "A Flexible Tradition: South Italian Immigrants Confront a New Work Experience," *Journal of Social History* 7 (1974): 429–46, and *Family and Community: Italian Immigrants in Buffalo, 1880–1930* (Ithaca: Cornell University Press, 1977); Olivier Zunz, *The Changing Face of Inequality: Urbanization, Industrial Development and Immigrants in Detroit, 1880–1920* (Chicago: University of Chicago Press, 1982).

9. See, for instance, Bonacich and Modell, *The Economic Basis of Ethnic Solidarity*; Harley Browning and Nestor Rodriguez, "The Migration of Mexican Indocumentados as a Settlement Process: Implications for Work," in *Hispanics in the U.S. Economy*, ed. George Borjas and Marta Tienda (Orlando, Fla.: Academic Press, 1985), pp. 277–97; Evelyn Glenn, "Split Household, Small Producer and Dual Wage-Earner: An Analysis of Chinese-American Family Strategies," *Journal of Marriage and the Family* 45 (1983): 35–47, and "The Dialectics of Wage Work: Japanese American Women and Domestic Service, 1905–1940," in *Labor Migration under Capitalism,* ed. Lucie Cheng and Edna Bonacich (Berkeley: University of California Press, 1984), pp. 561–89; Ilsoo Kim, *New Urban Immigrants: The Korean Community in New York* (Princeton: Princeton University Press, 1981); Kwang Chung Kim and Won Moo Hurh, "Ethnic Resource Utilization of Korean Immigrant Enterprises in the Chicago Minority Area," *International Migration Review* 19 (1985): 82–112; Ivan Light, *Ethnic Enterprise in America* (Berkeley: University of California Press, 1972), and "Asian Enterprise in America: Chinese, Japanese and Koreans in Small Business," in *Self-Help in Urban America*, ed. Scott Cummings (Port Washington, N.Y.: Kennikat Press, 1980), pp. 33–57; Suzanne Model, "Ethnic Bonds in the Workplace: Blacks, Italians and Jews in New York City" (PH.D. diss., University of Michigan, 1985), "Comparative Prespectives on the Ethnic Enclave: Blacks, Italians and Jews in New York City," *International Migration Review* 19 (1985): 64–82, "Italian and Jewish Intergenerational Mobility New York, 1910," *Social Science History*, 12 (1988): 31–48, and "Mode of Job Entry and the Ethnic Composition of Firms," *Sociological Forum*, 3 (1988): 110–27; Ewa Morawska, *For Bread with Butter: Life-Worlds of East Central Europeans in Johnstown, Pennsylvania, 1890–1940* (New York: Cambridge University Press, 1985), "The Modernity of Tradition: East European Peasant-Immigrants in an American Steel Town, 1890–1940," *Peasant Studies* 12 (1985): 259–79, and 'East European Laborers in an American Mill Town, 1890–1930s: The Deferential-Proletarian-Privatized Workers?" *Sociology* 19 (1985): 364–84; Roger Waldinger, "Immigrant Enterprise in the New York Garment Industry," *Social Problems* 32 (1984): 60–72, "Immigration and Industrial Change in the New York City Apparel Industries," in *Hispanics in the U.S. Economy*, ed. George Borjas and Marta Tienda (Orlando, Fla.: Academic Press, 1985), pp. 323–49, and *Through the Eye of the Needle: Immigrants and Enterprise in New York Garment Trades* (New York: New York University Press, 1986).

10. For exposition, review, and critique of the classical and new interpretations of international labor migrations in the literature, see Klaus Bade, "German Emigration to the United States and Continental Immigration to Germany in the Late Nineteenth and Early Twentieth Century," in *Labor Migration in the Atlantic Economies*, ed. D. Hoerder (Westport, Conn.: Greenwood Press, 1985), pp. 117–43; Cheng and Bonacich, *Labor Migration under Capitalism*; J. D. Gould, "European Intercontinental Emigration, 1815–1914: Patterns and Causes," *Journal of European Economic History* 8 (1979): 593–681; Martin Heisler and Barbara Schmitter Heisler, "Transnational Migration and the Modern Democratic State: Familiar Problems in New Form or a New Problem?" *Annals of the American Academy of Political and Social Science* 485 (1986): 12–23; Dirk Hoerder, "Immigration and the Working Class: The Reemigration Factor," *International Labor and Working Class History* 21 (1982): 28–42, and (as ed.) *Labor Migration in the Atlantic Economies* (Westport, Conn.: Greenwood Press, 1985); Mary Kritz et al., eds., *Global Trends in Migration* (New York: Center for Migration Studies, 1981); Petersen, "International Migration"; Michael Piore, *Birds of Passage* (New York: Cambridge University Press, 1979); Portes, "Migration and Underdevelopment" and "Modes of Structural Incorporation and Present Theories of Labor Immigration"; Alejandro Portes and John Walton, *Labor, Class and the International System* (Orlando, Fla.: Academic Press, 1981); Saskia Sassen-Koob, "The International Circulation of Resources and Development: The Case of Migrant Labor," *Development and Change* 9 (1978): 509–45, and "The Internationalization of the Labor Force," *Studies in Comparative International Development* 15 (1980): 3–26; Charles Wood, "Equilibrium and Historical-Structural Perspectives on Migration," *International Migration Review* 16 (1982): 298–319.

11. See, for instance, Lourdes Arizpe, "The Rural Exodus in Mexico and Mexican Migration to the United States," in *The Border That Joins,* vol. 1, ed. Peter G. Brown and Henry Shue (Totowa, N.J.: Rowman & Littlefield, 1984), pp. 162–87; Josef Barton, *Peasants and Strangers: Italians, Rumanians and Slovaks in an American City, 1890–1950* (Cambridge: Harvard University Press, 1975); Ivan Berend and Gyorgi Ranki, *The European Periphery and Industrialization, 1780–1914* (New York: Cambridge University Press, 1982); Celina Bobinska and Andrzej Pilch, eds., *Employment-Seeking Emigration of the Poles World-Wide XIX and XX Centuries* (Krakow: P.W.N., 1975); Bodnar, *The Transplanted*; Briggs, *An Italian Passage*; Albert Camarillo, *Chicanos in a Changing Society: from Mexican Pueblos to American Barrios in Santa Fe and Southern California, 1848–1930* (Cambridge: Harvard University Press, 1979); Lawrence Cardosa, *Mexican Emigration to the United States, 1897–1931* (Tucson: University of Arizona Press, 1980); Dino Cinel, "The Seasonal Emigration of Italians in the Nineteenth Century: From Internal to International Destinations," *Journal of Ethnic Studies* 19 (1982): 43–69; Arthur Corwin, ed., *Immigrants and Immigrants: Perspectives on Mexican Labor Migration to the United States* (Westport, Conn.: Greenwood Press, 1978); William Fogel, "Twentieth-Century Mexican Migration to the United States," in *The Gateway: U.S. Immigration Issues and Policies*, ed. Barry Chiswick (Washington, D.C.: American Enterprise Institute, 1982), pp. 193–222; Hoerder, *Labor Migration in the Atlantic Economies*; Mary Kritz, "International Migration Patterns in the Caribbean Basin," in *Global Trends in Migration*, ed. Mary Kritz et al. (New York: Center for Migration Studies, 1981), pp. 181–207; Sucheta Mazumdar, "Colonial Impact and Punjabi Emigration to the United States," in *Labor Migration under Capitalism*, ed. Lucie Cheng and Edna Bonacich (Berkeley: University of California Press, 1984), pp. 316–37; Mei, "Socioeconomic Origins of Emigration"; Morawska, *For Bread with Butter,* "The Modernity of Tradition," and "East European Laborers in an American

Mill Town, 1890-1930s"; Alan Moriyama, "The Causes of Emigration: The Background of Japanese Emigration to Hawaii, 1885-1894," in *Labor Migration Under Capitalism*, ed. Lucie Cheng and Edna Bonacich (Berkeley: University of California Press, 1984), pp. 248-77; Linda Pomerantz, "The Background of Korean Emigration," in *Labor Migration under Capitalism*, ed. Lucie Cheng and Edna Bonacich (Berkeley: University of California Press, 1984), pp. 277-316; Portes and Bach, *Latin Journey*; Juliana Puskás, *From Hungary to the United States, 1880-1914* (Budapest: Akademiai Kiado, 1982); Theodore Saloutos, "Causes and Patterns of Greek Emigration to the United States," *Perspectives in American History* 7 (1973): 381-441; Saskia Sassen-Koob, "Formal and Informal Associations: Dominicans and Colombians in New York," *International Migration Review* 13 (1979): 314-31; Miriam Sharma, "Labor Migration and Class Formation among the Filipinos in Hawaii, 1906-1946," in *Labor Migration under Capitalism*, ed. Lucie Cheng and Edna Bonacich (Berkeley: University of California Press, 1984), pp. 337-359; Mark Stolarik, *Slovak Migration from Europe to North America, 1870-1918* (Rome: Slovak Institute, 1980); Antonio Ugalde et al., "International Migration from the Dominican Republic: Findings from a National Survey," *International Migration Review* 13 (1979): 235-54; Yasuo Wakatsuki, "The Japanese Emigration to the United States, 1866-1924: A Monograph," *Perspectives in American History* 12 (1979): 271-99; Eric Wolfe, *Europe and the People without History* (Berkeley: University of California Press, 1982); Ewa Morawska, "Labor Migrations of Poles in the Atlantic World Economy, 1880-1914," *Comparative Studies in Society and History* 31 (1989): 237-72.

12. Barton, *Peasants and Strangers*; Paula Benkart, "Religion, Family and Community among Hungarians Migrating to American Cities, 1890-1930" (Ph.D. diss., Johns Hopkins University, 1975); Bodnar, *The Transplanted*; Briggs, *An Italian Passage*; Johan Chmelar, "The Austrian Emigration, 1900-1914," *Perspectives in American History* 7 (1973): 275-381; Cinel, *From Italy to San Francisco* and "The Seasonal Emigration of Italians in the Nineteenth Century"; Mei, "Socioeconomic Origins of Emigration" and "Socioeconomic Developments among the Chinese in San Francisco, 1848-1906"; Morawska, *For Bread with Butter*, "The Modernity of Tradition," and "East European Laborers in an American Mill Town, 1890-1930s"; Moriyama, "The Causes of Emigration"; Pomerantz, "The Background of Korean Emigration"; Puskás, *From Hungary to the United States*; Saloutos, "Causes and Patterns of Greek Emigration to the United States"; Sharma, "Labor Migration and Class Formation among the Filipinos in Hawaii, 1906-1946"; Stolarik, *Slovak Migration from Europe to North America, 1870-1918*. For discussions of some of these issues regarding the local context of present-day migrations to the United States, see Francisco Alba, "Mexico's International Migration as a Manifestation of its Development Pattern," *International Migration Review* 12 (1978): 502-14; Arizpe, "The Rural Exodus in Mexico and Mexican Migration to the United States"; Wayne Cornelius, "Outmigration from Rural Mexican Communities," Interdisciplinary Committee Program Occasional Monograph 5 (Cambridge: M.I.T., 1976), pp. 1-39, and "Mexican Migration to the U.S.: Causes, Consequences, and U.S. Responses," Migration and Development Monographs 78-79 (Cambridge: M.I.T., 1978); Charles Keely, "Philippine Migration: Internal Movements and Emigration to the United States," *International Migration Review* 7 (1973): 177-87; Massey et al., *Return to Aztlan*; Piore, *Birds of Passage*; Portes and Bach, *Latin Journey*; Joshua Reichert and Douglas Massey, "History and Trends in U.S.-Bound Migrations from a Central Mexican Town," *International Migration Review* 14 (1980): pp. 475-91; R. D. Shadow, "Differential Outmigration: A Comparison of Internal and

International Migration from Villa Guerero, Jalisco (Mexico)," in *Migration across Frontiers: Mexico and the United States*, ed. Fernando Camara and Robert van Kemper (Albany: SUNY Press, 1979); William Stinner, *Return Migration and Remittances: Developing a Caribbean Perspective* (Washington, D.C.: Smithsonian Institution, 1982); Morawska, "Labor Migrations of Poles."

13. U.S. Immigration Commission, *Abstracts of Reports*, 2 vols. (Washington D.C., 1911), and *Immigrants in Industries. Iron and Steel Manufacturing*, part II, vol. 1, "Community A" (Washington, D.C., 1911); Simon Kuznets, "Immigration of Russian Jews to the United States: Background and Structure,"*Perspectives in American History* 9 (1975): 35–127.

14. Lucie Cheng and Edna Bonacich, eds., *Labor Migration under Capitalism* (Berkeley: University of California Press, 1984).

15. On the socioeconomic characteristics of arriving "old" and "new" immigrants, see Bean and Tienda, *The Hispanic Population of the United States*; Bobinska and Pilch, *Employment-Seeking Emigration of the Poles World-Wide*; Bodnar, *The Transplanted*; Bonacich and Modell, *The Economic Basis of Ethnic Solidarity*; Monica Boyd, "The Changing Nature of Central and Southeast Asian Immigration to the U.S.," *International Migration Review* 8 (1974); 507–19; J. A. Bustamente, "Undocumented Migration from Mexico," *International Migration Review* 11 (1971): 149–77; Cafferty et al., *The Dilemma of American Immigration*; Cardosa, *Mexican Emigration to the United States, 1897–1931*; Cheng and Bonacich, *Labor Migration under Capitalism*; Corwin, *Immigrants and Immigrants*; Roger Daniels, *Asian America: Chinese and Japanese in the United States since 1850* (Seattle: University of Washington Press, 1988); Easterline, "Immigration"; Paul Ehrlich et al., *The Golden Door. International Migration: Mexico and the United States* (New York: Ballantine Books, 1979); Fogel, "Twentieth-Century Mexican Migration to the United States"; Gardner et al., "Asian Americans"; Hirschman and Wong, "Trends in Socioeconomic Achievement among Immigrant and Native-Born Americans, 1960–1976," and "Socioeconomic Gains of Asian Americans, Blacks, and Hispanics, 1960–1976," *American Journal of Sociology* 90 (1984): 584–86; Hoerder, *Labor Migration in the Atlantic Economies*; Keely, "Philippine Migration"; Charles Keely and Patricia J. Elwell, "International Migration: Canada and the United States," in *Global Trends in Migration*, ed. Mary Kritz et al. (New York: Center for Migration Studies, 1981), pp. 181–208; G. P. Kelly, *From Vietnam to America: A Chronicle of Vietnamese Immigration to the United States* (Boulder, Colo.: Westview Press, 1977); Harry Kitano, "Japanese Americans: The Development of a Middleman Minority," *Pacific Historical Review* 43 (1974): 500–519; Frank Bean et al., "Undocumented Migration to the United States: Perceptions and Evidence," *Population and Development Review* 12 (1987): 671–90; Kuznets, "Immigration of Russian Jews to the United States"; Stanford Lyman, *Chinese Americans* (New York: Random House, 1974), "Conflict and the Web of Group Affiliations in San Francisco's Chinatown, 1850–1910," *Pacific Historical Review* 43 (1974): 473–99, and *The Asians in North American* (San Francisco: ABC-Clio Books, 1977); Massey, "Dimensions of the New Immigration to the United States and the Prospects of Assimilation"; Massey et al., *Return to Aztlan*; Darrel Montero, *Vietnamese Americans: Patterns of Resettlement and Socioeconomic Adaptation in the United States* (Boulder, Colo.: Westview Press, 1980); Pedraza-Bailey, *Political and Economic Migrants in America*; G. Poitras, *International Migration to the U.S. from Costa Rica and El Salvador* (San Antonio: Border Research Institute, 1980); Portes and Bach, *Latin Journey*; Puskaś, *From Hungary to the United States, 1880–1914*; Moses Rischin, *The Promised City: new York's Jews, 1870–1914* (Cambridge: Harvard University Press, 1962); Sassen-Koob, "Immigrant

and Minority Workers in the Organization of the Labor Process" and "The Internationalization of Labor Force"; U.S. Immigration Commission, *Abstracts of Reports* and *Immigrants in Industries*; Fernando Camara and Robert Van Kemper, eds., *Migration Across Frontiers: Mexico and the United States* (Albany: SUNY, 1979).

16. U.S. Immigration Commission, *Abstracts of Reports*, and *Immigrants in Industries*. On collectivism in the migration patterns among South and East European immigrants and their regional concentration, see Barton, *Peasants and Strangers*; Bodnar, *The Transplanted*; Briggs, *An Italian Passage*; Cinel, *From Italy to San Francisco* and "The Seasonal Emigration of Italians in the Nineteenth Century"; Branko Čolakovic, *Yugoslav Migrations to America* (San Francisco; R&E Research Associates, 1973); Micaela Di Leonardo, *The Varieties of Ethnic Experience: Italians in Northern California* (Ithaca: Cornell University Press, 1984); Gabaccia, *From Italy to Elisabeth Street*; Hareven, *Family Time and Industrial Time*; Hoerder, *Labor Migration in the Atlantic Economies*; Irving Howe, *World of Our Fathers* (New York: Simon & Schuster, 1976); Arcadius Kahan, "Economic Opportunities and Some Pilgrims' Progress: Jewish Immigrants from East Europe in the United States, 1830–1914," *Journal of Economic History* 38 (1978): 235–52; Stanley Lieberson, *A Piece of the Pie: Blacks and White Immigrants since 1880* (Berkeley: University of California Press, 1980); Morawska, *For Bread with Butter*, "The Modernity of Tradition," and "East European Laborers in an American Mill Town, 1870–1930s"; Puskaś, *From Hungary to the United States, 1880–1914*; Rischin, *The Promised City*; Saloutas, "Causes and Patterns of Greek Emigration to the United States"; Smith, *Family Connections*; Donald Tricarico, *The Italians of Greenwich Village* (New York: Center for Migration Studies, 1984); Rudolph Vecoli, "Contadini in Chicago: A Critique of 'The Uprooted,'" *Journal of American History* 51 (1964): 404–17; David Ward, "Immigration: Settlement Patterns and Spatial Distribution," in *Harvard Encyclopedia of American Ethnic Groups*, ed. Stephan Thernstrom et al. (Cambridge: Harvard University Press, 1980), pp. 71–84; Morawska, "Labor Migrations of Poles."

17. Bonacich and Modell, *The Economic Basis of Ethnic Solidarity*; Monica Boyd, "Oriental Immigration: The Experience of the Chinese, Japanese and Filipino Population in the U.S.," *International Migration Review* 5 (1971): 48–61; Camarillo, *Chicanos in a Changing Society*; Cardosa, *Mexican Emigration to the United States, 1897–1931*; Cheng and Bonacich, *Labor Migration under Capitalism;* Roger Daniels, "The Japanese-American Experience, 1890–1940," in *Uncertain Americans: Readings in Ethnic History*, ed. Leonard Dinnerstein and Frederick C. Jaher (New York: Oxford University Press, 1977), pp. 250–77, and *Asian America*; Marie Garcia, *Desert Immigrants: The Mexicans of El Paso, 1880–1920* (New Haven: Yale University Press, 1981); Harry Kitano, *Japanese Americans* (Englewood Cliffs, N. J.: Prentice-Hall, 1976); Light, *Ethnic Enterprise in America*; Lyman, *Chinese Americans* and "Conflict and the Web of Group Affiliations in San Francisco's Chinatown, 1850– 1910"; Mei, "Socioeconomic Origins of Emigration"; Moriyama, "The Causes of Emigration"; Sharma, "Labor Migration and Class Formation among the Filipinos in Hawaii, 1906–1946."

18. The data on family networks used by Mexican immigrants is in Portes and Bach, *Latin Journey*. On collectivism among present-day immigrants and their regional concentration in the United States, see Mario Barrera, *Race and Class in the Southwest* (Bloomington: Indiana University Press, 1979); Bean and Tienda, *The Hispanic Population of the United States*; Browning and Rodriguez, "The Migration of Mexican Indocumentados as a Settlement Process"; Elsa Chaney, "Caribbean Migration to New York," *International Migration Review* 13 (1979): 204–13; Ina Dinerman, "Patterns of Adaptation among Households of U.S.-Bound Migrants from Michoacan, Mexico,"

International Migration Review 12 (1978): 485–511; Gardner et al., "Asian Americans"; Sherri Grasmuck, "International Stair-Step Migration: Dominican Labor in the U.S.," *Research in the Sociology of Work* 2 (1983): 149–73; Won Moo Hurh and Kwang Chung Kim, *Korean Immigrants in America* (Rutherford, N.J.: Fairleigh Dickinson University Press, 1984); Kim, *New Urban Immigrants*; Kim and Hurh, "Ethnic Resource Utilization of Korean Immigrant Enterprises in the Chicago Minority Area"; Kritz, "International Migration Patterns in the Caribbean Basin"; Peter Li, "Fictive Kinship, Conjugal Tie and Kinship Claim among Chinese Immigrants in the U.S.," *Journal of Comparative Family Studies* 8 (1977): 47–64, and "Occupational Achievement and Kinship Assistance among Chinese Immigrants in Chicago," *Sociological Quarterly* 18 (1977): 478–89; William Liu et al., "Asian American Families: Strategies of Domestic Groups in Migration" (Paper read at Annual Meeting of the American Sociological Association, August 30–September 4, 1986); Douglas Massey, *The Demographic and Economic Position of Hispanics in the U.S.: 1980* (Report to the National Commission for Employment Policy, 1982), "The Socialization of Mexican Migration to the United States," *Annals of the American Academy of Political and Social Sciences* 87 (1986): 102–13, and "The Settlement Process among Mexican Migrants to the United States," *American Sociological Review* 51 (1986): 670–85; Massey et al., *Return to Aztlan*; Darrel Montero and Marsha I. Weber, *Vietnamese Americans* (Boulder: University of Colorado Press, 1977); Sassen-Koob, "Formal and Informal Associations" and "Immigrant and Minority Workers in the Organization of the Labor Process"; Stinner, *Return Migration and Remittances*; Marta Tienda, "Familism and Structural Assimilation of Mexican Immigrants in the United States," *International Migration Review* 14 (1980): 388–408.

19. Data on South and East European peasant immigrants are in Price, "Methods of Estimating the Size of Groups"; U.S. Immigration Commission, *Abstracts of Reports* and *Immigrants in Industries*. On the Jews, see Jonathan Sarna, "The Myth of No Return: Jewish Return Migration to Eastern Europe, 1881–1914," *American Jewish History*, 1981, pp. 256–69.

20. Daniels, *Asian America*; Roger Daniels, *Concentration Camps North America* (Melbourne, Fla.: 1982); Harry Kitano, "Japanese Americans: The Development of a Middleman Minority," *Pacific Historical Review* 43 (1974): 500–519; Lyman, *Chinese Americans* and "Conflict and the Web of Group Affiliation in San Francisco's Chinatown, 1850–1910"; Price, "Methods of Estimating the Size of Groups."

21. Cardosa, *Mexican Emigration to the United States, 1897–1931* Massey, *The Demographic and Economic Position of Hispanics in the U.S.* and *Patterns and Effects of Hispanic Immigration to the U.S.*; Price, "Methods of Estimating the Size of Groups."

22. On circular migrations of the "old" immigrants, see Bodnar, *The Transplanted*; Briggs, *An Italian Passage*; Cardosa, *Mexican Emigration to the United States, 1897–1931*; Cinel, "The Seasonal Emigration of Italians in the Nineteenth Century"; Ivan Čizmič, "South Slavic Return Migration, 1880–1939: Economic, Social, and Cultural Consequences" (Paper presented at conference, "A Century of European Migrations, 1880–1930: Comparative Perspectives," Immigration History Research Center, St. Paul, Minn., November 6–9, 1986); Čolakovic, *Yugoslav Migrations to America*; Di Leonardo, *The Varieties of Ethnic Experience*; Monika Glettler, "Slovak Return Migrations from the United States to Hungary before the First World War" (Paper presented at conference, "A Century of European Migrations, 1830–1930: Comparative Perspectives," Immigration History Research Center, St. Paul, Minn., November 6–9, 1986); Clarence Glick, *Sojourners and Settlers: Chinese Migrants in Hawaii* (Honolulu: University Press of Hawaii, 1980); Gould, "European Intercontinental Emigration, 1815–1914"; Hareven, *Family Time and Industrial Time*; Hoerder, "Immigration and the

Working Class" and "An Introduction to Labor Migration in the Atlantic Economies, 1815–1914"; Frances Kraljic, "Croatian Migration to and from the United States between 1900–1914" (Ph.D. diss., New York University, 1975); Lyman, *Chinese Americans*; Mei, "Socioeconomic Origins of Emigration"; Morawska, "Return Migrations: Theoretical and Research Agenda" (Paper presented at conference, "A Century of European Migrations, 1830–1930: Comparative Perspectives," Immigration History Research Center, St. Paul, Minn., November 6–9, 1986), and "International Labor Migrations Within and Outside East Europe, 1880–1914" (Paper presented at the Annual Meeting of the American Sociological Association, August 17–21, 1987); Moriyama, "The Causes of Emigration"; Morawska, "Labor Migrations of Poles"; Piore, *Birds of Passage*; Puskas, *From Hungary to the United States, 1880–1914*; U.S. Immigration Commission, *Abstracts of Reports* and *Immigrants in Industries*.

23. Robert Warren and Jennifer Marks Peck, "Foreign-Born Emigrants from the United States, 1960–1970," *Demography* 17 (1980): 71–84.

24. Portes and Bach, *Latin Journey*.

25. Candace Nelson and Marta Tienda, "The Structuring of Hispanic Ethnicity: Historical and Contemporary Perspectives," *Ethnic and Racial Studies* 8 (1985): 49–75. On the circular migration of Hispanic Americans, see Fernando Camara and Robert van Kemper, eds., *Migration across Frontiers*; Wayne Cornelius, "Mexican Migration to the U.S.: The View from Rural Sending Communities," Working Paper (Cambridge: M.I.T., Center for International Studies, 1977); Juan Diez-Canedo, "Migration, Return and Development in Mexico" (Ph.D. diss., M.I.T., 1979); Dinerman, "Patterns of Adaptation among Households of U.S.-Bound Migrants from Michoacan, Mexico"; Charlie Hirschman, "Prior U.S. Residence among Mexican Immigrants," *Social Forces*, 56 (1978): 1179–1201; Kritz, "International Migration Patterns in the Caribbean Basin"; Massey, "Dimensions of the New Immigration to the United States and the Prospects for Assimilation"; Massey et al., *Return to Aztlan*; G. Poitras, *Return Migration from the U.S. to Costa Rica and El Salvador* (San Antonio: Border Research Institute, 1980); E. Sandis, "Characteristics of Puerto Rican Migrants to and from the United States," *International Migration Review* 4 (1970): 22–43; Sassen-Koob, "Formal and Informal Associations"; Ugalde et al., "International Migration from the Dominican Republic." On the rate of return migrations of particular immigrant groups during the first postwar decade, see Price, "Methods of Estimating the Size of Groups." On contemporary sojourn-migrations to the United States, see Piore, *Birds of Passage* and "The Shifting Grounds for Immigration," *Annals of the American Academy of Political and Social Science* 485 (1986): 23–34.

26. Frank Sheridan, "Italian, Slavic and Hungarian Unskilled Immigrant Laborers in the United States," *Bulletin of the Bureau of Labor* 72 (1907): 403–86.

27. Piore, *Birds of Passage*; Massey, "The Settlement Process among Mexican Migrants to the United States."

28. Kwang Chung Kim and Won Moo Hurh, "Korean Americans and the 'Success' Image: A Critique," *Amerasia Journal* 10 (1983): 3–21.

29. Francine Blau, "The Use of Transfer Payments by Immigrants," *Industrial and Labor Relations Review* 37 (1984): 222–40; Bodnar, *The Transplanted*; Briggs, *An Italian Passage*; Browning and Rodriguez, "The Migration of Mexican Indocumentados as a Settlement Process"; Cinel, *From Italy to San Francisco* and "The Seasonal Emigration of Italians in the Nineteenth Century"; Garbaccia, *From Italy to Elisabeth Street*; Glenn, "Split Household, Small Producer and Dual Wage-Earner"; Kraljic, "Croatian Migration to and from the United States between 1900–1914"; Light, "Asian Enterprise in America"; Lyman, *Chinese Americans* and "Conflict and the Web of Group Affilia-

tion in San Francisco's Chinatown, 1850–1910"; Massey et al., *Return to Aztlan*; Mei, "Socioeconomic Origins of Emigration" and "Socioeconomic Developments among the Chinese in San Francisco, 1848–1906"; Morawska, *For Bread with Butter*, "The Modernity of Tradition," "East European Laborers in an American Mill Town, 1890–1930s," and "Labor Migrations of the Poles in the Atlantic World-Economy, 1880–1914"; Moriyama, "The Causes of Emigration"; Victor Nee and Brett de Barry Nee, *Longtime California: A Documentary Study of an American Chinatown* (New York: Pantheon, 1973); Victor New and Herbert Wong, "Asian American Socioeconomic Achievement: The Strength of the Family Bond," *Sociological Perspectives* 28 (1985): 281–92; Jonathan Power, *Migrant Workers in Western Europe and in the United States* (New York: Pergamon Press, 1979); Puskás, *From Hungary to the United States, 1880–1914* and "Hungarian Overseas Migration: A Microanalysis" (Paper presented at conference, "A Century of European Migrations, 1880–1980: Comparative Perspectives," Immigration History Research Center, St. Paul, Minn., November 6–9, 1986); Stinner, *Return Migration and Remittances*.

30. Bodnar, *The Transplanted*; Nathan Goldberg, "Occupational Patterns of American Jews," *Jewish Review* 3 (1946): 262–91; Goldscheider and Zuckerman, *The Transformation of the Jews*; Arthur Goren, "Jews," in *Harvard Encyclopedia of American Ethnic Groups*, ed. Stephan Thernstrom et al. (Cambridge: Harvard University Press, 1980), pp. 571–98; E. P. Hutchinson, *Immigrants and Their Children, 1850–1950* (New York: Wiley, 1956); Kahan, "Economic Opportunities and Some Pilgrims' Progress"; Lieberson, *A Piece of the Pie*; Joel Perlmann, "Beyond New York: The Occupations of Russian Jewish Immigrants in Providence, R.I., and in Other Small Jewish Communities, 1900–15," *American Jewish History* 72 (1983): 369–94; Rischin, *The Promised City*; Gerald Rosenblum, *Immigrant Workers: Their Impact on American Labor Radicalism* (New York: Basic Books, 1973); U.S. Immigration Commission, *Abstracts of Reports* and *Immigration in Industries*.

31. Thomas Kessner, *The Golden Door: Italian and Jewish Immigrant Mobility in New York, 1880–1915* (New York: Oxford University Press, 1977); Edward Mazur, "Jewish Chicago: From Diversity to Community," in *The Ethnic Frontier*, ed. Melvin Holli and Peter d'A. Jones (Grand Rapids, Mich.: Eerdmans, 1977), pp. 263–93; Humbert Nelli, *Italians in Chicago, 1880–1930: A Study in Ethnic Mobility* (New York: Oxford University Press, 1970).

32. Zunz, *The Changing Face of Inequality*.

33. Caroline Golab, *Immigrant Destinations* (Philadelphia: Temple University Press, 1977); Theodore Hershberg, ed., *Philadelphia* (New York: Oxford University Press, 1981); Thernstrom, *The Other Bostonians*.

34. Howard Gillette and Alan Kraut, "The Evolution of Washington's Italian-American Community, 1890–World War II," *Journal of American History* 6 (1986): 7–28.

35. John Bodnar, *Immigration and Industrialization: Ethnicity in an American Mill Town, 1870–1940* (Pittsburgh: University of Pittsburgh Press, 1977); Morawska, *For Bread with Butter*; "The Modernity of Tradition," and "East European Laborers in an American Mill Town, 1890–1930s."

36. Bodnar, Simon, and Weber, *Lives of Their Own*; Michael Weber and Ewa Morawska, "East Europeans in Steel Towns: A Comparative Analysis," *Journal of Urban History* 11 (1985): 280–314.

37. Perlmann, "Beyond New York"; Rischin, *The Promised City*; Goren, "Jews"; Ewa Morawska, *Insecure Prosperity: Jews in Small-Town Industrial America, 1880–1940* (forthcoming).

38. Cinel, *From Italy to San Francisco*; Peter Decker, *Fortunes and Failures: White-Collar Mobility in Nineteenth Century San Francisco* (Cambridge: Harvard University Press, 1978); Di Leonardo, *The Varieties of Ethnic Experience*; Deanna Gumina, *The Italians of San Francisco, 1850–1930* (New York: Center for Migration Studies, 1978); Steven Hertzberg, *Strangers within the Gate City: The Jews of Atlanta, 1845–1915* (Philadelphia: Jewish Publication Society of America, 1978); Max Vorspan and Lloyd P. Gartner, *History of the Jews of Los Angeles* (Philadelphia: Jewish Publication Society of America, 1976).

39. J. Rogers Hollingsworth and Ellen J. Hollingsworth, *Dimensions in Urban History: Historical and Social Science Perspectives on Middle-Size American Cities* (Madison: University of Wisconsin Press, 1979); Ira Katznelson, *City Trenches, Urban Politics and the Patterning of Class in the United States* (Chicago: University of Chicago Press, 1981).

40. See Bean and Tienda, *The Hispanic Population of the Untied States*; George Borjas and Marta Tienda, eds., *Hispanics in the U.S. Economy* (Orlando, Fla.: Academic Press, 1985); Monica Boyd et al., "Status Attainment of Immigrant and Immigrant-Origin Groups in the United States, Canada and Israel," in *Comparative Social Research*, vol. 1, ed. R. Tomasson (Westport, Conn.: Greenwood Press, 1980), pp. 231–47; Barry Chiswick, "Sons of Immigrants: Are They at Earnings Disadvantage?" *American Economic Review* 67 (1977): 376–80, "The Effect of Americanization on the Earnings of Foreign-Born Men," "The Economic Progress of Immigrants," "Immigrant Earning Patterns by Sex, Race and Ethnic Groupings," and "An Analysis of the Earnings and Employment of Asian Men," *Journal of Labor Economics* 1 (1983): 197–214; David Featherman, "The Socioeconomic Achievements of White Religio-Ethnic Subgroups: Social and Psychological Explanations," *American Sociological Review* 36 (1971): 207–22; David Feathermann and Robert Hauser, "Changes in the Socioeconomic Stratification of the Races, 1962–1973," *American Journal of Sociology* 82 (1976): 621–51, and *Opportunity and Change* (New York: Academic Press, 1978); Gardner et al., "Asian Americans"; Hauser and Featherman, *The Process of Stratification*; Hirschman, "American Melting Pot Reconsidered"; Charles Hirschman and Ellen Kraly, "Racial and Ethnic Inequality and Labor Markets in the U.S., 1940 and 1950" (Paper presented at the Annual Meeting of American Sociological Association, August 30–September 4, 1986); Charles Hirschman and Morrison Wong, "Trends in Socioeconomic Achievement among Immigrant and Native-Born Asian Americans, 1960–1976," "Socioeconomic Gains of Asian Americans, Blacks, and Hispanics, 1960–1976," and "The Extraordinary Educational Attainment of Asian Americans: A Search for Historical Evidence and Explanations," *Social Forces* 65 (1986): 1–27; Robert Jiobu, "Earning Differentials between Whites and Ethnic Minorities: The Cases of Asian Americans, Blacks and Chicanos, " *Sociology and Social Research* 61 (1976): 24–39; Massey, "Dimensions of the New Immigration to the United States and the Prospects for Assimilation," *The Demographic and Economic Position of Hispanics in the U.S.,* and *Patterns and Effects of Hispanic Immigration to the U.S.*; Nee and Sanders, "The Road to Parity"; Neidert and Farley, "Assimilation in the U.S."; Dudley Poston et al., "Earning Differentials between Anglo and Mexican American Male Workers in 1960–1970: Changes in the 'Cost' of Being Mexican American," *Social Science Quarterly* 57 (1976): 618–37.

41. E. M. Beck, Patrick Horn, and Charles M. Tolbert II, "Industrial Segmentation and Labor Market Discrimination," *Sociological Problems* 28 (1980): 113–29; Peter Doeringer and Michael Piore, *Internal Labor Markets and Manpower Analysis* (Lexington, Mass.: Heath, 1971); Richard Edwards et al., eds., *Labor Market Segmentation*

(Lexington, Mass.: Heath, 1975) and *Contested Terrain: The Transformation of the Workplace in the Twentieth Century* (New York: Basic Books, 1979); David Gordon, *Theories of Poverty and Underemployment: Orthodox, Radical, and Dual Labor Market Perspectives* (Lexington, Mass.: Heath, 1972); Bennett Harrison and A. Sum, "The Theory of 'Dual' or Segmented Labor Markets," *Journal of Economic Issues* 13 (1979): 687–707; Paul Osterman, ed., *Internal Labor Markets* (Cambridge: MIT Press, 1984); Piore, *Birds of Passage* 1979; Michael Reich et al., "Dual Labor Markets: A Theory of Labor Market Segmentation," *American Academy Association: Proceedings* (1973): 359–65; Charles Tolbert et al., "The Structure of Economic Segmentation: A Dual Economy Approach," *American Journal of Sociology* 85 (1980): 1095–1116.

42. See Bonacich and Modell, *The Economic Basis of Ethnic Solidarity*; Portes, "Modes of Structural Incorporation and Present Theories of Labor Immigration"; Sassen-Koob, "The International Circulation of Resources and Development," "Immigrant and Minority Workers in the Organization of the Labor Process," and "The Internationalization of the Labor Force."

43. Gordon et al., *Theories of Poverty and Underemployment*.

44. David Gordon et al., *Segmented Work, Divided Workers: The Historical Transformation of Labor in the United States* (New York: Cambridge University Press, 1982). See also Osterman, *Internal Labor Markets*, particularly the essays by Stanford Jacobi, "The Development of Internal Markets in American Manufacturing (pp. 23–69), and Bernard Elbaum, "The Making and Shaping of Job and Pay Structures in the Iron and Steel Industry" (pp. 71–109).

45. Doeringer and Piore, *Internal Labor Markets and Manpower Analysis*.

46. Francine Blau, "Immigrant and Labor Earnings in the Early Twentieth Century," *Research in Population Economics* 2 (1980): 21–41; Paul McGouldrick and Michael Tannen, "Did American Manufacturers Discriminate against Immigrants?" *Journal of Economic History* 37 (1977): 723–46; Peter Shergold, "Relative Skill and Income Levels of Native and Foreign-Born Workers: A Reexamination," *Explorations in Economic History* 13 (1976): 451–61. On job insecurity in the experience of South and East European immigrants and the second generation before World War II, see Bodnar, *The Transplanted*; Bodnar, Simon, and Weber, *Lives of Their Own*; Hareven, *Family Time and Industrial Time*; Lieberson, *A Piece of the Pie*; Model, "Intergenerational Mobility among Italians and Jews in 1910 New York"; Morawska, *For Bread with Butter*, "The Modernity of Tradition," and "East European Laborers in an American Mill Town, 1898–1930s."

47. U.S. Immigration Commission, *Immigrants in Industries*, "Community A"; Morawska, *For Bread with Butter*.

48. Alejandro Portes and Cynthia Truelove, "Making Sense of Diversity: Recent Research on Hispanic Minorities in the United States," *Annual Review of Sociology* 13 (1987): 359–89; Marta Tienda and Lisa Neidert, "Segmented Markets and Earnings Inequality of Native and Immigrant Hispanics in the United States," *Proceedings of the American Statistical Association, Social Statistics Section* (1980): 72–81.

49. Portes and Bach, *Latin Journey*.

50. Poston et al., "Earning Differentials between Anglo and Mexican Male Workers in 1960–1970."

51. Tienda and Niedert, "Segmented Markets and Earnings Inequality of Native and Immigrant Hispanics in the United States."

52. Portes and Bach, *Latin Journey*.

53. C. Nelson and M. Tienda, "The Structuring of Hispanic Ethnicity; Historical and Contemporary Perspectives," *Ethnic and Racial Studies*, 1985, pp. 49–74.

54. Massey, *The Demographic and Economic Position of Hispanics in the U.S.*

55. Ibid. On the socioeconomic position of Hispanic Americans, see Bean and Tienda, *The Hispanic Population of the United States*; Massey, "Dimensions of the New Immigration to the United States and the Prospects for Assimilation" and *Patterns and Effects of Hispanic Immigration to the U.S.*; Douglas Massey and Kathleen Schnabel, "Recent Trends in Hispanic Immigration to the United States," *International Migration Review* 18 (1984); 212–44; Nelson and Tienda, "The Structuring of Hispanic Ethnicity"; Portes and Truelove, "Making Sense of Diversity"; Sam Rosenberg, "The Mexican Reserve Army of Labor and the Dual Labor Market," *Politics and Society* 7 (1977): 221–28; Sassen-Koob, "Immigrant and Minority Workers in the Organization of the Labor Process" and "The Internationalization of the Labor Force."

56. Bonacich and Modell, *The Economic Basis of Ethnic Solidarity*; Portes and Bach, *Latin Journey*; Alejandro Portes and Robert Manning, "The Immigrant Enclave: Theory and Empirical Examples," in *Competitive Ethnic Relations,* ed. Joanne Nagel and Suzanne Olzak (Orlando, Fla.: Academic Press, 1986), pp. 47–64; Jeffrey Reitz, *The Survival of Ethnic Groups* (New York: McGraw-Hill, 1980); Kenneth Wilson and W. Allen Martin, "Ethnic Enclaves: A Comparison of the Cuban and Black Economies in Miami," *American Journal of Sociology* 88 (1982): 135–60; Kenneth Wilson and Alejandro Portes, "Immigrant Enclaves: An Analysis of the Labor Market Experience of Cubans in Miami," *American Journal of Sociology* 86 (1980): 295–319.

57. Kuznets, "Immigration of Russian Jews to the United States."

58. Pedraza-Bailey, *Political and Economic Migrants in America*; Portes and Bach, *Latin Journey*.

59. Morrison Wong and Charles Hirschman, "Labor Force Participation and Sociological Attainment of Asian-American Women," *Sociological Perspectives* 26 (1983): 423–46. On "middleman minorities," "ethnic economic enclaves," and "ethnic economies," and for various explanations of them, see Stanislas Andreski, "An Economic Interpretation of Anti-Semitism," *Jewish Journal of Sociology* 5 (1963): 201–14; Ellen Auster and Howard Aldrich, "Small Business Vulnerability, Ethnic Enclaves and Ethnic Enterprise," in *Ethnic Communities in Business*, ed. Robert Ward and Richard Jenkins (New York: Cambridge University Press, 1984), pp. 139–57; Howard Becker, *Men in Reciprocity* (New York: Praeger, 1956); Hubert Blalock, *Toward a Theory of Minority Group Relations* (New York: Wiley, 1967); Edna Bonacich, "A Theory of Middleman Minorities," *American Sociological Review* 38 (1973): 583–94, and "Small Business and Japanese American Ethnic Solidarity," *Amerasia Journal* 3 (1975): 96–112; Bonacich and Modell, *The Economic Basis of Ethnic Solidarity*; Calvin Goldscheider and Francis Kobrin, "Ethnic Continuity and the Process of Self-Employment," *Ethnicity* 7 (1980): 256–78; Kim and Hurh, "Korean Americans and the 'Success' Image" and "Ethnic Resource Utilization of Korean Immigrant Enterprises in the Chicago Minority Area"; Kitano, "Japanese Americans"; Abram Leon, *The Jewish Question: A Marxist Interpretation* (New York: Pathfinder Press, 1970); Light, *Ethnic Enterprise in America* and "Ethnicity and Business Enterprise," in *Making It in America: The Role of Ethnicity in Education, Business Enterprise and Work Choices*, ed. Mark Stolarik and Murray Friedman (London and Toronto: Associated University Press, 1986), pp. 13–32; Lawrence Lovell-Troy, "Clan Structure and Economic Activity: The Case of Greeks in Small Business Enterprise," in *Self-Help in Cuban America*, ed. Scott Cummings pp. 58–85, and "Ethnic Occupational Structures: Greeks in the Pizza Business," *Ethnicity* 8 (1981): 82–95; Lyman, *Chinese Americans* and "Conflict and the Web of Group Affiliations in San Francisco's Chinatown, 1850–1910"; Model, "Ethnic Bonds in the Workplace" and "Comparative Perspectives on the Ethnic Enclave"; John Modell, *The Eco-*

nomics and Politics of Racial Accommodation: The Japanese of Los Angeles, 1900–1942 (Urbana: University of Illinois Press, 1977); Portes and Manning, "The Immigrant Enclave"; Jeffrey Reitz, *The Survival of Ethnic Groups* and "Ethnic Group Control of Jobs" (Paper presented at the Annual Meeting of the American Sociological Association, September 1–5, 1982); Irwin Rinder, "Strangers in the Land," *Social Problems* 6 (1958): 253–60; Tamotsu Shibutani and Kian Kwan, *Ethnic Stratification* (New York: Macmillan, 1965); Georg Simmel, "The Stranger," in *The Sociology of Georg Simmel*, ed. Kurt H. Wolff (Glencoe, Ill.: Free Press, 1950), pp. 243–59; Sheldon Stryker, "Social Structure and Prejudice," *Social Problems* 6 (1958): 340–54; Jonathan Turner and Edna Bonacich, "Toward a Composite Theory of Middleman Minorities," *Ethnicity* 7 (1984): 144–58; Robin Ward and Richard Jenkins, eds., *Ethnic Communities in Business* (New York: Cambridge University Press, 1984); Wilson and Martin, "Ethnic Enclaves"; Wilson and Portes, "Immigrant Enclaves"; Walter Zenner, "Middleman Minority Theories and the Jews: Historical Survey and Assessment" (Working Papers in Yiddish and East European Jewish Studies 31, 1978) and "American Jewry in the Light of Middleman Minority Theories," *Contemporary Jewry* 5 (1980): 11–31.

60. Bonacich and Modell, *The Economic Basis of Ethnic Solidarity*; Daniels, *Asian America*; Light, *Ethnic Enterprise in America*; Lyman, "Conflict and the Web of Group Affiliations in San Francisco's Chinatown, 1850–1910" and *The Asians in North America*; Mei, "Socioeconomic Origins of Emigration" and "Socioeconomic Developments among the Chinese in San Francisco, 1848–1906"; Modell, *The Economics and Politics of Racial Accommodation*.

61. Rischin, *The Promised City*; see also Howe, *World of Our Fathers*; William Mitchell, *Mishpokhe. A Study of New York City Jewish Family Clubs* (The Hague: Mouton, 1978); Model, "Mode of Job Entry and Ethnic Composition of Firms"; Shelly Tenenbaum, "Immigrants and Capital: Jewish Loan Societies in the United States," *American Jewish History* (January 1986): 67–77; see also "Jewish Landsmanshaften in America," Special issue of *American Jewish History* (January 1986).

62. See Decker, *Fortunes and Failures*; Goldscheider and Zuckerman, *The Transformation of the Jews*; Jacob Feldman, *The Jewish Experience in Western Pennsylvania: A History 1755–1945* (Pittsburgh: Historical Society of Western Pennsylvania, 1986); Hertzberg, *Strangers within the Gate City*; Kahan, "Economic Opportunities and Some Pilgrims' Progress"; Judith Kramer and Seymour Leventman, *Children of the Gilded Ghetto* (New Haven: Yale University Press, 1961); Marc Lee Raphael, *Jews and Judaism in a Midwestern Community: Columbus, Ohio, 1840–1975* (Columbus: Ohio Historical Society, 1979); Moses Rischin, ed., *The Jews of the West: The Metropolitan Years* (Waltham, Mass.: American Jewish Historical Society, 1979); Myrna Silverman, "Jewish Family and Kinship in Pittsburgh: An Exploration into the Significance of Kinship, Ethnicity and Social Class Mobility" (Ph.D. diss., University of Pittsburgh, 1976); Smith, *Family Connections*; Hertzberg, *Strangers within the Gate City*; Louis Swichkow and Lloyd Gartner, *The History of the Jews in Milwaukee* (Philadelphia: The Jewish Publication Society of America, 1963); William Toll, *The Making of an Ethnic Middle Class: Portland Jewry over Four Generations* (Albany: SUNY Press, 1984); Vorspan and Gartner, *History of the Jews of Los Angeles*.

63. See Bodnar, *Immigration and Industrialization, Workers' World*, and *The Transplanted*; Bodnar, Simon, and Weber, *Lives of Their Own*; Briggs, *An Italian Passage*; Milton Cantor, "Ethnicity in the World of Work," in *Making It in America: The Role of Ethnicity in Education, Business Enterprise and Work Choices*, ed. Mark Stolarik and Murray Friedman (London and Toronto: Associated University Press, 1986), pp. 98–115; Gabaccia, *From Italy to Elisabeth Street*; Tamara Hareven, "The

Dynamics of Kin in an Industrial Community," *American Journal of Sociology* 84 (1978): 271–89, and *Family Time and Industrial Time*; Christiane Harzig and Dirk Hoerder, eds., *The Press of Labor Migrants in Europe and North America, 1880s to 1930s* (Bremen: Universitat Bremen, 1985); Robert Harney, "The Padrone and the Immigrants," *Canadian Review of American Studies* 5 (1974): 101–18; Morawska, *For Bread with Butter*, "The Modernity of Tradition," "East European Laborers in an American Mill Town, 1890–1930s," and "Labor Migrations of the Poles in the Atlantic World-Economy, 1880–1914"; Model, "Mode of Job Entry and the Ethnic Composition of Firms"; Puskaś, *From Hungary to the United States, 1880–1914*; Tricarico, *The Italians of Greenwich Village*; Virginia Yans-McLaughlin, "Patterns of Work and Family Organization: Buffalo's Italians," *Journal of Interdisciplinary History* 2 (1971): 298–314, and *Family and Community*; Juliana Puskaś, "Hungarian Overseas Migration: A Microanalysis" (Paper presented at conference, "A Century of European Migrations, 1830–1930: Comparative Perspectives" [Immigration History Research Center, St. Paul, Minn., November 6–9, 1986]).

64. See Browning and Rodriguez, "The Migration of Mexican Indocumentados as a Settlement Process"; Hurh and Kim, *Korean Immigrants in America*; Kim, *New Urban Immigrants*; Kim and Hurh, "Korean Americans and the 'Success' Image"; Mary Kritz and Douglas Gurak, "Kinship Assistance and the Settlement Process: Dominican and Colombian Cases" (Paper presented at the Annual Meeting of the Population Association of America, May 3–5, 1984); Liu et al., "Asian American Families: Strategies of Domestic Groups in Migration"; Pyong Gap Min, "From White-Collar Occupations to Small Business: Korean Immigrants' Occupational Adjustment," *Sociological Quarterly* 25 (1984): 333–52; Nee and Nee, *Longtime California*; Paul Ong, "Chinatown Unemployment and the Ethnic Labor Market," *Amerasia Journal* 11 (1984): 35–54; Waldinger, "Immigrant Enterprise in the New York Garment Industry" and "Immigration and Industrial Change in the New York City Apparel Industries"; Morrison Wong, "Chinese Sweatshops in the U.S.: A Look at the Garment Industry," in *Research in the Sociology of Work* (ed. Ida Simpson and Richard Simpson) 2 (1983): 212–15.

65. Hirschman and Wong, "The Extraordinary Educational Attainment of Asian Americans."

66. Bonacich and Modell, *The Economic Basis of Ethnic Solidarity*; William Caudill, "Japanese American Personality and Acculturation," *Genetic Psychology Monographs* 45 (1951): 3–101; William Caudill and George De Vos, "Achievement, Acculturation and Personality: The Case of Japanese Americans," *American Anthropologist* 58 (1956): 1102–26; Roger Daniels, *The Politics of Prejudice* (New York: Atheneum, 1967), *Concentration Camps USA: Japanese Americans and World War II* (New York: Holt, Rinehart & Winston, 1982), and *Asian America*; Glenn, "The Dialectics of Wage Work"; Gardner et al., "Asian Americans"; Hirschman and Wong, "Trends in Socioeconomic Achievement among Immigrant and Native-Born Asian Americans, 1960–1976" and "The Extraordinary Educational Attainment of Asian Americans"; Kitano, "Japanese Americans"; Light, *Ethnic Enterprise in America*; Lyman, *Chinese Americans*, "Conflict and the Web of Group Affiliations in San Francisco's Chinatown, 1850–1910," and *The Asians in North America*; Darrel Montero, "The Japanese Americans: Changing Patterns of Assimilation over Three Generations," *American Sociological Review* 46 (1981): 829–39; Darrel Montero and Roland Tsukashima, "Assimilation and Educational Achievement: The Case of Second-Generation Japanese Americans," *Sociological Quarterly* 18 (1977): 490–503; Nee and Sanders, "The Road to Parity"; Neidert and Farley, "Assimilation in the U.S."; Petersen, "International Migration"; Daniels, *Concentration Camps North America*.

67. Nathan Glazer, "The American Jew and the Attainment of Middle-Class Rank: Some Trends and Explanations," in *The Jews. Social Patterns of an American Group*, ed. Marshall Sklare, (New York: Free Press, 1958), pp. 138–47; Charles Silberman, *A Certain People: American Jews and Their Lives Today* (New York: Summit Books, 1985).

68. See, for instance, Glazer, "The American Jew and the Attainment of Middle-Class Rank"; Fred Strodbeck, "Family Interaction, Values and Achievement" in *The Jews,* ed. Marshall Sklare (New York: Free Press, 1958), pp. 147–69; Sowell, *Ethnic America*; Joel Perlmann, *Ethnic Differences: Schooling and Social Structure among the Irish, Italians, Jews and Blacks in an American City, 1915-1935* (New York: Cambridge University Press, 1989).

69. See Stephen Steinberg, *The Ethnic Myth* (Boston: Beacon Press, 1981); Calvin Goldscheider, *Jewish Continuity and Change* (Bloomington: Indiana University Press, 1986); Goldscheider and Zuckerman, *The Transformation of the Jews*; Model, "Mode of Job Entry and the Ethnic Composition of Firms."

70. Model, "Intergenerational Mobility among Italians and Jews in 1910 New York" and "Mode of Job Entry and the Ethnic Composition of Firms"; Stephen Steinberg, "The Rise of the Jewish Professional: Case Studies of Intergenerational Mobility" (unpublished ms., 1986).

71. Selma Berrol, "Education and Economic Mobility: The Jewish Experience in New York City, 1880–1920," *American Jewish Historical Quarterly* 65 (1976): 257–72. See also Stephan Brumberg, *Going to America, Going to School: The Jewish Immigrant Public School Encounter in Turn-of-the-Century New York City* (New York: Praeger, 1986).

72. See Leonard Dinnerstein, "Education and the Advancement of Jews," in *American Education and the European Immigrants: 1840-1940*, ed. Bernard Weiss (Urbana: University of Illinois Press, 1982), pp. 44–61; Sherry Gorelick, *City College and the Jewish Poor: Education in New York, 1880-1924* (New Brunswick, N.J.: Schocken Books, 1982); Jeffrey Gurock, *When Harlem Was Jewish, 1870-1930* (New York: Columbia University Press, 1979); Elli Lederhendler, "Jewish Immigration to America and Revisionist Historiography: A Decade of New Perspectives," *YIVO Annual of Jewish Social Science* 18 (1983): 391–410; Moore, *At Home in America*; Perlmann, "Beyond New York."

73. The Johnstown data is from my research on the adaptation of East European Jewish immigrant families in western Pennsylvania, 1880-1940. For data on Jewish college attendance in other large American cities before World War II, see Marcia Graham Synnott, "Anti-semitism and American Universities: Did Quotas Follow the Jews?" in *Anti-Semitism in American History*, ed. David Gerber (Urbana: University of Illinois Press, 1986), pp. 233–75.

74. Portes and Bach, *Latin Journey*; Wilson and Portes, "Immigrant Enclaves."

75. Hirschman and Wong, "Socioeconomic Gains of Asian Americans, Blacks, and Hispanics, 1960-1976"; Li, "Fictive Kinship, Conjugal Tie and Kinship Claim among Chinese Immigrants in the U.S."; Kim, *New Urban Immigrants*; Jimmy Sanders and Victor Nee, "Limits of Ethnic Solidarity in the Enclave Economy," *American Sociological Review* 52 (1987): 745–67; Ong, "Chinatown Unemployment and the Ethnic Labor Market"; Min Zhou and John Logan, "Returns on Human Capital in Ethnic Enclaves: New York City's Chinatown," *American Sociological Review* 54 (1989): 809–20; Wong, "Chinese Sweatshops in the U.S."

76. Roger Waldinger, "Immigrant Enterprise in the New York Garment Industry," *Social Problems* 32 (1984): 60–72, and *Through the Eye of the Needle*.

77. Kim and Hurh, "Korean Americans and the 'Success' Image" and "Ethnic Resource Utilization of Korean Immigrant Enterprises in the Chicago Minority Area"; Light, "Asian Enterprise in America," "Immigrant and Ethnic Enterprise in North America," *Ethnic and Racial Studies* 7 (1984): 195–216, and "Immigrant Enterprises in America: Koreans in Los Angeles," in *Clamor at the Gates*, ed. Nathan Glazer (San Francisco: JCS Press, 1985), pp. 161–81; Lyman, *Chinese Americans*; Portes and Bach, *Latin Journey*; Philip Young, "Family Labor, Sacrifice and Competition: Korean Green-grocers in New York City," *Amerasia Journal* 10 (1983): 53–73.

78. Mark Rosentraub and Delbert Taebel, "Jewish Enterprise in Transition: From Collective Self-Help to Orthodox Capitalism," in *Self-Help in Urban America*, ed. Scott Cummings (Port Washington, N.Y.: Kennikat Press, 1980), pp. 191–214.

79. See, for instance, Daniel Bell, "Crime as an American Way of Life," in Daniel Bell, *The Edge of Ideology* (Glencoe, Ill.: Free Press, 1960), pp. 127–50; Francis Ianni, *A Family Business* (New York: Russell Sage, 1972); Jenna Weisman Joselit, *Our Gang: Jewish Crime and the New York Jewish Community, 1900-1940* (Bloomington: Indiana University Press, 1983); Ivan Light, "The Ethnic Vice Industry, 1880–1944," *American Sociological Review* 42 (1977): 464–79; Humbert Nelli, *The Business of Crime* (New York: Oxford University Press, 1976).

80. Chiswick, "Immigrant Earning Patterns by Sex, Race and Ethnic Groupings." See also Portes and Bach, *Latin Journey*; Poston et al., "Earning Differentials between Anglo and Mexican American Male Workers in 1960-1970"; Cordelia Reimers, "A Comparative Analysis of the Wages of Hispanics, Blacks and Non-Hispanic Whites," in *Hispanics in the U.S. Economy*, ed. George Borjas and Marta Tienda (Orlando, Fla.: Academic Press, 1985) pp. 27–75; Saskia Sassen-Koob, "Changing Composition and Labor Market Location of Hispanic Immigrants in New York, 1910-1980," in *Hispanics in the U.S. Economy*, ed. George Borjas and Marta Tienda (Orlando, Fla.: Academic Press, 1985), pp. 299–320.

81. Tienda, "Familism and Structural Assimilation of Mexican Immigrants in the United States."

82. Portes and Bach, *Latin Journey*.

83. Ibid. On the reliance on multiple earnings as a life strategy used by Colombian and Dominican immigrant families in New York, see Patricia Pessar, "The Linkage between the Household and the Workplace of Dominican Women in the U.S.," *International Migration Review* 18 (1984): 1188–1211; Giraldo Urrea, "Life Strategies and the Labor Market: Colombians in New York in the 1970s" (unpublished ms., New York University, 1982). On labor participation of Hispanic women, see Marta Tienda and Patricia Guhleman, "The Occupational Position of Employed Hispanic Women," in *Hispanics in the U.S. Economy*, ed. George Borjas and Marta Tienda (Orlando, Fla.: Academic Press, 1985), pp. 243–73.

84. Browning and Rodriguez, "The Migration of Mexican Indocumentados as a Settlement Process"; for Dominican immigrant families in New York, see Pessar, "The Linkage between the Household and Workplace of Dominican Women in the U.S."

85. Wong and Hirschman, "Labor Force Participation and Socioeconomic Attainment of Asian-American Women." On women's employment and familial collective economy among Asian Americans, see also Edna Bonacich, Ivan Light, and Charles Wong, "Koreans in Business," *Society* 14 (1977): 54–59; Gardner et al., "Asian Americans"; Glenn, "Split Household, Small Producer and Dual Wage-Earner"; Hurh and Kim, *Korean Immigrants in America*; Young, "Family Labor, Sacrifice and Competition."

86. On familism and ethnic collectivism as economic strategies among South and

East European immigrants before World War II, see Benkart, "Religion, Family, and Community among Hungarians Migrating to American Cities, 1890-1930"; Bodnar, *Workers' World* and *The Transplanted*; Bodnar, Simon, and Weber, *Lives of Their Own*; Briggs, *An Italian Passage*; Betty Caroli et al., eds., *The Italian Immigrant Woman in North America* (Toronto: Multicultural Historical Society of Ontario, 1978); Cinel, *From Italy to San Francisco*; Elisabeth Ewen, *Immigrant Women in the Land of Dollars* (New York: Monthly Review Press, 1985); Di Leonardo, *The Varieties of Ethnic Experience*; Gabaccia, *From Italy to Elisabeth Street*; Hareven, "The Role of Family and Ethnicity in Adjustment to Industrial Life," "The Dynamics of Kin in an Industrial Community," and *Family Time and Industrial Time*; Morawska, *For Bread with Butter* and "The Modernity of Tradition"; Maxine Schwartz-Seller, *Immigrant Women* (Philadelphia: Temple University Press, 1981); Smith, *Family Connections*; Tricarico, *The Italians of Greenwich Village*; Yans-McLaughlin, "A Flexible Tradition" and *Family and Community*.

87. On the impact of these and other factors affecting the socioeconomic achievement of white ethnics since World War II, see Alba, "The Twilight of Ethnicity among Americans of European Ancestry"; Featherman and Hauser, "Changes in the Socioeconomic Stratification of the Races, 1962-1973"; Greeley, "Immigration and Religio-Ethnic Groups"; Hirschman and Kraly, "Racial and Ethnic Inequality and Labor Markets in the U.S., 1940 and 1950"; Hutchinson, *Immigrants and Their Children, 1850-1950*; Lieberson, *A Piece of the Pie*.

88. For a review of the assimilation process and a bibliography of the literature, see Abramson, "Assimilation and Pluralism Theories"; Philip Gleason, "American Identity and Americanization," in *Harvard Encyclopedia of American Ethnic Groups*, ed. Stephan Thernstrom et al. (Cambridge: Harvard University Press, 1980), pp. 31-58; David Heer, "Intermarriage," in *Harvard Encyclopedia of American Ethnic Groups*, ed. Stephan Thernstrom (Cambridge: Harvard University Press, 1980), pp. 513-521; Hirschman, "American Melting Pot Reconsidered"; Massey, "Dimensions of the New Immigration to the United States and the Prospects for Assimilation"; Sowell, *Ethnic America*; Steinberg, *The Ethnic Myth*; Zunz, "American History and the Changing Meaning of Assimilation."

89. For a review of the data concerning the persistence of ethnicity as well as a bibliography, see Bodnar, *The Transplanted*; Nathan Glazer and Daniel P. Moynihan, *Beyond the Melting Pot* (Cambridge: Harvard University Press, 1970) and (as eds.) *Ethnicity*; Greeley, *Why Can't They Be Like Us?* and *Ethnicity in the United States*; Higham, "Current Trends in the Study of Ethnicity in the United States"; Hirschman, "American Melting Pot Reconsidered"; Hurh and Kim, *Korean Immigrants in America*; Michael Novak, *The Rise of the Unmeltable Ethnics* (New York: Macmillan, 1972); Rudolph Vecoli, "The Resurgence of American Immigration History," *American Studies International* 17 (1979): 17-28; Yinger, "Ethnicity."

90. See Bodnar, *The Transplanted*; Glazer and Moynihan, *Ethnicity*; Goldscheider and Zuckerman, *The Transformation of the Jews*; Michael Hechter, "Group Formation and the Cultural Division of Labor," *American Journal of Sociology* 84 (1978): 293-319; Eric Leifer, "Competing Models of Political Mobilization: The Role of Ethnic Ties," *American Journal of Sociology* 87 (1981): 23-48; Lieberson, *A Piece of the Pie*; McKay, "An Exploratory Synthesis of Primordial and Mobilizationist Approaches to Ethnic Phenomena"; Joanne Nagel, "A Structural Theory of Ethnicity" (Paper read at the Annual Meeting of the American Sociological Association, August 27-31, 1984); Susan Olzak, "Contemporary Ethnic Mobilization," *Annual Review of Sociology* 9 (1983): 355-74; Pedraza-Bailey, *Political and Economic Migrants in America*; Stein-

berg, *The Ethnic Myth*; Yancey et al., "Emergent Ethnicity"; Zunz, "American History and the Changing Meaning of Assimilation."

91. See Barton, *Peasants and Strangers*; Bodnar, *Immigration and Industrialization*; Bodnar, Simon, and Weber, *Lives of Their Own*; Briggs, *An Italian Passage*; Bonacich, "Small Business and Japanese American Ethnic Solidarity"; Bonacich and Modell, *The Economic Basis of Ethnic Solidarity*; Cheng and Bonacich, *Labor Migration under Capitalism*; Daniels, *The Politics of Prejudice* and *Asian America*; Gabaccia, *From Italy to Elisabeth Street*; Goldscheider and Zuckerman, *The Transformation of the Jews*; Hechter, "Group Formation and the Cultural Divisions of Labor"; Howe, *World of Our Fathers*; Hurh and Kim, *Korean Immigrants in America*; Kitano, "Japanese Americans"; Light, *Ethnic Enterprise in America*; Lyman, *Chinese Americans*; Douglas Massey, "Ethnic Residential Segregation: A Theoretical Systhesis and Empirical Review," *Sociology and Social Research* 69 (1985): 315–51; Modell, *The Economics and Politics of Racial Accommodation*; Moore, *At Home in America*; Morawska, *For Bread with Butter*; Nelson and Tienda, "The Structuring of Hispanic Ethnicity"; Portes and Bach, *Latin Journey*; Rischin, *The Promised City*; Jonathan Sarna, "From Immigrants to Ethnics: Toward a New Theory of 'Ethnicization,'" *Ethnicity* 5 (1978): 370–78; Lovell-Troy, "Clan Structure and Economic Activity"; Rudolph Vecoli, *People of New Jersey* (New Brunswick, N.J.: Transaction Books, 1969); Yans-McLaughlin, *Family and Community*.

92. See Bodnar, *The Transplanted*; Victor Greene, *The Slavic Community on Strike: Immigrant Labor in Pennsylvania Anthracite* (South Bend: Indiana University Press, 1968); David Montgomery, "Nationalism, American Patriotism and Class Consciousness among Immigrant Workers in the United States in the Epoch of World War I," in ed., *Struggle the Hard Battle: Immigrant Labor Militancy*, ed. Dirk Hoerder (Dekalb: Northern Illinois University Press, 1986), pp. 327–53.

93. Alejandro Portes, "The Rise of Ethnicity: Determinants of Ethnic Perceptions among Cuban Exiles in Miami," *American Sociological Review* 49 (1984): 387–97; Portes and Bach, *Latin Journey*.

94. On the instrumental-situational character of ethnicity, see Frederik Barth, *Ethnic Groups and Boundaries* (Boston: Little, Brown, 1969); Bodnar, *The Transplanted*; Bonacich and Modell, *The Economic Basis of Ethnic Solidarity*; Leo Despres, ed., *Ethnicity and Resource Competition* (The Hague: Mouton, 1975); Di Leonardo, *The Varieties of Ethnic Experience*; Hechter, "Group Formation and the Cultural Division of Labor"; Leifer, "Competing Models of Political Mobilization"; Light, *Ethnic Enterprise in America*, "Immigrant and Ethnic Enterprise in North America", and "Immigrant Enterprises in America"; Portes, "The Rise of Ethnicity"; Portes and Bach, *Latin Journey*; Yancey et al., "Emergent Ethnicity"; Yans-McLaughlin, *Family and Community*.

95. Bodnar, *Workers' World* and *The Transplanted*; Bodnar, Simon, and Weber, *Lives of Their Own*; Milton Cantor, ed., *American Workingclass Culture* (Westport, Conn.: Greenwood Press, 1972), and "Ethnicity in the World of Work"; Greene, *The Slavic Community on Strike* and *For God and Country*; Herbert Gutman, *Work, Culture and Society in Industrializing America* (New York: Vintage Books, 1976); Higham, "Current Trends in the Study of Ethnicity in the United States"; Gabriel Kolko, "The American Working Class: Immigrant Foundations,"in *Main Currents in Modern American History*, ed. Gabriel Kolko (New York: Harper & Row, 1976), pp. 67–98; David Montgomery, *Workers' Control in America* (New York: Cambridge University Press, 1979) and "Nationalism, American Patriotism and Class-Consciousness among Immigrant Workers in the United States in the Epoch of World War I"; Ro-

senblum, *Immigrant Workers*; Zunz, *The Changing Face of Inequality* and "American History and the Changing Meaning of Assimilation."

96. See Bonacich and Modell, *The Economic Basis of Ethnic Solidarity*; Cheng and Bonacich, *Labor Migration under Capitalism*; Goldscheider and Zuckerman, *The Transformation of the Jews*; Light, *Ethnic Enterprise in America*, "Immigrant and Ethnic Enterprises in America" and "Immigrant Enterprises in America"; Lyman, *Chinese Americans* and "Conflict and the Web of Group Affiliations in San Francisco's Chinatown, 1850–1910"; Moore, *At Home in America*; Portes and Bach, *Latin Journey*; Richard Thompson, "Ethnicity vs. Class: Analysis of Conflict in a North American Chinese Community," *Ethnicity* 6 (1979): 306–27; Toll, *The Making of an Ethnic Middle Class*; Sun Bim Yim, "The Social Structure of Korean Communities in California, 1903–1920," in *Labor Migration under Capitalism*, ed. Lucie Cheng and Edna Bonacich (Berkeley: University of California Press, 1984), pp. 515–47.

97. See Bonacich and Modell, *The Economic Basis of Ethnic Solidarity*; Hurh and Kim, *Korean Immigrants in America*; Light, *Ethnic Enterprise in America*; Portes and Bach, *Latin Journey*; Sassen-Koob, "Formal and Informal Associations"; Waldinger, *Through the Eye of the Needle*.

98. See Bodnar, *The Transplanted*; John Bukowczyk, "The Transformation of Working-Class Ethnicity: Corporate Control, Americanization and the Polish Immigrant Middle-Class in Bayonne, New Jersey, 1915–1925," *Labor History* 25 (1984): 58–83; Morawska, *For Bread with Butter* and "The Internal Status Hierarchy in the East European Immigrant Communities in Johnstown, Pa., 1890–1930s," *Journal of Social History* 16 (1982): 75–109; Zunz, "American History and the Changing Meaning of Assimilation."

99. Briggs, *An Italian Passage*; Bukowczyk, "The Transformation of Working-Class Ethnicity"; Morawska, *For Bread with Butter*; Puskas, *From Hungary to the United States, 1880–1914*; Robert Slayton, *Back of the Yards: The Making of a Local Democracy* (Chicago: University of Chicago Press, 1986).

100. See Light, "Ethnicity and Business Enterprise," on ethnic versus class resources in achievement strategies. See also Higham, "Current Trends in the Study of Ethnicity in the United States," for insightful comments regarding the problem.

101. See Zunz, "American History and the Changing Meaning of Assimilation," for a good discussion of this meandering development in American social history.

NEW APPROACHES TO THE STUDY OF IMMIGRATION

8

Cross-Cultural Comparison and the Writing of Migration History: Some Thoughts on How to Study Italians in the New World

Samuel L. Baily

George M. Fredrickson defines comparative history as "scholarship that has *as its main objective* [his emphasis] the systematic comparison of some process or institution in two or more societies that are not usually conjoined within one of the traditional geographical areas of historical specialization. It is only in work of this sort that comparison per se is consistently at the core of the enterprise."[1] Many historians would not agree with Fredrickson that all comparative history must be cross-cultural and must have systematic comparison "as its main objective," but most would accept the importance of this kind of approach. Although historians interested in Afro-American slavery and other subjects have used cross-cultural comparison with great effect, immigration historians have virtually ignored it. In this paper I want to argue for the use of systematic cross-cultural comparison in writing migration history and, by looking at the Italians in the New World as a case study, to suggest how it might be done.

Some years ago, when I first became interested in Italian migration, I was enormously impressed by the scope of Robert F. Foerster's classic 1919 work, *The Italian Emigration of Our Times.*[2] He wrote the book "to lay bare the grounds for a [United States immigration] policy." Because he placed his imme-

An early draft of this paper was presented at the international symposium "A Century of European Migration, 1830–1930 in Comparative Perspective," Immigration History Research Center, Minneapolis, Minnesota, November 6–9, 1986. I want to thank Michael Adas, Joan Baily, Greg Stone, and Virginia Yans-McLaughlin for reading this chapter and giving me the benefit of their comments.

diate interest in the broader context of Italian emigration to Europe, North Africa, and the other countries of the Americas, he greatly facilitated the possibility of cross-cultural comparative analysis. "In regard to Italian emigration," he noted in his preface, "a rare opportunity for comparative study is at hand, hitherto all but neglected. . . . "

Foerster, however, was reluctant to make these comparisons; he chose instead to present the extensive information he had gathered in separate country-specific chapters, leaving it to the reader to make the comparisons. "The available materials, however tempting, must not be forced," he warned, "and I have put into Book IV about as much as they have seemed to me to allow."[3] For example, Foerster treats the process of assimilation of the Italians in Algeria, Argentina, Brazil, and the United States in the separate chapters in which he discusses each country. Nowhere does he make specific or systematic comparison of the similarities and differences in the respective evolutions of the process. In Book IV, "Italy Among the Nations," Foerster presents the rather general comparisons he thinks warranted. His focus is on similarities among the emigrants to all destinations: motives, passion to save, practicality, sense of provincialism, and starting at the social bottom of the adopted country.[4] He completely leaves out of his comparison the significant differences. He does not discuss the differences in composition and function of mutual aid societies, impact of localism, social structure of the receiving society, and occupations of immigrants, among other characteristics. Foerster's book contains important information with which one could make significant cross-cultural comparisons, but this is not the central focus of his study. Those of us interested in comparative migration history are tantalized by the information, but unsatisfied because of the lack of specific and systematic comparison.

In the 1960s, more than three decades after the publication of Foerster's book, Frank Thistlethwaite and John Higham each published a provocative and suggestive essay in which he attempted to stimulate interest in cross-cultural comparative migration history.[5] George Fredrickson called Higham's essay "an open invitation for detailed [cross-cultural] comparisons of immigration and ethnicity," but no one has accepted this invitation and written a major cross-cultural comparative migration study.[6]

Nevertheless, within the past decade immigration historians have become increasingly interested in some forms of comparative history, if not cross-cultural comparative history, and this I find is an important step in the right direction. Since the publication in 1975 of Josef Barton's path-breaking work on Italians, Rumanians, and Slovaks in Cleveland, a number of book-length studies have appeared by authors who consciously use a comparative methodology.[7] These studies can be placed in several broad categories based on the number of immigrant groups and cities to be compared. Most of the authors, like Barton, focus on several immigrant groups in the same city: Thomas Kessner writes about Italians and Jews in New York City; John Bodnar and associates compare blacks, Italians, and Poles in Pittsburgh; Ronald Bayor discusses Italians, Germans, Irish, and Jews in New York City; and Gary Mormino and George Pozzetta analyze Spaniards, Cubans, and Italians in

Ybor City, Florida. Others focus on the same immigrant group in different cities of the same country. John Briggs, for example, studies Italians in Rochester, Utica, and Kansas City, Missouri; Robert Harney and Jean Scarpaci have edited a collection of studies on Little Italys in North America; and Timothy Meagher's anthology describes the Irish in a dozen cities in various parts of the United States. A few authors specifically compare one immigrant group in the sending country and the receiving city; Dino Cinel does this for Italians in Italy and San Francisco, and Dona Gabaccia does it for western Sicilians in New York City. The most neglected type of comparison is cross-cultural. To my knowledge there is no recent book-length historical study of the same migrant group in different host societies abroad.

Whatever the specific focus, these studies generally are not conceptually explicit or very systematic in their use of comparison. As Raymond Grew, longtime editor of *Comparative Studies in Society and History*, notes: "the validity of any comparison rests on careful definitions against which the elements compared must be systematically tested."[8] Frequently the discussion of comparison in historical migration studies is not related to the existing scholarly literature and does not therefore build upon it. The authors generally examine the various immigrant groups separately and often leave systematic comparison to the reader.

The field of migration history would benefit enormously from cross-cultural studies in which the historical comparisons are explicit, systematic, and methodologically rigorous. As is true of all systematic comparisons, cross-cultural comparisons would facilitate asking questions, identifying significant problems, formulating meaningful generalizations, demonstrating uniqueness, and establishing causal explanations. Especially important, however, cross-cultural comparisons would provide a corrective to the misleading assumption of U.S. exceptionalism. U.S. historians of migration frequently write as though the United States were the only possible destination for migrants and the U.S. experience with migration unique or exceptional. The value of cross-cultural comparison, Fredrickson explains, "is that it permits us to escape, at least to some extent, from the provincialism and limiting set of tacit assumptions that tend to result from perpetual immersion in the study of a single culture, a preoccupation that is especially constricting if that culture happens to be our own."[9]

What should we compare? How do we define terms such as *the process of migration*? What is the proper unit of analysis for the study of migration? What is the most accurate and informative spatial and chronological comparison? Is it, for example, more fruitful to compare Italians and Jews in New York City at the turn of the century, or Jews at the turn of the century with post-Castro Cubans in the New York area? What about Italians in two cities at the same time, or different ethnic groups in the same city at the same time? The answers depend on what we are looking for and how we set up our comparison, issues we will discuss below. Suffice it to point out here that as Magnus Morner notes, the units of comparison must be "representative of the universe about which generalizations will be made," and that "their significance in relation to their respective contexts must be similar or, at the least, made explicit and evaluated within the framework of analysis."[10]

It is especially when making comparison that immigrant historians need to be more explicit as to what they are doing and more systematic in how they do it. We must first define the kinds of variables to be used, something too few historians do: control variables, explanatory variables (independent), and variables to be explained (dependent). Every scholar who uses comparison consciously or unconsciously attempts to hold constant or control for some variables—thus limiting the number of independent variables to be considered—in order to be able to focus attention on the impact of other explanatory variables on the subject to be explained. In the comparative historical migration studies referred to above, most authors controlled for place and time (the same city during the same time period) in order to focus on the variables that explain the respective patterns of some phase of the migration process of different groups. A second category of authors controlled for the immigrant group and time (Italians or Irish during the same time period) in order to focus on the impact of different cities or host environments.

When we turn to the relationship between explanatory variables and the process to be explained, questions of theory, concepts, and analytical frameworks become important. Historical sociologist Victoria E. Bonell notes that "the comparative method is required in order to establish with certainty that a theoretical proposition applicable to one case sustains its explanatory power when applied to additional cases."[11] Historians need inductively based theoretical propositions that can be tested and refined in the process of comparative investigation, and that will reflect the essential empirical integrity of each case. A study of Italians in Buenos Aires and New York City, for instance, might indicate that kin- and village-based networks significantly influenced where immigrants lived, what jobs they held, and with whom they socialized. Thus, we might set forth the inductively based theoretical proposition that the stronger the kin- and village-based networks, the more likely an individual immigrant would be to live in a given neighborhood, hold a certain type of job, and socialize with a specific group of people. We would test this proposition by looking at Italians in other cities, and if necessary refine the proposition according to the new data.

All comparisons are not, however, based on the same "logic," as Theda Skocpol points out, and some approaches are more suited than others to the development of an inductively based analytical framework.[12] Skocpol distinguishes three logics of comparison. The *Parallel Demonstration of Theory* logic of comparison seeks to elaborate theoretical models and hypotheses and then turns to specific historical case studies to demonstrate that the theoretical arguments apply to multiple cases. Although some scholars of migration, such as Samuel Eisenstadt, have been attracted to this approach, its *a priori* commitment to a theoretical model makes it of little use to inductively predisposed historians.[13] On the other hand, Skocpol's second logic of comparison, the *Contrast of Contexts*, is designed to illustrate the uniqueness of each situation compared to any other, and thus maintains the historical integrity of every case. Grazia Dore's study of Italians in the Americas fits into this category. The author shows how different contexts can produce distinct results regarding democracy and fascism.[14] This logic does not, however, systematically link explanatory variables to the process or results to be explained and therefore does not help us build causal generalizations.

Skocpol's third logic of comparison, *Macro-Causal Analysis*, is promising from our point of view because it seeks causal explanations linking dependent and independent variables but at the same time is sensitive to the historical integrity of each case involved. This logic is "a kind of multivariate analysis to which scholars turn in order *to validate causal statements about macrophenomena for which, inherently, there are too many variables and not enough cases* [emphasis mine]. Macroanalytic comparative historians proceed by selecting or referring to aspects of historical cases in order to set up approximations to controlled comparisons. Always this is done in relation to particular explanatory problems and (one or more) hypotheses about likely causes."[15] The macroanalysts seek either to establish "that several cases having in common the phenomenon to be explained also have in common the hypothesized causal factors" (Method of Agreement), or to "contrast cases in which phenomenon to be explained and the hypothesized causes are present to other ('negative') cases in which the phenomenon and the causes are both absent (Method of Difference). . . . "[16]

If, for example, our concern is to explain the nature and degree of adjustment of immigrants in an urban receiving society—one of the important issues for historians seeking to describe and understand the migration process—we can employ either method. If we employ the Method of Agreement, we would compare Italians in Buenos Aires at the turn of the past century to Italians in São Paulo or San Francisco during the same period, or to Germans in Milwaukee during an earlier period, because the patterns of adjustment appear to be fairly similar. In so doing, we would look to similar explanatory causes of the common outcome. If, however, we employ the Method of Difference, we would compare Italians in Buenos Aires with those in New York City because the latter adjusted in a distinct manner. We would show that the New York pattern was the result of a set of explanatory variables that differed from those that explained the Buenos Aires pattern. The most effective approach would be to employ both methods and include sufficient additional cases to control for each explanatory variable in at least one comparison, and support cases of outcome and causal agreement with opposing negative cases in which neither the outcome nor the causes were present. However, because of the complexity of the migration process and the number of variables to consider, it is impossible to find enough cases to be able to control for all but one independent variable at a time, as we would like. Nevertheless, controlled comparison does permit us to eliminate at least some independent variables from consideration.

A few migration historians have done pioneering work that moves us toward the development of a systematic analytical framework of adjustment. Barton, for example, writes of the need for "a model of immigrant assimilation that accounts for the persistence of the relation between ethnicity and social status while it allows for the strength of assimilative forces." Nevertheless, he does not systematically relate the five aspects of immigration he considers most important (social structure and emigration in the societies of origin; different patterns of migration and social adjustment; ethnic settlements and the development of distinctive communities and values; ethnic origins and social mobility; and assimilation and generations) to one another or to the process as a whole.[17] Kathleen Conzen suggests that the experience of the Germans in antebellum Milwaukee constitutes a model of "painless adjustment and good living conditions for many but which also encouraged the postponement of assimilation. . . . " She explains the model of painless adjustment through such variables as skill levels of immigrants, size of immigrant group, and relationship between mass migration and growth of the receiving city. Her work, however, is not comparative.[18] John Bodnar and associates are perhaps the most explicit and systematic of recent migration historians in the use of a comparative framework. They argue, for example, that "comparing blacks with late-arriving European immigrants, those from eastern and southern Europe, in a single city provides the possibility of holding the variables of time and place somewhat constant and making comparisons more meaningful."[19] Yet even they could strengthen their work by more systematically relating the explanatory variables to the actual experience of each ethnic group in their target city, Pittsburgh.

Sociologists have done some suggestive work in developing explanatory models of at least parts of the migration process. In one such study, John Goldlust and Anthony H. Richmond set forth a multivariate model of adaptation in Toronto using interview data with recent Canadian immigrants.[20] The model theoretically relates to different kinds of adaptation the interaction of a variety of premigration characteristics and conditions (education and technical training, prior urbanization, demographic characteristics, auspices, and motivation), on the one hand, and situational determinants in the receiving society, (demography, urbanization, industrialization, government policies, pluralism, and stratification) on the other hand. It measures adaptation by both objective aspects (political, social, cultural, and economic) and subjective aspects (identification, internalization, and satisfaction). What emerge are five specific patterns (typologies) of adaptation based on the relative differences of two independent variables: the amount of education (more or less than ten years) and length of residence in the new country (more or less than ten years).

This model, however suggestive, raises problems for most historians. First, it assumes the use of interview data, which obviously cannot be replicated for historical situations. Second, it is a static model and cannot encompass changes over time essential for understanding the migration process. Third, it raises some important conceptual problems that confront all those who attempt to unravel historical processes: How, for example, can we distinguish the effects of length of residence from the normal aging process of any member of the locations being studied? And fourth, the model ultimately relies on a limited number of independent variables upon which to build the causal explanation (education and length of residence). We need to include the original variables listed by the authors and perhaps add others, such as occupation and membership in a social network. The results of the reductionism to two causal variables can only be to oversimplify and to distort the explanation.

Despite the problems of this study for comparative migration historians, it and similar studies suggest what we might be able to do. They specifically relate variables in the old country with variables in the new country in an attempt to explain adaptation, and they seek to measure the impact of these independent variables on adaptation. Equally important, they posit different outcomes that might be produced by different combinations of independent variables.

If migration history is to generate more comprehensive and sophisticated explanations, migration historians must frame their research in such a way that it can be useful to others in making comparisons; they must ask the same questions and develop and share the same inductively based analytical frameworks that systematically relate cause and effect. The use of the macroanalytic comparative approach will greatly facilitate this task.[21]

A Case Study of Cross-Cultural Comparison: The Adjustment of the Italians in the Americas, 1870–1914

I have been studying and writing about Italian migrants for some time and recently have attempted to explained, among other things, the respective patterns of their adjustment in Buenos Aires and New York City.[22] Implicit in this effort is an inductively based analytical framework of immigrant adjustment in an urban setting. The analytical framework, however, needs to be presented more explicitly and developed more systematically. In the pages that follow I will restructure my data on Italians in the two cities so that the relationship between the explanatory variables and the nature and degree of adjustment is clear and potentially usable for the analysis of immigrant adjustment in other urban areas.

My purpose is to explain in general the variation of immigrant adjustment in an urban receiving environment, and specifically the relative nature and degree of Italian adjustment in Buenos Aires and New York City at the turn of the century. *Adjustment* refers to a specific phase of the migration process. All immigrants, whether permanent or temporary, had to adjust to some degree to their new environment. To do this, they needed to find a job or some means of support, a place to live, and friends with whom to associate. In addition, however, because Italians going to New York and Buenos Aires did so primarily to increase their economic resources and those of their family, they also needed to develop organizations to articulate and defend their interests. We can measure the degree of adjustment by comparing in two or more locations the outcomes of the process by which Italian immigrants got jobs, found housing, became part of a social network, created protective institutions, and increased their economic resources. Because we do not have the kind of data that permit mathematical precision, we are looking for the relationship among our cases rather than the precise difference measured on some absolute scale.

In my analysis, I am controlling for some variables — country of origin of the immigrants (Italy), absolute size of the immigrant group within the urban receiving environment (over twenty-five thousand), and time (1870–1914) — in order to focus on the impact of other explanatory variables.[23] The variables that explain the different experiences of the Italians in Buenos Aires and New York City can usefully be clustered in three interrelated categories: immigrant characteristics at the time of migration, the kind of environment the immigrants entered, and the changing nature of the immigrant community over time.

We will look first at the dependent variables: the nature and relative degree of adjustment among Italians in New York and Buenos Aires up to 1914. Then we will evaluate the three clusters of explanatory variables to determine why the patterns of adjustment differed in the two cities. Finally, we will explore the relationship among the explanatory variables to see to what degree we can set forth in general a working analytical framework and typology of comparative urban immigrant adjustment. I will refer to data amassed during years of research in New York City, Buenos Aires, and Italy, but I will present it only in summary form. Anyone interested in greater detail and more extensive citations should consult my recent articles.[24]

The evidence on economic activity, residence, and immigrant community organizations makes it clear that the nature and degree of Italian adjustment in Buenos Aires differed significantly from that of their counterparts in New York City:

1. *Economic Activity*. In Buenos Aires, Italian workers and owners dominated the commercial and industrial sectors of this rapidly growing city (both in absolute terms and in proportion to their share of the population) throughout the period under consideration; in New York, the Italians, although numerous in a few occupations, never dominated any large sector of the economy. Similarly, although most Italians in both cities were blue-collar workers, a higher proportion in Buenos Aires were skilled workers and owners of small industrial and commercial establishments. In addition, although Italians in both cities experienced some upward occupational mobility, mobility among Italians in New York was confined to blue-collar occupations, whereas in Buenos Aires, limited mobility extended to white-collar occupations as well. Finally, Italians in Buenos Aires played a more significant role in organizations of workers (labor unions and federations) and employers (Argentine Industrial Union).

2. *Residence*. Although in both cities many Italians began their residence in crowded, low-rent districts, those in Buenos Aires were more dispersed throughout the city while those in New York were concentrated in Lower Manhattan and Harlem. Living conditions, poor in both cities, were somewhat better in Buenos Aires, where only one-quarter of Italians lived in crowded tenements, than in New York, where tenements sheltered three-quarters. The population density in the New York Italian districts was approximately 50 percent higher than in equivalent districts in Buenos Aires. Property ownership was also much higher among Italians in Buenos Aires than in New York.

Finally, Italians in Buenos Aires moved earlier than those in New York to the outer areas of the respective cities where there was less congestion and greater opportunity to buy a house.

3. *Immigrant Community Organizations.* Italians in both cities established a variety of community organizations to articulate their interests and meet their needs. In Buenos Aires these organizations were more highly developed, commanded greater resources, and were more representative of the diverse elements of the community. For example, the mutualist movement, an effort to create mutual-aid societies, started in the mid-nineteenth century in both cities but developed very differently. In New York, the overwhelming majority of societies were small (under five hundred members), poorly financed and managed, and confined to individuals from one town or region. In Buenos Aires, on the other hand, a number of large societies (one thousand members and more) open to all Italians provided leadership. These societies had substantial assets and performed more extensive services for their members. The divisive influences of localism, politics, and personal rivalries were present to some extent in Buenos Aires, but the leadership of the societies overcame this and developed a relatively united mutualist movement by 1914.

In terms of economic activity, residence, and community organizations the Italians in Buenos Aires adjusted more rapidly and completely in the four decades preceding World War I than Italians in New York City. Having established this difference, we must seek to explain it. The relationship among the three clusters of explanatory variables mentioned previously—the skills and attitudes the immigrants brought with them, the characteristics of the receiving societies, and the changing nature of the immigrant communities—is of primary importance in accounting for the patterns of adjustment. The variables that seem to explain the Buenos Aires pattern are (1) relatively high occupational and organizational skills among the immigrant group on arrival, and relatively high expectations that migration was to be permanent; (2) relatively good opportunity for employment throughout the receiving economy, positive attitude of host society toward immigrants, and a developed immigrant institutional infrastructure at time of arrival; and (3) a gradual pace of subsequent migration, numerical strength, and concentration; having to compete with only one other sizable immigrant group (the Spanish); and a dynamic and representative Italian elite with a strong middle-class component.

The variables that seem to explain the New York pattern are essentially the inverse of those for Buenos Aires: (1) relatively low occupational and organizational skills among the immigrant group on arrival, and low expectations that migration would be permanent; (2) employment opportunities restricted primarily to the lower levels of the economy, a negative attitude of the host society toward the immigrants, and a weak immigrant institutional infrastructure at the time of arrival; and (3) the concentrated arrival of subsequent migration, a relatively low numerical strength (negating the potential impact of concentration), numerous other immigrant groups with which to contend, and a two-tiered Italian social structure that seems to have produced an unrepresentative elite.

250 NEW APPROACHES TO THE STUDY OF IMMIGRATION

All of these variables interacted to produce the respective patterns of adjustment, but we cannot determine which variables were most important in the outcomes because we have only two cases. To do more, we would need to move beyond Buenos Aires and New York City. We might begin by setting up our two patterns (outcomes) as the extremes in a typology of urban immigrant adjustment, and hypothesize that Buenos Aires represented the most rapid and complete side of the spectrum and New York the least rapid and complete side. Then, with the aid of the secondary literature, we could place on the spectrum the respective patterns (outcomes) of Italian adjustment in other cities, as measured by an examination of economic activity, residence, and immigrant community organizations.

If this hypothesis were valid, all new cases would fall between those of Buenos Aires and New York City. If not, we would substitute the new polar case for one of the existing ones. For example, on the basis of the secondary literature, I would place San Francisco and probably St. Louis on the side of the spectrum close to Buenos Aires (rapid and complete adjustment), São Paulo in the middle, and Boston close to New York (slow and less complete adjustment). But perhaps San Francisco or Boston are really the respective polar cases.[25] If so, they would be moved to the appropriate position on the spectrum. In this way we could place Philadelphia, Chicago, Cleveland, Toronto, Melbourne, Paris, Lyon, and many other cities on the spectrum of Italian immigrant adjustment.

Once we developed our typology of adjustment with, say, a dozen or more cases, we would begin to seek the relationship between independent variables and the specific outcome to be explained. To do this, we would compare cases that allowed us to control for certain variables in order to focus on the impact of others. If, for example, we sought to determine which variables were most influential on rapid and complete adjustment, how could we confirm or deny the influence of the independent variables present in the Buenos Aires case? We could hypothesize that the variables present to a high degree were most influential to the outcome, but only through controlled comparison could we eliminate some independent variables from consideration.

If we compared Buenos Aires and San Francisco, we might well be able to control for a number of independent variables: (1) relatively high degree of occupational and organizational skills at time of arrival; (2) broader employment opportunities and a fairly well developed immigrant institutional structure when the large migration entered the receiving society; and (3) more even pace of migration, considerable numerical strength and concentration, and multilevel social structure developed over time. We could then explain the differences in terms of the independent variables: (1) expectations regarding permanency; (2) attitude of the host society toward immigrants; and (3) the presence of many other immigrant groups to contend with. If we had correctly selected control variables that were in fact highly similar, we could then conclude that some of these independent variables were more critical to the outcome than others.

There would, of course, be problems with this approach. In addition to the limitations imposed by the paucity of many kinds of historical data, perhaps the main difficulty would be in finding historical examples sufficiently similar to enable us to control for some independent variables. In my own work, when I attempt to control for country of origin, I sometimes find that origin becomes an important independent variable explaining outcome. Similarly, in an interesting article in *Comparative Studies in Society and History* comparing the assimilation of the Chinese in New York City and Lima, Peru, Bernard Wong attempts to control for cultural background and to focus on the respective host cultures as explanatory variables. Subsequent articles and comments in the same journal raise some questions about whether or not this is possible. Is the cultural background of the Chinese who went to New York and Lima sufficiently similar to allow the author to control for this variable? What about the impact of internal values on assimilation? What about a wide range of variables not discussed?[26]

Immigration historians can never develop and use mathematical models as do researchers working on contemporary society, who have different data at their disposal. Indeed, questions remain about whether mathematical models can effectively capture the complexity of the migration experience. Immigration historians can make cross-cultural comparisons, however, and in systematically doing so can determine which variables are important to a greater or lesser degree and then refine the findings through additional comparisons. The effort to be explicit, systematic, and rigorous will force the development and refinement of useful analytical frameworks for the study of migration that will provide a clearer view of the underlying relationships in the process of migration.

NOTES

1. George M. Fredrickson, "Comparative History," in *The Past Before Us*, ed. Michael Kammen (Ithaca: Cornell University Press, 1980), p. 458.

2. Robert F. Foerster, *The Italian Immigration of Our Times* (Cambridge: Harvard University Press, 1919).

3. Ibid., preface.

4. Ibid., pp. 415–44, 504.

5. Frank Thistlethwaite, "Migration from Europe Overseas in the Nineteenth and Twentieth Centuries," in *Population Movements in Modern European History*, ed. Herbert Moller (New York: Macmillan, 1964), pp. 73–92; John Higham, "Immigration," in *The Comparative Approach to American History*, ed. C. Vann Woodward (New York: Basic Books, 1968), pp. 91–105.

6. Fredrickson, "Comparative History," p. 471.

7. Josef Barton, *Peasants and Strangers: Italians, Rumanians, and Slovaks in an American City, 1890-1950* (Cambridge: Harvard University Press, 1975); Ronald H. Bayor, *Neighbors in Conflict: The Irish, Germans, Jews, and Italians of New York City, 1929-1941* (Baltimore: Johns Hopkins University Press, 1978); John Bodnar, Roger Simon, and Michael P. Weber, *Lives of Their Own: Blacks, Italians and Poles in*

Pittsburgh, 1900–1960 (Urbana: University of Illinois Press, 1982); John W. Briggs, *An Italian Passage: Immigrants to Three American Cities, 1890–1930* (New Haven: Yale University Press, 1978); Dino Cinel, *From Italy to San Francisco: The Immigrant Experience* (Stanford: Stanford University Press, 1982); Richard L. Ehrlich, ed., *Immigrants in Industrial America, 1850–1920* (Charlottesville: University of Virginia Press, 1977); Donna R. Gabaccia, *From Sicily to Elizabeth Street: Housing and Social Change among Italian Immigrants, 1880–1930* (Albany: SUNY Press, 1984); Robert F. Harney and J. Vincenza Scarpaci, *Little Italies in North America* (Toronto: Multicultural History Society of Ontario, 1981); Thomas Kessner, *The Golden Door: Italian and Jewish Immigrant Mobility in New York City, 1880–1915* (New York: Oxford University Press, 1977); Timothy J. Meagher, ed. *From Paddy to Studs: Irish American Communities in the Turn of the Century Era, 1880 to 1920* (Westport, Conn.: Greenwood Press, 1986); Gary R. Mormino and George E. Pozzetta, *The Immigrant World of Ybor City* (Urbana: University of Illinois Press, 1987).

    8. Raymond Grew, "The Case for Comparing Histories," *American Historical Review* 85 (October 1980): 765.

    9. Ibid., p. 769; Magnus Morner et al., "Comparative Approaches to Latin American History," *Latin American Research Review* 17, no. 3 (1982): 58; George M. Fredrickson, *White Supremacy: A Comparative Study in American and South African History* (New York: Oxford University Press, 1981), pp. xiv–xxv. The entire issue of the *American Historical Review* (October 1980) in which Grew's article appeared is devoted to comparative history.

    10. Morner et. al, "Comparative Approaches," p. 59.

    11. Victoria E. Bonnell, "The Uses of Theory, Concepts and Comparison in Historical Sociology," *Comparative Studies in Society and History* (hereafter *CSSH*) 22 (April 1980): 160.

    12. Theda Skocpol and Margaret Somers, "The Uses of Comparative History in Macrosocial Inquiry," *CSSH* 22 (April 1980): 174–97. See also Theda Skocpol, *States and Social Revolutions: A Comparative Analysis of France, Russia, and China* (Cambridge: Harvard University Press, 1979), especially pp. 33–39, and Fredrickson, *White Supremacy*.

    13. S. N. Eisenstadt, *The Absorption of Immigrants* (London: Free Press, 1954).

    14. Grazia Dore, *La democrazia italiana e l'emigrazione in america* (Brescia: Morcelliana, 1964).

    15 Skocpol and Somers, "Uses of Comparative History," p. 182.

    16. Ibid., p. 183.

    17. Barton, *Peasants and Strangers*, pp. 6, 8.

    18. Kathleen N. Conzen, *Immigrant Milwaukee, 1836–1860* (Cambridge: Harvard University Press, 1976), pp. 7, 225–28.

    19. Bodnar et al., *Lives of Their Own*, p. 4.

    20. John Goldlust and A. H. Richmond, "A Multivariate Model of Immigrant Adaptation," *International Migration Review* (Summer 1974): 193–225.

    21. It is important to note that I fully believe in the necessity of microstudies of migration as well as the macrostudies we are at present discussing. They complement each other; the macrostudies permit the development of explanatory hypotheses; the microstudies help us to test the limits of these hypotheses.

    22. This essay relies on the evidence developed in a larger study in progress on Italians in Buenos Aires and New York City during the period of mass migration from 1875 to 1925. The published parts of this study can be found in "The Italians and Organized Labor in the United States and Argentina, 1880–1910," *International Migra-*

tion Review 1 (1967): 55–66; "The Italians and the Development of Organized Labor in Argentina, Brazil and the United States, 1880–1914," *Journal of Social History* 3 (1969): 123–34; "The Role of the Press and the Assimilation of Italians in Buenos Aires and Sao Paulo, 1893–1913," *International Migration Review* 12 (1978): 321–40; "Marriage Patterns and Immigrant Assimilation in Buenos Aires, 1882–1923," *Hispanic American Historical Review* 60 (1980): 32–48; "Chain Migration of Italians to Argentina: Case Studies of the Agnonesi and the Sirolesi," *Studi Emigrazione* (Rome) 19 (1982): 73–91; "Las Sociedades de ayuda mutua y el dessarrollo de una comunidad italiana en Buenos Aires, 1858–1918," *Desarrollo Economico* (Buenos Aires) 21 (1982): 485–514; "The Adjustment of Italian Immigrants in Buenos Aires and New York, 1870–1914," *American Historical Review* 88 (April 1983): 281–305; and "Patrones de residencia de los italianos en Buenos Aires y Nueva York: 1880–1914," *Estudios Migratorios Latinoamericanos* 1 (Diciembre 1985): 8–47.

23. I Started with these control variables but subsequently realized that where migrants came from within Italy might be an important explanatory variable. My future work will take this into account. See comments, this chapter.

24. See note 22, and especially "Adjustment of Italian Immigrants."

25. For San Francisco, see Cinel, *From Italy to San Francisco*; Micaela Di Leonardo, *The Varieties of Ethnic Experience: Kinship, Class and Gender among California's Italian Americans* (Ithaca: Cornell University Press, 1984); Deanna Paoli Gumina, *The Italians of San Francisco, 1850–1930* (New York: Center for Migration Studies, 1978); Paul Radin, *The Italians of San Francisco, Their Adjustment and Acculturation* (New York: Arno Press, 1975); Rose Doris Scherini, *The Italian American Community of San Francisco, A Descriptive Study* (New York: Arno Press, 1980). For St. Louis, see Gary Mormino, *Immigrants on the Hill: Italian-Americans in St. Louis, 1882–1982* (Urbana: University of Illinois Press, 1986). For São Paulo, see Franco Cenni, *Italianos no Brasil* (São Paulo: Martins Editora, 1959); Michael M. Hall, "The Origins of Mass Immigration in Brazil, 1871–1914" (Ph.D. diss., Columbia University, 1969); Thomas H. Holloway, *Immigrants on the Land* (Chapel Hill: University of North Carolina Press, 1980); Gianfausto Rosoli, ed., *Emigrazione Europee e Popolo Brasiliano* (Rome: Centro Studi Emigrazione, 1987). For Boston, see William M. Demarco, *Ethnics and Enclaves: Boston's Italian North End* (Ann Arbor: UMI Research Press, 1981). A recent study that skillfully uses a comparative methodology to construct a similar typology for labor movements is Charles Bergquist, *Labor in Latin America: Comparative Essays on Chile, Argentina, Venezuela, and Columbia* (Stanford: Stanford University Press, 1986).

26. Bernard Wong, "A Comparative Study of the Assimilation of the Chinese in New York City and Lima, Peru," *CSSH* 20 (July 1978): 335–57; Stephen I. Thompson, "Assimilation and Nonassimilation of Asian-Americans and Asian Peruvians," *CSSH* 21 (October 1979): 572–88; Roger Daniels, "On the Comparative Study of Immigrant and Ethnic Groups in the New World: A Note," *CSSH* 25 (April 1983): 401–4; Bernard Wong, "On Assimilation of the Asians in the Americas. A Reply," *CSSH* 27 (January 1985): 171–73. See also the less systematic but informative effort of Christoph Klessmann, "Comparative Immigrant History: Polish Workers in the Ruhr Area and the North of France," *Journal of Social History* 20 (Winter 1986): 355–83.

9

Metaphors of Self in History: Subjectivity, Oral Narrative, and Immigration Studies

Virginia Yans-McLaughlin

This chapter explores subjective documents and their relationship to immigration and ethnic studies, fields that historically have found these sources both appealing and problematic. By "subjective documents" I refer to a broad class of evidence that reveals "the participant's view of experiences in which he had been involved."[1] They include autobiographies, life histories, letters, oral narratives, interviews, and court records. I wish to familiarize readers with some recent debates over the use and creation of this type of data, giving particular emphasis to phenomenology, hermeneutics, and textual analysis. I will focus here on one example, the oral interview or narrative; this strategy will expose both the unique peculiarities of these data and scholarly ambivalence about subjective sources.

As a demonstration of how recent debates may transform the meaning and use of personal documents for scholars in immigration studies and other fields, I will present my own analysis of oral interviews of New York City Jewish and Italian immigrants.[2] My study searches these life stories — these reconstructions of the self — at the symbolic level, not for what is remembered in them but for the ways in which memories themselves are structured. The methodologies suggested by ethnography and textual analysis prove powerful tools for analyzing these narratives, but as a historian, I am also inclined to argue that it is up to historians to expose the social processes and contexts from which these accounts of the self emerged. Textual analysts are not inclined to seek such

I would like to thank Rudolph Bell, Michael Frisch, Ronald Grele, the late Herbert G. Gutman, and Michael Seidman for their comments on earlier versions of this essay. Research for this essay was made possible by a grant from the National Endowment for the Humanities. The Rutgers University Faculty Research Grants Program also provided support.

relationships or to analyze groups of subjective documents as artifacts of social life. I will suggest that these personal narratives offer a means to establish political and cultural values as demonstrable phenomena emerging from the historical experience of groups, in this case, the historical experiences and narrative traditions of immigrant Italians and Jews.

Sensitized by the caveats of phenomenologists and ethnographers, I have exposed my own historical perspective as a context for my interpretation of these oral testimonies. I hope this chapter, in its attempt to join theory with practice, will aid researchers to evaluate the use of oral histories and other subjective documents in their own work.

Controversy over Subjective Documents

In the early 1940s, the Social Science Research Council published a summary review on the use of "personal" documents in history, sociology, anthropology, and social psychology. This publication has been regarded as a major authoritative source ever since. As one would expect, the review demonstrated that each discipline placed different emphases upon written and oral documentation. Each understood the personal document—what I prefer to call the "subjective document"—as one that reveals "the author and his view of events."[3] Acknowledging the appeal of these data, social scientists of the day complained, nevertheless, that they had problems knowing what to do with them. Were they acceptable evidence, and for what? How could social scientists and historians use them to develop generalizations about social and historical processes, or even to establish facts? The social psychologist Gordon W. Allport responded that personal documents were especially adapted to research on the "complexities of phenomenal consciousness." Anticipating the "scorching displeasure of behaviorists and objectivists," Allport offered the following simple defense: If we want to know how people feel, what they experience and what they remember, what their emotions and motives are like, "Why not ask them?"[4] Why not, indeed. Allport's question struck at the heart of objectivist epistemological notions concerning evidence, notably what is considered the appropriate, and the actual, distance between the observer and the observed. By insisting upon the significance of how things appear to people, Allport also challenged the behaviorists' insistence that autonomous mental states cannot be understood as known determinants of human behavior.

A survey of the relevant literature almost fifty years after the Social Science Research Council report reveals that controversy about subjective documents still rages.[5] Behaviorists continue to prefer statistics and other "hard data" to these sources. Necessity, in the case of some historians, and method, in the case of field ethnographers, explain their continuing acceptance of personal testimony. Historians, of course, must rely on what precious documents the past leaves behind. Although they are by convention accustomed to dealing with written sources, historians include accounts by living eyewitnesses in the category of acceptable evidence. Traditionally, ethnography relies upon direct observation for its data. Since the 1920s and even before, field ethnographers have also relied upon various "native texts" — oral exchanges such as interviews and life histories — to learn how the informant, through manner, presentation, and information offered, yields data about the culture being studied.[6] In an interesting turn of events, these and other scholars who value subjective data are questioning objectivist assumptions about their use and interpretation. They emphasize that many subjective documents, whether written or orally produced, as well as the edited texts that scholars create or synthesize and inject into scholarly publications, are all actually collaborations coauthored by informants and investigators. The primary texts and edited versions of them are not, they insist, simple and direct testimony, but must be understood as products of historical experiences and relations of power.

It should come as no surprise that this challenge to scientific authority emerges within anthropology, a discipline that in its postcolonial period is acutely aware of its objectification of colonized peoples. The fieldwork methods of ethnography, which often rely on the personal testimony of informants, make it a likely focus for the initiation of this extraordinary self-scrutiny. Remedies proposed include exposure of the "hidden" authority within the interview situation and behind the ethnographic text, as well as experimentation with ethnographic texts to make them overtly "polyvocal" (admitting not one but several "authoritative" voices). Both of the creators of the text — the ethnographer and the informant — are the newly acknowledged authorities.[7]

Historians have long recognized their writing as "literature," but this admission has not produced a restructuring of formal historical texts nor a radical critique of historical knowledge.[8] Historians generally use oral interview materials (even if they are considered of a somewhat suspicious, subjective character) as they would other data, and they generally do not acknowledge oral narratives or edited versions of oral narratives as collaborations. Excepting a small group of oral historians, the dominant view insists upon the historian's distance from, and authority within, the text.

Alternative Approaches

Those who find the objectivist interpretation of oral history and other subjective documents wanting seek an alternative approach in a phenomenological perspective and the allied methods of hermeneutics, the art of interpreting texts. Among social scientists and philosophers, the phenomenological perspective, grounded in the work of Edmund Husserl, Alfred Schutz, Maurice Natanson, and others, assigns major importance to the interpretations that people themselves place on their experience. It examines these subjective interpretations — not the investigator's constructs and models, recognized as alien to the individual life under construction — as explanations for behavior. This is obviously troublesome to positivist social scientists and historians who use the natural sciences as their model.

Phenomenologists insist upon a fundamental distinction between the social and natural sciences. If social scientists and historians did nothing but engage in silent observation of human subjects, they argue, perhaps the natural science model would suffice. But the moment we begin to commune with living persons who lived events—or dead persons who set down their responses to those events in writing—we are entering the special realm of social science where, in Schutz's terms, "human intersubjectivity," not "objectivity," reigns.[9] The observer/observed dichotomy does not apply here. Instead, a dialogue between the observer and "the other" creates a "world, or an understanding of the *differences between* two worlds, that exists between persons who are indeterminately far apart, in all sorts of different ways, when they started the conversation."[10] The "betweenness," as anthropologist Denis Tedlock calls it, does not disappear in the armchair when the social scientist or historian, now distant from the interview or field material, is tempted to believe he or she is analyzing data as a natural scientist would. As Schutz claims, the objectivity of the social scientist is really "nothing more than the 'subjectivity' of the observer making his own claims over and beyond the observed."[11] A contemporary anthropologist put it simply: the social scientist is "playing god with his constructs."[12]

The phenomenological approach explicitly recognizes the "status of the text or the object of interpretation"—life history, oral interview, and so on—as a "subjective bag of understandings."[13] That bag would, of course include categories such as "motivation," "hegemony," "class," "ethnicity," "class consciousness," and so forth. Although the use of constructs and models might be useful, even necessary, in scientific investigation, phenomenologists acknowledge them as "arbitrary acts" that, once initiated, generate their own "appropriate meanings and outcomes." Without attention to intersubjectivity, they warn, the integrity of the biographical account or other narrative product is "violated in the very act of interpretation."[14] This does not preclude the interpreting of oral histories and other subjective documents; rather, it is asserted that without reference to our own prejudices, "preunderstandings," or worldview—which those committed to natural science models keep on insisting do not exist or should not exist in the evidence—it would not be possible to understand the object or event under investigation.

A small group of ethnographers, sociologists, and historians offer hermeneutics, which operates very comfortably within the phenomenological frame, as an alternative way to interpret evidence. Practically speaking, hermeneutics brings two fundamental concerns to social and historical inquiry. The first is the relationship between the investigator and the object of inquiry. A brief discussion of oral narration illustrates the hermeneutic method. The interviewer is not understood as ferreting out data to be discovered only in the recesses of the informant's memory. Rather, the interviewer is actually creating a text *with* the informant. The interview is understood variously as a "social act," a "dialogue," and a "circular feedback" process in which the investigator and the informant continually influence one another.[15]

A second principle of hermeneutics would be that the object of interpretation must always be understood within the larger context from which it obtains meaning. The object might include the informant, but also the interviewer—

both in the field and in the armchair — and the interview situation itself. Hence, in approaching the interview, it is necessary to know as much as possible about the larger social and cultural context, family life, educational experience, and narrative traditions of the informant and the interviewer. We would also want to be aware of the context of the interview itself and of the investigator's and the informant's relationship to it. Dominant and submissive relationships, as well as cross-class and cross-cultural relationships, might well be involved. From the informant's point of view, the researcher requesting an interview might be making an entirely familiar or very peculiar request. The informant's perception of the situation and the role to be played could also be influenced by the existence, or lack, of other oral storytelling forms in his or her culture. We would like to know, as well, about the informant's notions of rhetoric, authorship, humor, irony, and comedy. We would want equivalent information about the interviewer, if only as an estimate of how his or her questioning might encourage departures from the informant's ordinary interpretation of events.

Immigration and Ethnic Studies

Phenomenology has had its most favorable reception on the European continent, where it was born. It has, however, occasionally surfaced in American sociology and anthropology. Insofar as immigration studies are concerned, sociologists seem to have introduced both the phenomenological perspective and, not coincidentally, the use of subjective and oral documents. In their multivolume work *The Polish Peasant in Europe and America* (1918–1920) William Thomas and Florian Znaniecki first called attention to autobiographies, letters, and other subjective sources as valuable evidence for social research.[16] They presented such documents in their study in an effort to connect objective conditions to the individual experience of those conditions. Their effort to include individual experiences placed them in direct communication with the phenomenological tradition. Now better known for their emphasis upon "social disorganization" and ethnic-group adjustment, Thomas and Znaniecki's emphasis upon personal documents was initially accepted as a model by the dominant Chicago school of sociology. During the 1940s and 1950s, however, as American sociologists substituted more "scientific" survey research, interviews, and structured observation, Thomas and Znaniecki's emphasis upon subjectivity fell out of favor.[17]

Although both sociologists and anthropologists had since the 1920s been developing methodologies for exploring subjective experience through personal documents, historians did not consult them until later. Perhaps the focus of most ethnographic interviews and life histories upon individuals from "exotic" cultures or upon American Indian cultures inhibited the exchange.[18] During the depression both historians and folklorists collected slave narratives and interviews of white ethnics for the Works Progress Administration (WPA), but historians did not even turn to these as source material until much later.[19] Some thirty years after Thomas and Znaniecki had published their study, its influence surfaced in the work of the influential historian Oscar Handlin.

Handlin's *The Uprooted* (1951),[20] recognized as a major work in the historiography of immigration, is told from the perspective of a first-generation newcomer. Handlin, however, did not cite actual interviews as the basis for his book. He seems rather to have used the first person as a literary device. Although Handlin's Pulitzer Prize-winning book was widely read, and its emphasis upon social disorganization remained unquestioned for decades, few immigration historians adopted its personal perspective. Instead, nearly the entire field of immigration history moved in the opposite direction, toward quantification and sociological positivism. In retrospect, this apparent contradiction appears logical; even though Handlin and many of his followers took immigrants as their subject matter in the 1950s and afterward, their primary concern was actually the process and the goal of Americanization, and quantitative techniques were ultimately deemed more appropriate tools for analysis of this subject. These authors were far removed from recent works, which stress the immigrants and the immigrants' perspectives as the objects of inquiry.[21]

The revival of ethnic consciousness in the 1960s, joined with a search for new methods of documenting the history of "inarticulate" groups, sparked historians' interest in fieldwork among workers and immigrants. Historians finally began communicating with colleagues in anthropology and area studies who worked among Third World or indigenous American peoples. They learned that whether oral narratives coexist with ancient literary traditions, as they do in southeast Asia, or stand on their own, as in Africa and among American Indians, many researchers relied upon them as primary sources for historical and cultural information.[22] They also learned that the same culture might contain competing popular visions of the past, some based upon mythic visions, some more closely allied to modern historiography.

One of the most insistent and creative uses of subjective oral history documentation came from those studying the history of American slaves, individuals who left few written documents. Cultural historian Lawrence Levine, for example, was one of the first to explore the WPA slave narratives along with Afro-American folk tales and musical expression. In *Black Culture, Black Consciousness* (1977),[23] Levine presented a great deal of his material to emphasize the slaves' perspectives rather than the perspectives of white owners or observers. Where Handlin's immigrants were victimized by their new environment, Levine's Afro-Americans used their cultural resources to shape and interpret their world as they saw it. As a typical example of the tone of the book, Levine described a rural Mississippi black's response to someone who told him he was not singing a song correctly: "Look-a-heah, man, dis yere *mah song*, en I'll sing it howsoevah I pleases."[24] In the late 1960s and 1970s, several efforts were also made to interview living southern blacks; one of the most impressive was the epochal oral narration of the life of Nat Shaw, *All God's Dangers*.[25] At Duke University, William Chafe and Lawrence Goodwyn initiated their biracial history of the South; newly created oral histories constituted one of their major resources.[26]

Among a group of social and labor historians also interested in the history of immigrant workers, disillusionment with positivistic methods, quantification, and what they considered a rigid, conventional Marxism, coupled with a desire to "write history from the bottom up," encouraged exploration of oral interviews and other subjective documentation. These efforts did not escape the political environment of the 1960s and 1970s. In some instances, the interview was being used as part of a community-organizing effort by liberal or radical historians who wanted to return history to the people; still others saw these interviews as "therapeutic."[27] For some scholars, then, the new emphasis upon subjectivity contained a possibility of uniting politics and method.

Oral History Projects

One group of historians persisted in examining immigrant, working-class, and Afro-American cultures from the perspective of traditional ethnic cultures, despite protests from certain Marxists who insisted that class analysis proceed through the study of the relations of production or the power of ruling-class hegemony. Subjectivity proved as offensive to traditional Marxists as it was to behaviorists. Eli Zaretsky was one of the few Marxists to appreciate that when researchers emphasized ethnicity as a point of protest, rather than as a means of entry into American culture, they overturned the consensual notion of "ethnicity as adjustment" first introduced by Thomas and Znaniecki and imported into immigration history by Oscar Handlin. This revisionist position was established by the distinguished historian of American labor and slavery Herbert G. Gutman.[28]

Gutman, like many of those who were rewriting immigration and working-class history in the 1960s and 1970s, was himself the child of Jewish immigrants. One might see the role of Gutman and scholars like him within immigration history as analogous to contemporary "indigenous ethnographers," who reject imperialist investigators and begin to study their own culture from the inside. The "object" of historical investigation had become the investigator. Moved by the political and academic battles of the 1970s over black culture and the black family, Gutman turned from labor history and wrote *The Black Family in Slavery and Freedom*,[29] a work revealing both the value of quantitative sources, such as plantation records, and a deep commitment to the use of personal documents and narratives. The extraordinary quality of Gutman's historical work rested upon his sympathetic reading of workers' and slaves' recollections, written or oral. In a significant anticipation of what was to follow in the 1980s, Gutman also used the work of anthropologists, particularly Sidney Mintz's *Worker in the Cane*, an oral narrative of a Puerto Rican sugarcane worker. Gutman strongly believed that it was possible and necessary to understand how ordinary individuals experience social change. This belief led him to initiate the City University of New York's oral history project, which was supported by the National Endowment for the Humanities in the early 1970s.[30]

Along with Gutman, I directed what was one of the first university-spon-sored oral history projects in the United States. I had studied briefly with him as a graduate student, and in 1970 I joined him to organize this two-year project, from which the interviews I will discuss in this essay were drawn. Like most of Gutman's other students, I shared his interest in subjectivity and in anthropology, and his uneasiness with deductive models and quantitative meth-ods. My book *Family and Community*,[31] a study of first-generation Italian immigrants, called "culturalist" by certain scholars who thought of the family and the values governing its behavior as epiphenomena, was, nevertheless, acknowledged as a revision of Handlin's consensus immigration history. My idea that traditional ethnic culture could function during the transitional peri-od of first-generation immigrant adjustment troubled those sociologists who preferred a social-structural analysis. As the child of immigrant parents, I was interested in examining the immigrants' perspective on social experiences, and I believed that heavy reliance on structural conditions almost inevitably resulted in a picture of immigrant workers as reactive agents. My approach, of course, made me sympathetic both with investigators who were interested in cultural analysis and with those interested in phenomenology. Along with Gutman, I believed that oral narratives, as subjective recollections, offered a fertile area for exploration.

Neither Gutman nor I had worked extensively with oral sources. We sought the assistance of Ronald G. Grele, now head of the Columbia University Oral History Research Program, noted for its archive and training program in oral narration. One of the first historians to commit himself full-time to oral histo-ry methodology, Grele became an activist in bridging the chasm between soci-ologists, historians, anthropologists, folklorists, and professional writers who used interview techniques to uncover the past. Grele would be among the first historians to refer to interviews as "conversational narratives" between two participants, and to understand the historian's role as one of "discovering the assumed structure of the informant's presentation." He was also one of the first to use oral history narration as evidence for ideological constructs.[32] At the time he joined the City University project, he was only beginning to formulate these notions. With Grele acting as the special consultant, Gutman and I supervised graduate students and a small group of undergraduates at City University.

We interviewed almost three hundred immigrants and migrants to New York City and their children: Afro-Americans, most of whom were casual laborers or domestics; Jews, all of whom were garment workers; Italians who were either garment workers or longshoremen; and a few Irish, Germans, and Puer-to Ricans in a variety of occupations.[33] Utilizing a flexible set of questions rather than a strict questionnaire, we intended our work to be "topical," along the lines of Studs Terkel's books on work and the Depression.[34] Certainly, we understood ourselves to be creating historical evidence, not literary texts. Sev-eral project participants went on to do their own work in labor or immigration history, but no major synthetic work emerged from the project. Individual persons involved with the project and others used details from the interview materials just as any historian consulting an archive of written sources would. Influenced by phenomenology, textual analysis, ethnography, and folklore, some oral historians, like Grele, traveled a different route. They took the individual interviews themselves as their data.[35] At a time when oral sources were so poorly understood by historians, the textual analysis was sorely needed. Despite their acknowledgment that the material conditions of life must explain them, Grele and his colleagues, did not, however, explain the process by which these narrative forms, or the ideologies expressed in them, came into existence.[36]

A brief discussion of other oral history projects suggests in a general way additional currently approved uses of oral history documentation. About ten years after the City University project began, two historians of American labor and immigration—Tamara Hareven and John Bodnar—did attempt fully developed uses for immigrant oral narratives. Hareven, who supervised a large collaborative project and used researchers to conduct many of the interviews, published two books—one a collection of edited interviews; the other, a historical monograph—in which she attempted to synthesize quantitative, qualitative, and oral history sources.[37] Hareven's approach in the latter publication typifies the use of multiple sources by historians. An appendix to the work titled "The Subjective Reconstruction of Past Lives" explains her methodology:

> Whereas the quantitative analysis provides structural evidence concerning the organization and behavior of kin, the oral history interviews offer insight into the nature of relationships and their significance to participants. The empirical analysis reported here—though attempting to weld both types of evidence—at times presents two levels of historical reality, each derived from a distinct type of data.[38]

Hareven makes the usual positivist bows to problems of representation, accuracy, and distance from the event. Although she intends to weave together the two "levels" of historical analysis, throughout most of the book, except when she uses oral interviews to document workers' recalled feelings, she uses them just as she would use qualitative evidence or written evidence: to offer factual information about hiring processes, neighborhood, and work relations.[39]

John Bodnar's *Worker's World: Kinship, Community and Protest in an Industrial Society, 1900–1940*, a collection of edited interviews, takes an entirely different approach to the use of oral evidence.[40] The interviews were gathered under thirty different projects, but Bodnar conducted most of them. He rejects outright the notion that anything these immigrant workers say is meaningless until the historian, as scientific investigator, gives it meaning. He also rejects historians' attempts to impose their own models upon the worker, including the notion that workers' lives were being acted upon "solely by larger societal forces, . . . that worker protest is shaped solely by the dynamics of the workplace" or state intervention. Although he elected to develop a guiding questionnaire to trigger respondents' memories and to generate "meaningful historical data," Bodnar asserts he avoided "too rigid an imposition of historical models," which would have threatened the possibility of the respondents' bringing a perspective model of their own. Since Bodnar edited the interviews and excluded his own voice from the text, it is difficult to know precisely how this came about. Nevertheless, he argues that the value of his book of oral interviews is that it demonstrates that workers are "culture bearing individuals," that we must uncover their "internally established goals" to "obtain an accurate picture of their consciousness and understand the ultimate thrust of their behavior."[41]

Bodnar's interpretation of oral documentation, clearly compatible with the phenomenological perspective, hermeneutics, and recent critiques of ethnographic texts, has not been widely adopted by American historians. They seem to prefer Hareven's positivist synthesis of several "levels" of historical analysis and the historian's solitary voice as authority. This is a deeply rooted attitude. A survey of over one hundred books published between 1985 and 1987 in American social history revealed that approximately 10 percent used oral history methods. Not one departed from the pattern Hareven established, although not all of them were as sophisticated about the use of oral evidence.[42]

This review of recent uses of oral narrative and other personal documents suggests certain conclusions about their use. The difficulty with these sources does not seem to be only what can be done *with* them. One group of scholars weaves the data into the fabric of historical narratives like any other kind of archival material. Rather, the difficulty resides in a failure to acknowledge how oral narratives are produced and how their method of production, not just their subjectivity, distinguishes them from other kinds of data, and should distinguish their use. At the other extreme, scholars like Grele and other oral history specialists, well aware of these difficulties, dwell on the narratives themselves, upon their structure and production. Although they insist that oral narrations are products of history, they have generally not situated these interviews within their social and historical context nor attempted to make generalized statements about groups of oral narratives that might lead to an understanding of the connections between material conditions and these narrated ideological constructions.[43] They have not, therefore, convinced sociologists, Marxists, or many historians of the value of their textual analysis.

I will proceed with an analysis of the interviews of New York City immigrants that attempts to come to terms with some of these difficulties. The preceding review has revealed the context of my own and my City University colleagues' approach to the interpretation of these oral documents, even as we oversaw a project that produced them. We thought we were creating an archive of empirical data. In hindsight and with the assistance of the scholarly literature just reviewed, I understand these personal narratives in a dramatically different fashion. These oral narratives offer more than empirical documentation about the past; they present popular historical consciousness expressed at the invitation of professional historians and their students, all of whom brought their own ideological scripts and understandings of history to the interviews of immigrants.

The Italian and Jewish immigrants, of course, also brought their own historical scripts to the interview. And their visions of the past are fundamental to our analysis. Although literary, ethnographic, and hermeneutic approaches calling for the exploration of narrative structure, metaphor, allegory, and rhetoric prove powerful instruments for defining the morphology of historical consciousness in these interviews, some effort will be required here to locate this ethnohistory in its real historical circumstances. It is to that task that we can now proceed.

Italians and Jews in the Garment Industry and on the Docks

The primary evidence I will deal with in the rest of this chapter was culled from about one hundred Italian and Jewish immigrants, and a few of their children, who labored in New York City between 1900 and 1930. All the Jews were garment workers or members of garment workers' families. Their role in this New York industry is legendary. Among Italians interviewed, longshoremen, garment workers, and a few of their wives and children were equally represented. By the early twentieth century, Italians, most of them living and laboring along the Brooklyn waterfront, were the largest single ethnic group among New York's forty-five to fifty thousand dockworkers. During the same period, Italians also entered the garment industry in great numbers.

Even those who are not immigration specialists have some idea of the different backgrounds of Italian and Jewish workers. Our informants fit typical patterns. All the Jewish garment workers had come from *shtetls* in eastern Europe or from moderately large cities in the Russian Pale. The Italian longshoremen and garment workers left southern villages and seaside towns to work in New York City.

Striking facts about Jewish culture and history must be kept in mind when interpreting Jewish immigrants' approach to the interview situation. For thousands of years, the history of the Jewish people, chronicled as events and acts of individuals, had been a part of Jewish scripture. The Jews also had biblical narrative traditions and the Talmudic recitations and interpretations, and eventually they also achieved a democratization of learning, all of which instilled familiarity with the interpretation of texts, respect for learned knowledge, and an awareness of the past. Jews did not regard the recording of historic events, or history itself, as intrinsically valuable[44] since they viewed history as a theophany, an unfolding of God's will, which consisted of God's interventions and man's responses to them as these were interpreted by priests and prophets, not by historians. But if Jews did not value historiography, they were certainly concerned with the *meaning* of history. Irving Howe argues that the Jews' sense of living in a biblical past and for a redeeming future changed only when the destruction of the *shtetl* in the nineteenth century forced upon them an "obsession" with their own history, a more "modern idea of time" as something that could not be held back.[45] This modern, secular notion was added to their mythical and traditional Jewish notions of history.

Secular experiences in the Old World likewise stimulated the Jews' particular comprehension of social and historical reality.[46] European Jewish culture developed within an interlinguistic and bicultural context, something that Italians experienced only after they immigrated.[47] In reaction to persecution and pogroms, the European Jews evolved a sense of responsibility to others within the *shtetl* community, an understanding of external power relationships, and the skills for dealing with them. What is more, persecution knew no sexual preferences: it touched women and men together.

Many from *shtetl* communities, small commercial towns, and cities came to the United States already having worked in small shops or factories, where they had been exposed to trade unions, to workers' newspapers, and to popular socialist interpretations of economic life.[48] Since in Europe they could not legally hold land, many had been forced into moneymaking occupations as traders, peddlers, merchants, speculators, or skilled craftsmen. Artisans in the garment and other trades had worked for wages in small shops; they had entered the modern relationships of industrial production. Although Jewish women by no means had equal status with Jewish males, they did belong to a culture that valued education, and some of them had attended schools.[49] They entered the market as laborers, vendors, or as members of organizations serving the community. *Shtetl* culture allowed expressions of female autonomy that easily translated into both labor activism and an ideology of a worker community in the United States. In short, recent experiences had prepared Jewish men and women to understand the symbols and organization of capitalist life, including its labor organizations, class relations, and radical critiques. Political movements among East European Jews, particularly socialism, social democratic unionism, and Zionism, were congruent with modern notions of history because they assumed the possibility that human action could bring about change in this world.[50] The Jewish past, with its unique class and intercultural character and its special historical consciousness, may also have shaped an understanding of the process and purposes of our interviews.

The immigrants from southern Italy brought very different social experiences and attitudes to the past and to their interviews. Although the Italian South was dragged into the flow of capitalist expansion, most obviously evident in the streams of migrants crossing the Atlantic, premigration rural Italy, like all traditional societies, had low agricultural productivity and technological innovation, high mortality and fertility, limited communication networks, and low living standards. Chronic underemployment, depression, increased land fractionalization, and scarce resources for purchasing land created a landless or nearly landless agricultural proletariat.[51] Agricultural laborers and peasants — and most immigrants came from these groups — all learned to give priority to family and personal interests; the possession of land, a tangible asset and their most cherished goal, seemed out of reach. These conditions hardly encouraged understanding of work as a rewarding, profitable, or hopeful activity. In many areas of the South, a long-standing *mafia* control of village relationships with outside economic and political structures curbed contact with modern urban centers and forestalled political protest. Italian women had even fewer opportunities than men to communicate with institutions outside the family. Although they occasionally participated in the harvest or the market, they rarely, if ever, became involved in political life.[52] Radical labor organizations, unions, strikes, syndicalism, and anarchism existed in some regions and cities of southern Italy, but regarding areas marked by high rates of out-migration, historians generally agree that the preferred strategy was emigration, not labor activism.[53] The idea was to earn scarce cash abroad that would allow land purchase upon return. Thousands, of course, remained in the United States.

Italians had limited exposure to religious or secular literary traditions; Italy did not establish public schools until after the great migrations began in the 1870s, and the overwhelming majority of South Italians were illiterate. Literacy was not required to practice their religion, a mixture of folk and Christian beliefs.[54] The Catholic church, conservative ally of the state, opposed labor radicalism. If the messianic idea of redemption buoyed the Jewish political spirit, Catholicism offered no alternative to the peasant's resignation to worldly fate.

In a recent study of rural South Italian villages, historian Rudolph M. Bell identified a collective history fully consonant with these political and economic circumstances. Oral narration, storytelling, his own structured interviews, and spontaneous discourse revealed one version of the Judeo-Christian sense of history: an "uncritical and often anti-analytical reliance on the past as an alternative to a dismal present, . . . [without] any linear, developmental, directional predictive sense."[55] Popular local history referred to Roman roots, Hannibal's attack in the third century B.C., diluvial rains, earthquakes, neighboring towns best known for their consistent production of cuckolds, and continuing family feuds.[56] Though precise names and even dates filled these stories, nature, fate and the past defined history's direction. Human agency and human beings controlled neither the past nor the future.

In the strict theological sense, neither Catholic nor Jewish theology encouraged historical understanding or emphasis upon human agency. If an all-powerful God sent the Messiah or granted salvation solely at his own discretion, the deeds and actions of men were of trivial consequence. Although Jews and Italians shared this fundamentally ahistorical theological heritage, the actual historical experience of Italians reinforced a theological tradition that led to fatalism and unwillingness to engage in collective efforts for change; the Jews' experience negated that tradition. The actual experiences of each group, then, encouraged strikingly different beliefs about human agency.

It is important to emphasize also that by the time Jews left eastern Europe, many had already been exposed to secular, linear notions of time and history. The Italians, of course, awaited a dramatic change in their circumstances—either in Italy or in places to which they emigrated—before this exposure could occur.[57] In the rest of this chapter, I wish to explore the possibility that the oral interviews with immigrants also reveal popular conceptions of history that imply explanations of and solutions to the circumstances in which Italian and Jewish immigrants found themselves in the United States.

Such propositions are not merely conjectural. An abundant literature, for example, relates cultural perceptions of time and history to political ideology. Primitive cultures believing in a mythic past, or highly sophisticated religions of the East that regard time and history as illusions from which humankind

must seek liberation are not likely to develop a logic for historical reconstruction and change. Consciousness of historical time and the idea of history itself,
both of which arrived relatively late in human civilization, have had profound
effects. Attempts to reconstruct the past can and often do result in an activist
posture to the present and the future.[58] Historical cultures, then, are distinguished by their use of the past as a basis for political philosophy and a
springboard for social action. And, as the late historian Warren Susman had
noted, historical consciousness is ideological. History "structures the consciousness of individuals and their conceptions of their relations to the conditions of existence."[59]

The search for possible sources of immigrant political ideology and beliefs
about history must extend to the American scene. An abundant literature
confirms that as groups, Italians and Jews met their status as American workers differently.[60] While the circumstances of their work may have been the
cause, our interviews confirmed, for example, the presence of a strong tradition of democratic socialism and unionism among Jews but not among Italians. Before we analyze the interviews themselves, it is important to understand
how the social relations and conditions surrounding New York City's longshore
and garment industries could have contributed to these self-described differences between the two immigrant groups, and to their historical and political
ideologies.

To be sure, laborers in the longshore and garment industries performed
distinct kinds of work in different social settings. By the early twentieth century, small-scale machine production, greater differentiation of labor, and the
presence of skilled workers distinguished New York City's garment industry
from longshore work. Immigrants entering the garment trade encountered a
unique development. Up until about 1910, small sweatshops employing a few
persons and run by subcontractors dominated; in the 1920s, when other industries were consolidating, the New York trade moved toward decentralization,
and smaller shops. The various branches of the industry employed men and
women: skilled cutters, pressers, finishers, handworkers, and home workers.
Still, by the 1920s, the unskilled factory operative had become the typical
garment worker.[61]

The ethnic composition of labor and management produced different situations for Italians and Jews in the industry. Jews predominated as both employees and employers. In small shops requiring little capital investment, artisan
bosses worked beside their workers; often the boss himself had just climbed out
of the ranks of wage labor and could easily slide back to his former status. For
the Jews particularly, networks of family, village, and neighborhood ties laced
together the upper and lower levels of the labor force and management; ethnic
identification blurred the relationships of production. As the industry expanded, and more unskilled workers were required, the more highly skilled Jewish
workers looked down upon the Italians as "Columbus tailors," who had discovered their needles in the United States. Ethnic divisions varied according to the
branch of the industry. By the 1920s, most employers in men's wear were
Jewish, and the largest percentage of the labor force was Italian. In other

branches, Jewish bosses presided over a predominantly Jewish work force. Italians were hired as scab labor, and formed their own union locals. Latecomers and less likely to be skilled, Italians did not share the Jews' privileged position in the garment industry.

The garment industry was one of the most successfully unionized in the nation. It boasted active union leaders, many of whom were Jews radicalized by the failed Russian Revolution of 1905 and committed to a social democratic agenda. By 1905 the New York State commissioner of labor had determined that the garment industry was the most strike-prone of all industries and the most successful at winning its objectives. From 1911 through the 1920s, unions won higher wages and shorter work weeks. Although Italians earned one-third less on average than Jews, possibly a reflection of their lower skill level, garment workers' wages compared favorably to those of other American workers.

The burly longshoremen relied upon brute strength to haul two- to three-hundred-pound weights on, off, and around ships, assisted only by primitive tools, pulleys, winches, and hooks.[62] By World War I, one of the nation's largest ports still did not boast one moving crane. Casual laborers hired daily on the docks, the men usually worked in gangs of sixteen to twenty. Certain physical abilities were required to load and unload ships, to balance a cargo, to traverse gangplanks, and to handle hooks and pulleys. But safety counted more than skill. This was a dangerous occupation, carried on over long hours, when work was available. Longshoremen between the ages of thirty-five and fifty-four were almost twice as likely to die as all other workers. Yet in the 1920s, the United States Supreme Court had ruled that as "maritime" workers, the men were not eligible for state compensation.[63] They earned better hourly wages than many skilled workers, but they were usually underemployed. These were not, to say the least, positive work conditions.

Immigrant newcomers were not warmly welcomed by fellow workers or longshore unions. Racial and ethnic competition influenced the formation of hiring gangs, and strikes occurred when a foreman hired a worker of the wrong nationality. Italian longshoremen settled in their own community, found work among their own in Brooklyn's Redhook waterfront district, and, like other ethnic groups, formed their own unions. Italians began entering the unions on May Day of 1907, when a Brooklyn strike drew 12,000 to join the Longshoreman's Union Protective Association (LUPA). Previously, the Italian local had withdrawn from the LUPA when the union refused to appoint an Italian as business agent. The Italians eventually returned to work with few gains except that one of their group, racketeer Paolo Vaccarelli (also known as Paul Kelly), became prominent in union circles and became vice-president of the International Longshoremen's Association (ILA) after it merged with LUPA.[64] In 1904, the ILA had twenty-one locals in New York, each representing a different kind of dockworker, city location, and ethnic group. The daily shape-up (line-up for work) required men to seek work by moving from pier to pier, an unlikely environment for labor force cohesion. The work itself was done in gangs, and many work gangs were tied together by local, family, ethnic, and personal ties. The men supplemented irregular wages by working at construction jobs, turning to loan sharks, or offering kickbacks to contractors for employing them. Since first the stevedores and later the gangsters controlled labor contracting, the unions in New York never achieved so strong a recognition among workers or shipping companies as did the unions elsewhere in the nation.

Differences existed between longshoring and garment work, yet it would be hasty to attribute workers' political behavior or ideologies solely to the more advanced stage of production and labor relations that immigrants encountered in the garment industry. Neither garment workers nor longshoremen were members of an ideal-type proletariat engaged in factory production. Neither the organization of work nor their workplaces fit this image. Strong personal bonds between co-workers and ties of patronage between workers and employers grounded in familial, ethnic, or village associations permeated both industries, coexisting with the union's more formal political ties. Longshoremen and garment workers, working seasonally and irregularly, depended upon those personal ties to find work. It is legitimate to argue, however, that these work experiences, like the entire Americanization process, increased the available repertoire of ideological orientations for immigrants participating in these trades, particularly for those of South Italian origin who had not been exposed through actual experience or oral traditions to unions, to labor radicalism, or to modern political ideologies and their historical corollaries.

The Interviews

Perhaps the best introduction to the immigrants would be to examine two interviews they helped to create. Although only excerpts, they will give the reader palpable examples of the actual dialogues, not merely the historian's reconstructions. Here, and in the rest of this essay, however, I have chosen to emphasize the immigrants' reconstructions of their work biographies. As an area where public and private, objective and subjective realities interact, the work world is an appropriate arena in which to explore one of our major themes: subjective history as an outcome of and reflection upon historical experience.

Born in Minsk, Russia, Abraham Bernstein,[65] a shoemaker's son, had known socialism and the Bund before coming to the United States. He began working in this country as a shoemaker, but by 1907 he had switched to the garment industry. He joined the union that year, early in its history.

Interviewer: How long did it take you to learn [garment work]?
Bernstein: I was used to the machine [from the shoe industry]. . . . In garment work, we have to hire a machine . . . to bring a machine to the factory and then I was eligible to work. . . . We had to have our own straps, our own needles, our own everything. . . . So I started asking: "Why are we doing it? Doesn't the employer supply these? Doesn't anybody know what there is that can be done?" . . . I started talking to people and people listened to

me. . . . I says, "Look . . . we have to do something to get machines . . . you have to carry on shoulder and then no good." . . . They throw me out with the machine. . . . I get together with representatives from other shops and the union sent someone to help organize. We organized half . . . mostly young immigrants from Russia. Many came from Russia as fighters . . . Socialists. . . . A bitter strike [the 1907 lockout] resulted. Finally, the employers signed a contract with the union and provided machines. The union become established. . . . A Jew believes in God and the Torah, like the union was to us. . . . We have kept the union a holy place. . . . It was a family of our own in every shop, and being that the union helped us, we were good union people. We wanted that the union should be strong.

Bernstein then went on, with little encouragement, to describe the formation of Local 17, the garment workers union, the 1910 general strike, the migration of the shops uptown in the 1920s, his succession to a job as business agent in 1929, and Communist infiltration of the union in the 1920s. Bernstein had an ideal image of the union in the formative era and later. He described Local 17 as "a brotherly gathering. They were so interested about the union and about the membership that they thought everybody was a brother and a father. . . . They progressed. They knew what they wanted, and they asked for more and more." Describing himself further, he summarized: "The union was my life." His job as a business agent, he continued, was to protect the people but not antagonize the boss, for you "need to get things from them." Individual agency, concerted action on the part of the workers who engaged in improving their lot, and progress over time figure prominently in Bernstein's story. The union seems to be at once a mythic, religious, and historical agent.

Mario Gelsemino was the son of a South Italian longshoreman who immigrated to the United States in 1880 without an education or a trade. Gelsemino remembered his father's coming home for lunch because he could not afford to eat out. His mother would give the man clean clothes because he was dirty. The interviewer asked about his employment history.

Interviewer: Why did you become a longshoreman?

Gelsemino: Being like my father, I had no trade. Knowing how to speak English, I got out of school young. We needed the money. I couldn't continue to go to school. I didn't have no aptitude. You know, no desire to continue going to school because of my home conditions. We kept shaping [lining up for work] every day, and couldn't find no work and a group of friends said: "Let's start shaping the piers." [He did so at age sixteen.]

Interviewer: Dockwork is passed from father to son?

Gelsemino: Among the Italians, definitely. My father wanted me to learn a trade. He was against it [dockwork]. Because of his suffering and what he went through. . . . There was no money. . . . I ran away and got married, so they had no choice. . . . I worked in a laundry a little while. . . . I had another job working in a factory and I didn't like this. I made up my mind. The work was hard, but I enjoyed it, the hard work, because it was outdoors.

Interviewer: What did people think of longshore work in the 1920s and 1930s?
Gelsemino: It was a good living, and they had no choice because they had no
   education.
Interviewer: I almost got the idea you wanted to work on the docks.
Gelsemino: Yes, I liked it. . . .

Asked to describe work conditions among Italians on the docks, Gelsemino
replied that there were Irish superintendents and timekeepers. The Italians
"didn't know how to read and write. . . . The Italians done most of the bull
work, the dirty work. Through no fault of their own. They were good, hard,
honest, conscientious, good citizens, loyal to America. They loved this country.
. . . Fifteen of 120 would get work. They keep [*sic*] coming back. . . . Whoever
grabbed a job didn't leave, unless he got sick, died." Gelsemino had only
vague, often inaccurate memories of union history. Queried about the Italians'
role in unions and strikes, he responded that he believed Italians began entering
unions about 1907, and took control of the leadership and delegates by World
War I. He asserted that until 1945, however, there were no major strikes:
"During the war they were very loyal . . . work was so scarce. . . . There was
nothing to strike about. Whatever work they had, they were lucky to have."
Asked if he knew any foremen, he expressed a clear understanding of status
differences. The foremen were "more aggressive . . . bigger in stature. . . .
They didn't take no guff. . . . The stevedore [hiring contractor] would come
around with his chauffeur, he was a big time in those days [1930s]. . . . They
were very wealthy. They would hang out in the athletic club . . . just like
Lloyds of London."

Interviewer: Why couldn't the union do as the stevedore did, as in hiring?
Gelsemino: Because it never did.
Interviewer: Why was there so much money in it?
Gelsemino: Because they work by tonnage. The men in Brooklyn were really
   hard workers, and they produced. . . . There was no hanging around playing cards and smoking or any of that crap. . . . When your work was
   finished, your time was cut, you went home. There was no more expense to
   the stevedore. You were being paid by the hour. It's the only way they could
   make money. They couldn't keep you full time. . . . [This was not] a WPA
   project.
Interviewer: The stevedore made money because he didn't have to keep a work
   force.
Gelsemino: Definitely. They didn't have no expenses. Of course they made
   money.
Interviewer: When you got hurt?
Gelsemino: At the time, compensation was very bad. Some stevedores were
   self-insured, or had insurance. In the 1940s when a guy died, [the workers]
   would make a collection. . . . The longshoremen have big hearts. . . . My
   mother would go next door or see a *comadre* or something and borrow
   $5.00 and that would carry us over. . . . Today we got all these little things
   we enjoy. . . . Thank God for Roosevelt!

Each of these excerpts typifies moments in the interactions between speaker and questioner in the City University oral history project. The form of each presentation merits some attention. Gelsemino responded to questions without much elaboration, laboring over the project which the interviewer set before him. Bernstein often offered spontaneous interpretations, and the narrative structure of his presentations often proceeded independently of the interviewer's queries. It is obvious, when listening to both tapes, that he felt more comfortable with the process than Gelsemino did. The two interviews reveal different attitudes toward work, toward unions, toward class relations, and probably even toward the interview situation itself. Instead of using class relations or a heroic union as explaining principles, Gelsemino's narrative appeals to what he appeared to think of as common sense, a primitive reality not requiring explanation. Although Gelsemino was aware of significant dates in the history of his union's formation, unlike Bernstein, he did not relish dramatic descriptions of its battles against injustices, nor attribute mythical or religious significance to it. Gelsemino was a union man, well aware of class relationships, but he never openly challenged them. Recognizing the grim realities of the longshoreman's life, competition for jobs and underemployment, he observed only: "There was nothing to strike about." He attributed some events to individual agency — getting married, leaving the factory; others, like having to work or quitting school, or being provided with job benefits, are attributed to God, Roosevelt, nature, lack of aptitude or money. Fate, not choice, takes the lead role here.

These are not, and could never be, absolute descriptions. Bernstein seemed fairly consistent in his themes and beliefs; Gelsemino sometimes seemed to vacillate. The fact is that no human being, or group of human beings, neatly adheres to an outside observer's categories. Within the same interview, a person will switch from one interpretation to another. So, for that matter, will the professional historian interviewing him or her. All of us have a wide repertoire of explanatory categories, folk and cultural beliefs, ideologies, and common-sense notions from which we choose in order to make sense of ourselves and the world around us. And we do not necessarily hold them in isolation from one another. These expressions, and related narrative strategies, emerge and are made evident in the interview process itself, a process consisting of an interaction between two or more repertoires — the historian's on one side and the immigrant's on the other.

Still, I think it is possible to use this textual analysis of the interviews heuristically, and apply what they suggest to a broader analysis of Italian and Jewish immigrants, to find out if these immigrant narratives reveal a collective sense of the past. Since I am looking to understand immigrant biographies on both the symbolic and factual levels. I will examine not only what is remembered but the structure of memory itself. My purpose is to show that these biographies, as metaphors of self, also function as metaphors for history as it is commonly understood by the narrators.

When immigrants express different visions of past time and of their own relationship to it, they are projecting these personal and political beliefs upon the past. In doing so, they relate beliefs about the impact of human action on environment—beliefs that, when generalized, also seem to be consistent with the historical narrative traditions of Italians and Jews. One scholar argues that self-representations in oral interviews

> do not "reflect" everyday life, though everyday life provides the raw material for the communication of complex cultural information. In other words, [everyday life] is used for symbolic purposes. . . . The self-images . . . introduce us to a narrative universe which revives traditions existing before the interview, adapting them and bringing them up to date. Real experience is subsumed by the symbolic framework, and is selected and interpreted according to its lights.[66]

Still, I would argue that in the case of these Italian and Jewish immigrants, whatever came to pass, or, more accurately, whatever speakers recall about what came to pass—does reflect both their subjectivity and the historical realities of their cultures. The immigrants' own descriptions of themselves as actors in the past, for example, correspond with the activism so commonly identified with the Jewish working class and the fatalism so often associated with Italian laborers and peasants. There is a congruence between how these immigrants conceptualize their pasts and how, as groups of workers, they responded to their environment. Jewish descriptions of the self in history correspond with the actual history of the Jews, who, in order to survive as a people and make their way in the New World, cultivated a sense of responsibility to themselves and to others as well as an appreciation of power relationships and skills for dealing with them. Italian interviews reflect a history in which Italian immigrant workers, like their European ancestors, created different understandings of and solutions for the world around them.

Interpreting Oral Interviews

Before attempting a group analysis of the interviews, a few guidelines should be set. Our analytic focus is upon the immigrants. It must be remembered, however, that the immigrants were defining their pasts as subjectively stated awareness in their interaction with interviewers who, we may presume, saw the past differently, according to various canons of modern historiography. This collaboration, this interaction of ethnohistory with history, could have produced a unique version of the immigrant past, one that would not have emerged were immigrants telling their stories without the intercession of "experts." Yet, analytic purposes justify examining Jewish and Italian interviews separately. We must acknowledge some accomplishment by the immigrant speakers who were narrating the work history or life history, for in one scholar's words, a connection exists between the "particular experience of ethnic groups and the techniques used to capture, reveal, and exorcise those experiences."[67]

As scholars develop their own rules for the interpretation of oral interviews, I would suggest four areas of temporal or self-representation that they might keep in mind: (1) the way in which the speaker organizes past, present, and future time during an interview; (2) the way in which the speaker describes himself or herself in relation to the past; (3) the way in which the speaker describes, or fails to describe, interaction with objects and persons of the past; and (4) the interaction of the two sets of scripts, the historian's and the speaker's.

I shall address first the matter of how subjects reveal temporal organization throughout their interviews. Victor Gioscia identifies two modes of patterning time, the *atomistic* and the *gestalt*. The former interprets past, present, and future as distinct, discrete, and discontinuous; the individual or culture viewing them atomistically does not perceive the self or society as an unbroken, linear development. This cognitive mode is essentially ahistorical. *Gestalt* reasoning, the psychological corollary of formal history, prepares individuals to see relations among the past, present, and future.[68] If past actions could influence the present, then present actions can influence the future. Borrowing from *gestalt* psychology, we see the "self" being presented in the interview as a "perceived object in the phenomenal field"[69] — the self against the ground of history. By this interpretation, the subject matter of oral interviews is not past reality; it is the way in which individuals perceive past reality and interpret their place in history. In other words, the interviews with Italians and Jews can be divided according to two styles of self-representation: the self *in* history and the history *of* the self. To be sure, the subjects themselves articulate no such distinction; moreover, autobiographical exercises and other personal documents often incorporate both styles, and as collaborative constructions they are influenced by the interviewer. As analytical tools, however, such self-representations offer a useful taxonomy for identifying strikingly different group portraits of Italian and Jewish men and women. How the subject perceives the self in relationship to the past can also be a significant clue to political and ideological views.

In discussing their work histories, Jewish garment workers like Bernstein volunteered long, complicated job descriptions reporting the duties they performed, how much they were paid, and why they left each place of employment. They presented a clear conception of what a job history is, and portrayed themselves as persons of worth, active in the center of their histories. Their accounts, often presented to the interviewer unsolicited, implicitly assumed the significance of the past in general and of their own pasts as workers in particular. And if the self emerges vividly in the Jewish interviews, so does the background against which it once moved: Jews embellished their stories with a sense of history and described successions of outside events to which they connected themselves and their people. They reported the European conditions — the pogroms, the persecutions, the exploitations — that forced them to flee native lands. Like Bernstein, many described labor activity as responses to or causes for change. Description of the union, of strikes, of political events, intruded upon personal histories.

We have no way of measuring whether these and other responses resulted from past influences or the bicultural character of the interview itself. But Jewish labor activism and class consciousness are congruent with an appreciation of such continuities, of connections between the self and the environment, and with the ability to conceptualize the self in a changing and changeable field. The obvious compatibilities between this historical sensibility and that of the expert interviewer may have contributed to the relative ease with which Jewish speakers related to the interview itself. Even if their methods of interpreting the past differed, the Jewish speaker and the trained historian could agree that the past contains answers for understanding the present, and that looking back to find them might be a useful exercise.[70]

When asked about their histories and work lives, Italian speakers journeyed less willingly into the past, resisted or failed to comprehend the task that the interviewer designed, and did not easily construct a work biography. These speakers apparently were not interested in the past — or at least they were not interested in discussing the past as the interviewer conceptualized and formulated it. In their accounts, they rarely connected themselves with historical background, balked at establishing sequential relationships, and acknowledged slight awareness of the public world in which they functioned. Personal relationships upstaged public events, and the connections between public and private life were not made evident. These atomistic and diachronic accounts suggest an idea of self *in* history, a perspective remarkably congruent with the comparatively apolitical working-class culture of these Italian immigrants. For, if to discern oneself is one thing, to discern oneself as part of a historical process is quite another: the first conception of self is personal, but the second is at once personal, political, and historical.

Further examination of how the immigrant speakers placed themselves in relationship to the past highlights other contrasts between the two groups. Jews and Italians described a past full of interaction with other people, but the significant others and the quality of the relationships they describe often differed. Jewish men and women generally portrayed themselves as active, autonomous agents, having functioned within a social tapestry heavily embroidered not only with personal but also with power relationships. Awareness of their own potential for power was matched by an awareness of power in the world around them. The Italian speakers typically recalled not political interaction but rather personal qualities and personal time; family relationships were a recurrent *leitmotif* of the Italian interviews. Family references are frequent in Jewish narratives, but as often as not in their accounts of life and work, the co-workers, *landsmen*, political allies, and bosses upstage mothers, husbands, and children. Many of the relationships that Jews chose to describe involve power and the play for it.

Jews evaluated themselves positively as workers; they were conscious of the value of their labor. Jews spoke of having educated themselves, of having struggled to get ahead, of having asked for raises. Though most union organizers were men and "big women," Rebecca Levine refused to be cowed: she tried to educate other workers by "talking to them . . . I was a tiny woman, but I tried to do it in my own way." Rebecca Cohen recalled her intellectual potential: mentally, "I was very good." Kiev-born Bessie Goldman once worried that her father's "ignorance would hinder" her "emotional development." This belief in the possibility for advancement was seldom expressed by the Italians. There is no way of knowing if the Jews' self-esteem and apparent confidence that they could manipulate environment for personal ends and needs preceded or resulted from their experiences as labor organizers, negotiators, and trade unionists. Once again, one could make a logical case for continuity of European precedents and narrative traditions.[71] The self-assurance emerging from the Jewish biographies seems related to a consciousness of the past and a confidence that individuals can exert some control over their environment.

Another outcome consistent with their Old World beliefs and values is the Jews' sensitivity to others. Not only did Jewish speakers recall themselves in association with people but many expressed self-esteem as a fulfilled responsibility to others: "For myself I have always been very independent and I have always been a person who never forgot other people."[72] The attitude that full personal functioning is derived from relationship to others, abstractly defined, finds formal expression among union organizers: "You must be a union man . . . otherwise you . . . are alone. . . . Working we have to organize."[73] Statements like these do not appear to be merely political or union rhetoric. Even those Jews not especially active in labor or political groups chose to remember themselves as socially conscious individuals. Hungarian-born Sylvia Gelb, for example, said of her years in Europe: "We had two classes, and I thought that was wrong . . . there is no reason for people to be hungry. . . . I would find a crime in that."

There are other levels of compatibility between the popular history of the Jews and that of the interviewers, most notably the Jews' tendency to think about human relationships abstractly, a possible analog of their acceptance of human agency as cause. In a study on middle-class life histories, the linguist Charlotte Linde observed the adoption of "expert systems," especially Freudian psychology and behaviorism, in popular discourse. The Jewish immigrants studied here chose explanations identified with liberal historiography or Marxist analysis, perhaps reinforced by their sensitivity to the interviewer's expectations but also because they carried them in their repertoire of historical explanation.[74]

Many Jewish complaints about working conditions and environment reflected an understanding of the power underlying social relationships. Jews' most common description of their work — "It was slavery" — indicates as much awareness of power relationships as it does of job conditions. One woman referred to her supervisor as a "Simon Legree . . . he would hold the whip over us."[75] Asked to define a sweatshop, Rebecca Levine depicted it not as a place to work, and not as a stage in the garment industry's evolution, but as a social relationship — and an exploitative one at that: "A sweatshop is when a foreman is in back of you, watching what you are doing — and God forbid you do just a little bit, he start screaming, he start yelling. . . . That's a sweatshop." The focus was power, and Jewish speakers were aware of their ability to manipulate or to be manipulated by it. Russian immigrant Stella Brodsky confided that the bosses "knew how to make tricks" on the workers. Asked how workers regarded their bosses, Jean Weinstein said: "We were indifferent. . . . We could not really feel very sympathetic. . . . I never felt personal dislike of my bosses, but I had the general feeling that they were doing something they shouldn't do."

Jews used abstract thinking to explain the world, to justify rights and union programs, and to organize workers, but political principles coexisted practically with personal commitments. The liberal or Marxist script was simply dropped at certain moments. Few lost sight of the class struggle existing beyond the home, yet few let political principles attenuate personal or family bonds. Socialist and union activist Bessie Goldman had a brother who was a boss, but "he didn't become less of a brother to me," she reported. "I didn't love him less. . . . I worked in a shop for a boss but I realize that's the system and I have to fight him in the union. But to say your brother is less worthy than I am, I couldn't see." Stella Brodsky described a shop where some employees got more work than others did, but instead of seeing only power or class inequities, she also perceived the personal ties that disposed the foreman to favor his *landsmen*: "He was for the people, the foreman. The bosses didn't have anything to do with it." These apparent dilemmas and the women's resolutions of them are not unusual. In an industry where heavy capital investment was not a requirement, Jewish families, communities, and shops often contained within themselves the conflicting interests of worker and entrepreneur.

Most Jewish men and women described themselves as capable of integrating their public and private values. Their language describing co-workers and shop in metaphors of family and home reflects the belief: "The shop became a family of our own"; "You knew the people, you felt at home"; "I made friends in the factory, we loved it; it was our home."[76] This tendency to personalize formal relationships eased the adjustment to work and city life: "Local 17 was actually a brotherly gathering. They were so enthused about the union and about the membership that they thought everybody was a brother or a father."[77] After living in the Midwest for a while, Bessie Goldman returned to New York City; knowing no one, she immediately went to the local Socialist club, for "once you are a comrade, even if you don't know them personally, you become friends." After recalling the old days when *landsmen* helped one another, Fanny Herman remarked, "Today there is no need for friends and community because you have the union."

Italian speakers likewise described a work world populated by friends and relatives. But none of them mentioned the union as a possible replacement for family ties, and none used language to reveal, more subtly, a transference of private bonds to public situations. Italian narrators resolved past conflicts in a different way. Like Gelsemino, they characterized their past selves as relatively passive agents, unable to control their environment, not terribly interested in doing so. They separated public and private worlds, and stressed personal values and relationships over formal organizational ones. Italian immigrant Vincent de Marco, admiring Jewish commitment to education and self-improvement, said: "The Jewish people know how to do it. They got the best jobs. Italians say, 'What are we going to do?' and that's it." Like Gelsemino, Italians described themselves as having fewer opportunities, and they took little credit for past achievements. Frank Levantino maintained steady employment in the United States but located his success outside himself: "What America did to me, Italy could never do in a million years. . . . When I was working . . . many times I knelt down and kissed the ground." *This happened to me*, not *I did this*. Both immigrant groups regularly cited the importance of friendly and family connections in securing work, but the Italian narrators, unlike the Jewish, reflected on a reality in which it was virtually impossible to obtain work on one's own: "If you had a relative who was a foreman, you'd be okay. . . . I think it's like everything else: it's who you know to get a position."[78] In the Italian presentation individuals did not function by will and autonomy, nor did they trust their ability to manipulate circumstances in order to obtain needs and ends. Fate, luck, America, even position in a kin network determined their past and their destiny.

Almost as often as referring to other people, the Italians mentioned places — neighborhoods, cities, homes, or work sites — to which they held firm association. Unlike Jews, who spoke with such relish of having moved from one job to another, Italians described favorably the long tenure at a single job. No Italians interviewed mentioned plans to move or work far from their neighborhoods; indeed, when they recalled opportunities for relocation, Italian speakers indicated that some deep identification would have been threatened by such a move. Agnes Mazza's match factory moved to Ohio. For sound financial reasons, Agnes did not follow it, but she described the job prospect in geographic rather than economic terms. She wouldn't "dare to go that far." She had chosen her job for the very reason that it was "close to home." Many of the jobs taken by women were preferred because they were "right in the neighborhood";[79] daughters and wives could be supervised more carefully if they lived and worked nearby. Joseph Serrano, an educated and skilled garment worker, explaining his refusal to follow his company outside New York, suggested that he too shared this attachment to place: "What good is it? I don't know anybody there. How am I gonna get workers? You got to be a local man." Communicated here and in other interviews was a fear that a person could not function away from home. The Italians' attachments to stable residences and jobs seems to have operated to maintain an identity, an identity dependent on associations with relatives and peers.

Nearly all immigrating Italian women were accompanied and then housed by relatives and friends. Jewish women more frequently arrived and settled on their own. These migration patterns reflected different cultural views about family identity and sense of place. How cultures manage women's departures from home and how women respond to their own detachment are one indicator of the degree to which autonomy is tolerated. The silence of Italian female speakers on this point suggests that self-assertion and initiative were not realistic considerations for most. Jewish women told, in great detail, a different story. Bessie Goldman was not forced to leave the Kiev area in 1912: "Being America [sic] is free, I can work as I please. . . . I used to envy people who can do as they please. . . . I felt suffocated. I couldn't stay." Sylvia Gelb came to New York in 1921 to work, to help her people, and to go to school: "I was freer. I was freed to do in my own way, in a respectful way. I wanted to be on my own." After arriving in the United States, many Jewish women moved into and out of relatives' homes and to cities outside New York: "To be on my own," or "to have more independence," or "to get out of my brother's house."[80] This free mobility across geographic space, this ability to locate oneself in different contexts, often coincided with expressions of a fiercely independent self-concept — one that surpassed the boldness even of men for its autonomy, and with no corollary in the Italian women's lexicon of memories. Fanny Abraham, for example, told how she quit jobs to move to work offering higher wages: "I never went to the union they should get me a job. I was an independent girl." Bessie Goldman, explaining her preference for socialism over communism, criticized the communist principle whereby "everything is given to you. I don't want to be given. That does not appeal to me." The same woman once spurned a suitor because she didn't *need* him: "I felt I could make a living for ten men." Yetta Braun took a husband, made "this sacrifice to get married . . . not to lose his friendship" — and also to "become independent" of her family of origin. In keeping with this spirit of self-reliance and personal adequacy, Jewish women, more often than Italian women, described their work lives as an outlet for personal identity: "I worked all my life, even when I got married. . . . I liked it. . . . I was among people."[81] Sensitivity to family permeated the Jewish woman's memory, without dominating her sense of self.

Jewish immigrant families and communities seem to have allowed outlets for women wanting activity outside the home as well as within it. They tolerated, in some cases even encouraged, self-reliant females who could find themselves in roles of worker or organizer — and who, individually and collectively, would make a mark on American labor history. Italian women, on the other hand, described themselves finding support in family and place. A search for autonomy was not one of their narrative themes; when they recounted difficulties in obtaining desired independence, they presented scenarios and issues different from those of the Jewish women. Italians reported conflicts occurring within the home, problems often revolving around control of the young women's income, but they never regarded leaving the family or developing an untried life-style as possibilities. Two examples illustrate this pattern. Complaining that her father expected her entire pay envelope, Betty Gnocchi reflected, "I never had anything for myself." When Agnes Mazza volunteered part of her pay if she could retain the rest of it, her mother "pretended at first she didn't know what board is." Italian families did not encourage female autonomy; indeed, the attitude underlying these conflicts is that single Italian women had no recognized existence outside the home. Restless daughters ultimately left parental homes to create their own families, only to encounter similar restrictions upon their individuality. "During the years I worked, I never said *I* did this or I did that. . . . I always tried to make it a *we*. Sometimes I'll slip and say 'I.' But there were an awful lot of people who made their husbands feel small about that kind of thing. . . . I don't think I ever did. I made a special effort not to."[82] Saying "I" was a "slip": the Italian woman faced social pressures to derive her identity from her family.

This was particularly apparent when Italian women described themselves as workers and as labor organizers. Angelina Mirabella, one of the few female activists among Italians interviewed, stated: "I went to work to produce." Later: "I left my children." For political as well as apolitical Italian women, family and children always intrude upon memories about work: they justified leaving home, striking, or demanding higher wages. It is as if these women had difficulty disassociating themselves or their actions from family life.

Despite their differences, both Jewish and Italian women — even the most liberated and political among them — accepted the notion that mothers and married women should not work. Both cited husbandly pressures as their reason for withdrawing from the work force. "What do you think I married you for?" asked one Italian husband; "Stay home and raise a family." An otherwise assertive Jewish woman and onetime labor activist reported: "I did want to work . . . but he was the man of the house . . . so I stayed home."[83] Many Italian women communicated internalized traditional values when explaining why they left the work force: "My mother said: 'Stay home and take care of your daughter. Your daughter is more important than money. Watch your daughter.'" Another commented: "Cuz you know those Italian people. You gotta starve: the *honor* is first"; "I didn't myself really approve of my working."[84] Jewish women implied a different basis for the decision. One articulated a common understanding:

> The man was ashamed [if his wife worked]. He felt like a *schlemiel* . . . if the wife worked, she was part of that household like a contributor and therefore she could not be domineered — let's face it — like a girl who depended on her husband to come home every week and give her money, and she could not do very much because that was restricted. Whereas if a girl worked, no matter, even in those days when there was no such thing as a woman's movement. . . .
>
> They [men] also didn't like the wife to work, and also when they come home they expect service, and if your wife was going to come home an hour later than you or a half hour before you, they weren't going to get the kind of service they wanted. Because they were kings of the house. They really were. They'd sit and order you, order you around, what to give them, and what they like and all that stuff. There wasn't too much you could do, especially if you had three kids.[85]

Note the relative neglect of considerations such as husbandly honor; the schlemiel image appears in its place. More frequently than Italian speakers, Jewish women externalized their motives by locating the withdrawal from work in a power struggle between man and wife — just one more manifestation of a reality penetrated by power relationships that generally appeared in the Jewish interviews.

Women's self-concepts conformed to cultural patterns and historical realities in still other ways. Few Italian women worked outside the home; their family roles were primary. Their memories generally did not describe public and private selves in conflict. Describing their pasts, Italian women indulged in an empathetic, often poignant relationship with themselves. Sharing an intimate moment, Lily Carpinello mourned the bygone Lily she never gratified:

As for myself, I didn't go to work. . . . I stayed home and raised my two little girls. I'd love to go to work now but I can't. . . . I sure would like to work to see what it is. . . . In my own mind I would have liked to try it out . . . to see if I can have a little bit more money . . . to have more leisure life. [She never told her husband of this desire.] I never did have a good time in my life . . . I read a lot . . . I used to read a lot of magazines when I was a young girl . . . they had these parties, you know . . . and I thought I'd missed a lot. Didn't have the proper clothes to wear or anything. My mother used to make my underclothes from chicken feed bags. . . . Sometimes when I am pressing, I think back and say, "My God! What a life I had!"

Angelina Mirabella was an exceptional case. Onetime union activist, mother, and wife, she drew from the usual cache of union slogans to describe her working past. But now and then she put aside the formula to talk about her interior self. She related to her past self with a kind of tenderness never admitted into the Jewish women's reminiscences. The garment shop's regimented routine and compartmentalized duties prevented Angelina from seeing customer reaction to her work. To compensate for this deprivation, she recalled:

I make stories in my mind when I am working. What kind of a person is going to wear this dress? Is she in good health? Is she a good person? Where it gonna go? What state? Is she gonna like it? Is she just gonna cast it aside . . . ? It was nice. That's why I like it. I kept creating something someone is gonna enjoy. What kind of person? Is she gonna be careful? Is she gonna keep it well? She's spending the money. It's not mine. I only made it. I got paid for it. Sometimes I tell the other operators. Making up stories, I'm living in a fantasy world.

Disassociation between worker and finished product prompted Angelina to connect her identity to the garments she made: "On each ticket you put your name or your number, so you know who has made it." In this assurance she typified her interpretation of both what was important to her about her work and the way in which she permitted the outside world to intrude upon her own sense of reality. Notice the purpose she ascribed to the label: the "ticket" was not the means used by a powerful boss to check up on his workers, nor a device for quality control, but an announcement to the world that Angelina Mirabella had made a dress.[86]

Yet Angelina, the worker, the union organizer, was well aware of power struggles in the world around her. The same woman replied to her boss's reprimand "Angelina, you talk too much" with "Nathan, I'm alive. I talk. When I'm dead, I won't talk." The personality she presented in the garment shop, a parody of Jewish phrasing, was absorbed in contact with her fellow workers. But private sensibilities exposed in memory remain strangely apolitical for a woman committed to union activism. Angelina seems to have operated with two selves—one public, the other private—that informed each other but did not easily coexist. Angelina, despite her activism, exemplifies an approach found in most of the Italian interviews: she did not really admit the world's power struggles into the privacy of her thought or family affairs. This approach, combined with familial restrictions and an emphasis upon dependence, did not encourage labor activism, or even memories of a public self, for most Italian female speakers.

We cannot conclusively know why Jewish women were less willing than Italians to share their interior worlds with interviewers, to admit their vulnerabilities into memory. Perhaps their reserve stems from the strong emphasis that their peers placed upon public, communal concerns, and their expectation that the interviewer would require the same. Certainly, their choice of language, which itself influences what is and is not available to human awareness, reveals a comfortable preference for political rhetoric. Most Italian women expressed no repertoire of union formulas, no ironic tradition that might have helped them to categorize past experience or to create an emotional distance from the past—and from their own frailties.

This discussion of popular history suggests how personal identity and inner life relate to thinking about the past and to political ideology. In their narratives, Italians and Jews created different stories about humanity's relationship to the world. Jewish women and Jewish men protested economic oppression. Italian women sought an end to confining personal relations. Most Italian men and women seemed disconnected from what politicized Jews saw as the emancipatory possibilities of work, political activity, unions, and geographic and occupational mobility. The Western scientific historiographical tradition regards the Jews' response as the more rational, sophisticated, and advanced. Our concentration upon the subjective experience related in these narratives points to the simplicity of that assumption. Plainly, both groups reveal themselves to be, for different reasons, profoundly alienated. Perhaps, after all, the Italians' skepticism about labor and political activity was different from but as subversive of capitalism and its institutions as the Jewish critique was.

Conclusions

The different self-concepts of Italians and Jews parallel their differing perceptions of the work world. Italian laborers saw poor work conditions as a given; individuals could do little to alter the environment. They described working life in personal rather than political terms. They conceptualized their unions largely in relation to their personal world, not as the agency that could bargain for power or manipulate class relationships in the outside world. Indeed, they frequently complained that union activism conflicted with personal obligations. "When it came to militancy," said longshoreman organizer Bruno Testa, Italians "were backward, and I don't blame them because they weren't about to spoil their families or anything else." Here we see the either/or attitude—shared by Italian men and women, garment workers and longshoremen—that work success and personal happiness were mutually exclusive. Thus, most female operators were politically uninvolved union members, and many used family responsibility as a reason for inactivity. Reversing the logic but committed to the same end, Italian activists sympathetic to the use of power used family responsibilities as their justification. Angelina Mirabella said that she organized her garment shop because "I was thinking of my children." Even the class-conscious and politically aware could not escape their personal, familial priorities. In contrast, an acceptable and popular route among Jewish laborers was to become union activists supporting the ILGWU negotiations for benefits and improved working conditions. This public behavior conformed to Jews' personal understanding of power relationships, to their faith in an ability to control environment, and to their comfort with public roles and abstract principles.

The words with which Jewish workers described working conditions indicate a belief in a better world, a world they thought obtainable through labor negotiations. Describing a Bleecker Street shop in which she worked, Yetta Braun carped that "you had to take out a policy" just to walk up the stairs, yet her sarcasm, ubiquitous in the Jewish accounts, implies the possibility of a better reality. Jewish laborers' ability to hypothesize another reality fit the ease with which they arranged and rearranged public and private lives in response to separate sets of rules and values. Experience gained as a persecuted minority straddling two cultural worlds may have contributed to this skill. Another factor, the Jewish reform mentality, which supported hope for a better world, was not exclusive to labor organizers, and found its roots in Jewish social, cultural, and political life.

One of the values of oral history is that in revealing how historical conditions are phenomenologically experienced, it can expose the interaction of objective history with consciousness. Even when these oral interviews do not describe an objective past, they bear its unmistakable imprint. Representations of the self in history, then, are at the same time reflections of the Jewish and Italian experiences and metaphors for their histories.

Some readers will find peril in this effort to make collective popular histories of these immigrant biographies. Interview material, like most human data, is sloppy. Speakers, like the creators of all subjective documents, bring many voices to their interviews. The narrators of the interviews described here were not always behaving and speaking as longshoremen, or Jews, or garment workers, or Italians. And historians do not always behave as historians should when they ask questions of their informants. The problems are especially complex for those who wish to use archival oral history materials such as those upon which this chapter relies: oral narratives created without benefit of the increasingly sophisticated methodologies offered by linguists, oral historians, and ethnographers.[87] Nevertheless, I think this exercise in collective biography suggests that historians and social scientists might do more with subjective documents. Historians who persist in using oral data as they would any other kind of data must be humbled by the complexities of recent work in phenomenology, ethnography, and textual analysis. At the same time, skeptics who rely only upon structural explanations and objective data might learn from the fact that subjective texts like these popular histories are themselves embedded in the historical processes they seek to describe. Perhaps it is possible and useful, after all, to understand a people's history not only as the experts describe it but also as it is conceived by those who lived it.

NOTES

1. Robert Angell, "A Critical Review of the Development of the Personal Document Method in Sociology, 1920–1940," in *The Use of Personal Documents in History, Anthropology, and Sociology*, ed. Louis Gottschalk et al. (New York: Social Science Research Council, 1945), p. 177.

2. The interviews were originally conducted under a grant from the National Endowment for the Humanities, "Family and Kinship, Work and Associational Life among Immigrants and Migrants to New York City, 1900–1930." The project, which was supervised by Herbert G. Gutman and me, is described below in the text of this essay. In order to maintain privacy, all names in these interviews, which are now deposited at the Robert F. Wagner Archives, Tamiment Institute Library at New York University, under the Immigration Labor History Collection of the City College Oral History Project, have been changed.

3. Gottschalk et al., *The Use of Personal Documents in History*, p. vii.

4. Gordon W. Allport, *The Use of Personal Documents in Psychological Science* (New York: Social Science Research Council, 1942), p. 37.

5. For recent literature on these controversies, see James Clifford and George E. Marcus, eds., *Writing Culture: The Politics and Poetics of Ethnography* (Berkeley: University of California Press, 1986); Daniel Bertaux, ed., *Biography and Society: The Life History Approach in the Social Sciences* (Beverly Hills, Calif.: Sage Publications, 1981); Charles L. Briggs, *Learning How to Ask: A Sociolinguistic Appraisal of the Role of the Interview in Social Science Research* (London: Cambridge University Press, 1986); L. L. Lagness and Gelya Frank, *Lives: An Anthropological Approach to Biography* (Novato, Calif.: Chandler & Sharp, 1981); Vincent Crapanzano, "Life Histories," *American Anthropologist* 86 (1984): 953–59; Gelya Frank, "Finding the Common Denominator: Phenomenological Critiques of the Life History Method," *Ethos* 7 (September 1979): 68–94; Michael Frisch, "Oral History, Documentary, and the Mystery of Power: A Case Study Critique of Public Methodology," *International Journal of Oral History* 6 (June 1985): 118–25. Ronald J. Grele, *Envelopes of Sound* (Chicago: Precedent, 1975) is essential reading for oral historians. For a discussion on narrative and history, see Paul Ricoeur, *Time and Narrative*, vol. 1 (Chicago: University of Chicago Press, 1984), and Johannes Fabian, *Time and the Other: How Anthropology Makes Its Object* (New York: Columbia University Press, 1983). See also "Memory and History," a recent special issue of the *Journal of American History* 75 (March 1989).

6. See Bernard L. Fontana, "American Indian Oral History: An Anthropologist's Note," *History and Theory* 8 (1969): 366–70; A. La Vonne Brown, "American Indian Oral Literatures," *American Quarterly* 33 (1981): 327–38; Sidney Mintz, "The Anthropological Interview and the Life History," *Oral History Review* 7 (1979): 18–26.

7. Clifford and Marcus, *Writing Culture*, passim.

8. There are a few exceptions. Perhaps the most notable is Martin Duberman, *Black Mountain* (New York: Dutton, 1972), in which the historian intrudes himself and his thoughts into the formal narrative. Because of their interest in textual analysis, oral

historians have also been aware of historical texts as "collaborations." Recent discussions of this approach may be found in Grele, *Envelopes of Sound*, and in recent issues of the *International Journal of Oral History*.

9. David Bidney, "Phenomenological Method and the Anthropological Science of the Cultural Life-World," in *Phenomenology and the Social Sciences*, ed. Maurice Natanson (Evanston: Northwestern University Press, 1973), 1: 109-40; Denis Tedlock, "The Analogical Tradition and the Emergence of a Dialogical Anthropology," in *The Spoken Word and the Work of Interpretation* (Philadelphia: University of Pennsylvania Press, 1983), pp. 321-38; Lawrence Watson, "Understanding a Life History as a Subjective Document," *Ethos* 4 (1976): 95-131; Paul Ricoeur, *Hermeneutics and the Human Sciences*, ed. and trans. John B. Thompson (London: Cambridge University Press, 1979). For an excellent discussion on recent debates among historians and social scientists, see Richard Harvey Brown's review article, "Positivism, Relativism, and Narrative in the Logic of Historical Sciences," *American Historical Review* 92 (October 1987): 908-20.

10. Tedlock, "Analogical Tradition," p. 323.

11. Ibid.

12. Bidney, "Phenomenological Method," p. 128.

13. Ibid., p. 101.

14. Ibid., p. 98.

15. Ibid.

16. William Thomas and Florian Znaniecki, *The Polish Peasant in Europe and America* 5 vols. (Boston: Gorham Press, 1919-1920).

17. See Herbert Blumer's *Critiques of Research in the Social Sciences: An Appraisal of Thomas's and Znaniecki's The Polish Peasant In Europe and America* (New Brunswick: Rutgers University Press, 1979). For a fine discussion of Thomas and Znaniecki, The Polish Peasant, see Eli Zaretsky's introduction in the abridged and edited edition (Urbana: University of Illinois Press, 1984). Some recent sociologists, mostly Europeans, are interested in life histories; see Bertaux, *Biography and Society*, especially his introduction and essays by Martin Kohli, "Biography: Account, Text, Method," pp. 61-76; Maurizio Catani, "Social-Life History as Ritualized Oral Exchange," pp. 211-24; Isabella Bertaux-Wiami, "The Life History Approach to the Study of Internal Migration," pp. 249-66.

18. A notable example of an early life history of an Indian is Paul Radin, *Crashing Thunder: The Autobiography of an American Indian* (New York: D. Appleton, 1926).

19. Ann Banks, ed., *First-Person America* (New York: Knopf, 1980), is a good source for WPA narratives. For examples of slave narratives, see George P. Rawick, ed., *The American Slave: A Composite Autobiography*, 19 vols. (Westport, Conn.: Greenwood Press, 1972). See also James Mellon, ed., *Bull Whip Days: The Slaves Remember* (New York: Weidenfeld & Nicholson, 1988).

20. Oscar Handlin, *The Uprooted* (Boston: Little, Brown, 1951).

21. One of the first major criticisms came from Rudloph J. Vecoli, "*Contadini* in Chicago: A Critique of *The Uprooted*," *Journal of American History* 51 (December 1964): 404-17. For some time since the 1960s, perhaps beginning with Stephan Thernstrom, *Poverty and Progress: Social Mobility in a Nineteenth Century City* (Cambridge: Harvard University Press, 1964), the field of immigration and ethnic studies was dominated by historians interested in quantification. Thernstrom was more concerned with property mobility as a means to Americanization than he was with ethnicity and immigration. Books like *Poverty and Progress* had much in common with American character studies, such as David Potter, *People of Plenty: Economic Abundance and the*

American Character (Chicago: University of Chicago Press, 1954). Thernstrom's *The Other Bostonians: Poverty and Progress in the American Metropolis, 1880-1970* (Cambridge: Harvard University Press, 1973), which relied heavily on statistical analysis of the social mobility of various ethnic groups, belongs squarely in the tradition of sociological positivism. Recent works are broadening their concerns and their sources. See, for example, Gary Mormino and George E. Pozetta, *The Immigrant World of Ybor City* (Urbana: University of Illinois Press, 1987). Samuel L. Baily's work attempts to utilize both empirical and subjective data. For an example of the former, see his "The Adjustment of Italian Immigrants in Buenos Aires and New York, 1870-1914," *American Historical Review* 88 (1983): 281-305; for an example of the latter, see Samuel L. Baily and Franco Ramella, eds., *One Family, Two Worlds; An Italian Family's Correspondence across the Atlantic*, trans. John Lenaghan (New Brunswick: Rutgers University Press, 1988).

22. The most influential work was Jan Vansina, *Oral Tradition: A Study in Historical Methodology* (Chicago: Aldine, 1961).

23. Lawrence Levine, *Black Culture, Black Consciousness* (New York: Oxford University Press, 1977).

24. Ibid., p. 207.

25. Theodore Rosengarten, *All God's Dangers: The Life of Nat Shaw* (New York: Knopf, 1974).

26. William Chafe's *Civilities and Civil Rights: Greensborough, North Carolina* (New York: Oxford University Press, 1980) utilized these interviews.

27. Gary Y. Okihiro, "Oral History and the Writing of Ethnic History: A Reconnaissance into Method and Theory," *Oral History Review* 9 (1981): 27-46, captures some of the concerns of "guerilla" historians and others who wished to document history from the point of view of those who lived it. See also Staughton Lynd, "Guerilla History in Gary," *Liberation* 14 (October 1969): 17-20. One of the best oral histories of working-class life is Peter Friedlander, *The Emergence of a UAW Local, 1936-1939: A Study of Class and Culture* (Pittsburgh: University of Pittsburgh Press, 1975).

28. Zaretsky, introduction to Thomas and Znaniecki, *Polish Peasant*, pp. 5, 36.

29. Herbert G. Gutman, *The Black Family in Slavery and Freedom* (New York: Pantheon Books, 1976). The strong presence of the grandchildren and children of white European immigrants in Afro-American history, including Gutman, Ira Berlin, Eric Foner, Eugene Genovese, Lawrence Levine, and Leon Litwack, appears to be not just a "colonization" of black history by whites but also an identification on the part of these immigrant descendants with Afro-Americans.

30. Sidney Mintz, *A Puerto Rican Life History* New York: Norton, 1974), originally published in 1960. Readers interested in other oral history projects existing at the time should consult Gary Shumway, comp., *Oral History in the United States: A Directory* (New York: Oral History Association, 1971). Paul Thompson, *The Voice of the Past: Oral History* (London: Oxford University Press, 1978), discusses oral history projects and methods.

31. Virginia Yans-McLaughlin, *Italian Immigrants in Buffalo, 1880-1930* (Ithaca: Cornell University Press, 1977). See Zaretsky's criticism of this book in his introduction to Thomas and Znaniecki, *The Polish Peasant*, pp. 5, 36, 46-47. Curiously, he condemns the book for its cultural relativism and culturalism while he praises historians such as Gutman for their understanding of the way in which workers maintained traditional cultural values.

32. See Grele's *Envelopes of Sound*, pp. 127-54, and his "A Surmiseable Variety: Interdisciplinarity and Oral Testimony," *American Quarterly*, (August 1975), pp. 275-95.

33. See note 2 for a description of original materials and their archival location. Neighborhood clubs and unions offered their assistance by inviting us to their senior citizen centers. Individuals volunteered for the interviews; after their initial cooperation, the unions and neighborhood agencies withdrew entirely from the process. We also interviewed a few individuals in private homes, some of whom were friends or relatives of project participants. Because we hoped to ground the interviews in actual historical experience, we developed preliminary research papers on the local history of work, community, and family and associational life. The interviewers were prepared to use a flexible set of questions related to these themes rather than a strict questionnaire.

34. Studs Terkel's *Hard Times: An Oral History of the Great Depression* (New York: Pantheon, 1970).

35. See Ronald Grele, "Listen to Their Voices: Two Case Studies in the Interpretation of Oral History Interviews," *Oral History Review* 7 (Spring 1979): 33–42. One project participant, Elizabeth Ewen, used oral testimony as she did other forms of evidence, by weaving it into her synthetic work, *Immigrant Women in the Land of Dollars: Life and Culture on the Lower East Side, 1890–1925* (New York: Monthly Review Press, 1985). In her fine book *Cheap Amusements: Working Women and Leisure in Turn-of-the-Century New York* (Philadelphia: Temple University Press, 1986), Kathy Peiss uses the project collection in the same way.

36. Charlotte Linde, "Explanatory Systems in Oral Life Stories," in *Cultural Models in Language and Thought*, ed. Dorothy Holland and Naomi Quinn (London: Cambridge University Press, 1987), pp. 343–51, discusses the absence of research on the origins of common-sense explanatory systems.

37. The collection of interviews is Tamara K. Hareven and Randolph Langenbach, *Amoskeag: Life and Work in an American Factory-City* (New York: Pantheon Books, 1978); the fine monograph by Hareven is *Family Time and Industrial Time: The Relationship between the Family and Work in a New England Industrial Community* (Cambridge: Cambridge University Press, 1982). Hareven's article "The Search for Generational Memory: Tribal Rites in Industrial Society," *Daedalus* 107 (1978): 137–49, is also of interest.

38. Hareven, *Family Time and Industrial Time*, p. 371.

39. Ibid., pp. 41–45, 71.

40. John Bodnar, *Worker's World: Kinship, Community and Protest in an Industrial Society, 1900–1940* (Baltimore: Johns Hopkins University Press, 1982).

41. Ibid., pp. 91, 3.

42. An example of Hareven's authorial voice appears in *Family Time, Industrial Time*, p. 372: "Without a historical and sociological imagination to guide the process [of interviewing] only hours of meaningless information are obtained." Some recent uses of oral interviews are Patricia A. Cooper, *Once a Cigar Maker: Men, Women, and Work Culture in American Cigar Factories, 1900–1919* (Urbana: University of Illinois Press, 1987); Peter Gottlieb, *Making Their Own Way: Southern Blacks' Migration to Pittsburgh, 1916–1930* (Urbana: University of Illinois Press, 1987). Typically, none of these books devote any attention to their oral history methods, and interviews are synthesized, along with the rest of the data, into the text. Jacquelyn D. Hall et al., *Like a Family: The Making of a Southern Cotton Mill World* (Chapel Hill: University of North Carolina Press, 1987), recent recipient of the distinguished Merle Curti Award in American social history, represents an effort to move beyond the conventional uses of oral narratives.

43. See, for example, Grele, "Listen to Their Voices," Notable exceptions are Henry Glassie, *Passing the Time in Ballymenone: Culture and History of an Ulster Community* (Philadelphia: University of Pennsylvania Press, 1982), and Louisa Passerini, *Fascism*

in Popular Memory: The Cultural Experience of the Turin Working Class (London: Cambridge University Press, 1984).

44. Yosef H. Yerulshalmi, *Zakor: Jewish History and Jewish Memory* (Seattle: University of Washington Press, 1982), presents a wonderful account of these themes. For a general discussion on learning in Jewish culture, see Mark Zabrowski, "The Place of Book-Learning in Traditional Jewish Culture," *Harvard Education Review* 19 (Spring 1949): 88–110.

45. Irving Howe, *World of Our Fathers* (New York: Harcourt Brace Jovanovich, 1976), p. 11.

46. See, for example, Abraham Menes, "The East Side and the Jewish Labor Movement," in *Voices from the Yiddish*, ed. Irving Howe and Eliezer Greenberg (Ann Arbor: University of Michigan Press, 1972), reprinted in Herbert G. Gutman and Gregory Kealey, eds., *Many Pasts*, vol. 2 (Englewood Cliffs, N.J.: Prentice-Hall, 1973), pp. 227–37.

47. On this point, see Michael J. Fischer, "Ethnicity and the Post-Modern Arts of Memory," in *Writing Culture: The Politics and Poetics of Ethnography*, ed. James Clifford and George E. Marcus (Berkeley: University of California Press, 1986), pp. 194–233.

48. Ezra Mendelsohn, *Class Struggle in the Pale: The Formative Years of the Jewish Workers' Movement in Tsarist Russia* (Cambridge: Cambridge University press, 1970); see also Howe, *World of Our Fathers*.

49. On Jewish women, see Charlotte Baum et al., *The Jewish Woman in America* (New York: New American Library, 1975).

50. See Menes, "East Side and the Jewish Labor Movement"; Nora Levin, *Jewish Socialist Movements, 1871–1917* (New York: Oxford University Press, 1978).

51. For treatments of premigration agricultural areas of Europe, see John Bodnar, *The Transplanted: A History of Immigrants in Urban America* (Bloomington: Indiana University Press, 1985); Josef Barton, *Peasants and Strangers: Italians, Rumanians and Slovaks in an American City, 1880–1952* (Cambridge: Harvard University Press, 1975). The following are especially useful for background on the Italian immigrants: John Briggs, *An Italian Passage: Immigrants to Three American Cities, 1890–1930* (Bloomington: Indiana University Press, 1978); Dino Cinel, *From Italy to San Francisco: The Immigrant Experience* (Stanford: Stanford University Press, 1982); Jane Schneider and Peter Schneider, *Culture and Politics in Western Sicily* (New York: Academic Press, 1976).

52. On *mafia* relationships, see Anton Blok, *The Mafia of a Sicilian Village, 1860–1960: A Study of Violent Peasant Entrepreneurs* (New York: Harper & Row, 1975), and Pino Arlacchi, *Mafia, Peasants and Great Estates: Society in Traditional Calabria* (London: Cambridge University Press, 1983). Several recent works have documented Italian women's economic roles in the cottage industry and outside the home; still, they were simply not so involved in public life as the Jewish women already discussed. For examples of literature on the Italians, see Schneider and Schneider, *Culture and Politics in Western Sicily*; Emiliana Noether, "The Silent Half: *Le Contadine del Sud* before World War I," in *The Italian Immigrant Woman in North America: Proceedings of the 10th Annual Conference of the American Italian Historical Association*, ed. Betty B. Caroli, Robert F. Harney, and Lydio Tomasi (Toronto: Multicultural Historical Society of Toronto, 1978), pp. 3–12; Jane Schneider, "Trousseau and Treasure," *Women and History*, no. 10 (1985): 81–119; Donna Gabaccia, "In the Shadows of the Periphery: Italian Women in the Nineteenth Century" in *Connecting Spheres: Women in the West: 1500 to the Present*, ed. Marilyn Boxer and Jean Quartet (New York: Oxford University Press, 1987), pp. 166–76; Donna Gabaccia, *Militants and Migrants: Rural Sicilians*

Become American Workers (New Brunswick: Rutgers University Press, 1988). Gabaccia documents the role of Sicilians in the United States as activists, and so challenges conventional images of Italian immigrants.

53. Two now-classic essays relating regional emigration and land tenancy patterns to labor militancy are John S. McDonald (*sic*), "Italy's Rural Social Structure and Emigration," *Occidente: Revista di Studi Politici* 12 (September–October 1956): 439–56, and J. S. and Leatrice D. MacDonald, "Institutional Economics and Rural Development: Two Italian Types," *Human Organization* 23 (Summer 1964): 113–18. Garbaccia, *Militants and Migrants*, questions this relationship.

54. Rudolph J. Vecoli, "Peasants and Prelates: Italian Immigrants and the Catholic Church," *Journal of Social History* 2 (Spring 1969): 217–68.

55. Bell, *Fate and Honor, Family and Village: Demography and Culture Change in Rural Italy since 1800* (Chicago: University of Chicago Press, 1979), pp. 30, 25.

56. Ibid., p. 25.

57. Bell, *Fate and Honor, Family and Village*, p. 33, considers the advent of the Communist party in the villages he studied as a possible instance of such a change. He argues that the exceptional appeal of the party to the Italian peasantry lies in Gramsci's sensitive reformulation of Marxism. Gramsci did not call on the peasants to reject the past but to "give purpose" to centuries of sacrifice by their forebears. The Communist peasants, Bell remarks, believe they are bound to succeed; history is on their side, it is beyond human control. So, he concludes, even in the present, "the past," not human agency,ontrols the future.

58. There is a very substantial literature on this subject. On Christianity and history, see Stephen Toulmin and June Goodfield, *The Discovery of Time* (New York: Harper & Row, 1965), p. 55; Leonard Doob, *Patterning of Time* (New Haven: Yale University Press, 1971); "Social Structure and the Multiplicity of Times," in *Sociological Theory, Values and Sociocultural Change*, ed. Edward Tiryakian (Glencoe, Ill.: Free Press, 1963), pp. 182–84; Joost Merloo, *The Two Faces of Man* (New York: International Universities Press, 1954); G. J. Whitrow, *Time in History: The Evolution of Our General Awareness of Time and Temporal Perspective* (New York: Oxford University Press, 1988); see also Edmund Leach's discussion of Lévi-Strauss on conceptions of historical time in *Claude Lévi-Strauss* (New York: Viking Press, 1970), pp. 7ff.; Marian W. Smith, "Different Cultural Concepts of Past, Present and Future: A Study of Ego Extension," *Psychiatry* 15 (1952): 395–400. Thomas Cottle and Stephen Klinebert, *The Present of Things Future: Explorations of Time in Human Experience* (New York: Free Press, 1974), is a fascinating study of the psychology of temporal perception. Warren Susman, "History and the American Intellectual: Uses of a Usable Past" in his *Culture as History* (New York: Pantheon, 1973), pp. 7–26, is an influential meditation on the uses of history. On ethnohistory, see Marshall Sahlins, *Islands of History* (Chicago: University of Chicago Press, 1985).

59. Grele, *Envelopes of Sound*, p. 140.

60. See Levin, *Jewish Socialist Movements*. Italians, of course, did have a tradition of labor radicalism, but the regional representatives from areas in which it predominated in Italy—the industrial North and certain areas of the South—did not predominate in the emigration stream. Gabaccia, *Militants and Migrants*, questions this correlation, originally drawn by the MacDonalds in "Institutional Economics." By treating the subject comparatively, Samuel Baily points to structural and cultural conditions that may explain why labor militancy was not as predominant in the United States as it was in Latin America. See his "The Italians and the Development of Organized Labor in Argentina, Brazil, and the United States, 1880-1914," *Journal of Social History* 3 (Winter 1969): 123–34.

61. I am grateful to one of the City University project participants, Louise Mayo, for her unpublished essay "Immigrant Jews and the New York Clothing Industry" (CUNY Oral History Project, Spring 1975). See also David Montgomery, *The Fall of the House of Labor: The Workplace, the State, and American Labor Activism, 1865–1925* (Cambridge: Cambridge University Press, 1987), p. 117.

62. On the longshore industry, see Montgomery, *Fall of the House of Labor*, pp. 96ff. Two City University Oral History Project participants prepared unpublished papers on the longshore industry in New York: Frank Faragasso, "The Italian Shoreman" (Spring 1975), and David Lightner, "Longshore Labor on the Brooklyn Waterfront, 1900–1932: Employers, Government, Technology, and the Work Environment" (Spring 1975).

63. Montgomery, *Fall of the House of Labor*, p. 99.

64. Ibid., pp. 106–7.

65. To protect the privacy of the persons interviewed, all names used here are fictitious. For a discussion of the sources, see note 2.

66. Passerini, *Fascism in Popular Memory*, p. 160.

67. Fischer, "Ethnicity and the Post-Modern Arts of Memory" p. 202; see also Cottle and Klinebert, *Present of Things Future*, p. 176.

68. See James Clifford, "Hanging up Looking Glasses at Odd Corners" in *Studies in Biography*, ed. Daniel Aaron (Cambridge: Harvard University Press, 1978), p. 42.

69. Carl Rogers, "The Process of Therapy," in *Client-Centered Therapy* (Boston: Houghton Mifflin, 1965), p. 136, discusses the self-concept useful for analysis of these interviews.

70. Alessandro Portelli, "The Peculiarities of Oral History," *History Workshop* 12 (Autumn 1981): 96–106, contains an interesting discussion of interview styles.

71. Passerini, *Fascism in Popular Memory*, p. 61, discusses the historical roots of Italian workers' narrative style, which, she hypothesizes, extend back through centuries of folk tradition. Elizabeth Mathias and Richard Raspa, *Italian Folktales in America: The Verbal Art of an Immigrant Woman* (Detroit: Wayne State University Press, 1985), is one of the few recent publications on Italian immigrant folk narrative.

72. Sylvia Gelb.

73. Isadore Opinski, a fur operator, describing his attitude to the Bund.

74. Linde, "Explanatory Systems."

75. Jean Weinstein.

76. Abraham Bernstein, Fanny Herman, Rebecca Levine.

77. Abraham Bernstein.

78. Agnes Moretti.

79. Leo Corso.

80. Stella Brodsky, Fanny Herman, Yetta Braun.

81. Jenny Goldberg.

82. Betty Gnocchi.

83. Adele Rossi, Belle Cohen.

84. Betty Gnocchi.

85. Jean Weinstein.

86. Compare Rebecca Levine's interpretation of the ticket. The tag was put there, she said, so the bosses would know who made the garment: "They know it's your dress. You're responsible for it."

87. See Briggs, *Learning How to Ask*, introduction, for a good summary of current positions.

THE POLITICS
OF IMMIGRATION

10

The Reactions of Black Americans to Immigration

Lawrence H. Fuchs

The myths that account for the origins of nations are usually tribal — based on genealogy or blood — as when God told Abraham to create a new nation, or when a favorite descendant of the Sun Goddess created the Japanese islands and became the first emperor, ancestor of all subsequent emperors. Such myths, which revolve around the dominant role of a favored or chosen people, have often provided a rationalization for the exploitation and oppression of subordinate groups in multiethnic societies. The founding myth of the American republic was not tribal but ideological, and became the basis of a sense of shared identity among peoples of diverse national backgrounds. But if the American founding myth was not tribal, it was implicitly racial. The new nation's spokesmen, when they explained that the United States was created by God as an asylum for liberty, opportunity, and reward for achievement, understood the myth (which to them was not a myth but reality) as an ideal meant especially, perhaps exclusively, for white men. Through the belief in the founding myth, white men in the United States created those new political institutions and practices that Alexis de Tocqueville saw in the 1830s as the basis of American patriotism.

Tocqueville in 1833 and the German immigrant Francis J. Grund in 1836 saw that immigrants quickly claimed principles of republican government as their own. They shared in the cult of the glorious Fourth of July, when the Declaration of Independence was read aloud on town greens and main streets, as well as in the worship of "God-like Washington," whose birthday was made a national holiday in 1799 and then became, like the Fourth, an occasion for preachers and teachers to discuss the virtues of American liberty and opportunity. But only two decades after Tocqueville's and Grund's panegyrics to American patriotism, the former slave Frederick Douglass, speaking of Independence Day, declared, "I am not included within the pale of this glorious anniversary . . . this Fourth of July is yours, not mine."[1]

Because the founding myth was stated in universal terms — *all* men are created equal — its appeal was universal, even or especially for blacks held in bondage, but it was inevitable that those shut out from freedom and opportunity would resent newly arrived immigrants, who were encouraged to take a clear and fast track to full membership in the society. In fact, most immigrants found their opportunities and even their freedoms limited through prejudice and discrimination. Nonetheless, in the eyes of successive generations of blacks, who were locked into the American system of caste pluralism, the myth seemed real enough for white immigrants and even some non-white immigrants. The buildup of slavery and the oppression of blacks paralleled the expansion of opportunity for whites from the seventeenth century on.

Edmund S. Morgan has demonstrated that American freedom and opportunity for poor immigrant whites in the seventeenth and eighteenth centuries was connected fundamentally with the spread of black slavery.[2] Every decade prior to the Civil War saw advances for immigrants while slavery was more harshly administered and the condition of free blacks generally made worse. In 1857, the year that saw a quarter of a million immigrants arrive in the United States, the Supreme Court, in *Dred Scott v. Sanford*, declared that because blacks were not citizens, they did not have the right to sue in court and that a citizen-master could take his property to wherever he liked, even to states that did not recognize slavery. After the Civil War and emancipation, when industrial expansion created new jobs and increased investment in the West opened new land for immigrants, blacks remained largely impoverished and without economic opportunity. Railroad companies received huge tracts of land to open up the West and recruited immigrants to settle around their lines. The Homestead Act of 1862 gave 160 acres to a settler if he or she would cultivate and reside on the land for five years. Although a small number of blacks became homesteaders in the West and some were permitted to purchase poor land on installment in five southern states, the result was free land for thousands of immigrant families in the West and only a tiny portion for blacks in the South. The economic dependency of blacks was assured with the deal made in 1877 between northern and southern whites that ended reconstruction in exchange for the election of Republican presidential candidate Rutherford B. Hayes. The South could once again rely on docile, cheap black labor to maintain a relatively static and highly stratified economic system; the North was free to expand its industry and commerce through the investment of capital and the importation of inexpensive immigrant labor.

Opportunity for blacks remained limited during the last quarter of the nineteenth century, at the same time that the United States provided more of it for newcomers. In 1883, when Emma Lazarus, a daughter of immigrants, wrote the impassioned words "Give me your tired, your poor, your huddled masses yearning to breath free," the Supreme Court undermined the last of the civil rights laws passed by Congress following the Civil War. The opening of Ellis Island as a reception-processing center for immigrants in 1892 was followed five years later by the Supreme Court decision in *Plessy v. Ferguson* sanctioning state-supported racial segregation. While Jim Crow laws reinforced the economic and political powerlessness of blacks during the first decade of the twentieth century, the United States received annually an average of 879,539 immigrants (not counting any of those who came illegally or who came lawfully across either land border), a migration unprecedented in world history. Some of the newcomers were even permitted to vote as aliens (as late as 1926 in racially segregated Arkansas). Although immigrants struggled against prejudice and job discrimination, the vast majority of them were not segregated by law, as were blacks. And with initiative and courage they could break the bounds of class, unlike blacks throughout the South and in much of the North, who remained tightly restricted by caste.[3]

Blacks React: The Issue Is Jobs

Even free blacks were passed over in favor of white immigrants for better jobs. In a typical nineteenth-century complaint, Frederick Douglass wrote, "Every hour sees the black man elbowed out of employment by some newly arrived immigrant whose hunger and whose color are thought to give him a better title to the place."[4] After emancipation, blacks began to move into skilled and semiskilled jobs. In 1870, the New Orleans city directory listed 3,460 blacks as carpenters, cigar makers, painters, clerks, shoemakers, coopers, tailors, bakers, blacksmiths, and foundry hands, but by 1904 the number was below 340, even though the black population had grown by more than 50 percent.[5] It did not take Jim Crow laws to drive blacks out of such jobs in the North, which could draw on a huge pool of immigrant labor flowing into the cities. In 1870 almost 32 percent of all black males in Cleveland were employed in skilled trades, but by 1910 only 11 percent were so employed. In New York, black workers were steadily forced out of employment during the same period.[6] In the South, where more than 90 percent of blacks lived, there was concern that Chinese and other immigrants would be brought in to make certain that blacks were kept to the most menial, unskilled tasks. In his famous Atlanta address, delivered at the opening of the Cotton States Exposition in September 1895, Booker T. Washington admonished the white leaders in his audience not to "look to the incoming of those of foreign birth and strange tongue and habits for the prosperity of the South, . . . I would repeat what I say to my own race, 'Cast down your bucket where you are.' Cast it down among the eight million negroes . . . who have without strikes and labor wars tilled your fields, cleared your forests, builded your railroads and cities. . . . "[7] At Fiske University in Nashville that same year, Washington pointed out that twenty years earlier barbershops all over the country were run by blacks but that he no longer could find a single large or first-class barbershop operated by them.[8]

For seventy years after the Civil War, when immigration to the United States expanded enormously, the Afro-American press and black leaders repeated the sentiments expressed by Douglass in 1853 and Washington in 1895 about immigrants' taking jobs that they thought should rightfully go to black Americans. The general attitude, as put by one writer in the *Washington Colored American* in 1902, was that "Negro labor is native labor and should be preferred to that of the offscourings of Europe and Asia. Let America take care of its own."[9] From 1900 to 1935 the pages of Afro-American newspapers warned against Greek and Italian immigrants, who would steal jobs from black Americans, and especially against the Mexicans and Asians, who also were alleged to be unassimilable. Immigrants, said the *Norfolk Journal and Guide* in 1928, were "crude, illiterate, and hopelessly unsympathetic with American institutions and ideals," and were "used to press us further down the economic ladder . . . in spite of our proved loyalty to America."[10]

Black leaders and the Afro-American press leveled some of their harshest criticism at Asian and Mexican immigrants. With the expansion of the West and Southwest after the Civil War, railroad builders, mine owners, ranchers, farmers, and factory managers and owners sought cheap labor from the Far East and Mexico, workers who were to be prevented or discouraged from becoming full members of the society. More than 322,000 unskilled Cantonese-speaking male workers arrived from China between 1850 and 1882; most worked on railroads, plantations, and ranches, and in mines, logging camps, vineyards, and orchards, with no expectation by them or their employers that they would ever be anything but sojourners who would return to their families when their labor was no longer wanted. Following the exclusion of Chinese laborers by federal law in 1882 — a law supported vigorously by the Afro-American press — employers then looked to Japan for temporary alien workers, and then, after the agreement in 1907 to limit the number of Japanese immigrants, they sought workers from Korea, the Philippines, and especially Mexico.

Under legislation passed in 1902, federally funded construction of large reservoirs encouraged labor-intensive irrigated farming, especially in Texas and California. By 1920 the demand for labor was growing not just in agriculture but in railroads, mining, the oil industry, textile manufacturing, and chemical production. In addition to the nearly half million Mexicans who entered the United States lawfully as resident aliens in the 1920s, probably a comparable number came illegally, establishing a pool of particularly exploitable workers who, like the Asians, were ineligible for citizenship.

Black opposition to these workers was strenuous. Booker T. Washington thought the Chinese particularly objectionable because, unlike blacks, they "lacked moral standards and could never be assimilated to occidental civilization."[11] Black leaders were also extremely negative about Mexican immigrant workers, alleging that because of their low standard of living they worked for practically nothing. Black historian Carter G. Woodson saw Mexican laborers taking jobs on farms and railroads and as busboys, cooks, and garbage men, work previously done by blacks. The Mexicans lived with their families, "boarded up in Fords like so many cattle en route to the cotton fields."[12] Many Afro-American leaders and newspapers strongly endorsed proposals to bar Mexicans from the United States during the late 1920s and early 1930s, and even supported the sometimes brutal roundup of over 400,000 Mexicans between 1929 and 1935 that sent them back to a country that the black press regularly depicted as backward and dirty.[13] The black journalist George Schuyler wondered, "If the million Mexicans who have entered the country have not displaced Negro workers, whom have they displaced?"[14]

Although the question was rhetorical, the emotion behind it was understandable. Blacks had made slight economic progress during the period of heaviest immigration, the first few decades of the century. In 1900 about 33 percent of all blacks were employed in jobs categorized as domestic or personal service, and thirty years later 28.6 percent of all black workers held the same occupations, nearly three times the percentage of all American laborers.[15] There is no question that in some instances employers favored Asian or Mexican immigrant workers over blacks. The Pullman Company, for example, hired relatively well-educated Filipino workers in the 1920s, partly in an effort to destroy A. Philip Randolph's attempts to organize black workers,[16] and Chinese workers, brought to Mississippi under contract to work on plantations, were permitted to settle in nearby towns and cities, where they had some success in small business.[17]

The Depression deeply hurt blacks, who were the first laid off from skilled and semiskilled jobs in the industrialized North because immigrants were favored not only by the racial attitudes of employers but by the rules of white-dominated or exclusively white unions. Whatever the overall impact on blacks as a group over time, many Afro-American leaders and the public generally, as reflected in black newspapers, saw immigrants as taking jobs from blacks, and not the Mexicans, Chinese, or Filipinos escaped resentment. Most black leaders supported the movement for restriction, which culminated in congressional legislation in 1917 and 1921 and included a total ban on Asian immigration in 1924. The leaders made no distinction between immigrants and refugees because the law made none, and they did not discuss illegal immigrants at all, although the latter existed. They simply opposed immigrants on the grounds that they were taking jobs that rightfully should go to blacks.

A Historic Reversal: Refugees

By the 1980s a complete change had taken place in the attitudes of black leaders toward immigrants and immigration. Despite tension between blacks and refugees, blacks and illegal aliens, and even native-born American blacks and black immigrants, national black leaders expressed sympathy with refugees, made no effort to restrict lawful immigration, and by 1984 actually gave strong support to Mexican-American groups in opposing legislation to curtail illegal immigration.

During the late 1970s, when large numbers of Indochinese refugees started arriving in the United States, black leaders had to worry about the reaction of their constituents, particularly those in the cities where the newcomers settled. It was an issue that Martin Luther King, Jr., had pondered in the 1960s, when Cuban newcomers in Miami became visibly entrenched in many service occupations. Hoping that the Cubans would expand economic opportunity for everyone, King decided not to pit black needs against Cuban aspirations by making an issue of the near-term displacement of black workers.[18] In part because of King's inspiration, almost every major black leader in the country, including the mayors of several large cities and the leaders of national organizations, signed an advertisement for the International Rescue Committee in 1978, headlined: "Black Americans Urge Admission of the Indo-Chinese Refugees." Acknowledging the economic troubles of the black community, these leaders, whose ethos of compassion had been shaped in the struggle for civil rights under the leadership of King, insisted on opposing the "dehumanizing tendency of placing price tags on the heads of Indo-Chinese refugees." Calling the refugees "an embattled minority," they argued that as blacks they knew that "the battle against human misery is indivisible " and that "our continuing struggle for economic and political freedom is inextricably linked to the struggle of Indo-Chinese refugees who also seek freedom."[19]

The humanitarian point of view was expressed frequently by leaders of black organizations, such as Vernon Jordan (president of the Urban League) and Benjamin Hooks (president of the National Association for the Advancement of Colored People—the NAACP). During a conversation with Hooks at his New York City office in the fall of 1980, he told me that although some members of the board of the NAACP were deeply apprehensive about competition between refugees and blacks for jobs and services, he and others on the board "did not have it in their hearts" to urge restriction of refugees. He spoke of having been raised in a household in which even during the depression his struggling family would share corn bread with those less fortunate.[20]

The importance of keeping a humanitarian perspective also informed the remarks of Congresswoman Cardiss R. Collins (D-Illinois) when in February 1980 she spoke for the Congressional Black Caucus before the Los Angeles meeting of the Select Commission on Immigration and Refugee Policy, a group established by Congress and the president to make recommendations about immigration and refugee policy. Collins declared that "Americans must continue to have an overriding loyalty to mankind as a whole."[21] Also speaking for the Congressional Black Caucus, Congressman Mickey Leland (D-Texas) urged the commission, at its public hearing in San Francisco, to recommend federal help for refugees because "our passionate commitment to human rights for blacks at home requires an overriding loyalty to mankind as a whole. . . . "[22]

The humanitarian outlook of black civil rights leaders, stemming in part from their own background of struggle for basic human rights under Martin Luther King, Jr., was also consistent with the cosmopolitan, humanitarian ideology of most social service professionals. It was a point of view, however, not shared by all or perhaps even most blacks. During visits to major cities and at public hearings, the Select Commission learned of black resentment toward the refugees. In Los Angeles, the director of the Afro Media Service, Wendell Green, speaking for the black organization Committee for Representative Government, charged that formerly black-owned and -operated gasoline stations had been taken over by Indochinese refugees, who were willing to accept the "exorbitant demands" made by oil companies to remain open at all hours and provide unusual services.[23] Green spoke of a black dentist who was unable to obtain a business-improvement loan, although, he asserted, two Asian refugee dentists had obtained large loans at low interest. A black man, speaking before the open microphone in Los Angeles during a time set aside for anyone who wished to testify declared that landlords were giving preference to groups of aliens, who were willing to pay more than blacks.[24]

In New Orleans, Dr. Marguerite Bryan asserted that refugees and blacks competed for housing and public assistance programs as well as jobs. It was little wonder, she concluded, "that many in the New Orleans black community are skeptical and even antagonistic to the new Indo-Chinese presence."[25] James Hayes, the black executive director of the TREME Community Improvement Association in New Orleans, expressed strong resentment that the black community in his city had never received the kind of federal support given to the Indo-Chinese. "I think when the issue boils down," said Hayes, "it goes back to the point that within a five-year period, the Indo-Chinese have been able to receive and get grants of such a nature that they have . . . become a part of mainstream America . . . and the American black community has been overlooked." Professor Wade Ragas of the University of New Orleans testified that he told the city government in November 1978, in a report on the local housing market, that the severe competition for low-cost housing was aggravated by the presence of refugees.[26] In Denver, the white director of the Indo-Chinese Development Center acknowledged that blacks resented what they believed was preferential treatment in housing for the Indochinese.[27]

In Miami, black resentment against Cuban refugees, already considerable in 1979, intensified in 1980 when large numbers of Cubans arrived by boat from Mariel and were quickly processed and given parole status and economic assistance, in contrast to the treatment of black Haitian boat people, most of whom were denied asylum and many of whom were held in detention. Nearly half a million Cubans were admitted to the United States along with nearly half a million Indo-Chinese refugees in the 1960s and 1970s. Indeed, the United States arranged an airlift to speed Cuban migration in October of 1965, in sharp contrast to decisions in the Justice Department not to grant work authorization to Haitian asylum claimants. Except for Congresswoman Shirley Chisholm (D-New York), national black leaders did not give prominence to the Haitian issue prior to the exodus of Cubans from Mariel Harbor in 1980. Blacks (especially Haitians) in the Miami area did not wait for Mariel. Led by the Reverend Gerard Jean-Juste, the director of the Haitian Refugee Center, they pleaded with the Select Commission during its hearings in Miami on December 4, 1979, that asylum be granted to the 9,871 undocumented Haitians then reported by the Immigration and Naturalization Service to be in the Miami area.[28] The different treatment given to Cubans and Haitians the following year sharpened the feelings of many blacks that racism was still a factor in refugee policy. A member of my staff at the Select Commission, after contacting local black leaders in ten cities in 1980, reported that each of them expressed outrage that Haitians were being held in detention or deported while Cuban asylum claimants and Indo-Chinese were being welcomed. That was the view of William R. Perry, Jr., president of the Greater Miami Branch of the NAACP, who told the Select Commission, "We in the NAACP think categorically, that the present immigration and refugee policy is based on historical racial prejudice . . . which we can clearly see as it related to more than 10,000 Haitian boat people." Perry asked, "Doesn't it seem unusual that the only persons that have been denied entrance to this country are black people?"[29] Marsha Sonders, director of the Office of Black Affairs in metropolitan Dade County, repeated the sentiment. She was not opposed to U.S. help for destitute Cambodians but she was upset that "all the boat people were welcome except black people."[30]

Despite these feelings of bitterness and resentment, most national black leaders did not give the Haitian issue priority as the debate on immigration and refugee policy unfolded during the early 1980s. They were much more concerned with domestic economic questions and were becoming increasingly involved in making common cause with Mexican-American leaders against legislative proposals to curtail illegal migration. Their stance regarding immigration contrasted sharply with the traditional views of the black leadership, and it was at variance with some of the testimony received from blacks in different communities.

Coalition Building: Illegal Aliens

Some of that testimony reflected the point of view expressed in an *Ebony* magazine article entitled "Illegal Aliens: Big Threat to Black Workers," published only a few months before the Select Commission began its work.[31] Reuben Green argued that in the Los Angeles area the negative impact was greatest on black teenagers in the food service industry. The garment industry, he said, had seen the replacement of black women by illegal aliens, and black car-wash employees had been displaced by aliens who worked long hours for short pay. He also told of a demonstration by about one hundred blacks in front of a large plastics concern protesting the layoff of black employees and their replacement with illegal aliens, and he maintained that a major hotel in the Hollywood area had replaced its black staff with a substantial number of foreigners.[32] One woman from Oakland complained, "My two younger brothers and other blacks would apply for jobs at the local factories only to be turned away. . . . The majority of the workers in unskilled positions were Mexicans. . . . The Mexican workers were cheaper and easier to have around, many of the employers saw blacks as asking for too many things, such as equal wages, benefits, improved safety conditions, and unions."[33]

Not all of the testimony given by blacks before the Select Commission was hostile to illegal immigration. Evillo Grillo, president of the Resource Center of Community Institutions in Oakland, California, who is both black and Hispanic, emphasized the number of black Hispanics who recently arrived in the United States and the importance of cooperation between native-born blacks and the newcomers.[34] Representative Leland, who had been elected with the backing of a coalition of blacks and Hispanics, acknowledged that "many of the black community have fears about the number coming into the country and about the possible negative effect it may have on the employment opportunities of black Americans." Leland told the Select Commission that it was an "age old myth that the entrance of foreigners into the U.S. economy during a recessionary period has a negative impact on job availability and earning capacity of the lower skilled segments of the population. . . . "[35]

As well as anyone, Leland knew that the coalition of blacks and Mexicans that he had so carefully nurtured in his own congressional district could come apart on the issue of immigration, and in my conversations with national black leaders, I found them extremely eager to prevent conflict between the two groups. In 1978 Carl Holman, chairman of the National Urban Coalition, together with Raul Yzaguerre, president of the National Council of La Raza, initiated three national meetings of blacks and Hispanics to talk about common problems and opportunities. Holman told me in 1979 that the tensions were serious and that one should not expect perfect agreement on issues such as immigration. It was a little early to speak of national coalitions. He and several other black leaders spoke of "going together," as boys and girls do in high school, of the two groups just getting to know one another a little better before making strong commitments. In 1979 black leaders were still somewhat sympathetic to the idea of deterring illegal migration by penalizing employers who hired them, but Mexican-American leaders strongly objected to President Carter's 1977 proposal calling for such sanctions. They urged an amnesty for the undocumented workers already in this country; black leaders reported that many of their constituents feared such an amnesty would be at their expense. At the meeting initiated by Holman in 1978, blacks tended to hold back from committing themselves on the issues of employer sanctions and amnesty.

In the spring of 1980 Benjamin Hooks told me that black leaders wanted to do something to deter illegal migration, which undoubtedly had a negative impact on young blacks entering the labor market. He thought it was unreasonable that employers should be exempt from penalties for hiring illegal aliens. When Congresswoman Collins testified before the Select Commission that she too was worried about the impact of illegal aliens on black employment, she argued that blacks and other minorities were being displaced by undocumented workers. Collins was careful to express strong concern for all of humanity, but she pointed out that "we must not forget the poor Americans who struggle within our shores."[36] Nevertheless, Collins, Hooks, and other national black leaders were increasingly reluctant to do anything that would directly conflict with the leadership of Mexican-American national organizations. As a consequence, national black leaders began to move toward supporting Mexican-American leaders on the illegal immigration issue. That was partly because of their strong common interest in other political issues, but also a result of the fact that nearly all of them were Democrats.

At Carter's White House, where there was considerable worry about a possible black-Mexican rift over immigration, Frank White, a black member of Carter's Domestic Council who worked closely with the Select Commission as a key member of the Staff Advisory Group, argued that although some blacks believed undocumented aliens depressed U.S. wages and took jobs away from them, most blacks would support an amnesty provision for illegal aliens already in the country, an opinion borne out by subsequent public opinion polls.[37] At the national level, he said, most "major black groups understand, appreciate and sympathize with the position articulated by most Hispanics — that there must be an assurance that new [immigration] laws will not promote discrimination against Hispanics." On the key issue of sanctions against employers who hire illegal aliens, White predicted that blacks "will support employer sanctions [only] if it is done in a way that Hispanics will also support."[38] By "Hispanics," White meant the leaders of Mexican-American advocacy groups and not general Hispanic public opinion, which a national poll showed in the summer of 1983 was remarkably supportive of employer sanctions, although not as much as black public opinion.[39] Three years later a national poll showed black and Hispanic views diverging on employer sanctions, as a majority of Hispanics shifted against them to come more into line with the leadership of Mexican-American organizations.[40] When the Select Commission made its report in April 1981, however, recommending employer sanctions as a principal method of deterring illegal migration, the unemployment situation for blacks was grave. By the spring of 1982, after the introduction of the Simpson-Mazzoli Immigration Reform Bill, which incorporated the employer-sanctions provision, unemployment among blacks had reached a record 18 percent compared to 7.9 percent for whites, with an extremely high level of unemployment among black teenagers (49 percent in August 1981).[41]

William Raspberry, the perceptive black columnist, concerned that the black and Mexican minorities might become "bitter political opponents" over the immigration issue, was reassured when he learned that the first national poll on the question of employer sanctions in 1983 indicated that both black and Hispanic citizens favored them by substantial margins. Because the major Mexican-American advocacy groups officially opposed employer sanctions, Raspberry was surprised to discover that Hispanic voters generally supported them by nearly two to one.[42] To Raspberry, usually astute at political analysis, the data suggested that blacks and browns might not have to fight over this issue.

Raspberry was half right. Black and brown leaders did not fight. They united against the sanctions proposal in 1984 when the Simpson-Mazzoli bill came before the House of Representatives, despite the national Peter Hart survey in 1983 and the national Gallup poll in 1984 that showed substantial majorities of black respondents favoring employer sanctions. A majority of Hispanic respondents also agreed that it should be against the law to hire illegal aliens, and that everyone in the United States should be required to have a reasonably secure form of identification, such as a counterfeit-resistant Social Security card, in order to get a job. On the other likely sticking point between the two groups — granting amnesty to illegal residents the data from the two national polls were more ambiguous. In the Hart poll, 48 percent of blacks favored amnesty for any illegal alien who had been in the country five or more years, compared to 60 percent of Hispanics. In the Gallup poll, a majority of blacks did not think amnesty should be given to those who had lived in the United States continuously for six years, in contrast to Hispanic voters, who endorsed amnesty for such persons by 59 to 32 percent.[43] Three years later, as already indicated, a national *New York Times*/CBS survey showed that 65 percent of blacks opposed deporting any illegal alien who had lived in the United States for several years without breaking the law; this response, though not expressing support for granting amnesty, indicated sympathy for the undocumented foreigners.

Regardless of the reservations of a substantial number of black voters on legalization (as amnesty was called by the Select Commission and by Senator Simpson and Congressman Mazzoli), and despite substantial black popular support for employer sanctions, all twenty members of the black caucus followed the Mexican-American members of the House on every crucial vote having to do with employer sanctions and legalization when Simpson-Mazzoli came before the House in 1984. Far from breaking on the immigration issue, the coalition, at least on the congressional level, was reinforced by it. Mexican-American leaders repeatedly said that employer sanctions were their civil rights issue, and black leaders accepted that view in order to strengthen the nascent coalition. Discrimination, racism, and oppression would result from the passage of employer sanctions, they said. It made no difference, they declared, that several provisions of the bill would inhibit discrimination under employer sanctions: an eligible worker would have only to show identification, not prove it was valid; employers would have only to show that they had seen and noted the ID; several agencies of government and the judiciary committees of both Houses would put a spotlight on the discrimination issue through annual reports and hearings; and the employment eligibility system, the identifier, could not be used for any purpose other than to identify an eligible employee when a person was changing a job or seeking work for the first time. Despite these provisions, Mexican-American leaders predicted that employers would shy away from hiring aliens or citizens who looked or sounded foreign.

The objections of Mexican-American leaders were in conflict with one major finding of the Select Commission: a considerable amount of discrimination already existed against persons eligible to work, including many Hispanics, because they could not produce a reliable identifier to distinguish them from illegal aliens, and, more important from the point of view of black politicians, some black workers were affected adversely by the continued flow of illegal migration. Despite these findings, fear that an employer-sanctions bills would be used as a pretext for cracking down on brown-skinned, foreign-looking and -speaking persons led many Mexican-American leaders to oppose employer sanctions, to the delight of the U.S. Chamber of Commerce and other representatives of groups that employed illegal aliens.

Having asserted their opposition, Mexican-American leaders possessed a litmus test by which to judge the friendship of others. One of the most vigorous seekers of friendship in 1984 was the Reverend Jesse Jackson, a candidate for the Democratic presidential nomination. Four years earlier, it had not been clear where Jackson would stand on the illegal immigration issue. He had not come to any of the coalition-building conferences sponsored by Carl Holman. It was possible he might take a strong restrictionist position on immigration, should he make a populist run for the presidency. Instead, in his bid to enlist Mexican-American leaders to support him against Walter Mondale during the Texas and California primaries, Jackson became one of the most vigorous antagonists of Simpson-Mazzoli, which he labeled restrictionist and racist. Praising illegal aliens as helping to make the United States a better country, he marched to the Mexican border in July 1984 to tell a youthful gathering of blacks, women, and Hispanics that he opposed the employer sanctions. "Just as Jesus marched to Jerusalem, and Gandhi marched to the sea, and Martin Luther King marched to Washington, we must march to the border," he declared, to praise amnesty and peace between Mexico and the United States and to denounce employer sanctions and discrimination.[44] For black voters, neither legalization nor employer sanctions was a vital issue; for Mexican-American leaders, whose endorsements Jackson needed to do well in the California primary, legalization and employer sanctions seem to have been the major issues.

Jackson's hyperbolic opposition to Simpson-Mazzoli removed any possibility that national black leaders would support employer sanctions, and made virtually certain the unanimous vote of the Black Congressional Caucus for an amendment to eliminate sanctions altogether, which was defeated by an almost three-to-one margin in the House in June 1984. Two members of the caucus, Augustus Hawkins (D-California) and Edolphus Towns (D-New York) spoke vigorously against the measure, which had been endorsed by many black leaders only a few years before. Towns pointed out that in his district in New York City 38 percent of the people had Spanish surnames,[45] but he failed to note that the vast majority of them were Puerto Ricans, a group that had strongly supported the employer sanctions proposal in exit polls conducted on the day of the New York State primary in 1984.[46]

On all other key votes on Simpson-Mazzoli in 1984, the Black Congressional Caucus hewed to the line with Mexican-American congressional leaders. Not a single member of the caucus voted for an amendment to reduce the number of undocumented aliens to be granted lawful resident status, despite public opinion polls that showed black voters opposing legalization. Not a single member of the caucus, all of whom were Democrats, voted for an amendment introduced by Democratic Majority Leader Jim Wright of Texas to require illegal aliens who applied for legalization to show that they were making an effort to learn English, despite the fact that only about 325,000 of the nation's 28 million blacks speak either Spanish or French as a first language, and that most blacks actually resent the foreign-language advantage of Hispanics in obtaining jobs in Miami, Los Angeles, and other cities.[47] So strong was the desire for solidarity with Mexican leaders that the black members of the House supported them on the language issue even against the House Democratic leadership and in the face of contrary constituent opinion. They agreed with Walter Fauntroy of Washington, D.C., the twenty-first (and only nonvoting) member of the caucus, that the requirement would place too great a burden on undocumented workers.[48]

The Immigration Reform and Control Act of 1986

When the immigration bill came up in a revised form in 1986, members of the Black Caucus joined the Hispanic Caucus again on key amendments to strengthen legalization and to inhibit the potential discriminatory effects of employer sanctions. On the final vote, the Hispanic Caucus itself split, with four key members announcing that they would vote for the bill. Elected to the House in 1984, none of the four had voted on the immigration measure when it came before the House in 1983 or 1984. They justified the break with their Hispanic colleagues by stating that the revised legislation was superior to any on which they might be called to vote in the future.

In fact, the Immigration Reform and Control Act of 1986 was a proimmigration bill and not a restriction measure as generally reported in the press. Although employer sanctions remained a part of the bill, almost everyone acknowledged that it would take years for them to become effective because the legislation did not provide a secure method of identifying those eligible to work, and it gave employers an absolute defense if they could demonstrate they had been fooled by bogus identifiers. Moreover, in addition to a comprehensive legalization program, the legislation contained wording to protect aliens against potential discrimination related to employer sanctions; a system for recruiting agricultural workers that gave them the chance to become permanent resident aliens and citizens; an upgrading of labor and legal protection standards for workers recruited under the temporary-worker H-2 visa program; and a special measure to legalize Haitians and Cubans whose status had been in limbo for several years.

With the ranks of Hispanics split in the final vote on the conference report, black members of Congress felt free to vote for the bill too, as did ten (of twenty) who came from districts with substantial majorities of black voters and few Hispanic voters.[49] Most of their constituents were probably less sympathetic to legalization, which would become a reality in May 1987, than to employer sanctions, which would take several years to be enforced effectively. But in black districts, and in those dominated by whites, where voters wanted action to enforce the immigration law, employer sanctions plus the authorization of more funds for the Border Patrol were the issues that representatives could comfortably stress.

Because the voting split in the Black Caucus was legitimized by the division in the Hispanic Caucus, the alliance between the two groups was probably not damaged by the vote over the Immigration Reform and Control Act of 1986. Blacks had demonstrated sensitivity on an issue of special significance to Mexican-American leaders during three series of votes on immigration in 1983, 1984, and 1986.

Black Immigration

The attention of black leaders to the illegal immigration issue contrasts with their relative lack of interest in policy questions concerning lawful immigration, despite the fact that blacks have been an increasing proportion of immigrants admitted to the United States in recent years. Before the turn of the century, free-black migration to the United States was low, and only in 1870 was the Naturalization Law amended to permit aliens of "African descent or African nativity" to apply for citizenship. Between 1891 and 1910, over 230,000 immigrants, most of whom were black, came from the British West Indies alone, and by the 1920s perhaps as much as one-fourth of Harlem's population was British West Indian.[50] Overall, more than half a million black immigrants have moved from the British West Indies to the United States since 1820, a larger number than the total number of blacks who came earlier as slaves. In 1972, 315,000 British West Indians were counted as living in the United States, 222,000 of them in New York and New Jersey.[51] Between 1967 and 1976, Jamaican immigration increased over the previous ten-year period from 14,853 to 130,404, and by 1980 Jamaica had become the fifth-largest immigrant-sending country to the United States, with 20,631 arrivals in that year. The increase for Trinidad and Tobago in the two ten-year periods was from 3,646 immigrants to nearly 60,000, and by 1980 Trinidad had become the eighteenth-largest sending nation, ahead of Greece and West Germany. Illegal migration of Jamaicans and other West Indians also increased tremendously in the 1970s; although precise figures are not available, West Indians may now constitute as much as 4 or even 5 percent of all blacks living in the United States. In addition, there are blacks from the Dominican Republic, Cuba, Puerto Rico, Guyana, and Haiti, the last two of which were thirteenth and fourteenth as senders of immigrants to the United States, ahead of Italy. The Dominican Republic especially became a major source of immigration, and by 1980 was the seventh-largest sending nation, with 17,245, ahead of Great Britain, Canada, and Portugal.[52]

For several decades many American-born blacks have resented the West Indians, whose American-born children actually have higher incomes than native-born whites, something that is also true for other immigrant groups.[53] Several factors encourage the economic mobility of West Indian blacks. From their early twentieth-century migrations on, British West Indian immigrants, a large proportion of whom have come from cities, have tended to be relatively skilled and educated. In addition to bringing with them communal institutions such as credit associations, they have carried forward strict educational standards learned under British rule. Like most immigrants, West Indians are a highly self-selected, ambitious, energetic, and healthy group. The resentment they meet because of their economic success led Afro-Americans to call them "Jew-maicans," as well as "monkey chasers" and "coconut climbers." As former NAACP head Walter White put it, "We have in Harlem . . . this strange mixture of reactions not only to prejudice from without but to equally potent prejudices from within."[54] Such negative feelings may account in part for the lack of interest by national black leaders in promoting immigration from the islands.[55] Perhaps the main reason that no national black leader spoke to the Select Commission as an advocate for West Indian immigration is that most of their constituents see such immigration as a take-away game in which they are the losers. That West Indian migrants generate jobs and provide leadership probably is obscured by the envy and resentment of many native-American blacks because of the newcomers' relatively rapid progress. Interestingly enough, West Indian groups themselves did not participate at the open-microphone hearing in New York City or otherwise present their views with respect to legalization of illegal aliens or other issues of immigration reform, even though it was estimated as early as 1975 that 250,000 Barbadians and 220,000 Jamaicans lived in the New York area.[56]

The Select Commission did hear from the West Indian Federation Government, particularly through the discreet importunings of Ambassador Harold Edwards, who represented the British West Indies in protecting the interest of West Indian migrants in the U.S. temporary-worker (H-2 visas) program. Although the program was small, about 30,000 in all, 95 percent of the nonimmigrants admitted for agricultural work (10,000 to 12,000 per year) were British West Indians, imported annually to help harvest the eastern apple crop and Florida's sugarcane, to work in the lumber industry, and to herd sheep in the West.

Summary: Four Perspectives

For eighty years after the Civil War, one major perspective shaped the opinions of black leaders and, it seems from the Afro-American press, of black public opinion, too: immigrants displaced black workers and made it difficult for blacks to rise from poverty.[57] That perspective has persisted and been enlarged by the concern about immigrants' displacing blacks from housing, health, and other services, as expressed in articles by blacks in newspaper accounts.[58] But this negative perspective now competes with three others that promote much more sympathetic views on immigration.

Within the past twenty years, many black Americans have become conscious of their special role in holding U.S. public policy to a high level of concern for the rights and needs of all human beings. The human rights perspective, so eloquently espoused by Martin Luther King, Jr., applies to persons seeking asylum, refugees, and, in the opinion of some, to immigrants. King's legacy was bequeathed to many of the black leaders who followed him, including Patricia Roberts Harris, the sole black member of the Select Commission, who never spoke on the Haitian issue or on the immigration of blacks specifically, but who, on the general question of immigration, clearly revealed her view that the United States should give opportunity to the poor from other countries, even though she must have known the strong views of many blacks that Asian and Hispanic immigrants take jobs from black Americans. At one of the meetings of the commission, she called for a generous immigration policy for those "who want new opportunity." She spoke about people who came to the United States as ditch-diggers and whose children became doctors. "That's the kind of opportunity I want to keep open," she said.[59] Even when, as noted earlier, Congresswoman Collins expressed her concern about job displacement, she said that the loyalty of Americans must be "to mankind as a whole." Though Benjamin Hooks was aware of his board's concern about competition between blacks and immigrants for jobs and services, he spoke of the human aspirations and rights of the refugees.

The humanistic perspective probably helps lead to the positive response of many black civil rights leaders and black churches to the Haitian asylum claimants, and so does a black immigrant perspective. There is ample self-interest to encourage black leaders to take a positive view toward black immigrants, who represent potential constituents. Whether they become constituents who identify with a broad black political agenda depends not only on the response of black leaders to their needs but also on the extent to which whites identify immigrant blacks as black Americans regardless of nationality. The extent to which black Dominicans, Haitians, Jamaicans, Nigerians, Ethiopians, and others will identify with native-born blacks whose ancestral identities are not known is unclear, but the image projected onto them as blacks by whites is likely to promote a merging of identities over time, as it has for other immigrant groups. Ilocanos, Visayans, and Tagalogs were all Filipinos to most native-born Californians. The Chinese, whether Punti or Hakka, were Chinese to the whites of the West. Immigrants from Calabria, Abruzzi, and Sicily were Italians to the Irish and Yankees, no matter how different they thought they were from one another.

Whether the grandchildren of black immigrants and refugees from Africa and the Caribbean will align themselves with blacks as a group will depend on many other factors, including patterns of settlement, language differences, and the similarity of educational levels and skill backgrounds between newcomers and natives. It will also depend on the extent to which immigrant ethnic communities retain strong ties to their home countries, something that is likely to vary according to other considerations, including the volume of continued migration from those countries and rates of emigration back to them. However slowly or quickly native-born black Americans develop an interest in continued black immigration, the increased flow of black immigrants to the United States will become more important in shaping the opinions of blacks on immigration issues.

Finally, and probably most important, there is the perception that despite differences at the local level on many issues, including redistricting, school desegregation, and bilingualism, blacks and Mexican-Americans share a large political agenda, which obliges blacks to adopt a coalition perspective that leads them to become more sympathetic to immigration. The congressional debates on immigration reform during the first six years of the 1980s saw black leaders using the immigration issue mainly to build a coalition with Mexican-American leaders, in the hope that their strong support on employer sanctions and legalization might translate into significant trade-offs of benefit to blacks on other issues. It is not clear what political gains have been achieved, but the commitment to forging an alliance with Mexican-American leaders was unshakable up to the vote on immigration reform in 1986, and probably was not reduced by that vote.

The combination of perspectives, including the fear that immigration is harmful to black workers, was reflected in the ambivalent views blacks expressed regarding immigration in a poll taken in June 1986 by the *New York Times* and the Columbia Broadcasting System. The survey did not distinguish between lawful and illegal immigration when asking respondents if they thought immigration should be increased, kept at current levels, or decreased. Nevertheless, most blacks said they thought immigration should be either kept at the current level (41 percent) or increased (11 percent), compared to only 39 percent who thought that immigration should be decreased.[60] What is surprising is that the relatively favorable black response to immigration came at a time of increased press accounts of illegal border crossings and tension between blacks and Asians or Hispanics in many cities. Even more significant, opinion on immigration became less favorable as one moved down the family income ladder. In all families making less than $12,600, and among those respondents with less than a high school education, solid majorities favored a decrease in immigration levels. Despite the historic resentment of such black leaders as Douglas and Washington toward immigration and immigrants; despite tensions in many communities between native-born black Americans and immigrants; despite the widespread perception among blacks that immigrants take old jobs away and make it difficult to get new ones; and finally, despite the fact that sympathy toward immigration among whites and blacks tends to rise with education and family income, and even though 59 percent of black respondents believed (incorrectly) that "most recent arrivals are here illegally," blacks were more sympathetic to immigration and immigrants than were whites. According to the *New York Times*/CBS poll, 44 percent of the blacks believed that immigrants "take jobs from Americans," and 48 percent believed that "most new immigrants end up on welfare" (only 34 percent of the whites believed that immigrants take jobs away from Americans and 47 percent believed that most end up on welfare). Yet, 38 percent of blacks surveyed believed that "most recent immigrants contribute to the U.S.," compared to 32 percent of the whites; and 77 percent of the blacks said that "new immigrants would be welcomed in their neighborhoods," compared to 67 percent of the whites.[61]

This dramatic shift in black public opinion, following a radical change in the views of black leaders on immigration from the negativism of Douglass and Washington to the positive views of the Congressional Black Caucus in the 1980s, is not likely to be permanent. With a downturn in the economy, public opinion among blacks could and probably would turn against immigrants. But the shift probably reflects the same underlying and substantial changing perspectives that came to black leaders earlier. The older feelings of displacement and competition still exist, but the views of blacks on immigration probably were more favorable in the late 1980s than at any time since emancipation. The founding myth of the United States as an asylum open to all who seek freedom and opportunity remains a cruel lie for millions of blacks, but immigrants are not seen by blacks so directly as an enemy of freedom and opportunity as they once were.

NOTES

1. Frederick A. Douglass, West Indian Emancipation Speech of August 18, 1853, "What to the Slave Is the Fourth of July?" in *Black on Black*, ed. Arnold Adolph (New York: Macmillan, 1968), p. 2.

2. Edmund S. Morgan, *American Slavery, American Freedom* (New York: Norton, 1975).

3. For the best analysis of data that compare blacks with white immigrants for this time period, see Stanley Lieberson, *A Piece of the Pie: Blacks and White Immigrants since 1880* (Berkeley: University of California Press, 1980). The complexity of black-white relations in the South is told by Joel Williamson, *The Crucible of Race: Black-White Relations in the American South since Emancipation* (New York: Oxford University Press, 1986). Blacks were not in a strictly caste position, as were the Untouchables of India, but compared to the situation of white immigrants, their choices in employment and in other respects were sharply limited. For other analytical comparisons, see John Bodnar, "Impact of the 'New Immigration' on the Black Worker: Steelton, Pennsylvania, 1880–1920," *Labor History* 17 (1976): 214–29: Also see John J. Appell, "American Negro and Immigrant Experience: Similarities and Differences," *American Quarterly* 18 (1966): 95–103; Niles Carpenter, *Nationality, Color and Economic Opportunity in the City of Buffalo* (Buffalo: University of Buffalo Press, 1927).

4. Quoted in Adrian Cook, *The Armies of the Streets: The New York City Draft Riots of 1863* (Lexington: University Press of Kentucky, 1974), p. 205.

5. Herbert Hill, "Race, Ethnicity and Organized Labor: The Opposition to Affirmative Action," *New Politics* (1987): 50.

6. Ibid., pp. 50, 51.

7. *Selected Speeches of Booker T. Washington*, ed. E. Davidson (Garden City, N.Y.: Doubleday, 1932), p. 38.

8. Ibid., p. 38.

9. Arnold Shankman, *Ambivalent Friends: Afro-Americans View the Immigrant* (Westport, Conn.: Greenwood Press, 1982), p. 156.

10. Ibid., p. 50.

11. Ibid., p. 16.

12. Ibid., p. 72.

13. Ibid., p. 74.

14. Ibid., p. 73.

15. Ibid., p. 151.

16. Barbara M. Posadas, "The Hierarchy of Color and Psychological Adjustment in an Industrial Environment: Filipinos, the Pullman Company, and the Brotherhood of Sleeping Car Porters," *Labor History* 23 (1982): 350–55.

17. James W. Loewn, *The Mississippi Chinese: Between Black and White* (Cambridge: Harvard University Press, 1971). Also see a more recent study of 1,400 Chinese in the northwest corner of Mississippi: Robert Seto Quan, in collaboration with Julian B. Roebuck, *Lotus among the Magnolias: The Mississippi Chinese* (Jackson: University Press of Mississippi, 1982).

18. Conversation between Monsignor Bryan Walsh, director of Catholic Community Services, Dade County, and the author, January 1985. King and Monsignor Walsh had several conversations on the subject.

19. Author's files.

20. Conversation with author, author's files.

21. Testimony of Cardiss R. Collins before the Select Commission on Immigration and Refugee Policy (hereafter cited as Select Commission), public hearing, Los Angeles, February 5, 1980, author's files, original transcripts. The author served as executive director of the staff of the Select Commission.

22. Testimony of Representative Mickey Leland (D-Texas) before the Select Commission, public hearing, San Francisco, June 9, 1980, author's files, original transcript.

23. Testimony of Wendall Green, vice chairman, committee for Representative Government, before the Select Commission, public hearing, Los Angeles, February 5, 1980, author's files, original transcript.

24. Testimony of Reuben Vaughn Green III (no relation to Wendall Green) before the Select Commission, public hearing, Los Angeles, February 5, 1980, author's files, original transcript.

25. Testimony of Marguerite Bryan before the Select Commission, public hearing, New Orleans, March 24, 1980, author's files, original transcript.

26. Testimony of James Hayes and Wade Ragas before the Select Commission, public hearing, New Orleans, March 24, 1980, author's files, original transcript.

27. Testimony of Lawrence Aylesworth before the Select Commission, public hearing, Denver, February 25, 1980, author's files, original transcript.

28. Testimony of the Reverend Gerard Jean-Juste, before the Select Commission, public hearing, Miami, December 4, 1980, author's files, original transcript.

29. Testimony of William R. Perry before the Select Commission, public hearing, Miami, December 4, 1980, author's files, original transcript. Actually, 20 to 40 percent of the Cuban Marielitos were black or mulatto. See Herberto Dixon, "Black Cubans in the United States," *Unveiling* (1984): 20–24.
Boatloads of Jewish refugees were turned back in the late 1930s, and in 1939 Congress actually refused to admit 20,000 refugee orphans because the quota for Germany was full. In 1981 and 1982 Salvadoran refugees were detained regularly and not awarded asylum.

30. Testimony of Marsha Sonders before the Select Commission, public hearing, Miami, December 4, 1980, author's files, original transcript. Policy toward the Haitians is complicated by factors that do not have to do with race. One is the close proximity of Haiti to the Florida coast. The U.S. government under Presidents Jimmy Carter and Ronald Reagan did not want the claim of asylum to create a side door for large-scale economic-opportunity migration from Haiti.

31. Jacquelyne J. Jackson, "Illegal Aliens: Big Threat to Black Workers," *Ebony*, April 1979, p. 33.

32. Testimony of Reuben Vaughn Green III, Select Commission, public hearing, Los Angeles.

33. Letter from Joyce Reitter, Oakland, California, author's files.

34. Testimony of Evillo Grillo before the Select Commission, public hearing, San Francisco, June 9, 1980, author's files, original transcript.

35. Testimony of Congressman Leland, Select Commission, public hearing, San Francisco. Leland was successful in coalition building in his district, but there are many difficulties in forming coalitions between blacks and Hispanic groups. See Albert Camarillo, "Blacks and Chicanos in Urban America: Some Comparative Perspectives" (Paper presented to the Fourth Annual Irvine Seminar on Social History and Theory,

University of California at Irvine, (March 28, 1981); National Council of La Raza, "Perspectives on Undocumented Workers: Black and Hispanic Viewpoints" (Washington, D.C., 1980).

36. Testimony of Congresswoman Collins, Select Commission, public hearing, Los Angeles.

37. There have been three major national polls of black opinion on immigration issues. The first, a nationwide survey for the Federation for American Immigration Reform by Peter D. Hart Research Associates, was conducted in June–July 1983. The second was the Gallup poll for November 1984. The third was a public opinion poll conducted by the *New York Times* and CBS in June of 1986. In subsequent footnotes these will be referred to as the Hart survey, the Gallup poll, and the *New York Times* survey. In each of these surveys, a majority of blacks was surprisingly sympathetic to the general idea of amnesty, although not as much as Hispanics. For example, in June of 1986 the *New York Times* survey showed that 65 percent of the black respondents, compared to 55 percent of the white and 79 percent of the Hispanic respondents, said that "illegal aliens who have lived here several years without breaking laws should not be deported" (*New York Times*, July 1, 1986, p. A21).

38. *U.S. Immigration Policy and the National Interest, Appendix H to the Staff Report,* Select Commission on Immigration and Refugee Policy, Public Information Supplement. (Washington, D.C.: April, 1981), p. 601.

39. The Hart survey. By a margin of 60 percent to 33 percent, Hispanics supported adopting legal sanctions against employers who hire illegal immigrants. Blacks favored penalizing employers who hire illegal immigrants by 66 percent to 27 percent, with 56 percent strongly supporting employer sanctions.

40. *New York Times* survey (*New York Times*, July 1, 1986, p. A21). Whereas only 34 percent of the Hispanics polled in the June 1986 national survey said that "government should penalize employers for hiring illegal aliens," 59 percent of the blacks and 73 percent of the whites agreed with that position.

41. *Wall Street Journal*, May 5, 1982, sec. 2, p. 1.

42. William Raspberry, *Washington Post*, September 16, 1983, p. A12.

43. Gallup poll, November 1984, Report No. 218. Seventy-seven percent of the black respondents said they thought it should be against the law to hire a person who has come to the United States without proper papers, compared to 62 percent of the Hispanic respondents.

44. *New York Times*, July 2, 1984, p. A13.

45. *Congressional Record*, 98th Cong. 2d sess., vol. 130, no. 80, June 13, 1984, p. 5714.

46. Ibid., June 11, 1984, p. 5558.

47. Ibid., p. 6076.

48. Ibid.

49. Of the ten black members of the House who voted for the bill, only two represented districts with substantial numbers of Hispanic voters: Julian C. Dixon (D-California), with 19 percent in 1980, and Cardiss Collins (D-Illinois), with 28 percent. Most of them came from districts with 1 percent or less Hispanic voters. In contrast, most of the black members who voted against the bill had substantial numbers of Hispanic voters in their districts, four of them with 23 percent or more. The final vote saw an even split in the Congressional Black Caucus among the twenty voting members. For the percentage of Hispanic and black populations in each district, "Rating Congress on Black and Hispanic Issues," *Congressional Ledger*, (Washington, D.C.: Congressional Education Associates, 1983).

50. Reed Ueda, "West Indians," in *The Harvard Encyclopedia of Ethnic Groups*, ed. Stephen Thernstrom (Cambridge: Harvard University Press, 1980), p. 1026. Ueda provides a brief summary of West Indian migration and an excellent bibliography on the subject. Particularly helpful is the classic book of Ira D. Reid, *The Negro Immigrant: His Background, Characteristics and Social Adjustment, 1899-1937* (New York: AMS Press, 1970). Also helpful is Gilbert Osofsky, *Harlem: The Making of a Ghetto*, 2nd ed. (New York: Harper & Row, 1971). To bring the story up to date, see Nancy Foner, ed., *New Immigrants in New York* (New York: Columbia University Press, 1987).

51. Ueda, "West Indians," p. 1020.

52. U.S. Department of Justice, *The 1983 Statistical Yearbook of the Immigration and Naturalization Service* (Washington, D.C.: Government Printing Office, 1985), p. 8. By 1983 immigration from the Dominican Republic was 22,058, and from Jamaica, 19,535. The McCarran-Walter Act of 1952 had been racially motivated in barring all inhabitants of British colonial possessions from entering under the large quotas of the mother country. A quota of only 800 was given for British possessions in the West Indies. But with the passage of liberalizing amendments in 1965, visa quotas were abolished for the islands that become independent. After 1976 all new countries and those soon to become independent were given an annual upper limit of 20,000 along with every other nation in the world.

53. For data comparing the mobility of West Indian blacks and native-born blacks, see Thomas Sowell, *Ethnic America: A History* (New York: Basic Books, 1981), pp. 216-220. Also see Ivan H. Light, *Ethnic Enterprise in America* (Berkeley: University of California Press, 1972). See Sowell's earlier *Race and Economics* (New York: Basic Books, 1975), which provides more detail than *Ethnic America*. Also useful is Virginia Dominguez, *From Neighbor to Stranger: The Dilemmas of Caribbean Peoples in the United States* (New Haven: Yale University Press, 1975).

54. Ueda, "West Indies," p. 1025.

55. The pioneering work on West Indian migration is Ira D. Reid, *The Negro Immigrant, His Background, Characteristics and Social Adjustment, 1899-1937* (New York: Arno Press, 1969; reprint of the 1939 edition).

Although many West Indians are sojourners who do not identify with native-born black Americans, they have played a disproportionate role in the cultural and intellectual leadership of blacks in the United States, stemming in part perhaps from the gap between the attainments, ambitions, and self-confidence of the immigrants and those of native-born blacks in northern cities, who by the 1920s increasingly were made up of recently transplanted rural southerners with low education and occupational skills.

Cultural and intellectual leaders from the West Indies include James Weldon Johnson, Claude McKay, Kenneth B. Clark, Nobel Prize winner W. Arthur Lewis, Arthur Schomburg, Sidney Poitier, and Harry Belafonte. Johnson, who also was a leader of the NAACP, was a major architect of the black renaissance in Harlem in the 1920s. Claude McKay was regarded by many as the leading poet of the Harlem renaissance and also one of the most vigorous critics of American racism. Even more remarkable has been the political leadership given to blacks by West Indian immigrants. Marcus Garvey, the Pan-African leader of the 1920s, was a Jamaican, and Malcolm X's mother came from Grenada. Their hostility to integrationist politics, copied by West Indian-born Stokeley Carmichael, contrasts sharply with the leadership of native-born Americans such as Martin Luther King, Jr., and, in times past, Frederick Douglass and Booker T. Washington. Other West Indian immigrants, including James Farmer and Shirley Chisholm, while ardent in their defense of the rights of black Americans, have taken the path of integrationist politics.

56. The estimates for Barbadians and Jamaicans are reported in Nancy Foner, "West Indians in New York City and London: A Comparative Analysis," *International Migration Review* 13 (1979): 289.

57. In addition to Shankman and the citations from Douglass and Washington, see W. E. Burghardt DuBois, *The Philadelphia Negro: A Social Study* (New York: Schocken Books, 1967); and Sterling D. Spero and Abram L. Harris, *The Black Worker* (New York: Columbia University Press, 1931).

58. In addition to the already-cited articles by Jacquelyne J. Jackson and William Raspberry, see the following by William Raspberry: "Our Own Wretched Refuse," *Washington Post*, July 4, 1979; "Their Tired, Their Poor—Our Jobs," *Washington Post*, July 4, 1980; "Cutting Off Jobs Is the Only Way to Cut Off Illegal Immigration," *Washington Post*, September 9, 1980; "Our Huddled Masses," *Washington Post*, April 8, 1981; "Are Blacks Better Off?" *Washington Post*, December 15, 1982; "Immigration Reform: Do Something," *Staten Island Advance*, June 21, 1985; and "Honest Talk about Illegal Aliens," *Washington Post* February 24, 1986. Also see Carl T. Rowan, "What to Do about the Flood of Illegal Aliens?" *Washington Star*, August 29, 1976; June Brown, "It's Time We Curtailed Immigration," *Detroit News*, August 3, 1980; Dorothy Gilliam, "Exploited," *Washington Post*, January 23, 1982. Black journalists and columnists, in the tradition of an earlier Afro-American press, spoke out much more openly from a jobs-displacement and services-competition perspective than black civil rights leaders and national political figures. The press frequently reported stories of conflict between blacks and newly arrived aliens with respect to jobs. See Patrick Oster, "Refugees Get Jobs—Blacks Get Angry," *Chicago Sun-Times*, September 24, 1979, p. 4; Michael Hirsley, "Hispanics Overwhelm Blacks in Miami Jobs Fight," *Chicago Tribune*, January 18, 1983, p. 4.

59. Select Commission on Immigration and Refugee Policy, *U.S. Immigration Policy and the National Interest, Appendix H to the Staff Report*, "Public Information Supplement" (Washington, D.C., April 1981), p. 630.

60. *New York Times*/CBS survey, *New York Times*, July 1, 1986, p. A21.

61. Ibid.

11

Reforming the Back Door: The Immigration Reform and Control Act of 1986 in Historical Perspective

Aristide R. Zolberg

Immigration into the United States today consists of three distinct flows, each shaped by its own transnational dynamics and governed by unique institutional arrangements in the receiving country. Participants in two of the flows — relatives of U.S. citizens or permanent residents, and those who qualify as refugees — are welcomed through the main gate of the United States. Those in the third flow, however — mainly poor people from adjoining countries who come in search of work and in response to the call of U.S. employers — pass surreptitiously through a "back door." This threefold division of immigrants and their passage through two very different doors are recent innovations, which arose as unplanned consequences of changes in immigration policy that would favor or hinder some entering groups over others. From this perspective, the Immigration Reform and Control Act of 1986 is the culmination of a reform process that began after World War II, and represents the most recent in a series of political settlements that have attempted long-term solutions to the perennial tensions and problems of immigration.

The significance of these developments can be better understood by considering them in the context of the goals of the reform efforts.[1] In the wake of World War I, the United States passed the most sweeping change in the history of its immigration laws and regulations. New measures drastically reduced the number of immigrants and favored certain ethnic groups over others. The motivation behind these laws was a desire by the guardians of the established social and cultural order to reduce the heterogeneity of the population and reinforce the values that were seen as the traditional bulwark of American society. This xenophobic movement, bearing the air of a crusade, paralleled the one that concurrently imposed its moralism on the country at large by way of Prohibition. Quite independently, organized labor also sought to reduce immi-

315

gration so as to minimize perceived unfair competition by newly arrived workers used to a lower standard of living and with a more docile attitude toward authority. Seeking to keep the door open were industrial capitalists, who had long relied on immigration to provide cheap unskilled labor, and the recent immigrants themselves — including institutions associated with them, such as the Catholic church and Jewish philanthropies — for whom it would become more difficult to bring over relatives, and who correctly perceived the measures as part of a concerted effort to erect obstacles to their social mobility and political influence.

Conflict over immigration creates "odd couples" whose pairings cut across the usual ideological alignments of left and right. This is because immigration evokes two very different sets of concerns: one pertaining to national identity and the composition of the political community, the other having to do with economic considerations, mostly the effects on the labor market. Some who favor immigration on the first grounds may oppose it on the second, and vice versa, yet the two sets of considerations are indissociable because as human beings immigrants are both economic and political actors.[2]

The best-known features of the new policy, completed in 1924, pertain to immigration from Europe, which amounted at the time to approximately one million arrivals a year, most of them from economically less developed countries and those in the throes of political upheavals, then, as now, often overlapping categories. This was reduced to a maximum of 150,000, with numbers allocated according to national origins so as to minimize the "new immigration" from eastern and southern Europe; within these categories, preference went to immediate relatives. These provisions extinguished European immigration as a source of disposable industrial labor, and narrowed it into a process of family reunion. However, for eastern and southern Europeans, because the number of available entries was small in relation to demand, this usually entailed a wait of many years, so that the family members might die before reunion ever took place. In light of subsequent developments, it is noteworthy that the law provided no priority to refugees, victims of persecution or of violence, for whom the immediate availability of a haven might constitute a matter of life or death. The only concession was to exempt them from the literacy test imposed on all immigrants in 1917.

The system institutionalized in the 1920s also encompassed what we would today call the Third World; but whereas Asian immigration was prohibited altogether, immigration from the independent countries of the Western Hemisphere — Canada, Latin America (including Cuba), and Haiti — was subject to "qualitative" restrictions only, with no limit on annual numbers.[3] Despite their opposite character, both stances rested on the same principle, whose elucidation provides a key to understanding the dynamics of the "back door" in U.S. history.

The first Asians to come to North America in modern times were Chinese, drawn to California, like many others, as aspiring gold miners in the 1850s. Soon excluded from this activity by their white competitors, many Chinese in the mining camps fell back on performing services such as laundry and cooking that were usually provided by wives or servants. A decade later great numbers of Chinese workers were imported for railroad construction throughout the West Coast region; most were indentured by Chinese labor contractors, but with the collusion of U.S. employers and public officials.[4] In the eyes of employers, such bondage was a necessary feature of labor importation because the chronic labor shortage in new territories gave workers many alternatives, and only through coercion could employers recoup the very high costs of transporting their labor and keeping the labor force intact. It should be noted as well that under prevailing U.S. law, the Chinese were ineligible for naturalization and hence membership in the national community.[5] Although this provision of naturalization law was designed originally to exclude blacks and native Americans, the courts held that it applied to Asians as well, a view that reflected widespread beliefs that their racial characteristics put them beyond the limits of assimilation.

Status as bound labor and ineligibility for citizenship were mutually reinforcing features that distinguished people thus categorized from immigrants properly speaking. The U.S. Constitution distinguishes between "migration" and "importation," in a section discussing the abolition of the slave trade (mandated to end in 1808). It stands to reason that slaves were not thought of as migrating in the normal sense but, rather, of being imported, like "goods," including chattels. Although the slave trade and later slavery itself were abolished, the broader category of importation persisted, and the people who fell within it continued to be considered as not quite "persons" but *labor*, brought in for a specific economic purpose and easily disposed of when no longer needed — much like contemporary "guest workers." The very characteristics that made them desirable as *workers* made them undesirable as *members* of the receiving society. These institutional arrangements created a "back door" through which American employers imported successive groups of temporary workers after the slave trade and slavery were abolished, including in the later decades of the nineteenth century not only Asians but also European "birds of passage" from the southern and eastern parts of the continent.[6]

Once the transcontinental railroad was completed in 1869, California opened up to white laborers, who as citizens of a populist frontier democracy were in a position to exclude their Chinese competitors. At the same time, the railroad made it possible for eastern employers to bring Chinese from the West as substitutes for their own unruly workers, propelling Chinese exclusion to the forefront of the concerns of organized labor. Concurrently, there was increased concern with the "yellow peril"; in addition to the understandable objections of organized labor, the general public saw the Chinese as a source of drugs, disease, and immorality — the more dangerous because they came from a populous land perennially subject to famine. By the early 1880s, when anti-Chinese sentiment had reached the national level, the first law was enacted barring "Chinese coolies" (for a ten-year period).

This was precisely the time when California — after the exhaustion of its mines — was discovering its vocation as an agricultural wonderland. As of 1886, when exclusion went into effect, the Chinese constituted approximately four-fifths of the state's farm labor; afterward, many more were brought in illegally. In the 1890s the growers steadfastly opposed exclusion, but when it proved impossible to secure additional Chinese, they turned to Japan and the Philippines. As Mary Coolidge observed in 1909, "The history of general labor in California since about 1886 is the story of efforts to find substitutes for the vanishing Chinese."[7] By the turn of the century, however, the definitive substitute was found: "While the immigration service makes desperate efforts to catch a few Chinamen crossing over without certificates, the pauper Mexican Cholos, by the hundreds, freely come and go under contracts of labor. . . . "[8] The cotton farmers of Texas also resorted increasingly to Mexican contract labor as an alternative to emancipated blacks from the southeastern states.

The flow of Mexicans vastly increased in the second decade of the twentieth century, due as much to the revolutionary upheavals in Mexico as to increasing demand in the United States, particularly during World War I when the supply of workers from Europe ground to a halt. Although organized labor secured as early as 1885 the enactment of a law prohibiting the importation of contract labor, wartime legislation lifted this prohibition for agricultural and railroad workers from neighboring countries, that is, Mexico and some of the Caribbean islands; and these workers were also excused from the literacy requirement, imposed in 1917 to reduce immigration from the less-developed countries of Europe.

From the perspective of the guardians of the traditional cultural order, Mexicans or Caribbean blacks were even more undesirable than Greeks or Russian Jews. In the 1920s, however, agricultural employers insisted they could not survive without them, and that in any case these were "migrants" rather than "immigrants," who usually returned whence they came once discharged, and if not, could easily be rounded up and shoved out. In their opposition to quantitative restriction on immigration from the Western Hemisphere, employers had the support of the State Department, which fought it on grounds of diplomacy, but this was hardly decisive, for the State Department lost the battle to prevent the exclusion of Japanese along with the Chinese and other Orientals. What mattered most was that given the structure of congressional representation and power at the time, agricultural interests fared better than industrial interests. Although qualitative controls included a prohibition on contract labor, a literacy requirement, and the obligation to demonstrate financial viability, which if enforced would operate as a quantitative restriction on the flow of Mexican peasants, immigration authorities had neither the organizational capacity nor the inclination to enforce these requirements in the Southwest.

It was obvious from the beginning that along the southern border, in sharp departure from the trend toward greater state control over immigration, laissez-faire would be allowed to prevail. In this manner, the system of the 1920s institutionalized the "back door" as a major feature of U.S. immigration policy. Unlike African blacks or Chinese, the workers involved were neither bound nor categorically ruled out of citizenship, but like their predecessors they were confined to a prescribed economic role and excluded from membership in the national society by virtue of their status as *illegal aliens*.

With the onset of the depression and in the face of new pressures to reduce immigration, administrative regulations were tightened up to minimize the flow from Europe; at the same time, Mexican agricultural workers were brutally dumped back over the border. As the dark shadow of authoritarianism spread over Europe, members of groups targeted for persecution turned to the United States and other liberal democracies for havens, but the gates were barely widened because the restrictionists remained adamant and even sympathizers hesitated to challenge them for fear of jeopardizing their own still precarious position within American society.[9]

In contrast with this, however, as soon as the war began to stimulate economic demand and because the draft and the attraction of higher wages in industry created a shortage of agricultural labor, the United States initiated a far-reaching program of labor importation from Mexico. Because organized labor was part of the New Deal coalition, this took the form of government-supervised contracts for temporary workers in agriculture and the railroads, generally known as the *bracero* program.[10] Discontinued after the war, the program was revived with relatively minor modifications at the outbreak of the Korean War (1950) and extended throughout the Eisenhower years. Still, because the *bracero* program imposed some controls on labor conditions, agricultural producers resorted all along to private recruitment in the traditional vein as well. Attempts by organized labor in the early 1950s to press for legislation prohibiting the employment of illegal aliens got nowhere. The informal system persisted, and whenever demand flagged, surplus workers were once again brutally expelled. Over 1.3 million were thus dumped across the Mexican border at the end of the Korean War in "Operation Wetback" (1954–1955), the most comprehensive deportation campaign in U.S. history.

At the end of World War II, pressures began to build up to reform general immigration by eliminating its discriminatory features and providing for refugees. Revelation of the horrors of the Holocaust placed advocates of a more generous refugee policy in a better bargaining position, but the decisive factor was the incipient cold war, which prompted U.S. policymakers to relieve Western Europe of the heavy burden of displaced persons, and to provide a haven for those fleeing the prospect of Communist rule in eastern Europe, or defecting from established Communist regimes. Initially implemented through a series of ad hoc executive and legislative measures, the differentiation of "refugees" from ordinary immigrants was more formally institutionalized in 1965, when 6 percent of annual entries from outside the Western Hemisphere were set aside for this purpose, and further in 1980, when the process of admitting refugees was separated from the remainder of the immigration system altogether. Although U.S. refugee policy remains highly problematic, what matters for present purposes is that the separation of the refugee flow from general immigration appears to have become firmly institutionalized.[11]

In the sphere of general immigration, the impulse for reform originated around 1950 among the "new immigrants" discriminated against by the national-origins quota system. By the 1950s they wielded considerable political weight in urban constituencies, particularly in the Northeast, and constituted an important component of the New Deal coalition within the Democratic party. They were concerned almost exclusively with family reunion, an objective that could be achieved by eliminating the quota system and attributing the highest priority to close relatives. Such an approach enabled the reformers to secure the support of their labor allies within the Democratic camp for an increase in annual entries as well. The legislative history of various proposals indicates that in keeping with the preferences of organized labor, the reformers were also planning to include immigration from the Western Hemisphere within the annual total, and thus move it from the "back door" to the "main gate." These plans became moot when reformers suffered a setback with the election of a Republican Congress in 1950, and were soundly defeated by the restrictionists, who reaffirmed the 1920s system in 1952 with but minor modifications. Nevertheless, the reformers chipped away at the status quo throughout the Eisenhower era, with some cooperation from the administration itself, and with the return of the Democrats to the White House in January 1961, the day of reform finally dawned.

Persuaded that labor importation worsened the plight of migrant agricultural workers, liberals in Congress decided to terminate the *bracero* program altogether. The Eisenhower administration, in its final year had agreed to only a six-month extension to December 31, 1961. Immediately faced with a concerted effort by agricultural interests to obtain yet another extension, the incoming Kennedy administration agreed to two more years, but exacted as its price a substantial reinforcement of the secretary of labor's statutory authority to regulate conditions in the fields. A final one-year extension extended the program until the end of 1964.

In the intervening period, Kennedy's political position improved somewhat with the election of the 88th Congress in the fall of 1962. The president announced the following January that his administration was planning to offer a recommendation on immigration and naturalization. Enacted in 1965 but scheduled to become effective in 1968, the "Kennedy-Johnson amendment" to the McCarran-Walter law of 1952 eliminated both the prohibition of Asian immigration and the quota system. It established an annual quota of 170,000 for areas outside the Western Hemisphere (Europe, Asia, and Africa), to be allocated without regard to national origin (but with a maximum of 20,000 per country) according to a system of priorities within which, in effect, the bulk would go to close relatives. In addition, *immediate* relatives were exempted from the annual quota limitation altogether. As noted earlier, the law also constituted a step in the direction of differentiating refugees from general immigration. With respect to immigration as labor procurement, one-fifth of the Europe–Asia–Africa quota was dedicated to immigrants with special skills, but strict positive certification was required to ensure that they would not compete with Americans.[12] Overall, however, the law clearly institutionalized family reunion as the leading principle governing general immigration, as indicated by the nickname it earned in Washington circles — the "Brothers and Sisters Act."

Celebrations over the demise of antiquated restrictionism obscured the fact that the Kennedy-Johnson amendment was itself significantly restrictive. It imposed for the first time in U.S. history a quantitative limit on immigration from the Western Hemisphere, scheduled to go into effect in 1968 unless Congress took action to the contrary. Fixed at 120,000 a year, without a preference system, the cap was somewhat below the level of the current flow. The legislative history indicates that issues pertaining to the Western Hemisphere became increasingly prominent as the proposals moved through Congress. The reformers themselves were divided on the advisability of a numerical ceiling, but even those who preferred continuing to regulate Western Hemisphere immigration through qualitative requirements alone agreed they should include the new, strict labor certification. Both approaches were in keeping with the objective of the postwar reformers to minimize the labor-procurement aspect of immigration; in this regard, the new arrangements regarding the Western Hemisphere should be viewed with the contemporaneous termination of the *bracero* program. The ceiling was included in the law as enacted at the insistence of traditional restrictionists, who sought to deter immigration of blacks from the West Indies and "browns" from south of the border more generally. Senator Everett Dirksen, the powerful Illinois Republican who was then minority leader, later affirmed that Western Hemisphere restriction was the price the administration agreed to pay for his support for elimination of the quota system.[13]

In retrospect, it is obvious that the Western Hemisphere provisions of the law were grossly inadequate for dealing with problems that had already surfaced at the time of enactment and would become much more pressing in the following decades. Some arose from the political upheavals that had already begun to trigger sizable waves of refugees, many of whom turned to the United States as a country of first asylum. Most of the problems were attributable to the conjunction of two powerful economic processes: the continued advantages "back-door" immigration afforded to U.S. employers in agriculture and some other sectors, and the push exerted upon the rapidly growing populations of Mexico, Central America, and the Caribbean by a reduction in agricultural employment without sufficient industrialization to provide enough new jobs. Even as the new law came into effect, the Immigration and Naturalization Service (INS) reported that the number of illegal Mexicans had nearly doubled since President Kennedy's message launching immigration reform five years earlier. Although the number of arrests cannot be taken as a reliable indicator of the overall number of undocumented border crossers, there is little question that with the elimination of the *bracero* program and the restriction of ordinary immigration from the Western Hemisphere, the flow of illegals grew steadily in response to opportunities provided by U.S. employers.

Little occurred in the decade that followed passage of the Kennedy-Johnson measure because the reform coalition that brought it into being had been formed essentially around the issue of European immigration, with respect to which its constituent groups got most of what they wanted. Few people were interested in the problems brewing along the southern border, and those who cared about them found it difficult to attract congressional attention. Attempts to control illegal immigration by penalizing employers repeatedly failed. Congressman Peter Rodino of New Jersey, a liberal Democrat who played an important role in the struggle to eliminate the national origin quotas, twice shepherded employer-sanction bills through the House, only to have them die in the more conservative Senate. In 1976 Congress belatedly extended to the Western Hemisphere the preference system and annual country limit of 20,000 already in effect for the rest of world but also closed a loophole that exempted parents of U.S. citizens or resident aliens under twenty-one from the labor certification requirement.[14] The major consequence was to make things even worse for Mexicans, whose flow in recent years had averaged 60,000.

Meanwhile, a period of economic stagnation in the United States helped increase public concern about the economic and social consequences of the illegal flow, awareness of which was vastly enhanced by a veritable media epidemic, aided and abetted by the INS for its own bureaucratic interests. Much was also said about the divisive potential of proliferating Spanish-speaking urban communities, reputed to assimilate more slowly than previous immigrant waves. On top of this, at the end of the 1970s the United States granted asylum to Vietnamese "boat people," whose numbers vastly exceeded refugee entries provided under the 1965 law. Congress, locked into a stalemate over immigration legislation, in 1979 enacted a law creating a Select Commission on Immigration and Refugee Policy to conduct a comprehensive study and evaluation of existing laws, policies, and procedures. Even as the commissioners carried out their task, reports suggested the number of undocumented newcomers was still expanding, and 125,000 Cubans landed in the United States as the result of the push-out from Mariel harbor. Although the commission, chaired by Notre Dame University's president, Father Theodore Hesburgh, and directed by Professor Lawrence Fuchs of Brandeis University, was scheduled to present legislative recommendations to the Carter administration, by the time its work was completed Ronald Reagan had become the president-elect.[15] In the intervening period Congress enacted the 1980 refugee law referred to earlier. With family reunion immigration now firmly anchored in U.S. practice, the commission's most important recommendations pertained to the perennial problems of the "back door." Despite the change of administration, the formula it suggested for resolving them shaped the path leading to the 1986 act.

The Wondrous Career of Simpson-Mazzoli

The Select Commission on Immigration and Refugee Policy made two recommendations that became the elements of a congressional package deal named after its sponsors, Senator Alan Simpson (R-Wyoming) and Congressman Roman Mazzoli (D-Missouri).[16] Advocates of its enactment referred to their ultimate objective euphemistically as "immigration reform"; the term was also appropriated by the leading restrictionist lobby, the Federation for American Immigration Reform, resulting in the clever acronym, FAIR. The package involved, on the one hand, the imposition of sanctions on employers of illegal aliens, and on the other, the grant of permanent resident status—providing access to citizenship — to illegal aliens who had become de facto permanent residents by entering the United States prior to some specified date. It was an ingenious trade-off between liberals and conservatives across the two dimensions of concerns mentioned. Sanctions appealed to organized labor as well as to restrictionist appalled at the "loss of control of our borders"; legalization — or "amnesty," as it was commonly termed — appealed to Hispanics and to civil rights liberals.

But the package deal left out agricultural employers, particularly on the West Coast, who remained the major users of illegal alien workers. These employers found the status quo preferable, and worked to block enactment of Simpson-Mazzoli. Another difficulty was that although the trade-off made cooperation initially very appealing, its complexity made it likely that one or more of the various interests might cease cooperating and choose to live with the status quo. In particular, Hispanic leaders and civil rights liberals were concerned that sanctions would lead employers to avoid the hiring of Hispanics altogether, which would outweigh any benefits conferred by legalization, and that the identification requirements associated with sanctions would foster an increase in state control over the lives of citizens.

A first version of Simpson-Mazzoli was enacted by the Senate in 1982 but not by the House. In the face of strong opposition from Hispanics and their civil rights allies on the issue of identity requirements, as well as from agricultural interests, the proposals died with the expiration of the 97th Congress. Both Simpson and Mazzoli again sponsored bills in the 98th Congress, each providing a more recent cutoff date for legalization and more federal funds to reimburse the states for the social benefits (health, education, welfare) to which aliens would become entitled once they were legalized. The House version addressed the concerns of agricultural employers by streamlining and liberalizing the existing H-2 program to expand it from the current 40,000 temporary foreign crop-pickers a year to between 300,000 and 500,000. The Senate version, approved in May 1983, granted agricultural employers a three-year transitional exemption from sanctions. Reported out by the House Judiciary Committee, "Mazzoli" was about to reach the floor in early October 1983, when further action was blocked by Speaker of the House Thomas P. O'Neill, who feared it would be used by President Reagan in the forthcoming presidential campaign to trap the Democrats between general pressures to restrict immigration and the contrary concerns of their Hispanic constituents. Although O'Neill later relented and indicated the House would vote on immigration in early 1984, renewed hints of a presidential veto led to further postponements.[17]

While the measure remained bottled up, the House Agriculture Committee approved an amendment sponsored by Congressman Leon Panetta (D-California) that authorized the attorney general to admit foreign crop-pickers on three days' notice. The workers would be allowed to stay up to eleven months and to move from farm to farm but would be confined to a prescribed region; although the measure did not specify numbers, the anticipated level was about 250,000 a year.[18] Behind the proposal was a decision by western growers, in the face of mounting restrictionist pressures that were especially strong in California itself, no longer to fight "immigration reform" but to seek instead accommodation to what they deemed to be their labor needs.[19] In retrospect, it is evident that this marked a turning point in the development of immigration policy, for by providing conditional support in this manner, the growers made an offer that those committed to enactment of the Simpson-Mazzoli package could not refuse.

The growers' campaign was remarkably well orchestrated. In the fall of 1982, Thomas J. Hale, a former president of the Grape and Tree Fruit League, whose three hundred members grow most of California's table grapes, peaches, plums, and pears, began pulling western farm groups dependent on illegal immigrants into the Farm Labor Alliance. Among the early supporters was the Nisei Farmers League, made up of fourteen hundred second-generation Japanese-American farmers, whose president took on the task of raising a war chest by way of a special assessment on every one of the millions of boxes produced by alliance members. Early in 1983 the alliance retained two Washington law firms to deal with each of the two major political parties. On the Republican side, the key adviser was James H. Lake, who had successfully represented California clients on the issue of federal water subsidies. A top aide in three of President Reagan's campaigns, he had close ties with two key Californians in the administration: Edwin Meese — then still in the White House — and Richard E. Lyng, deputy secretary of agriculture. To deal with the Democrats, the alliance retained the firm of former party chairman Robert S. Strauss; the partner in charge was Ruth Harkin, a former Department of Agriculture lawyer and the wife of Senator Tom Harkin (D-Iowa), then a member of the House Agriculture Committee. The National Council of Agricultural Employers, which had secured the concessions already mentioned, hesitated to endorse the alliance's proposal because it thought the westerners were overreaching, but it eventually went along.

As the campaign on behalf of the Panetta amendment got under way in the spring of 1984, the Reagan Administration's various departments responded in keeping with their differing institutional concerns: Agriculture was strongly supportive, Labor strongly opposed, and Justice objected because the program would be difficult to enforce.[20] However, with Meese's help the objectors were moved to a "neutral" — in effect benevolent — stance. Because the Senate had already passed a bill, the alliance concentrated on the House. Given the administration's declared neutrality, the alliance was able to secure the support of the Republican leadership, and thereby of most of the rank and file. On the Democratic side, however, in the face of Speaker O'Neill's hostility, the alliance had to seek out key individuals. Under the guidance of Congressman Tony Coelho, a Californian who was chairman of the Democratic Congressional Campaign Committee, they persuaded Congressman Leon Panetta, from California's Salinas Valley, to champion their cause. Panetta was variously described as a moderate or liberal Democrat with ambitions for a leadership role. As a lobbyist put it to the *New York Times*, "If he put his name on [the guest worker proposal], they knew it could not be a horrible, abusive type of program."[21] to the surprise of the alliance, organized labor failed to mount a serious campaign against the amendment; Hispanic groups opposed it vehemently, but this mattered little because they opposed Simpson-Mazzoli as a whole. Mazzoli himself, whose opposition might have been fatal, objected but not very strongly. The amendment was adopted by a comfortable 228 to 172 vote in June, with the Republicans 138 to 15 in favor, and the Democrats 90 to 157 against. To balance this and assuage the fears of Hispanics, "Mazzoli" was further amended to prohibit employers from discriminating against legal aliens in hiring or recruiting workers (404 to 9, with 150 Republicans in support).[22] The bill finally squeaked by a few days later, on the eve of the Democratic convention, 216 to 211.

In later months the alliance's victory appeared quite hollow. The normal procedure for reconciling differences between the Simpson and Mazzoli bills would be to form a conference committee, which would send its compromise bill back to each chamber for final approval. New developments, however, made it unlikely that the House would go along. Urged on by the Gary Hart and Jesse Jackson camps, Hispanic delegates at the Democratic National Convention threatened a boycott of the first ballot on the immigration issue, which caused the party's presidential nominee, Walter Mondale, to characterize Simpson-Mazzoli as "harmful." Mondale promised to communicate his opposition to the congressional leadership, and negotiations were shortly reported under way with Speaker O'Neill to kill the bill when it emerged from conference.[23] Mondale's running mate, Geraldine Ferraro, had little difficulty with this stance, having already voted against the bill in the House, although for the reason that "the voters back home did not like the idea of giving amnesty to illegal aliens."[24] By the end of July over forty House Democrats who had voted for the bill demanded the Panetta amendment be dropped.[25]

In the face of this, the alternative for Simpson-Mazzoli supporters was to have the Senate pass the House version. But when the Republican leader informed the White House they were considering this approach, they were told the president found the House version unacceptable because it was too expensive, and later the attorney general indicated that it also went too far in protecting the rights of legal aliens and Hispanic workers. Simpson and the Senate therefore had no choice but to risk going into conference with the House.

As the conferees met in early September, prospects for passage of immigration legislation in 1984 appeared very bleak, because the Democrats would be better off avoiding a final showdown altogether. The conferees readily agreed on a compromise on sanctions, dropped provisions in "Simpson" that would reduce the availability of visas for brothers and sisters of citizens — as insisted upon by committee chair Rodino — and split the difference between the 1980 and 1982 cutoff dates, but as adjournment approached, they remained stuck on the issue of protection for the rights of aliens and on guest workers. That stumbling block was removed on September 21 by dropping the Panetta amendment but expanding the H-2 program. Panetta himself found the compromise acceptable, as did Mazzoli, but a spokesman for the National Council of Agricultural Employers indicated that although an improvement over the current arrangement, it fell far short of meeting the needs of Western agriculture. The committee then went on to include the Senate's three-year exemption as well. But in the end, the American Farm Bureau Federation opposed the bill because it did not meet the needs of producers of perishable commodities, and the AFL-CIO opposed it because the concessions to agricultural employers already went too far.[26]

The conferees adjourned on September 26, unable to agree on the issue of protection of aliens' rights and leaving the financial aspects of the bill unresolved as well. The *New York Times* suggested someone was "looking for a molehill big enough to hide behind"—the Democrats to win favor among the Hispanics; the Republicans because the measure would cost too much—and urged the conferees to try one more time to turn the molehill back into a molehill.[27] The conferees did meet again on October 9, and approved (15-8) a compromise on the rights issued drafted by Congressman Schumer (D-Brooklyn), but the matter of federal payments to the states remained as an insurmountable mountain.

The bill's demise evoked widely divergent assessments. Immigration historian Oscar Handlin of Harvard University deplored the loss of "a more liberal measure than any we've had in 90 years." Richard Wade, the City University of New York's distinguished historian of urban America, found the bill in essence "identical with the restrictive legislation of the 1920s."[28] Less extravagantly, Lawrence Fuchs, former executive director of the Select Commission, characterized the conferees' Simpson-Mazzoli "an improvement over earlier versions." The *New York Times*, deploring "the Death of a Humane Idea," laid most of the blame on Hispanic leaders and warned that theirs might be a bitter victory because the new Congress was likely to pass a bill calling for sanctions without amnesty.

The Final Inning

The 99th Congress, elected at the end of 1984, opened on a promising note for advocates of immigration reform when Senator Simpson became assistant majority leader. In April 1985 the senator—who early in the history of "immigration reform" had said, "The American people suffers from compassion fatigue"—unveiled a third revised edition of his bill. While keeping to the package deal, the new "Simpson" significantly changed the balance between its two elements. It limited the amnesty provision by making it contingent upon improved enforcement of the immigration laws, as determined by a presidential commission on the basis of indicators such as a reduction in the number of illegal entries or of overstayers. When the senator formally introduced his bill on May 23, he indicated the legalization program might start "within a year" after the law was passed, but in fact there was no guarantee the requirement would ever be met.[29] Employer sanctions remained, but the burden of verification imposed on the employer was lightened, and the penalties were to be civil rather than criminal. Once again the bill allowed farmers to continue employing illegal aliens for three years after enactment.

The shift was evident to all concerned. The Chamber of Commerce, which had opposed earlier versions and had been denounced by Simpson in 1982 for being selfishly concerned with profitability alone, endorsed the bill as an improvement. The League of United Latin American Citizens and the Mexican-American Legal Defense and Educational Fund said they would oppose the new version even more adamantly than the old. It drew praise from Attorney General Meese and Commissioner of INS Alan Nelson, who welcomed postponement of amnesty, but was criticized by the ACLU as "an unfortunate compilation of some of the worst elements of the original Simpson-Mazzoli bill."[30]

As the senatorial process got under way, the *New York Times* complained in an editorial that "Simpson-Mazzoli" had become "Simpson-Nobody" because the House had not yet begun to act. Pointing out that the new version was close to what was on the conference table at the end of the previous Congress, the editorial also raised the possibility that the curtailment of amnesty was included "to provide bargaining grist."[31] What the editorial failed to point out, however, was that this ploy weighted the process toward the restrictionist camp and put the liberals on notice about what might occur unless they made greater concessions.[32] Meanwhile, the alliance resumed its lobbying blitz on behalf of an extensive program of foreign guestworkers. Complaining that "their greed knows no bounds," Simpson exclaimed in dismay, "I don't what the hell to do with them. I don't know how I can accommodate them. I'll never be right for them; they're the toughest guys to deal with."[33]

On the House side, prospects for enactment were unexpectedly enhanced when Rodino, chairman of the House Judiciary Committee, and fourth in overall seniority within the Democratic majority, announced on July 18 that in the following week he would introduce a bill of his own, jointly with Mazzoli, and would make the issue one of his top legislative concerns. As one of the architects of the 1965 law, Rodino strongly objected to a recommendation by the Select Commission for eliminating the high priority given to married brothers and sisters of U.S. residents, which had been incorporated in the original Simpson-Mazzoli; for this reason, he did not stir when it faced defeat. It is reasonable to surmise, however, that now nearing the end of his long career in Congress, he wished to have his name attached to a piece of legislation. Publicly, he justified his shift as a move designed to preempt more restrictionist measures: "What's going to happen if we don't act, is that a psychology will develop that says, 'Don't let anybody in.'"[34] This was also the tone of the *Times* editorial that welcomed Rodino's commitment.[35] As introduced on July 25, the Rodino-Mazzoli bill was closer to the old package: it included immediate amnesty and did not provide for guest workers.

Simpson, meanwhile, attempted to maintain control over his bill, turning back an amendment proposed by Senator Edward Kennedy (D-Massachusetts) to expand amnesty, as well as attempts to include a guest-worker program. On July 30, however, in order to secure sufficient support for passage in the committee, he accepted a relatively liberal amendment providing for the legalization program to begin not later than three years after enactment, and possibly earlier, and another initiating criminal penalties for repeated employer offenders. The bill also established an expedited procedure for farmers to bring aliens into the United States under the H-2 program, without imposing a numerical limit. The Judiciary Committee then approved a final version, 12 to 4, with ten Republicans and two Democrats supporting it. The opponents were all Democrats, including Kennedy.

When floor debate began in the Senate on September 11, strong support emerged for guest workers along the lines advocated by the alliance. As set forth by its chief proponent, Senator Pete Wilson (R-California), the program would allow annually for 200,000 to 300,000 workers, who would be admitted for a period of nine months and confined within a particular region, with 20 percent of their wages held in a trust fund, to be returned only after they returned home. Although Commissioner Nelson declared the administration did not support the Wilson proposal, it did urge passage of a "self-financed, limited seasonal worker program" for harvesting perishable commodities, and it was reported that President Reagan supported that provision more strongly than any other element of the bill.[36]

Despite the opposition of Simpson as well as of liberal Democrats such as Kennedy, who said the proposed system resembled the pass laws of South Africa, the proposal was endorsed by twenty-eight Republicans and eleven Democrats. Although it was rejected on September 12 by 50 to 48, with thirty-three Republicans and fifteen Democrats in support, five Republicans were persuaded to switch their votes and the Senate reversed itself on September 18, voting 51 to 44 to establish a guest-worker program for perishable crops, with an upper limit of 350,000 workers a year.[37] An attempt was made to render the program more palatable by specifying it would end after thirty-three months unless a law was passed to extend it.[38] The delay for amnesty was reinstated, and the Senate also approved — with administration support and over the objections of both Simpson and Kennedy — a provision requiring states to check the legal status of aliens applying for social benefits.[39] Conservatives and liberals joined to pass another amendment, in this case opposed by the administration, that required federal law-enforcement officers to obtain a warrant before searching open fields for illegal aliens. The amount of federal aid to states was set at $3 billion over a three-year period. Thus amended, the final bill was approved by a vote of 69 to 30 on September 19: forty-one Republicans and twenty-eight Democrats voted for, nineteen Democrats — including all the Senate liberals — and eleven Republicans against.

The Senate's action drastically reduced prospects for enactment of a law because Rodino remained adamantly opposed to guest workers. Although the Immigration Subcommittee approved the bill in November, it delayed a decision on how to treat agricultural interests, and Rodino decided no further action would be taken during the remainder of 1985.[40] Meanwhile, Schumer began searching for a compromise with the help of two fellow Democrats from California, Panetta and Howard Berman, the latter of whom was close to the United Farm Workers and a vociferous critic of the guest-worker program.[41]

As the year of the Statue of Liberty's centennial began, the administration remained ambivalent toward the new bill, unable to resolve the contradiction between the dictates of law and order and those of economic growth as envisaged by free-market advocates. The INS publicized the upsurge of illegal entries occasioned by Mexico's deteriorating economy, and linked the flow to crime, drugs, and later on, to terrorism. Shortly before a meeting between the presidents of Mexico and the United States, Mexican officials reaffirmed their opposition to tighter controls, an act that did not ease political tensions between the two countries. In January the Los Angeles County Board of Supervisors, at the initiative of a member seeking the Republican nomination for the U.S. Senate, enacted a resolution asking the president to dispatch troops to the border. Later in the year the INS commissioner himself hinted the time might come when this would be necessary, a view echoed by Senator Wilson as well.[42] On the even of the Statue's centennial celebrations, there were further reports that the United States was poised to act with new means to stop illegal flows of drugs and people across the southern border, while specialists warned such measures might have a counterproductive effect by undermining Mexico's stability.

On the other hand, a draft report of the Council of Economic Advisors, leaked to the *New York Times* in January, said there was no firm evidence that illegal aliens displaced native-born workers but that instead they contributed to an overall economic expansion whose benefits were widely diffused in the form of lower prices, new job opportunities, and higher profits for investors. Imposing sanctions on employers for hiring illegal aliens would reduce the national output of goods and services and would impose a new "labor-market tax" on employers on the order of $1.6 to $2.6 billion a year in screening costs. As Robert Pear observed in the *New York Times*, "The report undermines the rationale for a comprehensive immigration bill. . . . "[43] These views were first advanced at a July 1985 meeting of the Domestic Policy Council by Beryl Sprinkel, the recently appointed chairman of the Council of Economic Advisors, as a critique of the Simpson bill; reflecting the often-voiced conclusions of the Chicago economists, with whom Sprinkel has long been associated, the conclusions were then included in the first report prepared under his direction. It aroused furious argument within the administration, in the course of which the draft chapter was leaked to the press. The INS, in particular, insisted the economists' reports failed to isolate the separate economic effects of illegal as against legal alien workers.[44] The *Economist* commented that although the report was not a position paper, it could be taken as a signal "that the Reagan administration is of two minds about immigration reform. Since the same can be said of both parties in Congress, the outlook for action this year has begun to look poor."[45]

The day after the leak, however, the White House reaffirmed Reagan's commitment to the Senate bill, now awaiting action by the House Judiciary Committee, and indicated the contested section of the council's report would be deleted from the report submitted to Congress. But Chairman Rodino — still concerned with avoiding a trap — said the draft placed a major obstacle in the path of enactment and urged the president to take an actively supportive role.[46] The *New York Times* editorialized to the same effect on January 24, pointing out that earthquakes and recession in Mexico had further swollen the tide of illegal aliens. On March 11 the president finally met with Simpson and Rodino, who now agreed to proceed with further consideration. The *New York Times* at this time published an op-ed piece by Father Theodore Hesburgh, chairman of the Select Commission, who advocated enactment lest greater restrictions come up. This was balanced by publication of a letter from Cushing Colbeare, chairman of the American Friends Service Committee's working group on the Mexico-U.S. border program, urging a more humanitarian outlook and a policy that took into consideration causes of the "push" to emigrate.[47]

The House Judiciary Committee was scheduled to take up the legislation in early May, but on May 1 Rodino decided to postpone action for five weeks until the issue of the guest workers could be resolved.[48] A compromise announced by Schumer on June 9, with indications that it was acceptable to Rodino, was designed to guarantee farmers a ready supply of labor while preventing exploitation of the foreign workers by providing them with the opportunity to become permanent residents. The compromise extended the amnesty to any illegal aliens who could prove they had been working in agriculture for at least twenty full days from May 1, 1985, to May 1, 1986. It permitted the government to admit additional agricultural workers if the secretary of labor and the secretary of agriculture determined there was a shortage of labor for farms producing fruits and vegetables. These workers would be admitted as permanent residents on condition they work in agriculture at least forty days in each of their first two years in the country; they would qualify for citizenship after five years' residence, like ordinary immigrants, but must in addition work in agriculture for at least forty days a year during the entire period.[49] The compromise was endorsed by the *New York Times* in a June 18 editorial, with the suggestion that the qualifying period for amnesty be made somewhat longer. (Subsequent negotiations increased it to 60 days.)

The Schumer proposal was a remarkable feat of congressional horse-trading, which secured the support of the United Farm Workers because "it gives the workers a fighting chance," as well as that of the Farm Labor Alliance — but subject to the condition that further amendments require immigration officers to secure warrants before entering open fields. Beyond this, however, it got a mixed reception. Mazzoli called it unprecedented and unacceptable, and the ACLU both objected to the sizable importation of foreign workers and acknowledged that if there were to be an immigration bill, the Schumer proposal was "by far the best way of guaranteeing some protection for farm workers." Prolabor Democrats such as Berman of California went along. Conservative Republicans such as Lungren of California and Sensenbrenner of Wisconsin objected vehemently to the "give-away" of permanent resident status to illegal aliens who worked just sixty days. Similarly, the administration had told the Judiciary Committee in February that the admission of alien agricultural workers as permanent residents would adversely affect the U.S. labor force.[50]

Overall, however, the trade stuck. The compromise was endorsed by the Judiciary Committee on June 25 on a vote of 19 to 15, and the bill itself was reported out immediately afterward, 25 to 10, in time for the Independence

Day recess. This was the third time in five years a bill had gotten this far in the House. On its way to the finish, it had also acquired a provision barring the government from deporting Nicaraguans and Salvadorans for eighteen months after the bill became law.

As congressional consideration resumed after the recess, Robert Pear, the immigration specialist in the Washington bureau of the *New York Times*, concluded an extensive review of the situation by remarking that public sentiment in favor of restricting immigration appeared to have increased in recent years, and that therefore liberals who opposed previous versions of the proposed law "may reckon that they will never get a better deal than the one they could negotiate this year."[51] What was the evidence? As a prelude to the Statue of Liberty celebrations, the media gave considerable attention to immigration and took the nation's pulse on the subject. Wide publicity was accorded to dramatic manifestations of hostility, such as the capture and detention of a group of illegal Mexicans by a vigilante group in Texas, but that could hardly be taken as a reliable indicator of the general will. More significantly, the *New York Times*, in a story headlined "New Restrictions on Immigration Gain Public Support," reported on July 1, 1986, that according to a *New York Times*/CBS poll, 49 percent of the public thought the immigration level should be decreased, and 43 percent thought it should be kept the same or increased.[52]

In a special effort to tap Hispanic opinion, the survey established, not surprisingly, that Hispanics were much more favorable to immigration than whites, with only 31 percent favoring a decrease as against 52 percent. Blacks were slightly closer to Hispanics than to whites on this issue (39 percent); mirroring this, 61 percent of Hispanics thought immigration should be the same or increased, as against 39 percent of whites, with blacks again in the middle (52 percent). People of old American stock most strongly supported a decrease (50 percent), and most recent arrivals least strongly (29 percent). Of all the categories surveyed, people born abroad or from a family arriving in the United States after 1941 were the most favorable to immigration. All the regions but the Northeast favored a decrease. Conservatives most strongly favored a decrease (57 percent); moderates, least (45 percent); and liberals were in the middle (48 percent). Given sampling error, the intermediate position of liberals is consistent with the ambiguous position of immigration issues in relation to left/right alignments. With regard to pending legislation, the public supported the broad outlines of the original Simpson-Mazzoli package but strongly disapproved of guest workers (58 to 36 percent).

Pear interpreted the poll to indicate a "strong and growing public support for new restrictions on immigration despite widespread sympathy for both legal and illegal immigrants as individuals." He supported this contention by pointing out the contrast with 1965, the year of the Kennedy-Johnson amendment, when only 33 percent thought immigration levels should be decreased and 46 percent thought they should remain the same level or be increased. The comparison was somewhat misleading. In the intervening period, legal immigrants increased from 296,697 a year to 621,444; concurrently, apprehensions of illegals escalated even more spectacularly, from 110,371 to 1,251,357.[53] As presented in the national media at the time, the main issue in 1965 was to abolish the national-origins quota that discriminated against immigrants from southern and eastern Europe, who had by then entered the American mainstream. The restrictive aspects of the law with respect to the Western Hemisphere were hardly discussed outside Hispanic communities, which were in any case much less visible at the time and did not yet participate in the national political process.

Pear's conclusions, however, are much less solid than might seem at first glance. After a decade and a half of public attention to illegal immigration, the appointment of a presidential commission, the "refugee crisis" of 1979–1980, and the multiseason Simpson-Mazzoli playoffs, the proportion of "don't knows" in the polls decreased by about half, from 20 percent to 9. The proportion of those favoring a reduction of immigration increased by about half, from 33 to 49 percent. While there is no gainsaying the significance of this change, the significance should not be exaggerated. The proportion of the U.S. public that accepted the much higher level of immigration of the 1980s or wanted it increased was only four points lower than the equivalent in 1965 (down from 46 to 42 percent). As noted in *U.S. News and World Report*, this revealed no evidence of an upsurge of xenophobia. But congressional actors — particularly in an election year — do not operate on the basis of a long-term view, and what mattered to them was not "reality" but a particular reading of it imposed on the attention of Congress by high-stakes players.

As the House Rules Committee considered the bill for inclusion in the legislative agenda in the months remaining, the Schumer compromise emerged as the most controversial issue. As proposals to modify the bill proliferated, the architects of the compromise urged the Rules Committee to bar hostile amendments that might upset the bill's "delicate balance." Rodino said he continued to support the compromise but would allow the House to vote on a motion to delete it; Speaker O'Neill remained unconvinced.[54] With the administration's antidrug campaign swinging into action, both Attorney General Meese and INS Commissioner Nelson again linked drugs to immigration and urged O'Neill to put the bill to a vote. Finally, on September 24, the Rules Committee sent the bill to the floor, having barred from consideration a substitute amendment by Lungren of California, the ranking Republican on the Judiciary Committee, to drop the Schumer compromise in favor of the Senate's "Wilson Workers." Some members warned, however, that this decision might endanger chances of passage, and, indeed, two days later, by a vote of 202 to 180, the House defeated a resolution to bring the bill to the floor under these conditions; only thirteen Republicans supported the rule. With Congress now scheduled to adjourn by October 10, Rodino called for the administration to intervene and declared he had no intention of asking for another rule. The bill was dead.

The *New York Times* once again deplored the House's inaction, allocating the blame even-handedly to both the Democratic leadership, which allowed the issue to drag into the final days of the session, and to the Republicans for rejecting the Schumer compromise. It pointed out that the task could still be completed, if the president intervened to secure Republican support for a further compromise, thus putting partisan Democrats on the spot, as he had done with tax reform.[55]

The administration now swung into action. Meese urged the Rules Committee to send the measure back to the floor "in a way that allows the full House to vote its conscience"—that is, with the possibility of amendments hostile to the Schumer compromise.[56] In a surprise move on October 1, the Republicans tried to circumvent the Rules Committee and bring the bill to the floor, but this time it was the Democrats who blocked the effort by a vote of 235 (230 Democrats, 5 Republicans) to 177 (167 Republicans, 10 Democrats). Again, the bill appeared dead because even if it were enacted by the House, time would be needed to iron out significant differences between this version and the Senate's.

In a change of tactics, Senate and House supporters now worked out a compromise despite the lack of final action by the House, and then used this achievement to persuade the House Rules Committee to reconsider. The modified version reflected concessions to restrictionist opponents of the "give-away" of permanent resident status to foreign workers, and to agricultural interests. In short, the possibility of bringing in foreign workers was maintained, but was limited to a transitional three-year period, fiscal years 1990 to 93. The work period requirement to qualify for amnesty under the Schumer provision plan was raised to ninety days in each of the last three years, leading to a one-year status of "temporary resident," after which workers would attain permanent-resident status. The number eligible for the entire transition period was limited to 350,000. Lungren found the new version acceptable; Senator Wilson still did not, yet he did not rule out a further splitting of the difference were the House to enact the bill.[57] The following day, the House agreed 278 to 129 to take up the bill and consider fourteen amendments.

By a narrow vote of 199 to 192, the House rejected the proposal advanced by a Florida Republican to eliminate the amnesty provision altogether. The Schumer qualification period was reduced once again to ninety days in one year, and the provision prohibiting the deportation of Nicaraguans and Salvadorans survived intact as well. Agricultural interests secured an amendment (221 to 170)—opposed by the Reagan administration—prohibiting the INS from entering farms without warrants or the owner's permission. Finally, in a dramatic reversal, the House approved the bill, 230 to 166. Despite heavy Democratic support (168 to 61), the bill would not have passed without the contribution of a sizable minority of Republicans (62 for, 105 against). In keeping with our "odd-couple" hypothesis, the opposition was made up of liberal Democrats, who warned of discrimination, and conservative Republicans, who objected to the overly generous treatment of illegal aliens and future guest workers. For the first time, however, five Hispanic representatives out of eleven voted *for* the bill, out of fear "that any immigration bill in a future Congress would be even more restrictive and might omit the amnesty."[58] Overall, thirty more Democrats supported the bill than in 1984, and twenty-nine fewer Republicans did. Quipped Senator Alan Simpson, "I guess we just jump-started a corpse."

Simpson's country-boy trope was chosen by the *New York Times* as the title for its editorial. It urged the liberals, who in an ironic historical development had shifted since the 1950s from strong support of employer sanctions to objection, to accept the Senate's indefinite version over the House's six-and-a-half-year "sunset" provision, as well as to drop the "incendiary provision" to grant temporary haven to Central Americans. On the other side, the *Times* urged acceptance of the House's more generous cutoff date for amnesty, and the provision of assistance from Legal Services lawyers. Congressional adjournment was again postponed, and House and Senate conferees met on October 10 to iron out remaining differences. As a token of the administration's concern, the INS commissioner attended the opening meeting. Items to be worked out included the cutoff date for amnesty (Senate: 1980; House: 1982); details of employer sanctions, including the amount of fines and the indefinite versus the sunset provision; and provisions in the House bill, but absent from the Senate's forbidding discrimination against legal aliens, obliging employers to ask for identification documents of all applicants, and allowing employers to give preference to citizens if applicants were equally qualified.[59]

The administration, seeking maximum leverage while last-minute negotiations were under way, publicly stated for the first time its objections to the Schumer amendment, which it characterized as a "well-intentioned" but "inequitable, ineffective, and costly scheme for meeting the needs of domestic agricultural employers." Officials from the INS and the Office of Management and Budget (OMB) provided details of these objections. Despite this, the conferees sketched the terms of possible meeting grounds: the House would accept the Senate's indefinite period for sanctions, and in return the Senate would agree to the House's antidiscrimination provisions despite the administration's opposition. A major issue was aid to localities that contained illegal aliens who, once legalized, would qualify for social benefits. Under both bills, they would be ineligible for at least five years for most types of public assistance provided by the federal government. The conferees also proposed $1 billion a year for four years in federal funds, and the administration committed itself to less than half of this, $1.8 billion for a four-year period.[60]

The final compromise came on October 14, 1986. Conferees agreed to drop the bar to deportation of Salvadorans and Nicaraguans. On the matter of sanctions, for a first offense, the employer would be subject to a civil penalty of $250 to $2,000 for each illegal alien hired, but a "pattern of practice" would give rise to criminal penalties, a fine of up to $3,000, and six months in prison. Sanctions would go into effect six months after final enactment, without the "sunset" provision; however, the General Accounting Office (GAO) would report to Congress on the effects of sanctions, and if they were found to create severe discrimination or problems for employers, Congress might reexamine and even repeal this portion of the law. On the issue of amnesty, the conferees adopted the House's more generous 1982 cutoff date. Aliens could apply for legal status within an eighteen-month period starting six months after the bill became law. They would move into the transitional status of "lawful temporary residents," and after a year be eligible to apply for status as permanent residents if they could demonstrate "minimal understanding of ordinary English" and a basic knowledge of U.S. history and government—requirements not imposed on ordinary immigrants, and usually reserved for those seeking U.S. citizenship after five years' residence. The Schumer compromise survived in altered form, with illegal aliens who worked in agriculture for at least ninety days in 1985–1986 eligible for permanent residence after a two-year period as "temporary residents", an option available also to any seasonal farm workers admitted in the fiscal years 1990 to 1993 should the domestic supply prove inadequate. While stopping short of issuing a national identity card, the bill required employers to verify the status of all job applicants. Federal reimbursement would be provided for at the $1 billion level.

What Mazzoli called "the least imperfect bill we will ever have before us" was approved by a vote of 238 to 173. The majority included seven fewer Democrats and fifteen more Republicans than the previous House version. Liberal Democrats objected, and members of the Hispanic caucus remained about evenly divided.[61] When the Senate took up the conference bill, Simpson reported assurances from President Reagan that he would sign. By a vote of 75 to 21, the Senate crushed an attempt to prevent consideration of the bill. Simpson then filed a precautionary motion to prevent a filibuster, and on October 17 the bill was approved by a vote of 63 to 24. The majority included thirty-four Democrats and twenty-nine Republicans; against were sixteen Republicans and eight Democrats, including both conservatives and liberals. Senator Phil Gramm (R-Texas) denounced the amnesty provisions and the Schumer arrangements; Senator Kennedy, the measure's potential for discrimination.[62] Keeping his promise, on November 6 Reagan signed the bill into law (PL 99-603).[63]

Conclusion

The *New York Times* hailed passage of the Immigration Control and Reform Act of 1986—Simpson-Mazzoli—as Freedom Day. Having perennially allocated blame to the various actors in the drama of immigration reform, the *Times* now dispensed praise to Schumer and Mazzoli, Lungren, and many others, but above all to Senator Alan Simpson: "Ten and 20 years from now, when the children of Freedom Day hear his name, they'll think grateful, noble thoughts."[64] In the country at large, however, pronouncements ranged as widely as they had while the law was in the making. Hispanic leaders appeared deeply divided. Many continued to denounce the act, but the president of the National Council of La Raza said that although he could not endorse it, it was "probably the best immigration legislation possible under current political conditions." Robert Conner of FAIR, a prominent restrictionist lobby organized to fight the Select Commission's balanced recommendations, said that the bill "could be the turning point in regaining control of our nation's borders, or it could turn into an immigration disaster," depending on how sanctions and amnesty were implemented and what, if any, steps were taken to reduce *legal* immigration.[65] The county executive of El Paso, who thought that amnesty would encourage others to come and sanctions would hardly stop employers, predicted that "after the initial shock it will be business as usual on the border."[66] Such skepticism is warranted, for the significance of the law will be fully revealed only by its consequences, and these will depend largely on how the executive branch implements the legislation. It has considerable leeway in this respect, and there is reason to doubt whether legislation such as Simpson-Mazzoli can fundamentally alter a social process as complex as international migration. Nevertheless, the *enactment* of the law is itself an accomplished social fact whose historical significance can be assessed in its own right. Overall, the episode reveals the tensions and contradictions of a particular type of international migration, involving the temporary relocation of people from the Third World as workers in affluent capitalist democracies. Although the present study has been concerned exclusively with the United States, the pattern is a very widespread one, and similar stories could be told with different collectivities as the leading characters: French and Algerians, Germans and Turks, Belgians and Moroccans, or if we go back in time, British and Irish, Germans and Poles. In all these cases, the flow was fostered by a relationship of structural inequality between two countries, forming the complementary sectors of a transnational economic system within which the dependent country served among other things, as a labor reserve.[67] Leaving aside the costs and benefits to the sending country and the individual migrants, from the perspective of the receiving country, the balance sheet is difficult to establish. On the economic side, the benefits of alien labor used in this manner spill over from the specific sectors where it is employed to the economy as a whole, by reducing the prices of certain widely used commodities such as, in the case of the United States, fruits and vegetables. However, the costs are borne unevenly by the lowest income groups of the receiving society, whose wages are depressed by the additional supply of labor, and perhaps as well by local communities, which must provide additional services without concomitant income.

Yet, although there are indications that resentment of immigration of this sort runs high among lower-income groups, it is quite evident that, by virtue of their powerlessness, they cannot constitute a source of *effective* opposition. Movements to close the "back door" do tend to broaden their base of support in periods of depression and unemployment, when economic insecurity is more widespread. But the most recent attempt to do so confirms the validity of the "odd-couple" hypothesis suggested by earlier episodes in U.S. history. The movement involves the formation of a coalition drawn from groups activated by two distinct concerns, the economic and the cultural-political, usually located at opposite ends of the liberal–conservative continuum.

Thus, it is quite in accord with expectations that the restrictionist coalition did get employer sanctions, desired by one party of the couple to protect American workers against "unfair" competition from abroad, and by the other to protect American society from Hispanicization. What is remarkable about this episode is that the other half of the odd couple got much of what it wanted as well: civil libertarians and Hispanics secured the amnesty, and employers managed to keep the "back door" from closing altogether. But precisely because all four actors did so well, it is likely that they will soon return to center stage.

NOTES

1. The historical background material is taken from "The Main Gate and the Back Door," a paper presented by the author at a workshop of the Council on Foreign Relations, Washington, D.C., April 1978; this is itself part of a larger work in preparation, a preview of which has been presented in "Patterns of International Migration Policy: A Diachronic Comparison," in *Minorities: Community and Identity*, ed. Charles Fried (Berlin: Springer-Verlag, 1983), pp. 229–46. Research for that work was supported by a grant from the Population and Development Policy Research Program of the Rockefeller and Ford foundations.

2. For an elaboration of these concepts, see the author's "International Migrations in Political Perspective," in *Global Trends in Migration: Theory and Research on International Population Movements*, ed. Mary M. Kritz, Charles B. Keely, and Silvano M. Tomasi (New York: Center for Migration Studies, 1981), pp. 3–27.

3. Immigrants from the colonial countries of the Western Hemisphere fell under the quota assigned to their imperial masters. This was especially relevant for British West Indians because the British quota was the largest and usually remained unfilled; however, they had to meet "qualitative" requirements, such as the literacy test, and provide evidence of financial viability.

4. For an elaboration of this analysis, see Aristide R. Zolberg, "Wanted but Not Welcome: Alien Labor in Western Development," in *Population in an Interacting World*, ed. William Alonso (Cambridge: Harvard University Press, 1987), pp. 36–60.

5. The "free-and-white" requirement for naturalization was legislated in the early nineteenth century; however, persons of African descent became eligible by virtue of the post-Civil War amendments.

6. On this subject more generally, see Michael Piore, *Birds of Passage: Migrant Labor and Industrial Societies* (Cambridge: Cambridge University Press, 1979).

7. Mary R. Coolidge, *Chinese Immigration* (New York: Holt, 1909), p. 384.

8. Ibid., p. 330.

9. See, on this subject, Henry Feingold, *The Politics of Rescue: The Roosevelt Administration and the Holocaust, 1938-1945* (New Brunswick, N.J.: Rutgers University Press, 1970); and the two books by David S. Wyman, *Paper Walls: America and the Refugee Crisis* (Amherst, Ma.: University of Massachusetts Press, 1968), and *The Abandonment of the Jews* (New York: Pantheon, 1984).

10. Unless otherwise indicated, information pertaining to the program is based on Richard B. Craig, *The Bracero Program: Interest Groups and Foreign Policy* (Austin: University of Texas Press, 1971). For a more extensive and critical discussion, see Manuel Garcia y Griego, "The Importation of Mexican Contract Laborers to the United States, 1942-1964: Antecedents, Operation, and Legacy," in *The Border That Joins: Mexican Migrants and U.S. Response*, ed. Peter G. Brown and Henry Shue (Totowa, N.J.: Rowman & Littlefield, 1983), pp. 49–98.

11. For a thorough overview of the subject, see Gil Loescher and John A. Scanlan,

Calculated Kindness: Refugees and America's Half-Open Door, 1945 to the Present
(New York: Free Press, 1986), and the author's "The Roots of American Refugee Policy"
(Paper presented at the Lehrman Institute, Immigration and U.S. Foreign Policy Series,
April 1987).

12. In the short run this had the effect of fostering a brain drain toward the United
States, mostly of professionals from Asian countries; once the first wave was established, its members began to bring in relatives, whose number rapidly expanded to fill
the annual country maximum, shutting out "independent" immigrants.

13. Interview, *New York Times*, October 29, 1968.

14. This category, which accounted for between 25 and 35 percent of Western
Hemisphere immigration, resulted from the well-established practice of women's crossing the border at any cost to give birth on U.S. soil.

15. For a detailed account, see *U.S. Immigration Policy and the National Interest*,
Staff Report of the Select Commission on Immigration and Refugee Policy (Washington, D.C., April 30, 1981).

16. This account should be seen as a *preliminary* rather than a *definitive* history,
based on reports in the daily press, publications of the organizations concerned, and
numerous conversations with participants in the legislative process over a period of
several years. Specific references have been provided to document quotations and specific actions attributed to groups and individuals.

17. Martin Tolchin, *New York Times*, November 30, 1983; Robert Pear, ibid.,
January 19, 1984.

18. *Forum Information Bulletin* March 19, 1984, p. 11.

19. As reported by Bill Keller, *New York Times*, July 21, 1984.

20. Secretary of Agriculture Block expressed his support at a cabinet council meeting in mid-January *New York Times*, January 19, 1984).

21. Keller, *New York Times*, July 21, 1984. "Liberal" is from the *Times*; "moderate"
is from the *Forum Information Bulletin*, March 19, 1984, p. 7.

22. The enactment of the bill in effect killed the prospects of H.R. 4904, sponsored
by Congressman Edward Roybal (D-California), introduced in the House on February
23, 1984. In an attempt to make border control more acceptable to Hispanics, the
Roybal bill provided for amnesty without employer sanctions; instead, it called for
stricter enforcement of appropriate labor laws, as well as reinforcement of INS services.

23. *New York Times*, July 18, 1984.

24. As reported by Jane Perlez, *New York Times*, July 13, 1985.

25. Robert Pear, *New York Times*, July 30, 1984.

26. Robert Pear, *New York Times*, September 22, 1984.

27. *New York Times*, September 28, 1984.

28. Ibid., October 12, 1984.

29. Ibid., May 24, 1985.

30. Ibid., April 18, May 24, and June 14, 1985. Unless otherwise indicated, all
reports are by Robert Pear. Senator Simpson's critique of the Chamber of Commerce
appeared in an op-ed piece, *New York Times*, August 10, 1982, p. 27.

31. *New York Times*, May 24, 1985.

32. Ibid., June 14, 1985.

33. Ibid., July 18, 1985. See also *Economist*, September 28, 1985.

34. *New York Times*, July 18, 1985; Stephen Engelberg reporting.

35. *New York Times*, July 25, 1985, p. 20E.

36. Robert Pear, *New York Times*, May 4, 1986.

37. *New York Times*, September 18, 1985.

38. ibid., September 19, 1985.

39. Ibid., September 14, 1985.

40. In the course of the hearings, Attorney General Meese objected to its amnesty provisions as dangerously permissive, as well as to the establishment of an office of alien protection in the Justice Department. He also cautioned that the president might veto any bill that provided for too much federal aid to the states, and deplored the absence of a guest-worker program. A further sticking point was the truculence of OMB regarding federal reimbursement to state and local governments for costs associated with amnesty (The *New York Times* editorial, January 24, 1986; *FAIR/Immigration Report* 6 (May 1986):1.

41. *New York Times*, September 10 and 29, 1985.

42. Ibid., February 15, and 21, and April 29, 1986; *Wall Street Journal*, May 14, 1986; *FAIR Immigration Report*, May 1986.

43. *New York Times*, January 23, 1986.

44. *Economist*, February 1, 1986, p. 22.

45. Ibid., pp. 22–23.

46. *New York Times*, January 24, 1986.

47. Ibid., March 20 and April 30, 1986.

48. Ibid., May 2 and 4, 1986.

49. Ibid., June 10 and September 14, 1986.

50. Ibid., July 15, 1986.

51. Ibid.

52. Similarly, another survey cited in *U.S. News and World Report* found 51 percent favored a decrease.

53. This is the 1983 figure, latest available at this time; it includes the now separately counted refugee admissions.

54. *New York Times*, September 14, 1986.

55. Ibid., September 29, 1986.

56. Ibid., September 27, 1986.

57. Ibid., October 9, 1986.

58. Robert Pear, *New York Times*, October 10, 1986.

59. *New York Times*, October 11, 1986.

60. Ibid., October 12, 1986.

61. Ibid., October 16, 1986.

62. Ibid., October 17, 1986.

63. It became Public Law 99-603. In addition to the text, see House Committee on the Judiciary, *The Immigration Reform and Control Act of 1986. A Summary and Explanation* 99th Cong. 2d sess. December 1986, Serial No. 14.

64. *New York Times*, October 19, 1986, p. E22.

65. *FAIR/Immigration Report* 7 (November 1986).

66. *New York Times*, October 16, 1986.

67. The dynamics governing the formation of international labor supply networks are analyzed by Alejandro Portes and John Walton in *Labor, Class, and the International System* (New York: Academic Press, 1981), especially pp. 21–65.

CONTRIBUTORS

Samuel L. Baily teaches Latin American history and immigration history at Rutgers The State University of New Jersey in New Brunswick. He specializes in comparative studies of immigration, and is currently at work on a forthcoming book *The Italians in Buenos Aires and New York City: 1875-1925*. With Franco Ramella as co-editor and John Lenaghan as translator, Professor Baily recently edited *One Family, Two Worlds: An Italian Family's Correspondence: 1901-22* (1988). His research on immigration has been supported by grants from the Social Science Research Council and the American Philosophical Society.

Sucheng Chan, professor of history and director of Asian-American studies at the University of California at Santa Barbara, specializes in comparative Asian-American history and sociology. Her book, *The Bittersweet Soil: The Chinese in California Agriculture, 1860-1910* (1986) won the 1986 Saloutos Memorial Book Award in Agricultural History, the 1987 American Historical Association Pacific Coast Branch Award, and the 1988 Association for Asian American Studies Outstanding Book Award. She has held postdoctoral fellowships from the National Endowment for the Humanities and the John Simon Guggenheim Foundation.

Philip D. Curtin, Herbert Baxter Adams Professor of History at Johns Hopkins University, is well known for his studies of the African slave trade. His publications include *Africa Remembered* (1967), *The Atlantic Slave Trade: A Census* (1969), and *Economic Change in Pre-Colonial Africa* (1975). Professor Curtin, who has received much recognition for his contributions to historical research, was a MacArthur Foundation Prize Fellow and a past president of the American Historical Association.

Lawrence H. Fuchs is a political scientist who has published widely in immigration and ethnic studies. His books include *The Political Behavior of American Jews* (1955), *Hawaii Pono: A Social History* (1961), and, most recently, *The American Kaleidoscope: Race, Ethnicity and the Civic Culture* (1990). Dr. Fuchs served as executive director of the Select Commission on Immigration and Refugee Policy from 1979 to 1981, and he was the first overseas director of the Peace Corps in the Phillipines from 1961 to 1963. He was chair of the politics department and the American studies department at Brandeis University, where he is Meyer and Walter Jaffe Professor of American Civilization and Politics. He has received research grants for his work from the Ford Foundation, the Rockefeller Foundation, and the Alfred P. Sloan Foundation, among others.

Kerby A. Miller, professor of history at the University of Missouri-Columbia, is an authority on Irish immigration. His *Emigrants and Exiles: Ireland and the Irish Exodus to North America* (1985), for which he was made a finalist for the Pulitzer Prize in history, received both the Merle Curti Award in Social History from the Organization of American Historians and the Theodore Saloutos Memorial Book Award in Immigration History from the Immigration History Society. He is currently editing a collection of Irish immigrants' letters and memoirs, *"Out of Ireland Have We Come,"* for Oxford University Press. Professor Miller has received fellowships from the American Council for Learned Societies, the National Endowment for the Humanities, and the Institute of Irish Studies at Queens University, Belfast.

Suzanne W. Model, assistant professor of sociology at the University of Massachusetts at Amherst, has written on ethnicity and occupational status. Her current research, an investigation of patterns of ethnic and racial stratification in New York City between 1880 and 1980, is supported by the Russell Sage Foundation.

Ewa Morawska is herself a recent immigrant to the United States from Poland. Dr. Morawska, who teaches at the University of Pennsylvania, holds graduate degrees in both sociology and history. She is a specialist on contemporary eastern Europe and on East European immigration to the United States, the subject of her *For Bread with Butter: The Life-worlds of East Central Europeans in Johnstown, Pennsylvania, 1890-1940* (1985). She is at work on *Insecure Prosperity: Jews in Small Town Industrial America: 1880-1940*. Recently, she has held research grants from the American Council for Learned Societies, the National Endowment for the Humanities, the John Simon Guggenheim Foundation, and the Institute for Advanced Study in Princeton, New Jersey.

Alejandro Portes, John Dewey Professor of Sociology and International Relations at the Johns Hopkins University, is a specialist on urbanization in the world economy, international migration, and class, race, and ethnicity. Professor Portes has served as chairman of the expert review board, Hemispheric Migration Program, under the Intergovernmental Committee on Migration; he has also served a number of U.S. House subcommittees during hearings on Latin-American migration. With Manuel Castells and Lauren Benton, he recently published *The Informal Economy: Studies in Advanced and Less Developed Countries* (1989), and with Robert Bach, he published *Latin Journey: Cuban and Mexican Immigrants in the United States* (1985). He has also published many essays on ethnic labor markets, ethnic communities, and Third World development. Professor Portes has been awarded postdoctoral research grants by the National Institute of Mental Health, the National Science Foundation, the Rockefeller Foundation, the Ford Foundation, and the Alfred P. Sloan Foundation.

Charles Tilly is Distinguished Professor of Sociology and History and director of the Center for Studies of Social Change at the New School for Social Research. He studies large-scale social change, including migration, in Europe and America. His most recent books are *Big Structures, Large Processes, Huge Comparisons* (1985), *The Contentious French* (1986) and *Coercion, Capital, and European States* (1990). Professor Tilly has received grants from the Russell Sage Foundation, the Alfred P. Sloan Foundation, and the Social Science Research Council.

Virginia Yans-McLaughlin teaches history at Rutgers The State University of New Jersey in New Brunswick. Her book *Family and Community: Italian Immigrants in Buffalo, 1880–1930* (1977) won the American Historical Association's Harold R. Marraro Prize and the American Association of State and Local History Award. She is especially interested in the history of immigrant women and the immigrant family. She is currently at work on a book and a film on the anthropologist Margaret Mead. Professor Yans-McLaughlin has received grants from the Rockefeller Foundation, the National Endowment for the Humanities, and the American Philosophical Society.

Aristide R. Zolberg has written extensively in the fields of comparative politics and historical sociology. Recent major works include *Working-Class Formation in Western Europe and the United States* (1986, co-edited with Ira Katznelson), and *Escape from Violence: Conflict and the Refugee Crisis in the Developing World* (1989, co-authored with Astri Suhrke and Sergio Aguayo). He is currently completing a book on the politics of international population movements from the sixteenth century to the present, and continuing research on the globalization of contemporary politics. Professor Zolberg has received grants from the Ford, Rockefeller, and MacArthur foundations. He has taught at the University of Chicago, and has been a visiting professor at the Institute for Political Studies of the University of Paris as well as the École des Hautes Études en Sciences Sociales and the Collège de France. He currently holds the University-in-Exile chair at the Graduate Faculty of the New School for Social Research.